Contributions to Social Ontology

Recent years have seen a dramatic re-emergence of interest in ontology. From philosophy and the social sciences to artificial intelligence and computer science, a range of different ontological projects have emerged that are having significant implications for the manner in which each discipline conceives of itself and for how applied research is carried out. This book focuses upon the nature of these developments in the social sciences. As the contributions collected here show, however, this interest in social ontology involves far more than an unquestioning acceptance application of the concepts and methods of academic philosophers. Rather, something quite different appears to be emerging. This book attempts to contribute to this emerging field by not only illustrating the diversity, relevance and sophistication of the ontological projects currently being pursued in the social sciences, but by explicitly considering the relationship between these projects and more traditional approaches to ontology.

Clive Lawson is Fellow of Girton College Cambridge and an affiliated Lecturer in the Faculty of Economics and Politics, University of Cambridge.

John Latsis is the Jean Monnet Fellow at the Robert Schuman Centre for Advanced Study, European University Institute in Florence.

Nuno Martins is a member of the Portuguese Catholic University, Faculty of Economics and Management, Porto.

Routledge studies in critical realism

Edited by Margaret Archer, Roy Bhaskar, Andrew Collier, Kathryn Dean, Nick Hostettler, Jonathan Joseph, Tony Lawson, Alan Norrie and Sean Vertigan

Critical realism is one of the most influential new developments in the philosophy of science and in the social sciences, providing a powerful alternative to positivism and post modernism. This series will explore the critical realist position in philosophy and across the social sciences.

1 **Marxism and Realism**
A materialistic application of realism in the social science
Sean Creaven

2 **Beyond Relativism**
Raymond Boudon, cognitive rationality and critical realism
Cynthia Lins Hamlin

3 **Education Policy and Realist Social Theory**
Primary teachers, child-centred philosophy and the new managerialism
Robert Wilmott

4 **Hegemony**
A realist analysis
Jonathan Joseph

5 **Realism and Sociology**
Anti-foundationalism, ontology and social research
Justin Cruickshank

6 **Critical Realism**
The difference it makes
Edited by Justin Cruickshank

7 **Critical Realism and Composition Theory**
Donald Judd

8 **On Christian Belief**
A defence of a cognitive conception of religious belief in a christian context
Andrew Collier

Also published by Routledge:

Critical realism: interventions

Edited by Margaret Archer, Roy Bhaskar, Andrew Collier, Kathryn Dean, Nick Hostettler, Jonathan Joseph, Tony Lawson, Alan Norrie and Sean Vertigan

Critical Realism
Essential readings
Edited by Margaret Archer, Roy Bhaskar, Andrew Collier, Tony Lawson and Alan Norrie

The Possibility of Naturalism 3rd edition
A philosophical critique of the contemporary human sciences
Roy Bhaskar

Being & Worth
Andrew Collier

Quantum Theory and the Flight from Realism
Philosophical responses to quantum mechanics
Christopher Norris

From East to West
Odyssey of a soul
Roy Bhaskar

Contributions to Social Ontology

Edited by
**Clive Lawson, John Latsis
and Nuno Martins**

Routledge
Taylor & Francis Group

LONDON AND NEW YORK

First published 2007
by Routledge
2 Park Square, Milton Park, Abingdon, Oxon, OX14 4RN

Simultaneously published in the USA and Canada
by Routledge
270 Madison Ave, New York, NY 10016

Routledge is an imprint of the Taylor & Francis Group, an informa business

Transferred to Digital Printing 2007

Typeset in Times by Keyword Group Ltd

British Library Cataloguing in Publication data
A catalogue record for this book is available from the British Library

Library of Congress Cataloging in Publication Data
A catalog record for this book has been requested

ISBN10: 0-415-40373-1 (hbk)
ISBN10: 0-415-44238-9 (pbk)

ISBN13: 978-0-415-40373-3 (hbk)
ISBN13: 978-0-415-44238-1 (pbk)

Contents

Figures and tables

Figures

Table

Contributors

Margaret S. Archer is a Professor of Sociology at the University of Warwick, a past-President of the International Sociological Association and a Council Member of the Pontifical Academy of Social Sciences. Her last book was *Structure, Agency and the Internal Conversation* (CUP 2003). Under an ESRC award she has completed a book entitled *Making Our Way through the World: Human Reflexivity and Social Mobility* (2007 forthcoming). This will be followed by a companion volume *The Making and Braking of Human Reflexivity*. The issue of 'reflexivity' obviously raises questions about the ontological status of subjectivity.

Lorenzo Bernasconi-Kohn is currently completing his doctorate in the Department of History and Philosophy of Science at Cambridge. His research interests span the philosophy of the social sciences and the later Wittgenstein. Prior to this, he studied economics and philosophy at the London School of Economics.

Ram Roy Bhaskar was educated at Balliol College, Oxford, and Nuffield College, Oxford. He is best known as the originator of the philosophy of critical realism. He helped found the Centre for Critical Realism in 1995, which gave rise to the various international and interdisciplinary organizations such as the International Association of Critical Realism, the *Journal for Critical Realism* and the Routledge book series Critical Realism: Interventions. He is the author of *A Realist Theory of Science* (1975), *The Possibility of Naturalism* (1979), *Scientific Realism and Human Emancipation* (1986), *Reclaiming Reality* (1989), *Philosophy and the Idea of Freedom* (1990), *Dialectic: The Pulse of Freedom* (1993), *Plato Etc.* (1994), *From East to West* (2000), and *Reflections on Meta-Reality, From Science to Emancipation,* and *Meta-Reality* (all 2002). He is currently patron of the Centre for Critical Realism, London; president of Meta-Reality (UK, USA); Guest Professor in Philosophy and Sociology, Department of Health, Örebro University (Sweden); Adjunct Professor in Philosophy at the Centre for Peace Studies in Tromsø (Norway); Guest Professor in Philosophy of Science and Social Science, Department of Development and Planning, University of Aalborg (Denmark); and Visiting Fellow of the Lancaster University Institute of Advanced Studies (UK), where he has recently given the first series of the Annual Bhaskar Lectures on the Formation, Development, Application and Frontiers of Critical Realism.

Michaeline A. Crichlow is Associate Professor in African and African American Studies at Duke University in Durham, North Carolina, US. Her most recent book is *Negotiating Caribbean Freedom: Peasants and the State in Development* (2005). Her latest book, *Globalization and the Post-Creole Imagination: Notes on Fleeing the Plantation*, is currently under review. She is also co-editor of *Informalization: Process and Structure* (2000) and is currently editing *The Art and Cultural Politics of Carnival*. Collaborative work with Patricia Northover, on Rurality and State Configuration in Contemporary Globalisation, has led to her engagement with critical realism and ontological issues.

Mário Duayer is Professor of Political Economy at the Universidade Federal Fluminense, Rio de Janeiro State, Brazil. Working from within the Marxist tradition, he has written on methodological issues in economic science, conceptions of history and the role of subjectivity, and ontological relativism. In particular, he has been trying to show, in his lessons and works, the way the late G. Lukács' contributions could be very helpful in the relatively recent attempt to restore ontology.

Dave Elder-Vass recently completed his doctorate in sociological theory at Birkbeck College, University of London. He works on the theory of emergence and its application to the ontology of the social sciences. His thesis and recent papers relate emergence to the questions of structure, agency, cause, and method-ology, and he plans to develop an emergentist account of language, meaning, and culture. For further information, see his web site: www.eldervass.com.

John Latsis was educated in philosophy of economics and the history of economic thought at Oxford, the London School of Economics and finally Cambridge. He is currently a Jean Monnet Fellow at the Robert Schuman Centre for Advanced Study, part of the European University Institute in Florence.

Clive Lawson is a Fellow of Girton College Cambridge, Assistant Director of Studies at Gonville and Caius College and an Affiliated Lecturer in the Faculty of Economics and Politics, Cambridge. He has a PhD in Economics from Girton College, Cambridge and was a Research Fellow at the Centre for Business Research in Cambridge. He has published on American institutionalist economics and regional economics. His current research is in the philosophy of technology.

John Lawson is Director of Studies for Social and Political Science at Girton College, Cambridge. senior research associate at the Autism Research Centre, University of Cambridge and a senior lecturer in the department of Psychology at Oxford Brookes University. He has worked and published within the field of autism research for the last seven years. More recently he's become interested in how cognitive tendencies rooted in autism may influence and shape the way that all humans think and engage with the world. These ideas will appear in his forthcoming book, *The Role of Autism in Shaping Society*, to be published by Routledge.

Nuno Martins has a PhD in Economics from the University of Cambridge (Magdalene College), was a research scholar of the Portuguese Foundation for Science and Technology, and is currently a member of the Portuguese Catholic University, Faculty of Economics and Management, Porto. Current research interests include the methodology of economics, social ontology, philosophy of science, history of economic thought and development economics. These academic research interests stem from an engagement with projects like critical realism in economics, Sen's capability approach and human development.

João Leonardo Medeiros teaches various courses on the history of economic thought and political economy at the Universidade Federal Fluminense, Rio de Janeiro State, Brazil. He is interested in Lukác's late work on social ontology and particularly in the relationship between ethics and ontology. He has published articles (in Portuguese) on these subjects and on the ontology implicit in mainstream economic theories.

Eleonora Montuschi is Deputy Director at The Centre for Philosophy of Natural and Social Science and Visiting Fellow in the Department of Philosophy, Logic and Scientific Method at the London School of Economics. She has a BA and post graduate degree in philosophy from the University of Pavia (Italy) and a D.Phil in philosophy of science from Oxford. Her areas of teaching and research include the philosophy and methodology of social science, the philosophy of science and the history of philosophy. She directs the CPNSS project 'Objectivity, Human Values and Social Inquiry'. Her most recent book in English is *The Objects of Social Science* (Continuum Press, 2003).

Margaret Moussa lectures in political economy and economic theory at the University of Western Sydney. Her research area is the ontological and epistemological basis of economic theory.

Patricia Northover is a Fellow at the Sir Arthur Lewis Institute of Social and Economic Studies, University of the West Indies, Mona, Jamaica. Her interest in ontology was sparked by her doctoral study of growth theory and subsequent research on development processes which stimulated her engagement with critical realism and poststructuralism. She is a co-author of the ACS study, *The Future of Special and Differential Treatment in the FTAA* and editor of a special double issue of the Journal of Social and Economic Studies, on Arthur Lewis' Theory of Economic Growth. She is currently engaged in an interdisciplinary project, spearheaded by Michaeline Crichlow at Duke University, addressing 'Race, Space and Place: The Making and Unmaking of Freedom in the Atlantic and Beyond'.

Stephen Pratten is Lecturer in Economics at the Department of Management, King's College, London. His main research interests are in the methodology of economics, focusing particularly on issues relating to social ontology and realist theorising. He is a coeditor of the *Cambridge Journal of Economics*.

Lynn Savery is a Postdoctoral Fellow in the Department of International Relations at the Australian National University. She completed a PhD in International Relations at Monash University in 2004 and is the author of *Engendering the State: The International Diffusion of Women's Human Rights Norms* (forthcoming Routledge). She is also the author of 'Women's Human Rights and Changing State Practices: A Critical Realist Analysis', *Journal of Critical Realism* (2005). She has a longstanding interest in the ontology of international life. Her current research examines the responses to states and the international community to the moral imperative of redressing historical injustices committed against women.

Brad Shipway teaches Human Society and Environment in the School of Education at Southern Cross University, Australia. He is also a researcher for the Centre for Children and Young People at the same institution, where he is currently researching children's conceptions of citizenship and spirituality. He has a keen interest in critical realism, the philosophy of education, the interface between science theology, and home schooling. Brad has previously worked as a primary school teacher in both government and independent school systems, and currently serves on the board of a small rural independent school.

Tone Skinningsrud is associate Professor and Chair of the Department of Education, University of Tromsø in Norway. She is also General Secretary of the Academy of Science in Northern Norway. Her research interest is in comparative education, and she teaches the history of Norwegian education, sociology of education and methods in social research. Her interest in critical realism was a result of getting to know Margaret Archer's work in the sociology of education.

David Tyfield is completing his PhD in philosophy and sociology at the Centre for Philosophy of the Social Sciences, Exeter University, after studying biochemistry at Oxford and philosophy at London School of Economics. His research is on the contribution of realist social theory to the economics of science, focusing on changes in the production and ownership of knowledge in the life sciences. He is also interested in the productive interaction of philosophy and social science, as posited by critical realism, and the relationship between critical realism and Kant, Wittgenstein, Schumpeter and Marx. He is a qualified lawyer.

Nicholas Wilson is Principal Lecturer in Entrepreneurship at Kingston University. He studied music at Clare College, Cambridge and went on to train as a singer in London and Berlin. Changing career path in the mid 1990s, Nicholas worked in concert promotion and festival management before joining the Small Business Research Centre, Kingston University in 2000. Nicholas's interest in social ontology is informed by his own particular experience of the highs and lows of life as a freelance musician, as well as the challenges of lecturing in entrepreneurship. His current research focuses on critical realist accounts of creativity, entrepreneurship and emergence.

Acknowledgements

We are very grateful to all those who assisted in the preparation of this volume. In particular we would like to thank Andy Brown, Andrew Collier, Ben Fine, Steve Fleetwood, Francesco Guala, Mervyn Hartwig, Geoff Hodgson, Nick Hostettler, Branwen Jones, Martin Kusch, Tony Lawson, Peter Lipton, Caroline New, Alan Norrie, Nigel Pleasants, Doug Porpora, Antti Saaristo, Andrew Sayer, Phil Sharpe, Charles W. Smith, Phil Walden and Colin Wight,

We would also like to thank the members of the Cambridge Social Ontology Group, not only for the many helpful comments and ideas that helped shape this volume, but for their help in organising the original conference at Girton College, Cambridge at which the papers in this volume were first presented. We would also like to thank the Cambridge Political Society Trust, and the Centre for Research in the Arts, Social Sciences and Humanities, for financial help with this conference as well as those at Girton who made the conference so enjoyable.

1 Introduction: ontology, philosophy and the social sciences

John Latsis, Clive Lawson, Nuno Martins

Ontology, understood broadly as a concern with the nature of being, is currently enjoying a revival. Indeed, the recent rekindling of interest in ontological matters has prompted the perception of ontology as the latest buzzword or even paradigm shift.[1] Whereas this interest is evident across the disciplinary spectrum – from philosophy to artificial intelligence and computer science[2] – this book focuses upon the recent developments that have taken place within the social sciences. Until recently, social scientists tended to treat ontology with a great deal of suspicion. In large part, this may have arisen from the identification of ontology with metaphysics, which tends to be seen both as inaccessible to social scientists without the correct philosophical training and, in any case, as quite irrelevant to their concerns.[3] In this context, it is perhaps surprising to see just how much of a comeback ontology has made in recent years. Indeed it is now common for researchers in a range of social science disciplines not only to refer explicitly to ontology but to describe their work as in some sense ontological or as part of an ontological project. It is this turn to ontology in the social sciences that forms the central focus of this book. As will become clear, however, in practice this turn has taken a variety of different forms and can be understood from quite different vantage points.

The papers collected in this book are the outcome of a conference organised in Cambridge during the summer of 2004, which was dedicated specifically to ontology. The broad theme of the conference, 'theorising ontology', was intended to provide an interdisciplinary forum for new research in ontology that would both give space to very different approaches to ontology as well as facilitate the further development of such projects. Over the course of the conference it became clear that there were three broad categories of contribution being made. The first and largest group of contributions was concerned with the social sciences directly and in particular with social theory. The second group of contributions engaged directly with philosophical argument, focusing upon the historical uses of the term within standard philosophy texts. A third set of contributions was more grounded in empirical research and focused upon the relationship between ontology and the application of specific theoretical or empirical models within the social sciences.

These distinctions between types of contribution serve to provide the basic structure of this book. However, these distinctions not only allow us to present a very diverse set of contributions in a relatively natural way, they also highlight significant differences in the kinds of ontological projects being pursued. Moreover, the details of these differences, we believe, prompt some important rethinking of the relationships that exist between the different kinds of ontological projects currently thought possible. In short, these broad groupings do more than organise the contributions, they raise important issues of their own. For example, the nature of ontology has often been seen to involve a particular, top down or *a priori*, relationship between philosophy and the social sciences. Alternatively, it is often suggested that ontology must primarily be taxonomic and so without direct implications, i.e., it must be supplemented with empirical claims to be of any use to applied social scientists. In which case, how is ontology to make a difference to social science? Before proceeding to the contributions, we first, in the remainder of this introduction, consider this relation between philosophy, social theory and empirical research in the context of a focus on ontology. Specifically, we provide some historical and philosophical context to the emergent literature on social ontology, thereby showing how it alternatively builds on, or breaks with, older traditions within philosophy. A central consideration is that modern social ontology cannot be seen simply as an application of philosophical categories or techniques to the social sciences.

Several qualificatory remarks are perhaps best made at this point. First we have no desire to impose an artificial homogeneity onto the 'ontological turn' within the social sciences. In fact, we hope to emphasise the diversity of ontological orientations currently in play. Secondly, we do not seek to defend one or other orientation, but rather to illustrate the distinctiveness and sophistication of approaches currently being developed within the social sciences. Ontology is more than a buzzword, it implies a range of concerns that have been neglected in the traditional disciplines and are rarely discussed in philosophical circles, as we shall see below.

Ontology in historical perspective

The term 'ontology' is a philosophical term of art. Coined by late scholastic writers during the seventeenth century,[4] it entered philosophical terminology as a sub-category of the broader domain of metaphysics. The word derives from the Greek 'onto' (being) and 'logos' (study or science); so that ontology, as traditionally understood, is the science or study of being. The word 'being' itself has two senses in this context: firstly it refers to the entities or things that exist; secondly it refers to what it is to exist, i.e., to what (if anything) all things have in common.

Defined in this way, ontology amounts to the study of anything and everything. In practice, the following narrower ontological concerns have tended to dominate. First, ontology is only the study of anything under the aspect of its being, of what is involved in its existence. In light of this, ontology has tended to be distinguished broadly in terms of a concern with existence claims in contrast to other domains of philosophical enquiry such as epistemology (the study of knowledge), and methodology (the study of method). Secondly, ontology tends to be preoccupied with the study of those entities or things that are regarded as in some sense the most basic or significant. Although such an orientation is some-times viewed negatively (typically as the first step towards some form of essen-tialism[5]), such a focus tends to involve little more than a particular limiting of scope to those features of being that might be expected, in some historical con-text, to be of most interest.

The first major reference to ontology came with the publication of *Philosophia Primasive Ontologia* by the German rationalist philosopher Christian Wolff. Wolffian ontology was an application of the deductive method to philosophical problems generated by the Aristotelian distinction between substance and acci-dent. Beginning with indubitable first principles such as the principle of non-con-tradiction, rationalist metaphysicians like Wolff hoped to deduce the contents of the world without dirtying their hands in messy and inherently dubitable empiri-cal research. Wolff's *a priori* arguments concluded that the world was made up of simple, distinct, imperceptible and shapeless substances of which physical objects were complex composites. Though it persists today in some scholastic manuals, the Wolffian argument quickly lost its philosophical respectability dur-ing the eighteenth century, principally as a result of the critical contributions of Immanuel Kant. In his *Critique of Pure Reason* (1781), Kant demonstrated that *a priori* methods could be used to deduce both the thesis and the antithesis of Wolff's argument from the same premises, thus dealing a fatal blow to the earli-est modern tradition of ontology. After Kant, metaphysics survived and continued to be an integral part of philosophy, but the study of being *qua* being was treated with increased caution.

From the mid-seventeenth century onwards, British empiricists argued in favour of the precedence of the first-person perspective and licensed an over-whelming emphasis on human perception, resulting in a declining emphasis on ontology within Western academic philosophy. This reached its apotheosis in the first half of the twentieth century with the emergence of logical positivism and logical empiricism. Taking their cue from Hume and Berkeley, and associating metaphysics with unfalsifiable speculation, positivists and empiricists adopted a 'flat' ontology of sense data. This went largely unrecognised by both the authors and their critics. It was in this period that metaphysics, as noted, became a pejo-rative term, used to undermine unpopular philosophical positions and attack one's opponents. As a result the ontological import of philosophical and scientific thought was rarely discussed and was left largely unarticulated.

The middle of the 20th century saw a reversal of this trend and the reintroduc-tion of ontology into respectable academic philosophy. The main figure respon-sible for this renaissance was Willard Van Ormen Quine, whose collection of essays *From a Logical Point of View* (1953) drew attention to the crucial role of ontological commitment in the construction of both scientific and philosophical theories. Quine's project, though intimately tied to the tradition of logical empiri-cism, made a decisive break with orthodoxy by affirming that speculation about the contents of the universe was not hocus-pocus but rather an integral part of successful scientific practice. At least in the early years, Quine appeared to have been concerned with traditional ontological questions and his discussions of

ontology were grounded in a type of physicalism that many of his empiricist contemporaries would have shared.

Subsequently, philosophers of science such as Harré and Madden (1975), Fine
(1986), Cartwright (2000), Ellis (2001) helped to reintroduce ontology into
respectable philosophical discourse. These post-Quinian philosophers recognise
that scientific activity presupposes particular ontological conceptions and that
these are (in some sense) implied by our best scientific descriptions of the world.
Thus, modern ontology within the philosophical mainstream takes its cue from
the study of the natural sciences.

Perhaps unsurprisingly, therefore, modern philosophers mostly assume that
natural science provides our best epistemic practice and hence assume that we
should look to the natural sciences for our ontological commitments. Recent contributions often begin with the perceived success of natural science and try to elucidate (a) what it tells us about the world, and consequently (b) what the status of
scientific knowledge is. Thus protracted discussions of truth, verisimilitude and
rationality are common, yet mainstream philosophy rarely commits itself to a
specific ontological outlook. Philosophers do not see their main job as being one
of active interaction with the sciences but rather as outside observers of a spe-
cialised and privileged knowledge-generating activity.

This external, non-interactive role for ontology is not universally applied however. The philosophical approach to ontology has recently generated considerable
non-philosophical research in artificial intelligence and the computer sciences,
where 'formal ontology' is currently the central organising concept of a growing
research programme. The aim is to construct formal representations of entities
and relations in a given domain that can be shared across different contexts of
application. At least part of the attraction is that 'philosophy offers rigour'.
However in information science, the objective is not to model reality *per se* but
to make it possible to integrate different data systems into a single or more
encompassing framework. Philosophers have been teamed up with software specialists in the hope of providing all-encompassing top-level or 'backbone'
'ontologies' that all data systems could be translated into.

Irrespective of the outcome of this particular development in the use of ontology, two observations are germane to the issues raised in this book. First, formal
ontology can be directly related to the philosophical literature, and yet it involves
a fundamental shift away from the descriptive work of philosophers and towards
active engagement with a specific field of human knowledge (computer science).
Formal ontology draws unashamedly on the philosophical literature whilst going
well beyond what philosophers would normally attempt. Secondly, the desire for
such a single, top-level, ontology appears to have been impossible to maintain
alongside an explicitly realist orientation. Whilst the initial attraction of involving philosophers in data management and artificial intelligence lay in developing
a meta-language that really would capture general features that could be univer-
salisable in some sense, in practice such aims disappeared as prominent information systems ontologists have rather embraced a view of ontology as an inwardly
directed discipline (so effectively adopting an epistemologised reading of ontol-

ogy analogous to that of Carnap and Putnam – see Smith 2003). Ontology has, rather, come to be understood simply as referring to a 'conceptual model' (see Gruber 1995). In this latter case, ontology does not deal with or refer to reality as such, only 'alternative possible worlds' which are defined by the information systems themselves. Thus formal ontologies are shown to be artificial, deliberately constructed to achieve some predefined programming goal.

Formal ontology is in stark contrast to a second modern trend in ontology that is the locus of this book: social ontology. Social scientists have tended to approach ontology quite differently. On the one hand, for this group of contributions, references to traditional philosophical texts and concerns are few and far between. The genetic link between the literature on social ontology and the debates of academic philosophy is tenuous at the best of times. On the other hand, social ontologies are not deliberately constructed in the same way as formal ones. They are intimately related to the body of social scientific theory and the world it is supposed to describe and explain. At this point it is necessary to go into more detail about some general features of the social ontology projects that have emerged in recent years, and which provide the focus for much of the discussion in the contributions to this book.

Philosophy for the social sciences?

As already noted there has been a dramatic increase in interest in ontology within the social sciences in recent years and this interest has not simply amounted to an unquestioning acceptance of the concepts and methods of academic philosophers. Rather, something quite different appears to have emerged.

First, there has not been a simple or straightforward adoption of philosophical terms. Where terms have been adopted from philosophical discourse, the meanings are often quite different. For example, for social scientists the term scientific realism is intimately linked to discussions of ontology, and more specifically to discussion of the particular ontologies presupposed or implicit in the doing of science, whereas the term in philosophy conveys a more epistemological preoccupation with discussions of truth and its reliability. Secondly, social scientists have been concerned with a *philosophy for social science* rather than of it. There is clearly a practical interest here. Social scientists tend to be much more concerned with the nature of social being, focusing upon categories such as social structure, social institutions, rules, conventions and norms, rather than warrants for knowledge, identity conditions, etc. It is perhaps no surprise, then, that social scientists have tended to be more concerned with the work of philosophers such as Searle and Bhaskar, rather than Quine, Carnap or Putnam. The development of particular ontological conceptions has been the main attraction for social scientists, rather than epistemic problems raised by ontological explanations of the success of science.

This form of reasoning characterises the contributions in the first and largest part of this volume. In it, the authors do not examine the ontological assumptions and presuppositions of social theories in order to fit them into a pre-ordained philosophical straight-jacket. Instead, they choose to highlight the importance of fundamental (and often unarticulated) elements of social explanation and to use them for the critique and development of existing social scientific theories. These contributions are quite clearly motivated by concerns that are generated *within* the social sciences, problems that relate to social material as studied by practicing scientists. In contrast to philosophers' discussion of physics (for example), theory is not necessarily assumed to be epistemically privileged: the questionable empirical credentials of most social scientific disciplines exclude this as a universally legitimate starting point.

This does not mean that the study of existing scientific theories, and their ontological presuppositions, is not an important, and often far from straightforward, exercise. However, social ontologists have not tended to take scientific theories and their ontological presuppositions for granted regardless of their empirical record. It is one thing to identify the presuppositions of scientific theories, and another to accept the plausibility of those theories and so their ontological presuppositions. The study of scientific theories and the identification of ontological presuppositions is part of the job of modern social ontology, but social ontologists have also sought to establish descriptive, evidential or empirical criteria for assessing those theories. Moreover, general accounts of social ontology have often been brought to bear either in establishing such criteria or in providing directionality or clarification to social theorising. In these ways, ontological insights, occasionally informed by philosophical debate, are used to enrich, develop, or criticise existing theoretical approaches. In the first section of the book, all such ontological strategies are represented in different contexts and in differing degrees. The first two contributions emphasise the advantages of developing an existing account of social ontology within a particular domain. The next four are relatively more concerned with drawing out the specific ontological assumptions and tensions of particular authors and approaches within the social sciences.

In Chapter 2, Margaret Archer tackles a central category of modern social scientific discourse, subjectivity. In particular, Archer focuses upon the role that subjectivity plays in mediating between structure and agency. Archer argues that existing accounts of the structure–agency relation, including her own, have tended to emphasise the objective aspect of structure impinging upon agents, and have largely failed to explore the (responsive) role played by human subjectivity. Archer attempts to rebalance such accounts by explicitly considering the role of reflexivity in enabling agents to design and determine their responses to the structured circumstances in which they find themselves. Central to Archer's argument is the importance of personal powers, which are exercised through the process of reflexive internal dialogue (what Archer terms the Internal Conversation). This internal dialogue serves to delineate our concerns, define our projects and ultimately determine our practices.

Technology is the focus of Chapter 3. Here Clive Lawson draws upon the critical naturalism of critical realism and the transformational model of social activity to develop a conception of technology that has a series of advantages in relation to the existing literature on technology. Specifically, Lawson develops a transformational and relational conception of technology based upon the dual nature of technical objects. Lawson then attempts to re-cast claims made by a range of commentators, such as Heidegger and Habermas, who are often criticised as technological determinists. Lawson argues that this label is something of a straw person that serves to hide the fact that these so-called technological determinists, on closer inspection, seem to be posing important ontological questions that simply cannot be addressed by their, usually constructivist, critics.

In Chapter 4, Stephen Pratten questions the unity of the ontological turn in economics. Taking three major proponents of ontological theorising within economics (Tony Lawson, Nancy Cartwright and Uskali Mäki) as examples, Pratten argues that despite some similarities in language and overall concerns, a number of quite different ontological projects are being pursued. In the case of economic methodology, these projects yield both differing methodological advice and contrasting views of the future development of economics. Pratten highlights the differences between the ontologically orientated projects of Cartwright, Maki and Lawson through a discussion of their varying responses to the well known 'realism of assumptions' issue.

Lorenzo Bernasconi examines the theoretical and philosophical reflections of one of the dominant figures in modern social thought, Pierre Bourdieu, in Chapter 5. The locus of Bourdieu's theory of practice is the perceived opposition between subjectivist and objectivist theories in the social sciences. With the aid of Wittgenstein's rule-following considerations and the revolutionary concept of the 'habitus', Bourdieu claims to have finally transcended this age-old debate. Not so according to Bernasconi. He uses Saul Kripke's interpretation of Wittgenstein to show that Bourdieu's praxeological theory cannot be used to explain our normative practices adequately. Bernasconi proposes a sceptical solution to the problem of rule following: the explanation of social order can simply do without the sorts of justifications typically proposed by social theorists.

In Chapter 6, Margaret Moussa argues that, against Humean claims to the contrary, natural necessity is implied in a conception of purposive or reasoning activity. In order to make this argument, Moussa focuses upon two important theories of action, Habermas' theory of communicative action, and Luhmann's action system theory. Although both are attempts to develop a Weberian idealist theory of action, Moussa argues that they both contain a logic that stems from the fact that natural necessity is implied in purposive activity. Moussa's account operates at two levels. First, she shows that neither Habermas nor Luhmann can resolve the Weberian problems they attempt to deal with because neither theory completely rejects the idealist premises on which it is grounded. Second, she claims that purposive activity of the sort discussed by both authors presupposes the objective existence of generative mechanisms operating in open systems of cause and effect.

In Chapter 7, Mário Duayer and João Medeiros use Lukács's discussion of labour to illustrate how ontology can play a central role in underlabouring for a realist ethics. The genesis of value is to be found in the production and reproduction of social life, therefore in labour itself. Given the separation between needs and their satisfaction, the human subject is constantly faced with the need to judge. Duayer and Medeiros trace out the way use value serves to change the direction of causation in things. Thus conceptions of what 'ought' to be done become a determining factor in subjective praxis. But it is the social objectivity of values, reacting back on subjects as the internal criterion of the adequacy of practices, which is important for Duayer and Medeiros. Values, realised in practices, appear to human beings in practice as (ethical) reasons to act.

Distinguishing these ontological projects within the social sciences from philosophical concerns is a first step towards conveying the character of recent developments in social ontology. However, it would be a mistake to portray philosophical issues as being of no interest or significance to social ontologists. Many philosophical debates turn out to be of relevance to the emerging debates within social ontology, and it is hard to imagine that being informed about the traditional concerns of philosophy might not be of some help in developing social ontological projects. Moreover, the very relationship between traditional philosophy and the newly emerging social ontological projects is something that social scientists need to consider in some depth. Thus, for example, if philosophical caution is indeed necessary, the question arises as to whether recent developments within the social sciences be seen as misguided or presumptuous. The reverse may also be true: if it is possible for social scientists to develop specific ontological systems relatively unhampered by the epistemological concerns identified by traditional philosophy, is it not the case that there is something wrong with the traditional concerns of philosophy – that they are overcautious or even misguided?

In keeping with the older traditions of metaphysics and ontology, the contributors to the second section draw upon the philosophical literature in order to inform and supplement the expanding social scientific literature. The first three chapters explore some tensions that arise when social scientific enquiry and metaphysics come into contact, while the following paper ventures a metatheoretical elaboration of emergence, one of the central concepts of modern social ontology, and the final paper calls for a supplementation of ontology.

Chapters 8 and 9 explore the continuities and discontinuities between critical realism in the social sciences and the ontological tradition of modern analytic philosophy. In his chapter, John Latsis compares the contributions of Willard Quine and Tony Lawson. Latsis argues that the ontological turn advocated in Quine's early work was part of a conscious and concerted attack on contemporary philosophers who claimed to transcend metaphysics. In the same vein, Latsis argues, Lawson takes economists to task for not recognising their own implicit ontological commitments. Thus both authors advocate the recognition and elaboration of ontological commitments, but they propose very different criteria for admission into an acceptable ontology. For Quine the question of the legitimacy of ontic commitment flows from our ability to specify identity conditions for the entity in question. Within Lawson's transformational model on the other hand, the specification of identity conditions is not required. Social phenomena that appear to lack the boundaries usually attributed to entities are nevertheless recognised.

David Tyfield's chapter invokes a different interpretation of Quine's work as he investigates the nature of the transcendental argument and the validity of synthetic *a priori* truths. Tyfield argues that opponents of the synthetic *a priori* can be divided into two camps: the 'disillusioned trackers' who have attempted to find it but have ultimately failed; and those who never even pursued it, believing that any attempt would be futile. Tyfield refers to the writings of Peter Strawson and Quine respectively as examples of these two positions. He goes on to argue, against Quine, that the validity of the transcendental argument (and the synthetic *a priori*) has nothing to do with the logical form of the proposition that the argument attempts to establish. Instead, it has to do with the *presuppositions or premises* of the proposition. Tyfield further argues, this time against Strawson, that the synthetic *a priori* is not just about actual, but also about possible referents. Thus, Tyfield claims that the transcendental argument should be re-interpreted as an enquiry into the conditions of intelligibility of a phenomenon which constitutes the premise of the argument. Finally, Tyfield argues that it is not possible to understand either the transcendental argument or the synthetic *a priori* from an empiricist viewpoint, for any explanation of these requires the use of terms that are not available for the empiricist. Both concepts fall within the intentional theory of meaning, hence the discussion is better approached from a critical realist stance. To address the problems of the transcendental argument and the synthetic *a priori* from an empirical realist ontology (like both Quine and Strawson) leads to intractable problems from the onset.

A more recent contribution to the history and philosophy of science provides the backdrop to Eleonora Montuschi's reformulation, in Chapter 10, of the realist/constructivist debate. According to an increasingly influential account due to Lorraine Daston ('applied metaphysics') examples from the history of science show that the opposing poles of 'real' and 'invented' are over-emphasised in current philosophical debate. Montuschi shows how, in order to sustain her position, Daston embraces a strong distinction between quotidian and scientific objects, implicitly relying on the former as prior to and more fundamental than the latter. According to Montuschi, this spells problems for Daston's all-embracing, 'catholic' approach and her desire to account for both the natural and the social sciences using the same basic framework. Social scientific objects do not bear the same relations to quotidian objects as their natural scientific counterparts and thus the wide scope of applied metaphysics is threatened. A new historically grounded and practice-based conception of scientific objectivity flows from this discussion.

In Chapter 11, Dave Elder-Vass addresses the issue of emergence. One of the key distinguishing characteristics of critical realism in social theory is the insistence on emergent properties. Elder-Vass addresses the implications of two views of emergence for Bhaskar's three ontological domains: the empirical, the actual and the real. He distinguishes between a 'level abstracted view' and a 'downwardly inclusive view' of emergence. A level abstracted view analyses an entity as a whole regardless of its parts, whilst a downwardly inclusive view takes into account the existence and effects of its parts. He goes on to argue that causal explanation requires a downwardly inclusive view, which takes into account lower level entities. Elder-Vass recognises that this requires level stratification (the stratification of the world into emergent explanatory levels), when analysing lower level parts of an entity. Furthermore, he notes how Bhaskar's domains are also important since they allow a distinction between actual causation and causal powers. Elder-Vass argues that the dichotomy between actual causation and causal powers should be seen as *methodological* rather than ontological.

The final chapter of this section, Chapter 12, is by Roy Bhaskar. Although Bhaskar has perhaps contributed more than most to the recent interest in ontology, in this chapter he emphasises the need for ontological projects (in particular critical realism) to be supplemented with more epistemological and, what he terms, axiological concerns. After summarising and contextualising some of his own contributions to ontology, Bhaskar turns to various epistemological and moral problems, especially with what he refers to as the problem of the 'other'. Although critical realism has been right to combine ontological realism with epistemological relativism and judgemental rationality, Bhaskar argues, there has been a general failure to develop the issues relating to the latter, judgemental rationality. This can be done, Bhaskar argues, by grounding judgemental rationality upon two transcendental capacities: the capacity to identify with others (universal solidarity) and the capacity to reconcile with others (axial rationality).

Bhaskar's chapter focuses upon a series of themes, especially the relationship between ontological realism, epistemological relativism and judgemental rationality, which recur in many of the contributions to the last section of the book. These contributions illustrate the different ways in which ontological contributions have begun to have an impact on the practice of empirical social science. This section is made up of contributions to applied research that have been developed in close connection with the study of social ontology. The dialectical and interactive nature of these ontological projects is manifested in the authors' willingness to engage in the revision of previous ontological assumptions whenever empirical research provides descriptive or evidential criteria to do so.

On the one hand, social scientific practice can benefit from being ontologically informed. On the other, empirical analysis and social scientific practice can have an impact on the basic assumptions of scientific theories. By engaging in concrete and empirically orientated work, the chapters in this section demonstrate how modern trends in social ontology go beyond the traditional concerns of philosophers. Here the revisionary nature of social-ontological projects can be brought to the fore: ontological work involves an interactive process where empirical analysis and ontological conceptions have mutual implications, and jointly contribute to the formation of scientific (social) theory.

Patricia Northover and Michaeline Crichlow address the problematic of competitiveness of the countries of the Caribbean Community in Chapter 13. In order to do so, they develop a model of social power which moves beyond the traditional approaches to development that have been used in this region. This model explains the ontology and dynamics of social power within a context of social change, and is applied to concrete issues related to the historical transition from feudalist systems to capitalist societies, and to the formation of political identities and social power that occur as a consequence, while also addressing the present challenges for the Caribbean countries that arise within the process of globalisation.

In Chapter 14, Lynn Savery discusses the diffusion of international norms of sexual non-discrimination, especially at the level of the state. More specifically, the social ontology of critical realism is drawn upon to conceptualise this diffusion process in ways that transcend existing accounts which either, in emphasising the importance of utility maximisation, tend to be preoccupied with the activities of agents to the neglect of structural constraints, or, in emphasising the importance of socialisation, fail to distinguish between structure and agency at all.

Savery applies these ideas to an analysis of the gender-biased identity of the state, understood as a corporate agent. The processes that constitute identity, and the internal and external pressures exerted on the state by various actors, are then unpacked and the implications that follow for the diffusion into domestic state practices, mitigating the gender-biased corporate identity of the state, are drawn out. The cases of Germany and Japan are drawn upon to illustrate the particular dynamics and determinants of norm diffusion to the domestic practices of states. Savery shows that whilst the gender-biased corporate identity of the state is a serious impediment to diffusion, diffusion does take place under specific conditions that depend on the nature of local social interaction. This points to the need to understand how gender-bias is created and maintained, which, she suggests, itself depends on how gender is conceptualised and on how power relations emerge and become reproduced in particular situations.

Chapters 15 and 16 address the role that critical realism can play in the field of education. First, Tone Skinningsrud draws upon Margaret Archer's morphogenetic theory in order to explain the development of the state educational system in Norway. Grounded in the author's historical research, Skinningsrud argues that the appropriate framework for conceptualising the emergence of the Norwegian educational system is not a model where education is mono-integrated with the church, but rather a model in which there is a dual integration both with the state and the church.

Skinningsrud explains how even though a mono-integrated relation between education and the Roman Catholic Church is appropriate as a description of the Norwegian and wider Scandinavian situation in the Middle Ages, after the Lutheran Reformation education became integrated both with the church and the state. This leads to a reformulation of Archer's theory. Whilst in the case of mono-integration one morphogenetic cycle would provide an appropriate account of the emergence of state educational systems, in the case of dual integration one needs a model which comprises two morphogenetic cycles.

In Chapter 16, Brad Shipway draws directly upon Bhaskar's dialectical critical realism to investigate the problematic of emancipation and rational agency in compulsory schooling. Shipway notes how Bhaskar's notion of rational agency comprises cognitive, empowered and dispositional components. It is then argued that these components are possessed in degrees, as opposed to possessed or not. Thus, an agent always has some degree of rationality, and hence all agents are involved in emancipation to some extent. According to Shipway, the universal moral worth of the agents' emancipatory process and the agent's being are not dependent on any imposed, social or biological limitations. However, before acquiring rational agency, there is also a pre-rational stage in infancy. Following Bhaskar, Shipway notes how the process of emancipation is present since infancy, even before the realisation of cognitive emancipation.

Shipway describes teachers and carers who work with students at this pre-rational stage as 'custodians'. He goes on to provide an example of how dialectical critical realism can be applied to a concrete example of a kindergarten class. The paper finishes with some further considerations on how dialectical critical realism can facilitate the emergent rationality of students towards emancipation. The author argues that attempts to be neutral on these issues often lead to the perpetuation of oppressive structures, and advocates the supported perspective as a promising alternative for education.

In Chapter 17, John Lawson investigates the reasons for modern economics' preoccupation with mathematical modelling. Drawing on his research in the social psychology of autism spectrum conditions, Lawson suggests that the drive towards mathematisation in economics is symptomatic of the dominance of 'closed system thinking'. This diagnosis links the widely criticised ontology of mainstream economics to an underlying set of cognitive and biological factors that might explain its persistence in the face of empirical and theoretical setbacks. In laying out his argument, Lawson extends critical realist ontological analysis to the domain of psychology and shows how open and closed systems might correspond to different styles of thought.

In the final chapter, Nicholas Wilson draws from an in-depth empirical study and personal experience in his analysis of the emergence of a labour market. He uses a small, recently formed professional community as his subject; tracing the establishment and development of the market for early music performers in the United Kingdom. Wilson's chapter goes beyond the standard critical realist ontological analysis in showing how familiar insights might be used to inform detailed empirical case studies within the social sciences. In so doing, he shows how ontological reflection can facilitate the study of labour markets in general. Margaret Archer's morphogenetic approach provides the basic toolkit for a re-conceptualisation of labour markets and a new account of their emergence.

Contributions in each of the three sections of this book demonstrate the partial independence of current social science ontological projects from the traditional concerns of academic philosophy. These contributions also show that social ontologists have tended to adopt a revisionary and interactive role within the social sciences. Given the lack of general agreement upon successful social science theories and the lack of empirically convincing test cases, it is hardly surprising that ontologists have not resigned themselves to purely descriptive roles. Yet, as the papers in this volume demonstrate, the alternative to description or unravelling the implicit ontologies of the sciences, is not the pursuit of Wolffian, infallible, or indubitable deductions from secure ontological premises. And it is this middle ground between description and deduction that recent ontological projects have attempted to occupy.

Our intention in this brief introduction has been to illustrate some of the issues that currently motivate those engaged within ontological projects in order both to provide points of entry into the current debate and to stimulate further discussion. The structure of the book, we believe, serves to highlight the different nature of the ontological projects currently emerging within social science. Making such distinctions helps to contextualise the diverse, often conflicting current contributions to social ontology, whilst maintaining their legitimacy as specifically ontological projects. We do not intend to imply that the contributions that follow are an exhaustive selection of all the research currently being pursued within the social sciences. Nevertheless, we do believe that they ably illustrate the diversity and sophistication of modern social ontology.

Notes

1 See for example Winter 2001.
2 For example recent years have seen the establishment or further funding of such projects as the Buffalo Centre for Ontological Research, the Laboratory for Ontology in Turin and the Institute for Formal Ontology and Medical Information Science in Saarland. Much of the interest within Artificial Intelligence has been in relation to data organisation; for a good discussion see Poli (1996) and Smith (2003).
3 The term meta in Greek means over or after and the term physis translates as nature. The term metaphysics gained currency from Aristotles' The Metaphysics (ta meta ta phusika) which was placed immediately after the book called Physics. The term seems to have gained wide appeal as denoting the *purpose* of metaphysics, which is (or includes) reaching above or beyond nature (physis) to uncover its most basic components of fundamental features. It is this status as in some sense 'over and above' science which seems to lie at the root of much of the deep suspicion that scientists have for metaphysics, often using the term to convey the idea of idle or detached speculation. See for example the essays on ontology in Burkhardt & Smith (1991).
4 'Ontology', or rather 'ontologia', appears to have been coined in 1613 by two philosophers writing independently of each other: Jacob Lorhard in his *Theatrum Philosophicum* and Rudolf Göckel in his *Lexicon Philosophicum*. Its first occurrence in English seems to be in Bailey's Dictionary of 1721, where ontology is defined as 'an account of being in the abstract'. See for example Smith (2003), or Lawson (2005).
5 Where essences are usually understood rather dismissively as unchanging and deterministic.

References

Burkhardt, H. and Smith, B. [eds.] (1991) *The Handbook of Metaphysics and Ontology*, vol. 2, Munich, Germany: Philosphia Verlag.

Cartwright, N. (2000) *The Dappled World: A Study of the Boundaries of Science*, Cambridge: Cambridge University Press.

Ellis, B. D. (2001) *Scientific Essentialism*, Cambridge and New York: Cambridge University Press.

Fine, A. (1986) *The Shaky Game: Einstein, Realism and The Quantum Theory*, Chicago, IL: University of Chicago Press.

Gruber, T. R. (1995) 'Towards Principles for the Design of Ontologies Used for Knowledge Sharing', *International Journal of Human and Computer Studies*, 43 (5/6), pp. 907–928.

Harré, R. and Madden, E. (1975) *Causal Powers*, Oxford: Basil Blackwell.

Kant, I. (1781 [2003]) *Critique of Pure Reason*, N. Kemp Smith (transl.), London: Palgrave Macmillan.

Lawson, T. (2005) *A Conception of Ontology,* Cambridge: Mimeo.

Poli, R. (1996) Ontology for knowledge organization, in R. Green (Ed), *Knowledge Organization and Change*, Frankfurt/Main, INDEKS Verlag, pp. 313–319.

Quine, W. V. O. (1980 [1953]) *From a Logical Point of View* (2nd ed), Cambridge, MA: Harvard University Press.

Smith, B. (2003) 'Ontology', in L. Floridi (Ed), *Blackwell Guide to the Philosophy of Computing and Information*, Oxford: Blackwell, pp. 155–166.

Winter, S. (2001) *Ontology: Buzzword or Paradigm Shift,* in Geographical Information Science, Vol. 15, no. 7, 587–590.

Part I
Ontology and social theory

2 The ontological status of subjectivity: the missing link between structure and agency

Margaret S. Archer

Introduction

One of the few propositions upon which social theorists agree is the truism 'no people; no society'. Accord stretches a bit further because no one seriously maintains that 'society is like people'. Society remains different in kind from its component members, even if it is conceptualised as being no more than the aggregate effect of people's doings (and conceptions) or the pattern produced by them.

The crucial difference is that no aggregate or pattern truly possesses self-awareness,[1] whereas every single (normal) member of society is a self-conscious being. Thus, however differently the social may be conceptualised in various schools of thought (from an objective and emergent stratum of reality to an objectified social construct with the ontological status of 'facticity'), the social remains different from its component members in this crucial respect. It lacks self-consciousness. Therefore, it follows that a central problem for social theorists must be to provide an answer to the question 'What difference does the self-awareness of its members make to the nature of the social?'

Historically, the answers given have varied from 'all the difference', as the response common to idealists, to 'no difference at all', as the reply of hard-line materialists. Today, the variety of answers has increased but the question remains because it cannot be evaded. For example, social constructionists cannot dodge the issue by regarding any societal feature as a product of 'objectification' by its members. This is because each and every individual can mentally deliberate about what is currently objectified in relation to himself or herself (they can ask 'Should I take this for granted?'). Conversely, no objectified 'entity' can be reflexive about itself in relation to individuals (it can never, as it were, ask 'Could this construct be presented more convincingly?'). The ineluctability of this issue led Hollis and Smith (1994) to maintain that 'argument about [the] "objective and subjective", … is as fundamental as argument about [the] "collective and individual"'. Not only are these two issues of equal importance but also they are closely intertwined.

The 'problem of structure and agency' has a great deal in common with the 'problem of objectivity and subjectivity'. Both raise the same question about the relationship between their component terms, which entails questioning their respective causal powers. Once we have started talking about causal powers, it is impossible to avoid talking about the ontological status of those things to which causal powers are attributed or from which they are withheld.

However, a popular response to these two (recalcitrant) problems is the suggestion that we should *transcend* both of them by the simple manoeuvre of considering them to be the two faces of a single coin. Transcending the divide rests upon conceptualising 'structures' and 'agents' as ontologically inseparable because each enters into the other's constitution and therefore they should be examined as one mutually constitutive amalgam.[3] In a single leap-frog move, all the previous difficulties can be left behind. This manoeuvre has direct implications for the question of 'objectivity and subjectivity'. If 'structure' and 'agency' are conceptualised as being inseparable, because they are maintained to be mutually constitutive, then this blurring of subject and object necessarily and seriously challenges the possibility of reflexivity itself. If the two are an amalgam, it is difficult to see how a person or a group is able to reflect critically or creatively upon their social conditions or context.

Part 1: The impossibility of eliminating subjectivity

Critical Realists are necessarily 'against transcendence' precisely because, on ontological grounds, they are 'for emergence'. Ontologically both structure and agency are conceptualised as distinct strata of reality because they have different, irreducible and causally efficacious properties and powers. For example, structures can be centralised, whilst people cannot, and people can exercise reflexivity, which structures cannot do. In this case, there is no alternative to theorising about the interplay between 'structure' and 'agency' as strata of reality that are irreducible to one another. Moreover, as the above example shows, the same goes for 'objectivity' and 'subjectivity'.

My intention is to examine these interconnected issues of 'subjectivity and objectivity' and 'structure and agency' through briefly reviewing the answer given by Realists to the question 'how does structure influence agency?' Central to the Critical Realist answer is Roy Bhaskar's (1989, pp. 25–26) statement that 'the causal power of social forms is mediated through social agency'. This is surely correct, because unless the emergent properties of structure and culture are held to derive from people and their doings and to exert their effects through people, then Realism would obviously be guilty of reification. Nevertheless, it is not complete because what is meant by that crucial word 'through' has not been unpacked.

Generically, the word 'through' has been replaced by the process of 'social conditioning'. However, to condition entails the existence of something that is conditioned, and because conditioning is not determinism, then this process necessarily involves the interplay between two different kinds of causal powers – those pertaining to structures and those belonging to agents. Therefore, an adequate conceptualisation of conditioning must deal explicitly with the interplay between these two powers. Firstly, this involves a specification of *how* structural and cultural powers impinge upon agents, and secondly of *how* agents use their own personal powers to act 'so rather than otherwise' in such situations.

Thus, there are two elements involved, the 'impingement upon' (which is objective) and the 'response to it' (which is subjective). Realists, myself included, have concentrated upon the former to the neglect of the latter. This one-sidedness is illustrated in Figures 2.1 and 2.2.

The place of social conditioning in realist social theory

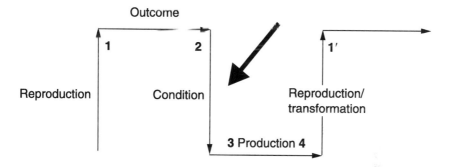

Figure 2.1
Source: Roy Bhaskar, *Reclaiming Reality*, Verso, London, 1989, p. 94.

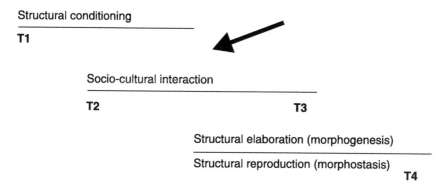

Figure 2.2
Source: Margaret S. Archer, *Realist Social Theory*, Cambridge University Press, 1995, p. 157.

On the whole, I think we have satisfactorily conceptualised the objective side by specifying that cultural and structural emergent properties impinge on people by shaping the social situations that they confront. Often this confrontation is involuntary, as with people's natal social context and its associated life-chances. Often it is voluntary, like getting married. In either case, these objective conditioning influences are transmitted to agents by shaping the situations that those agents live with, have to confront, or would confront if they chose to do x, y or z. Sometimes they impinge as constraints and enablements and sometimes by distributing different types of vested interests or objective interests to different groups of people in either reproducing or transforming their social conditions.

However, since Realists are not determinists, what we have omitted to examine is why people do not respond in uniform fashion under the same circumstances. Subjects who are similarly situated can debate, both internally and externally, about the appropriate course of action and come to different conclusions, which is one reason why Humean constant conjunctions are not found. At best, what are detected are empirical tendencies in action patterns, consonant with objective influences having shaped them. These must remain nothing more than trends, partly because contingencies intervene, but partly because a second causal power is necessarily at play, namely the personal power to reflect upon one's circumstances and to decide what to do in them or to do about them.

In short, the conceptualisation of this process of mediation between structure and agency has not been fully adequate because it has not fully incorporated the role played by human subjectivity in general. In particular, it omits the part of reflexivity in enabling agents to design and determine their responses to the structured circumstances in which they find themselves.

The process of 'conditioning' thus entails the exercise of two sets of causal powers: those of the property that 'conditions' and those of the property that is 'conditioned'. Let us look at this concretely in relation to constraints and enablements. The obvious point is that a constraint requires something to constrain and an enablement needs something to enable. These are not intransitive terms because if *per impossible* no agent ever conceived of any course of action then neither could be constrained nor enabled. This is impossible because by virtue of our biological constitution and life in society we have to conceive of courses of action (deciding what to eat tonight cannot be consigned to reflex or routine action, otherwise why are we aware of giving some thought to it?).

Similarly, the mere existence of a top heavy demographic structure does not constrain a generous pensions' policy at all, unless and until somebody advances the policy of giving generous pensions. Only when that project has been mooted does the top-heavy demographic structure in relation to a small active population become a constraint, *ceteris paribus*. Equally, in the cultural realm, if there is a contradiction between two beliefs or two theories it remains a purely logical matter, existing out there in the 'Universal Library',[4] until and unless someone wants to uphold one of those ideas or assert one of those ideas or do something with one of those ideas.

Consequently, the incorporation of agential powers into the conceptualisation of conditioning entails the following three points. First, that social emergent properties, or rather the exercise of their powers, are dependent upon the existence of what have been termed 'projects', where a project stands for any course of action intentionally engaged upon by a human being. These projects, *as subjectively conceived by agents*, are necessary for the activation of social emergent properties, i.e. their transformation into powers. Second, only if there is a relationship of congruence or incongruence between the emergent social property and the project of the person(s) will the latter activate the former. If there is congruence, this represents enablement and if there is incongruence, that constitutes constraint. Third, and most importantly for this paper, agents have to respond to these influences by using their own personal powers to deliberate reflexively over how to respond. This is the difference between human agents and other kinds of animate or inanimate matter. What is also unique about the reflexivity of human beings is that it can involve anticipation. A constraint need not have impinged or impacted, it could just be foreseeable.

Because the response of the agent to a constraint (or enablement) is a matter of reflexive deliberation, it can take very different forms: from compliance, through evasion and strategic action to subversion. The one thing that is rarely, if ever, found is a complete uniformity of response on behalf of every agent who encounters the same constraint or the same enablement.

Therefore, it is essential to distinguish between the objective existence of structural (and cultural) emergent properties and the exercise of their causal powers, since the realisation of their causal powers requires them to be activated by agents. Hence, the efficacy of any social emergent property is at the mercy of the agents' reflexive activity. Outcomes vary enormously with agents' creativity in dreaming up brand new responses, even to situations that may have occurred many times before. Ultimately, the precise outcome varies with agents' personal concerns and degrees of commitment, together with the costs different agents will pay to see their projects through in the face of structural obstacles and hindrances. Equally, they vary with agents' readiness to avail themselves of enablements.

Were someone determined to deny the independent influence of human subjectivity, the second mode of conditioning that Realists have conceptualised could be brought into play. It might be stressed that emergent properties also motivate us towards various courses of action. They do not just constrain and enable us. This is true, but it would not serve to sustain the above argument because these social properties are held to work precisely through agential subjectivity itself, by moulding it in a particular manner. Usually they are considered to work without full personal awareness and often as what sociologists call the 'unacknowledged conditions of action'. Yet, if they are genuinely unacknowledged then such causal influences should be exerted in blanket form on all people. There would be no difference in response, according to their subjective reception by different individual agents (or groups of agents) if all were totally unaware of them. Only a uniform response from the population in question would justify ignoring their personal subjectivity, on the grounds that this has been externally shaped. Yet, such differences are common. Therefore the examination of agential subjectivity and reflexive variability becomes even more important in order to understand differences of response under the same ('unacknowledged') conditions.

There are indeed structural properties, such as vested interests, that can motivate by encouraging and discouraging people from particular courses of action. However, these have first to be found good by a person before they can influence the projects she entertains. For a person to find a vested interest good does not entail that she has full discursive penetration of the property, as if she were endowed with all the qualities of a good sociologist. In fact, agents do not have to know everything that is going on, or there would be no such things as 'unacknowledged conditions'. There are indeed, but all those conditions need to do in order to shape her motivation is to shape her circumstances. Take a young academic, born in this country with English as her mother tongue. What she recognises or takes for granted about her situation are aspects of its ease: books are translated quickly, English is one of the official languages at conferences and used in the best known journals, etc. What she does not need to have is discursive penetration about why her situation is so comparatively easy and rewarding. She does not need to acknowledge that she is a beneficiary of neo-colonialism, which gives English the status it has today in academe. In order for her motivation towards her academic career to be enhanced, all she has to acknowledge is, for example, the ease and fluency with which she makes interventions at international conferences.

However, this same young academic may have a baby and then determine that babies and academic careers are incompatible. Our hypothetical social determinist might then argue that without the 'hegemonic discourse of maternity' she would not have so determined. Yet, given this (past) hegemony, how would one account for the minority of women who continued with their careers whilst others resigned? Of course, further social factors could be adduced, but the dogged social determinist then confronts infinite regress. The only way out of this impasse is to allow that personal emergent properties give us the ability to make variable responses under the same objective social circumstances.

Equally, structural factors do constitute deterrents, capable of depressing agential motivation. They do so by attaching different opportunity costs to the same course of action (such as house purchase) to different parts of the population. This is how 'life chances' exert causal powers, but their outcomes are only empirical tendencies. What they cannot explain is why x becomes a home owner and y does not, if both are similarly socially situated. That is a question of the agents' own concerns and deliberations which govern whether or not they find the cost worth paying. The simple fact that somebody is faced with a deterrent in the form of an opportunity cost does not mean they are necessarily deterred, any more than does the fact that people inherit vested interests mean that they are bound to defend them – Tony Benn renounced a knighthood in order to sit in the House of Commons.

Thus, there is no one-to-one relationship between social position and individual disposition in terms of actions and their outcomes. Instead, there is always

↑ potential
adopters.

some variability in the courses of action taken that is attributable to personal subjectivity. Without acceptance of this, we are thrown back upon empirical generalisations of the kind, 'the greater the cost of a project, the less likely are people to entertain it'. Not only is that no explanation whatsoever (merely a quest for Humean constant conjunctions) but also, far from having eliminated human subjectivity, it relies upon a banal and highly dubious form of it.

Because human subjectivity cannot be kept out of any such account, the overwhelming tendency has been for sociological investigators to insert their own subjectivity in place of the agents' reflexivity. Often we Realists have been guilty of putting things like vested interests or objective interests into our accounts of action as a kind of dummy for real and efficacious human subjectivity. There are many worse exemplars, and probably the worst is Rational Choice Theory, which imputes instrumental rationality alone[5] to all agents as they supposedly seek to maximise their preference schedules in order to become 'better off' in terms of some indeterminate future 'utiles'. Subjectively, every agent is reduced to a bargain hunter and the human pursuit of the *Wertrationalität* is disallowed.[6] Bourdieu (1977, 1990), too, was often guilty of endorsing an empty formalism about subjectivity, such that people's positions ('semi-consciously' and 'quasi-automatically') engendered dispositions to reproduce their positions. Such theoretical formulations seem to lose a lot of the rich and variable subjectivity that features prominently in *La Misère du Monde*.

Part 2: The ontological implications of incorporating subjectivity

Instead, let us explore the theoretical and practical implications of giving agential powers their proper due. This is what the rest of this chapter is about, namely conceptualising the interplay between personal subjective properties and powers and objective societal properties and powers. Specifically, what are the implications of maintaining that personal reflexivity mediates the effects of objective social forms upon us? In other words, 'reflexivity' is being advanced as the answer to how 'the causal power social forms is mediated *through* human agency'. It performs this mediatory role by virtue of the fact that we deliberate about ourselves in relation to the social situations that we confront, certainly fallibly, certainly incompletely and necessarily under our own descriptions because that is the only way we can know anything. To accord human reflexivity that role, even provisionally, means at least entertaining that we are dealing with two ontologies, the objective pertaining to social emergent properties and the subjective pertaining to agential emergent properties.

What is entailed by the above is that subjectivity is (a) real, (b) irreducible, and (c) possesses causal efficacy. Before examining these three implications, it is probably helpful to specify what kinds of subjective properties and powers are under consideration as constitutive of this mediatory process. I have termed this process the Internal Conversation (Archer, 2003), to designate the manner in which we reflexively make our way through the world. This is what makes (most of us) 'active agents', people who can exercise some governance in their lives, as opposed to 'passive agents' to whom things just happen.[7]

Being an 'active agent' hinges on the fact that individuals develop and define their ultimate concerns: those internal goods that they care about most[8] and whose precise constellation makes for their concrete singularity as persons.[9] No one can have an ultimate concern and fail to do something about it. Instead, each seeks to develop a concrete course(s) of action to realise that concern by elaborating a project(s), in the (fallible) belief that to accomplish the project(s) is to realise one's concern(s). If such courses of action are successful, which can never be taken for granted, everybody's constellation of concerns, when dovetailed together, becomes translated into a set of established practices. This constitutes their personal *modus vivendi*. Through this *modus vivendi,* subjects live out their personal concerns within society as best they can. In shorthand, these components can be summarized in the formula: Concerns → Projects → Practices. There is nothing idealistic about this, because 'concerns' can be ignoble, 'projects' illegal and 'practices' illegitimate.

These are the kinds of mental activity that make up the strange reality of reflexivity, as part of broader human subjectivity. Because the implication under consideration is ontological and not epistemological, its acceptance entails the endorsement of plural ontologies. This should not in itself be a problem for Critical Realism. The reality of what has been termed 'Internal Conversation' (also known as 'self talk', 'rumination', 'musement', 'inner dialogue', 'internal speech', etc.) does not mean that when we deliberate, when we formulate our intentions, when we design our courses of action or when we dedicate ourselves to concerns, that such mental activities are like chairs or trees, they are not. Yet, this has nothing whatsoever to do with whether or not they are real because reality itself is not homogeneous. The whole of reality cannot be confined to and defined in terms of the Enlightenment notion of 'matter in motion'. Indeed, in post-positivistic science, physical reality is made up as much by quarks and genomes as it is by old stagers like magnetism and gravity or even older stagers like rocks and plants.

Abandonment of that Enlightenment assumption paves the way to the acceptance of plural ontologies. It is now more than 30 years since Popper distinguished his Three Worlds, as ontologically distinct sub-worlds: the world of physical states, the world of mental states and the world of objective ideas. What is important about this for the present argument is that Popper put his finger on the genuine oddity about World Two, the world of mental states, namely that it is both objectively real and yet it has a subjective ontology.

1. Reality

Conscious states like holding an Internal Conversation can only exist from the point of view of the subject who is experiencing those thoughts. In other words, Internal Conversations have what John Searle (1999, p. 42) terms a first-person ontology. This means they have a subjective mode of existence, which is also the case for desires, feelings, fantasies, beliefs and intentions. That is, only as experienced by a particular subject does a particular thought exist. Just as there are no such things as disembodied pains, there are no such things as subjectively independent thoughts. Both are first-person dependent for their own existence. However, you might object that whilst I cannot share my toothache with you, what am I currently doing but sharing my thoughts with you? In fact I do not agree that it is possible to share my thoughts with you. Instead, what I am doing is sharing my *ideas* with you, as World Three objects, ones that will become even more permanently[10] part of World Three once they are published.

What I cannot share with you is something William James (1890, p. 254f) captured very well, the reflexive monitoring that is going on here and now as my thoughts are turned into the complete sentences that you will read at least 12 months hence. Internally, I am engaged in self-monitoring activities, which are an inextricable part of my thoughts, such as mundanely checking if a singular subject is accompanied by a singular verb or deciding on the words that seem best to capture an insight. That experience I cannot share with you any more than I can convey to my doctor or dentist what kind of toothache I have, except by metaphors like sharp and jagged, etc. What I cannot do is take my toothache out and say to the dentist 'Here you experience it for two seconds please and then you will know with what you have to deal'. So too, thoughts remain intransigently first-person in kind. However, the crucial point is not about sharing or epistemic access – the point is ontological. As Searle (1999, p. 43) puts it, 'each of my conscious states exists only as the state it is because it is experienced by me, the subject. That is what makes the ontology of subjectivity distinctive. Most other parts of reality have a third-person mode of existence, sometimes self-sufficient like mountains, sometimes dependent upon people at a prior time like books, but not necessarily dependent upon a knowing subject at this point in time. A thought, however, does require a present-tense subject doing the thinking in the first-person. That is the oddity of subjective ontology.

2. Irreducibility

If human reflexivity, in the form of Internal Conversations, has the causal power to mediate structural and cultural properties, then it must be irreducible to these emergent social forms. Moreover, reflexivity could not even be a candidate for performing this mediatory role if there was not first-person authority as well as a first-person perspective.[11] Indeed, there are schools of thought that are quite willing to entertain the existence of a first-person perspective but would not accept first-person authority. That would be true of social constructionists in general. In particular, Rom Harré (1983, p. 61f) maintains that we are merely sites of perception, that is we are just like the coordinates of Washington '39N 77W' – a standpoint from which we see things. Today, most social theorists can agree that there is no 'news from nowhere'. However, it is not sufficient simply to argue for the existence of a first-person perspective. First-person authority is needed too if subjectivity is to play a full part in social theorising. Such authority has to be part of a subjective ontology, otherwise utterances about internal mental activities are either reducible or lack causal efficacy because they are merely phenomenological 'froth'.

In other words, a claim has to be sustained that subjects alone have first-person authority to know their own minds about objective social factors better than can anyone else. This claim maintains that we have a special knowledge about ourselves in relation to society that cannot be replaced by a third-person account, such as that offered by an investigator. If the two were interchangeable, or the investigator's account was deemed to be superior to the subject's account in all respects (though it can be in some), then our reflexive Internal Conversations would be redundant in social theory. All theory and investigation could be conducted in the third-person. In that case, the notion of reflexivity playing any indispensable role, such as is being claimed for it as a mediatory mechanism, would necessarily fall to the ground.

To avoid this I am going to make a claim for the existence of a certain kind of first-person authority, whilst avoiding the excessive claims that have been made about first-person epistemic authority. Thus, I am not arguing for first-person infallibility with Descartes, nor for first-person omniscience with Hume, nor for first-person indubitability with Hamilton and nor for first-person incorrigibility with Ayer.[12] If there is anything in the psychoanalytic notion that we conceal certain beliefs, desires, etc. from ourselves and attribute other beliefs or desires to ourselves, then each of those four claims above is completely undermined. However, psychoanalysis itself does not undermine first-person authority, because recovery of authority by a patient over an attitude is often the only evidence that it was there prior to the therapeutic suggestion.[13]

Instead, it is argued that one can still claim first-person self-warrant. In other words one can make the claim, 'I enjoy self-warrant whenever I truly believe I am thinking (or feeling) X at the moment; *ipso facto,* I am justified in claiming to know the state of my belief, even if that belief itself turns out to be untrue'.[14] In other words, an agent can be granted self-warranted authority (not infallibility), whose importance is that she bases her public conduct on her own reflexive deliberations. These are known directly to her and only indirectly to a third-person (an investigator or interlocutor) through fallible interpretation. If that is the case, it follows that no investigator may properly substitute his or her interpretation for that of the agent. If I tell you 'I am happy to have two children', I know my meaning, its nuances and proper emphases when I produce that utterance – or its opposite. You can only interpret my meaning from my utterance and your notions, connotations and emphases are your interpretations, which may be very different from mine. What warranted first-person authority entails is that an agent may be wrong *in* her beliefs (and often is) but she cannot be wrong *about* her beliefs. This argument maintains that the agent therefore retains an irreducible property – and power – since she acts on her beliefs. Whenever there is acceptance of first-person authority and of its basic asymmetry with third-person accounts, then the contribution of agential subjectivity can never be bypassed in sociological accounts of action and its consequences.

Hence, the admission of first-person authority is a necessary stepping-stone for avoiding social 'hydraulics' and asserting instead that it is our deliberations about things structural and cultural, about the contexts and social situations in which we find ourselves, that determine exactly what we do. Certainly, because we are not infallible, it can be maintained that social factors affect agents' outlooks without people actually diagnosing this. That would be the case for ideological influences or for members of a social class overestimating an objective obstacle, like those working class parents who used to turn down Grammar School places on the grounds that 'they are not for the likes of us'. However, the key point is that we cannot know that this is the case without examining agents' subjectivity, their reflexive Internal Conversations. Without that we cannot discover what 'ideology' or 'social class' have encouraged one person to believe but failed to convince another to believe. What cannot be assumed is that every ideological effort will or can be victorious in instilling all people with the desired beliefs. Ideologies, however hegemonic, are not in themselves influences, but rather attempts to influence. They too, as a cultural counterpart of structural factors, involve both impingement upon the subject and reception by the subject. Reception is obviously heterogeneous, or no one would ever have accepted a Grammar School place for their working-class child and no counter-ideology would ever have been formulated.

Sometimes it seems even more tempting, in habitus theory or discourse theorising in general, simply to take reproduction as a passive act on the part of an agent that requires no investigation of his or her reflexive thought. However, reproduction in society rarely means replication and is equally rarely achieved through routine, non-deliberative action. In fact, successful 'reproduction' is usually heavily dependent upon reflexive activity because reproduction is not about staying put, it is about staying ahead. Some of the best examples Bourdieu himself gave depended upon self-conscious subjective ingenuity, such as middle class parents with non-academic offspring seeking out some form of niche training that could salvage the social status of their not-too-bright child. In sum, it is impossible to explain how agents reproduce or transform the objective social context without examining their subjectivity. This leads directly to the last crucial point, namely the causal powers of agents and the mediatory power of the Internal Conversation.

3. Reflexivity and its causal powers

It has been maintained that our personal powers are exercised through reflexive internal dialogue and that the Internal Conversation is responsible for the delineation of our concerns, the definition of our projects and, ultimately, the determination of our practices in society. It is agential reflexivity which actively mediates between our structurally shaped circumstances and what we deliberately make of them. There is an obvious caution here; agents cannot make what they please of their circumstances. To maintain otherwise would be to endorse idealism and the epistemic fallacy. Indeed, if people get their objective circumstances badly wrong, these subjects pay the objective price whether or not they do so compre-hendingly. What the Internal Conversation does do is to mediate by activating structural and cultural powers and in so doing there is no single and predictable outcome. This is because agents can exercise their reflexive powers in different ways, according to their very different concerns and considerations.

Thus, a three-stage process of mediation is being put forward, one that gives both objectivity and subjectivity their due and also explicitly incorporates their interplay.

(i)   Structural and cultural properties *objectively* shape the situations that agents confront involuntarily, and possess generative powers of constraint and enablement in relation to them.

(ii) Agents' own configurations of concerns, as *subjectively* defined in relation to the three orders of natural reality – nature, practice and society.

(iii) Courses of action are produced through the reflexive deliberations of agents who *subjectively* determine their practical projects in relation to their *objective* circumstances.

The first stage deals with the kind of specification that Realists already provide about how 'social forms' impinge and impact on people by moulding their situa-tions. This was summarised as follows in *Realist Social Theory:*

> Given their pre-existence, structural and cultural emergents shape the social environment to be inhabited. These results of past actions are deposited in the form of current situations. They account for what there is (structurally and culturally) to be distributed and also for the shape of such distributions; for the nature of the extant role array, the proportion of positions available at any time and the advantages/disadvantages associated with them; for the institutional configuration present and for those second order emergent prop-erties of compatibility and incompatibility, that is whether the respective operations of institutions are matters of obstruction or assistance to one another. In these ways, situations are objectively defined for their subsequent occupants or incumbents.[15]

However, these only become generative powers, rather than unactivated proper-ties in relationship to agential projects. Stage 2 examines the interface between the above and agential projects themselves, for again it is not the properties of agents that interact directly with structural or cultural properties but their powers as expressed in the pursuit of a project. It is Stage 3 that has been missing in social theorising to date, but which appears essential in order to conceptualise the process of mediation properly and completely. In Stage 3, agents, by virtue of their powers of reflexivity, deliberate about their objective circumstances in rela-tion to their subjective concerns. They consult their projects to see if they can realise them, possibly adapting them, adjusting them, abandoning them or enlarg-ing them in the deliberative process. They alter their practices, such that if a course of action is going well subjects may become more ambitious and if it is going badly they may become more circumspect. It is this crucial Stage 3 that enables us to try to do, to be or to become what we care about most in society – by virtue of our reflexivity.

This final stage of mediation is indispensable because without it we have no explanatory purchase upon what exactly agents do. The absence of explanatory purchase means settling for empirical generalisations about what 'most of the people do most of the time'. Sociologists can settle for even less: 'Under circumstances x a statistically significant number of agents do y'. This spells a return to Humean constant conjunctions and a resignation to being unable to adduce a causal mechanism.

Conclusion

Neglect of the subjective contribution to mediation has the consequence that social forms are treated as intransitive, simply as advantages or disadvantages. In effect, the presumption is that no one looks a gift horse in the mouth and that everybody gets down to cutting their coats to suit their cloth. Yet, 'advantages' are not intransitive because they have to be positively evaluated by the agent for some purpose. This is particularly relevant when the luck of having been dealt better life-chances than others is then presumed to mean that the advantages of 'keeping ahead' will dominate the activities of all who are so placed. This may be a common concern, but if it is, then it must have been subjectively adopted, for it is not one that can be blandly imputed to everybody. Once again, the conclusion is that if subjectivity is not properly investigated, it will be improperly imputed – for it cannot be eliminated.

When a subjective ontology is introduced and agential reflexivity is investigated, three points are acknowledged on the agential side of the equation.

- That our unique personal identities, which derive from our singular constellations of concerns, mean that we are radically heterogeneous as agents. Even though we may share objective social features we may also seek very different ends, when in the same social situation.
- That our subjectivity is dynamic, it is not psychologically static nor is it psychologically reducible because we modify our own goals in terms of their contextural feasibility, as we see it. As always, we are fallible, can get it wrong and have to pay the objective price for doing so.
- That as agents we are active, for the most part, rather than passive because we can adjust our projects to those practices that we believe we can realise.

Unless all of these points are taken on board, what is omitted are agential evaluations of their situations in the light of their concerns and agential re-evaluation of their projects in the light of the situations in which they find themselves – whether voluntarily or involuntarily. In short a full account of structure and agency and of the process mediating between them entails accepting and examining the interplay between two ontologies – the socially objective and the personally subjective.

Notes

1 If the statement that 'The British electorate now mistrusts Tony Blair' is true, it is only a statement about the views of the majority of people eligible to vote. To attribute a predicate like 'distrust' to the 'electorate' as such is to reify the latter.
2 See Nicos Mouzelis (2000).
3 Archer (1995, Ch. 4).
4 See Archer (1988, Ch. 5).
5 See Archer and Tritter (2001).
6 See Hollis (1989).
7 For this distinction, see Martin Hollis (1977).
8 See Harry Frankfurter (1988, Ch. 7).
9 Archer (2001, Ch. 9).
10 The sentence is expressed in this way because this paper was first delivered as a talk to the IACR annual conference, Girton College, Cambridge, 2004.
11 See Shoemaker (1996).
12 See William Alston (1971, p. 225f).
13 See Donald Davidson (1984, p. 105).
14 See Alston (1971, p. 236).
15 p. 201.

References

Alston, W. 'Varieties of Privileged Access', *American Philosophical Quarterly*, 8:3, 1971

Archer, M. S. *Culture and Agency*, Cambridge University Press, Cambridge, 1988

Archer, M. S. *Realist Social Theory*, Cambridge University Press, Cambridge, 1995

Archer, M. S. *Being Human: The Problem of Agency*, Cambridge University Press, Cambridge, 2000

Archer, M. S. *Structure, Agency and the Internal Conversation*, Cambridge University Press, Cambridge, 2003

Archer, M. S. and Tritter, J. (eds.). *Rational Choice Theory: Resisting Colonisation*, Routledge/Taylor and Francis, London, 2001

Bhaskar, R. *The Possibility of Naturalism*, Harvester Wheatsheaf, Hemel Hempstead, 1979, 1989

Bourdieu, P. *Outline of a Theory of Practice*, Cambridge University Press, Cambridge, 1977

Bourdieu, Pierre, *The Logic of Practice*, Polity Press, Oxford, 1990

Davidson, D. 'First-Person Authority', *Dialectica*, 38:2–3, 1984

Frankfurter, H. G. *The Importance of What We Care About*, Cambridge University Press, Cambridge, 1988

Harré, R. *Personal Being*, Basil Blackwell, Oxford, 1983

Hollis, M. *Models of Man; Philosophical Thoughts on Social Action*, Cambridge University Press, Cambridge, 1977

Hollis, M. 'Honour Among Thieves', *Proceedings of the British Academy*, LXXV: 163–180, 1989

Hollis, M. and Smith, S. 'Two Stories about Structure and Agency', *Review of International Studies*, 20:241–5, 1994

James, W. *The Principles of Psychology* (Vol. 1), Macmillan, London, 1890

Mouzelis, N. 'The Subjectivist-Objectivist Divide: Against Transcendence', *Sociology*, 34:4, 2000

Searle, J. *Mind, Language and Society*, Weidenfeld and Nicolson, London, 1999

Shoemaker, S. *The First-Person Perspective and Other Essays,* Cambridge University Press, 1996

3   Technology, technological determinism and the transformational model of social activity[1]

Clive Lawson

Introduction

The role that technology plays in social change is experienced by us all on a daily basis. Whether cleaning our home, purchasing an air ticket over the internet, paying for shopping at a supermarket or borrowing a book from the library, we continually experience changes to our normal or routine ways of doing things that can be attributed to the introduction of some new technology or other. But do such experiences provide evidence to support the thesis of technological determinism? One of the few sources of agreement in the recent technology literature, is that the answer to this question must be 'no' – technological determinism must be wrong. However, I want to suggest that this 'agreement' actually obscures a problem with the treatment of technology. Namely, I want to suggest that certain questions posed by so-called technological determinists remain unaddressed (and perhaps unaddressable) by technological determinism's critics, at least those most rooted in social constructivism. Implicitly, of course, I am suggesting that the questions asked by so-called technological determinists are important ones. And indeed I believe their importance explains why so many writers on technology are continually drawn to the 'flame' of technological determinism (see Smith & Marx, 1996).

I also want to argue that the issues at stake here are fundamentally ontological and that in this regard critical realism has much to contribute to the current study of technology. Although surprisingly little attention has been given by critical realists to the study of technology, it would seem that the social ontology developed within critical realist accounts has much to offer in developing a conception of technology that avoids the particular problems I address here.[2] More specifically the (transformational) conception of social activity, which of course is particularly well suited to the avoidance of both determinism and voluntarism with regard to social phenomena, can very fruitfully be applied to an account of technical activity. Furthermore, I shall argue that fundamental to an account of technology is a conception of its dual constitution in the social and natural domains. However, it is rare for technological commentators, especially recently, to attempt to elaborate an account of technology in terms of the differences between these domains. My intention here is to initiate this task by drawing upon the critical or qualified naturalism developed within critical realist accounts. In so doing, not only is it possible to provide a sketch of technology that incorporates what I see as the advantages of both (so-called determinist and constructivist) positions, but it is also possible (more speculatively) to re-cast the questions that technological determinists have posed.

Varieties of technological determinism?

It is fair to say that technological determinism is most usually referred to in a crude, undifferentiated manner. To the extent that different strands of the technological determinist argument are distinguished, it is most common to find discussions of hard and soft technological determinism (see Smith & Marx, 1996). The hard–soft distinction is based upon a spectrum of technological determinisms – with movement along the spectrum involving the degree of agency, or the power to effect change, attributed to technology. At the hard end, technology has certain intrinsic attributes that allow little scope for human autonomy or choice. At the other end of the spectrum, soft determinism simply emphasises the large scope for human interventions and choice. Indeed, for Smith and Marx at least 'the soft determinists locate [technology] in a far more various and complex social, economic, political and cultural matrix' (1996, p. xii). The immediate problem with such accounts, however, is that it is not clear why they should be considered to be deterministic at all. In what sense can either hard or soft determinism actually be deterministic in any sense, given that some scope for human choice is accepted in both, the disagreement being over how much?

Indeed, this point seems to be the motivation for Bimber's very useful, if rarely cited, distinctions between nomological, unintended consequences and normative uses of the term technological determinism (Bimber, 1996). And it proves useful to consider each of these in turn. The nomological is that which takes the 'determinism' in technological determinism most seriously: 'technological determinism can be seen as the view that, in the light of … the state of technological development and laws of nature, there is only one possible future course for social change' (1996, p. 83). There is no scope for human desires or choices.

Now, although this definition accords most closely with the philosopher's (or common sense?) meaning of the term, Bimber argues that it is actually almost impossible to find any examples of technological determinism if such a definition is strictly adhered to. The most likely candidates emanate from the economics domain. Marx is perhaps the most popular example, usually evidenced by the famous statement that 'the hand-mill gives you society with the feudal lord; the steam-mill society with the industrial capitalist' (Marx, 1971, p. 109). However, it is very difficult to attribute anything like a hard or nomological form of technological determinism once a wider reading of Marx is undertaken (especially see Dickson, 1974; Rosenberg, 1976; Harvey, 1999, pp. 98–136).

One sense in which Marx might be understood as encouraging such an interpretation is in his insistence that history or sequence matters, and indeed this can sound unduly mechanistic, and has been interpreted by later Marxists in an unduly mechanistic way (an obvious example is Heilbroner, 1967). But the point that Marx, and indeed Heilbroner, are making about sequence, amount to little more than highlighting that some kinds of technology could not happen without others and that some forms of social organisation could not happen without certain technological developments having taken place first. The idea that sequence matters recurs throughout accounts that have been held up as examples of technological determinism. Perhaps the most sustained of these is provided by the American Institutionalist Clarence Ayres. On par with Marx's handmill statement is Ayres's contention that given 'the shipbuilding and navigation skills in existence in 1492, America was bound to be discovered in a decade or two' (Ayres, 1952) – often read as betraying the worst kind of determinism. However, on closer reading, as with Marx, the point that emerges is that some technological development may be a necessary condition for some other technological development (or indeed social development). But nomological technological determinism requires that it is also a sufficient condition. And it is doubtful whether such a position can be found in any of the above contributors' work.[3]

Bimber's second use of the term, i.e. 'unintended consequences' technological determinism, is one that emphasises the process whereby human ideas, values, etc., become manifest in some particular technology so giving a fixity or concretisation to these ideas which is then hard to change. Perhaps the classic statement of this idea is made by Langdon Winner (1977, 1980). And as his account explicitly brings out, although there is a concern with explaining the fact that technology appears to be out of our control, the point is not that everything is strictly determined or that choice is precluded. Rather, the point is that choices about the design and building of technology have implications that are likely to require some living with. The call, from Winner at least, is for greater democratic involvement at an *earlier* stage in the development of some technology, not that it is not possible.[4] This general idea is also to be found in Marx with specific emphasis on the way that social relations become 'concretised' in particular technologies which then act to maintain or reproduce those social relations (MacKenzie, 1984).

However, neither the nomological nor the unintended consequences uses of the term are, Bimber argues, the most familiar face of technological determinism within the technology literature. Rather, in what he dubs the normative version of technological determinism, technology appears to us as autonomous because the norms by which it is advanced are 'removed from political and ethical discourse and … goals of efficiency or productivity become surrogates for value-based debate over methods, alternatives, means and ends' (Bimber, 1996, p. 82). Here technological development is an essentially human enterprise in which people who create and use technology are driven by certain goals that rely unduly on norms of efficiency and productivity. Thus other (ethical, moral) criteria are excluded, producing a process that operates independently of larger political processes and contexts. The end point is one in which society adopts the technologist's standards of judgement. Thus there is a technological domain, which includes elements of society generally, which not only acts as a constraint and causal force on other aspects of society, but is constantly encroaching upon them.

The main examples this time appear to be from the philosophy of technology. Bimber singles out the contribution of Habermas (see especially Habermas 1970). And although Habermas actually writes very little on technology, his position does clearly involve the more general features that Bimber has in mind, although at this level of generality it is perhaps as relevant to Mumford's 'megatechnics' (1967) and Ellul's 'technique' (1964). Habermas is attempting to ground what he sees as the negative or dystopian character of modernity in very general terms. Central to Habermas's contribution, of course, is a Weberian differentiation of society into the spheres of work (which is success oriented, purposive action concerned with controlling the world) and interaction (communication between subjects in pursuit of common understanding in the 'lifeworld'). Modernity is characterised by the colonisation of the system of objectifying (delinguifying) behaviour of the former on the latter lifeworld. Thus the problem of modernity amounts to the inappropriate extension of one domain to another.

Although Bimber fails to mention it, perhaps the most developed position of this sort is provided by the work of Heidegger. For Heidegger, our engagement with technology involves the transformation of the entire world (and ourselves) into 'mere raw materials' or 'standing reserves' (1977) – objects to be controlled. Central to Heidegger's account is a process in which methodical planning comes to dominate, destroying the integrity of everything. Rather than a world of 'things' treated with respect for their own sake, we end up with a collection of functions and resources. Heidegger's examples of the Greek jeweller making a chalice and a modern dam builder destroying the local environment show the difference Heidegger has in mind between (the older crafts-based activity of) bringing things together in harmony and the 'de-worlding' of modern technology. The central point is that technology itself is not neutral. Everything is sucked up into a particular kind of (technological) process and reduced to the status of a resource that has to be optimised in some way. Especially worrying is the idea that, in so doing, people grow to see themselves in the same way. Moreover, there is an obscuring not only of what is being lost, but of what the goals of such a process might be.

Although quite different in many respects, the concern of both Heidegger and Habermas is the same, i.e. with the reduction of meaning and value of humans in the 'lifeworld'. Human involvement is reduced to a minimum and the values of possession and control tend to dominate social life. The central ideas are that using technology not only makes us become something else, but that it creates a new lifeworld, which separates, de-worlds, isolates and impoverishes both the natural world as well as ourselves.[5]

The constructivist critique[6]

Criticisms of technological determinism, at least those made more recently, tend to be made by social constructivists, or at least by those drawing upon their arguments. There are though several dimensions to the constructivist rejection of technological determinism. There is an explicit rejection of the idea that technical change should be understood as being an autonomous or disconnected source of social change – and certainly a rejection of the idea that technical change can be seen as fixed, or on some monotonic 'trajectory'. Technological change is genuinely contingent and not reducible to some inner technological 'logic'. Constructivists also question the (accepted) relation between science and technology (in which science is the independent, non political source of technological ideas) along with the idea that technological change leads to (determines) social change and not vice versa. Instead, emphasis is placed, usually by drawing attention to a series of case studies, upon the contingent nature of technical change and on how technology is 'shaped', especially by different social groups in the process of settling a range of technological/social controversies and disagreements (MacKenzie & Wajcman, 1985).

However, as Winner famously argues, this emphasis on the social dimension of technology comes at a cost (Winner, 1991). In particular, because there remain no 'autonomous' characteristics of technology, he argues, technology becomes no different to any purely social phenomenon. To see why this might be, we need to consider the particular manner in which the technological is understood to be social and also the particular role played by the idea of symmetry.[7] Again the main idea is taken from the sociology of scientific knowledge literature (Bloor, 1976): that it is best to remain agnostic about the truth, falsity, rationality, etc., of competing claims in settling scientific controversies. Translated to the technological realm this means that the researcher should remain impartial with regards to the actual properties of the technology involved in determining which technologies become 'settled upon' (Pinch & Bijker, 1987). The researcher must, in other words, treat as possibly true or false all claims made about the nature of technology – such claims must be treated symmetrically (explaining them by reference to similar factors), since there is no independent way of evaluating the knowledge claims of scientists, technologists, etc.

As in the sociology of scientific knowledge literature, two ideas underlie these arguments. First, the 'real world' plays no role in settling controversies (in settling the form that technology takes) and, second, that the researcher has no independent access to the world – so that there is no way of evaluating competing claims. Thus claims about the relative efficiency or successfulness of different technologies or technical progress (or how some technology comes to be accepted) are to be avoided (see also Staudenmaier, 1995; Pels, 1996).

Given that the actual nature of some technology is thought to have little bearing upon whether it is accepted or emerges, if some technology is found to exist, that existence must be analysed purely in terms of the stabilisation of different controversies and disputes. Once stabilisation is achieved, controversy is removed and the properties of this stabilisation (how consensus is achieved) determines how that technology functions. The focus, as with the sociology of scientific knowledge literature, is upon how 'closure' is achieved. Crucial to the idea of closure is the idea that technology is not interpreted or understood in any fixed way. These different interpretations of some technology are not only of its social characteristics or relative functionality, but of its technical content – of how it works. Thus 'facts' about technology are simply the (different) interpretations of different social groups (Bijker, 1995). It is thus a rhetorical process of settling dispute via negotiation and social action that is understood in the term 'closure'. Technology is thus socially shaped and socially constructed.

But, at the same time, and this is Winner's point, the ability to distinguish technology from any other social phenomenon is lost. Thus it would seem to be impossible to explain the one feature of technology, noted at the outset, that motivates most so called determinist accounts – how is it the case that technology continually prods or provokes all manner of social changes?

Constructivists are clearly correct to argue, against nomological determinist accounts that contingency matters. However, little is said about the manner in which technology concretises particular values, ideas, etc., or the impact that this might have upon ideas of sequence or contingency, let alone the normative form noted by Bimber and others, in which the very values and ideas may take form because of something about the nature of technology itself. Unseating the privileged position of science in technology's development, whilst surely right, actually distracts from the very factors that Habermas, Heidegger and others are drawing attention to. That the use of technology may bring with it values of possession and control that dominate social life and drain it of meaning, are questions about which the constructivist must remain silent. At root there seems to be a failure to distinguish two quite different issues – the contingency and the irreducibly social nature of technology.[8] It is as if to establish the former, the latter has to be so thoroughgoing that technology ends up being reduced to the social. Questions concerning technology's special role in the social world then become impossible to ask.

It is these questions, however, that underlie and seem to motivate those accounts which are usually identified as examples of technological determinism. For example, how do we account for the extent to which technology appears to be 'out of control'? How do we make sense of the appearance of stages of development? How do we account for the constraining effect that technology has on social organisation? What do we mean when we talk of technology concretising or fixing values or ideas? Why should the technological domain impinge, if it does, on other domains? More generally, how are we to address such questions whilst maintaining the irreducibly social character and essential contingency of technological change which constructivists (rightly) insist upon. In what remains, I shall argue that these questions are best addressed by drawing upon recent developments in social ontology. Specifically, I want to argue that there are significant advantages to locating a conception of technology within the account of social activity developed by critical realists.

A transformational and relational conception of material artefacts

The account of social activity that I shall draw upon here has been formalised in terms of the transformational model of social activity (TMSA). The basic features of the TMSA have been presented in different ways, notably as a corrective to existing voluntaristic or reificatory accounts of social structure or as a transcendental argument from the existence of generalised features of experience of the social world, such as routinised practices.⁹ Either way, the main point that arises is that social structure only exists in and through the activity of human agents, even though it is not reducible to such activity. Put another way, against individualistic or voluntaristic accounts of social structure, structure pre-exists and is a necessary condition for all intentional agency, whilst, against reificatory accounts, structure only exists in virtue of the activity it governs. Thus if social structure always pre-exists actual behaviour this does not mean that individuals create structure in any sense but that it is actively reproduced or transformed. Similarly, if it is something that only exists in virtue of human activity, there is no sense in which it is outside of or external to human activity. However, neither are structure and agency simply moments in the same process – they are different kinds of thing. And it is this transformational nature of the connection between the two (interestingly, for my purposes, often conveyed by the Aristotelian metaphor of the sculpting artist fashioning a product out of the material and with the tools available) that lies at the heart of the TMSA. The resulting emphasis, then, is upon transformation.

Society, conceived of as the sum of the relations between agents is the ever present condition and continually reproduced outcome of social activity. Society acts as both an enabling and constraining influence on behaviour as well as, more constitutively, as a socialising force, thus impacting on how individuals react to the structural constraints and enablements they face. But as structure is only ever reproduced or transformed through human action, where such structure endures, its continuity as much as its change is a significant object of analysis. As such, social change is inherently non-deterministic. To capture this aspect of structure, following Giddens, the term duality of structure is often used. Similarly, it should be clear that although action, where it does reproduce certain structural forms, this will typically not be the intention of this activity. Thus, my speaking English is not intended to reproduce the grammar of the language, although it does generally do so. Following Bhaskar, the duality of practice is used to capture this dual aspect of action.

One more aspect of this account needs to be drawn out before we can return to a discussion of technology. Specifically, the TMSA can also be seen as an attempt to elaborate how the social and natural worlds differ, and especially as part of a qualified or critical naturalism.¹⁰ Both natural and social science are understood to involve a focus upon generative mechanisms that are not reducible to events or states of affairs (see Harré, 1970; Harré & Secord, 1972; Harré & Madden, 1975). Science, then, is concerned not primarily with induction or deduction at all, as modes of inference, but with forms of inference that lead from the observation or experience of events and states of affairs (e.g. falling apples) to the underlying structures and mechanisms that could give rise to them (gravity, curved space or whatever). The difference between the two kinds of science then rests on the differences between the kinds of structures or mechanisms that feature in the respective (social/natural) domains. For present purposes the important differences can be thought about from the perspective of what must be the case for (successful and replicable) experiment to have the status it does in the natural sciences but not in the social sciences. In natural science, it would seem, closures are possible to achieve. Thus it must be the case that some mechanisms or sets of mechanisms have a sufficiently consistent internal structure to behave the same way under the same circumstances. Additionally, such structures or mechanisms must be isolatable from other disturbing or countervailing factors. It would seem however that such possibilities rarely exist in the social world.

A major point of the TMSA is that social structures only exist by virtue of the activity they constrain or enable. Thus social structures depend, for their existence, on the activities of agents and the conception agents have of such structures. As such social structures will not tend to endure across time and space in the same way that natural mechanisms do. Such differences (or ontological limits to naturalism) can be summarised as the relatively greater activity–concept–time–space dependence of social structures (see Bhaskar, 1989, pp. 37–54, 174–179). The major epistemological limit is that whereas the differentiability of natural mechanisms means that the natural world may well be characterised very usefully in terms of closed systems, this is unlikely to be the case for much of the social world.

For those familiar with critical realism at least, this much should be familiar if not uncontentious. But how is any of this of relevance to a conception of technology? The relevance comes from the fact that technology is irreducibly social, so dependent upon social activity. The TMSA above is an attempt to draw out the main features of human agent's relationship with social structure through the medium of social activity. The focus is on the domain of social relations. However, such activity can be viewed under another aspect – as technical activity. Human activity of course is essentially the same: people act, always intentionally, in conditions not of their own choosing but transforming the materials to hand. But here a distinction can be made between technical objects, that act as the condition and consequence of technical activity and the technical subjects, those human agents engaged in technical activity. These can be combined in a similar way to that above to provide what I shall call a transformational model of *technical* activity (TMTA).

Here the technical subject and object are, similarly, not reducible to or derivable from each other, they are different kinds of things, even though both are, in some sense, the condition and consequence of each other. It should be clear that the state of technological development both enables and constrains human activity in a similar way to that noted in the TMSA. Perhaps the most developed literature on the enabling power of technology is that which views technology primarily as an extension of the human body.[11] And of course the idea that technology enables, or simply is, the control of nature is pervasive, at least since Bacon. But as new technological objects enable different sets of human actions to take place, this will always set new constraints, e.g. solar power enables cheap/sustainable electricity but must be located in sunny places, laptops allow me to work in the library, but only near electricity points, etc. But the idea of constraint can be understood more systemically too. For example, Hughes (1983) focuses on the fact that technical objects are not used, and do not exist, in isolation – people use or deal with systems of technical objects. At any point in time there will be a weakest link in these technological systems which effectively acts to constrain the working of the whole (Hughes refers to these as reverse salients). These constraints then act to give directionality to future technical activity.

It is particularly important for present purposes, however, to point out that technical objects do not simply constrain or enable particular human behaviour – but have some effect on the nature of the human actor also. Of course, this is a recurrent theme in the study of technology, whether in Veblen's account of the machine process, or Heidegger's comparison of craftsmanship and new technology, or the Amish Bishops' decisions about which technology to 'endorse', the question that recurs is 'what does using this technology make us become?' The term socialisation, which features in the TMSA, should no doubt be replaced by something like technologisation, but the idea is the same – technical objects (like social structure) do more than constrain or enable. They have a role in shaping the capabilities and competences of those agents engaged with some technology.

As with the social activity of the TMSA, technical activity can be understood in terms of transformation and reproduction (this time of technical objects), rather than creation from nothing. And indeed there are some clear advantages to thinking of technical activity this way. Viewing technical activity as transformational, as with social activity, affords a way between voluntarism and determinism. For example, it makes it possible to accommodate the insights of so-called technological determinists, noted above, who stress the importance of sequence, path-dependency, etc. But it should be clear that the point made is about necessary rather than sufficient conditions. In which case a focus on design as transformational captures what is essential to the argument in a fundamentally non-deterministic manner. In other words, talk of constraining, enabling or socialising no more requires (or reduces to) a form of determinism in the TMTA than it does in the TMSA.[12]

It is equally important, however, to point out that transformation in the TMTA does not play the same role that it does in the TMSA. First, there is much in design that cannot be transformed at all. I am referring here simply to the fact that technical objects are constituted by natural as well as social mechanisms. For example, gravity is not something that human beings can change, but something that must be drawn upon or used. The importance of this will depend on the kind of artefact in question. Both a pendulum clock and a book are subject to gravity, but although a book may be very difficult to use in the absence of gravity, for the pendulum clock gravity is essential to its way of working. The designer is thus *harnessing* the powers of existing mechanisms in the design and not transforming them in any sense (see Pickering, 1995). Secondly, we tend to see technology as 'designed' or 'engineered' on the one hand, and then simply 'used' on the other. Neither action seems to be a form of transformation or reproduction in the senses used above. For example, when we acquire a new CD player we read the instruction manual, which tells us who designed this particular player, what it is for and how it is to be used. We then simply use it in line with the designer's intentions. This is clearly different from, say, our use of language or our repro- duction and transformation of social relations.

If the role that transformation plays in technical action differs from the role it plays in specifically social action, then so too does the role of reproduction. For example, it is hard to believe that we reproduce a hammer by knocking in nails in the same way that we reproduce language by speaking. Technical activity is typically divided up into the stages of design or construction on the one hand, and use on the other.[13] The design stage involves primarily a process of abstracting various properties of existing things (artefacts or naturally occurring objects or mechanisms) and recombining them into objects with particular capacities or powers. Use is primarily concerned with identifying objects with particular capacities and powers and inserting them (or enrolling them), into particular net- works of social and technical interdependencies. In one sense then both types of technical activity share similar characteristics – they can be understood to involve two moments, one of isolation and one of reconnection. This idea is at the heart of the Instrumentalisation Theory developed by Feenberg (2000).

Thus although both design and use involve both moments, the kinds of isola- tion and connection involved at each end of the spectrum (design to use) do have different characteristics. At the design stage things are perhaps clearer. Particular functional capacities of things or mechanisms are isolated and (atomistically) reassembled in line with some prior criteria or functional requirements. Use, however, provides a more complex example of the isolation and reconnection moments, and centrally hinges on the relational aspect of technical objects. It is true that the form and content of the hammer would not disappear tomorrow if human societies ceased to exist (as say language would). But the hammer, in the eventuality of human societies ceasing to exist, would actually cease to be a ham- mer. Because part of what a hammer is exists only in relation to those using it. It is only by being used that a collection of wood and nails, or a tree trunk in the forest, become tables. In fact, use involves enrolment in two kinds of networks, both social and technical. For the telephone to work it must be connected to a telephone network, to an electricity supply, etc. But without human societies it is not a telephone at all. Such relations though are not simply concerned with the object's function. When I use my mobile on the train I am certainly reproducing the relation of this object to users in general as 'a communicating device', but I am also reproducing or transforming rules of politeness, etc., depending upon where I use it (in a mobile-free carriage?) and how (by speaking loudly?)

Viewed in this way, the TMSA has some role to play as a model for the kind of relation between technical object and subject, but its major role is that it is part of the relation itself. Alternatively put, the social activity that the TMSA is designed to capture is actually part of technical activity. It is the social relations of the TMSA that are reproduced and transformed in technical activity, as well as being enabling and constraining of that activity. However, technical activity is about more than simply reproducing or transforming social relations. Indeed, what appear to be essential to technical activity are the moments of isolation and reconnection which combine in different ways to produce all activities from design to use.

By focusing upon technical activity in this way it is possible now to pinpoint the ways in which technical objects may be understood to be social. By social I mean here only those things that depend on us in some way. The first sense in which technical objects are social derives from the design process in which technical objects take a particular form. How different natural mechanisms, existing artefacts, etc., are brought together reflects the values, desires, intentions, etc., of those designers and all the groups that have had some say in the nature of the design, which then become concretised in the very structure of the technical object. This is, of course, where the social constructivist approaches to technology have made such a strong contribution to the study of technology in recent years. How particular designs and formulations are settled upon is clearly a very social affair. However, as is brought out so well in the work of Marx, it is not just values, intentions, etc., that become concretised in this way, but social relations themselves. This is both because, as is brought out in the TMSA, the existing state of social relations are a condition as well as a consequence of social, including technical, action, but because, as constructivists ably demonstrate, so much technology takes the form it does because of the way that disputes between different groups are settled. Thus the very structure of technical objects is irreducibly social. However, this sense in which technical objects are social is worthy of note. To say that values, intentions and even social relations become concretised in this way is to talk of essentially social things becoming material. As such, given the relative concept–space–time independence of material things, there is a relative endurability and travel that is possible for those otherwise precarious aspects of the social world. Thus, and this seems to be centrally important for an understanding of technology, technology can be understood as the site in which the social achieves a different mode of existence through its embodiment in material things.

The second sense in which technical objects are social is the relational sense. Use involves the insertion or enrolment of technical objects into social and technical networks, which, in so doing, reproduces or transforms a variety of social relations along the way. Another way of saying this is that the duality of practice is as relevant for technical activity as it is for social activity. In a sense it is more relevant, in that the duality here not only captures the thin sense in which action to do something has unintended consequences, but that action to do one kind of thing (technical action) achieves another kind of thing (social action).

Underlining, and differentiating, these two senses in which technical objects are irreducibly social thus emphasises the importance of transformation and reproduction as types of technical activity. But they are not as central to technical action as they are in the TMSA. This is because material artefacts have a mode of existence (as physical objects) which is not *simply* reliant upon their transformation or reproduction through human activity. Thus transformation and reproduction, at the very least, need to be supplemented by the important moments of isolation and reconnection. And indeed it seems to be in terms of the latter that much of the changing nature of technology is best understood. For example, it is possible to characterise skills-based, tool-using technical activity in terms of the almost simultaneous acts of isolation and reconnection. By contrast, mass production is most often associated with an explicit and even institutionalised separation between processes of isolation and reconnection – where design or research departments often become quite disconnected from the details of how their (primarily isolative) research will be used by other designers (i.e. recombined with other technical objects into useful things), which are in terms disconnected in more far-reaching ways from those who may actually use the objects produced (contextualising or embedding these objects in particular social and technical networks). Focusing upon the separation of moments in this way also brings out the differences between the moments at different stages of technical activity (design and use). Where full or clear isolation is possible, recombination will tend to be more atomistic (which seems more likely at the design stage) whereas given the internal relatedness of the social networks in which technical objects are combined in use, the form of recombination will tend to be more organic.

To take stock briefly, I have attempted to give an account of a domain that is a particular mixture of both natural and social elements. Drawing upon the TMSA, I have given an account of social action that is engaged with material things, and how these material things must be understood as socially as well as materially constituted.[14] I have argued that what I have been calling technical objects are irreducibly social in two distinct senses. First, they are social in that the form they take is effectively a concretisation of past values, actions, social relations, etc. Thus to understand why they take the form they do, requires a consideration of human actions of various kinds. The second sense in which artefacts are to be understood as social is the relational sense. To understand the causal powers that some artefact has, some account needs to be taken of the relations in which the artefact stands to people, institutions, etc. This was addressed above by the sense in which technical action is reproduction as well as transformation, and by noting that both the TMSA and the TMTA are both in play simultaneously.

It was also noted that such technical activity can be viewed as having two moments – that of isolation and that of reconnection. And that the scope for separation of these moments would depend both on the nature of the artefacts involved and the institutional circumstances in which such activity takes place.

Implications of the TMTA

Although the implications of conceptualising technology and technological activity in the above terms turn out to be far reaching, I shall restrict the remaining discussion to a few of the issues raised in the discussion of technological determinism set out above. These fall briefly into two categories – the implications of a transformational conception and the implications of the dual nature of technical objects.

The emphasis on a transformational conception of technical action focuses attention upon conditions and consequences of action rather than creation out of nothing. This much is in line with a range of contributions (including for example those by Ayres) that emphasise that invention does not result from the whims of detached 'genius' inventors, but typically revolve around the re-combination of existing ideas or technical objects. Not only is the enquirer thus sensitised to the importance of historical context, but a conception of stages or sequence is accommodated in a way that does not exclude the essentially social nature of such a process. Indeed it would seem to amply accommodate positions, such as Winner's, in which the (social) consequences of action become the technical conditions for future action. Most importantly, as noted, this accommodation of the main insights of all these theorists is done without at all encouraging the label of technological determinism. Thus, just as the TMSA has clarified a relation between structure and agency that steers a course between determinism and voluntarism, the TMTA performs the same task in the technological realm. Additionally, focusing upon the transformational nature of technical activity underscores the important manner in which technical objects are continually shaped by human activity and so one sense in which technical objects are irreducibly social. But the TMSA as part of a model of technical activity itself also underscores the other sense in which technical objects are social in and through the reproduction and transformation of social relations which also constitute technical objects as artefacts of some kind.

This of course brings us to the implications that follow from the dual conception of technology outlined above. More specifically, a series of differences follow that relate to technology's being rooted in a different way in the natural domain via the relative concept–activity–space–time *in*dependence of the natural world and the relatively greater differentiability of natural mechanisms.[15]

First, this account provides a much more complex grounding of the positions of those such as Marx, Winner, etc., for whom technology concretises the social in some way. Ideas of endurability, fixity, etc., seem plausible but are notoriously difficult to pin down. However, locating the concreteness of technical objects in the relatively greater concept–activity–time–space independence of the natural world would seem to avoid such problems in a sustainable way.

An undoubtedly more contentious set of implications follows from a focus on the kinds of technical activity noted above. Specifically, a focus upon the moments of isolation and reconnection enables some rather different implications of the dual nature of technology to be drawn out. As noted, the idea central to this transformational conception of our engagement with technical objects is the manner in which aspects of the existing world of artefacts or natural objects are separated off, refined, developed and re-combined with other aspects and assembled into working technologies. All technical activity will involve both moments, but not to the same degrees. And the extent to which one moment or the other can dominate or to which the two moments can be separated will depend on a variety of factors. But a crucial factor will be the differentiability of the social and natural domains. For example, given the greater differentiability of the natural world there would appear to be greater scope for a concentration on the isolative moment in technical activity. Although much attention is given to (the relation between) science and technology (see Pickering, 1992) or the institutionalised separation of machines as opposed to tools (see Ingold, 2000, Ch 15), the grounds for such separations are rarely considered, but do seem to follow from consideration of the isolative moment of technical activity opened up by the greater differentiability of the natural world.

Such talk of separation suggests two further sets of implications. First, a domain emerges that is effectively preoccupied with the isolative moment. And there emerges the possibility of not only a set of methods or explanatory schema, but skills, ideas, values, mindsets, etc., which tend to emerge that are more appropriate to this domain. These methods, skills, values, etc., will, in short, be those most appropriate to situations where closed systems are a real possibility.

Secondly, the isolative moment is still only a moment. Thus technical objects always require reconnection or recombination to become functioning technologies. As such, as we have seen, technical objects, which concretise values, ideas, etc., of predominantly closed-system based isolation diffuse to peoples' everyday lives. Now given the irreducibly open character of social reality detailed in the TMSA, a potentially important feature of the second moment, of reconnection, involves transferring, capillary-style, values and mindsets appropriate for closed systems to situations that are irreducibly open – both as ideas are 'passed along' but also as ideas become embodied in different stages of the design process. Thus given technology's dual constitution, I am suggesting that the technological domain is a point of overlap or even 'battleground' for the competing mindsets, values, etc., attached to open and closed system ways of thinking about the world. Such a scenario would seem to provide a solid foundation for Bimber's normative technological determinists, such as Habermas or Heidegger. The invasion of the lifeworld by the technological can better be understood in terms of the mistaken application of ideas, values, methods, concerns, etc., of most direct relevance to closed systems to situations that are predominantly open. However, without a conception of these different moments of technical activity, and without some kind of sustained ontological elaboration of the social and natural domains, it is not clear that these concerns can even be posed in a sustainable way.

Conclusions

A series of important problems posed by so-called technological determinists simply cannot be addressed by critics wedded to a social constructivism that ultimately reduces technology to the social, thus making it impossible to consider the possible nature of any 'autonomous' qualities it may have. This paper, by drawing on the social ontology of critical realism, has attempted to provide a framework in which the insights both of so-called technological determinists and their constructivist critics can be accommodated without so reducing technology to just another social phenomenon or committing the error of 'nomological' determinism. Some of the more obvious characteristics of technology (its endurability, concreteness, etc.), seem to be unproblematically grounded by conceiving of technology in terms of its dual constitution, given the critical realist account of the differences between the social and natural domains. Lastly, the normative concerns of various philosophers of technology have been re-cast in terms of the different moments of technical activity suggested by the TMTA, i.e. of isolation and re-connection.

Notes

1 I would like to thank members of the Cambridge Social Ontology Group for helpful comments on earlier versions of this chapter; special thanks to Phil Faulkner, John Latsis, Tony Lawson, Nuno Martins and Stephen Pratten.

2 Although the point cannot be developed here, it may be argued that extending the ontology of critical realism to the study of technology is not simply an act of under-labouring for technology studies, but has various advantages for the ontological accounts being developed within critical realism itself. Given that society, as amongst others actor network theorists argue persuasively, is not simply a network of *social* relations, it is not clear how a conception of society can be sustained without socio-technical networks (see Brey, 2003).

3 Perhaps there is a case to be made that nomological technological determinism is alive and well in the writings of mainstream economists or in the more mathematical tech-nological trajectories literature of neo-Schumpeterians of those such as Dosi (see Dosi *et al.* 1988). However, in these accounts, the adoption of closed-system methods gen-erally imposes a determinism throughout the social world (see Lawson 1997, 2004). But there is nothing in these accounts that suggests that there is anything specific about technology that generates determinism of any sort (it is simply an implication of a par-ticular set of methods), and thus does not really seem relevant here.

4 Winner also argues that certain technologies have certain characteristics, e.g. that wind and solar power are likely to be more consistent with democratic political systems than nuclear power. But, again, there is nothing deterministic about this.

5 If not for limitations of space, I would also here address the more recent, and more social, re-workings of Heidegger's ideas, such as the work of Albert Borgmann (1984).

6 The main roots of social constructivist accounts of technology appear to lie in the soci-ology of scientific knowledge (for a good review see Bloor 1976; Shapin 1982). The term 'social constructivism' is most often used in a narrow sense to refer to the social construction of technology (SCOT) approach outlined by Pinch and Bijker (1987) by Bijker (1995) and related approaches (e.g. Woolgar 1991). However, I shall also include here the 'social shaping' approaches (MacKenzie & Wajcman 1985; Wajcman 1991) and the actor–network approach of Latour (1987) and Callon (1987). Although these approaches display some very significant differences in orientation, they are roughly in agreement over the following points.

7 Various accounts put this aspect as central stage (Collins 1985; Lynch 1992) some even present the field as a series of extensions of the symmetry principle (Woolgar 1988)

8 I am certainly not arguing that it is only social constructivists who make this mistake. Indeed, although I do not have space to pursue this here, I would argue that many explicit reactions to technological determinism have involved reduction of technology to a purely social phenomenon. For an example of such a reaction within Institutionalist thought see Brinkman (1997).

9 For a statement of the former see Bhaskar (1989), and Archer *et al.* (1998); and for a statement of the latter see Lawson (1997, 2003).

10 It is clearly impossible here to do justice to the complexities of the arguments involved. For a detailed account see Bhaskar (1989), Lawson (2003), Collier (1994.)
11 A useful introduction is provided by Brey (2000).
12 This point is returned to below.
13 See for example Mitcham (1994). Although intermediate stages clearly exist (e.g. the craft worker amending the design of his or her tools in practice to suit the job at hand), such hybrids can easily be understood as combinations of design and use.
14 It should be clear, however, that the discussion given so far does not really provide us with a definition of technology as such. By focusing upon that domain, the artefactual, where the social and natural come together, I have only actually been able to suggest broad features that seem relevant to a range of different artefacts. So far, nothing has been said that would help us distinguish between different kinds of artefacts (including art, toys, food, etc.) that traditionally have been contrasted with technology. Indeed nothing has been said that might distinguish material artefacts, such as technology from other phenomena, usually understood as social, which also can be understood as the material results of human doings (such as social institutions). Such further distinctions have been developed elsewhere (see Lawson 2006), and in any case are not necessary for the arguments that follow, i.e., technology can be understood as a subset of the above.
15 Again, any attempt at an exhaustive account of these implications is beyond the scope of the present chapter, but the following should at least be suggestive.

References

Archer, M, *et al*. *Critical Realism: Essential Readings*. London: Routledge, 1998.

Ayres, C. *The Industrial Economy*. Cambridge: Houghton Mifflin, 1952.

Bhaskar, R. *The Possibility of Naturalism*. Brighton, UK: Harvester, 1989.

Bijker, W. E. *Of Bicycles, Bakelites, and Bulbs: Toward a Theory of Sociotechnical Change*. Cambridge, MA: MIT Press, 1995.

Bimber, B. 'Three Faces of Technological Determinism.' In *Does Technology Drive History? the Dilemma of Technological Determinism*, edited by M. Smith and L. Marx, 79–100. Massachuetts: MIT Press, 1996.

Bloor, D. *Knowledge and Social Imagery*. London: Routledge and Kegan Paul, 1976.

Borgmann, A. *Technology and the Character of Contemporary Life*. Chicago, IL: University of Chicago Press, 1984.

Brey, P. 'Theories of Technology as Extension of the Human Body'. In *Research in Philosophy and Technology, Volume 19*, edited by C. Mitcham, pp. 59–78. New York: JAI Press, 2000.

Brey, P. 'Theorizing Mondernity and Technology'. In *Modernity and Technology*, edited by T Misa, P. Brey and A. Feenberg, pp. 33–72. Massachusetts and London: MIT Press, 2003.

Brinkman, R. 'Toward a Culture-Conception of Technology.' *Journal of Economic Issues* 31, no. 1027–1038, Dec, 1997.

Bunge, M. 'Ethics and Praxiology as Technologies.' *Techne* 4, no. 4, 1989.

Callon, M. 'Society in the Making: The Study of Technology as a Tool for Sociological Analysis.' In *The Social Construction of Technological Systems: New Directions in the Sociology and History of Technology*, edited by W. Bijker, T. Pinch, and T. Hughes. Massachusetts: MIT Press, 1987.

Collier, A. *Critical Realism: An Introduction to Roy Bhaskar's Philosophy*. London: Verso, 1994.

Collins, H. M. *Changing Order: Replication and Induction in Scientific Practice*. Beverly Hills, CA: Sage, 1985.

Dickson, D. *Alternative Technology and the Politics of Technical Change*. London: Fontana, 1974.

Dosi, G. *et al.. Technical Change and Economic Theory*. London: Frances Pinter, 1988.

Ellul, J. *The Technological Society (J. Wilkinson, Trans.)*. New York: Vintage, 1964.

Feenberg, A. *Questioning Technology*. New York: Routledge, 2000.

Habermas, J. *Towards a Rational Society*. Boston: Beacon Press, 1970.

Harré, R. *Principles of Scientific Thinking*. London: Macmillan, 1970.

Harré R. and Madden, E. *Causal Powers*. Oxford: Basil Blackwell, 1975.

Harré R. and Secord, P. *The Explanation of Social Behaviour*. Oxford: Basil Blackwell, 1972.

Harvey, D. *Limits to Capital*. London: Verso, 1999.

Heidegger, M. *The Question Concerning Technology (W. Lovitt, Trans.)*. New York: Harper and Row, 1977.

Heilbroner, R. L. 'Do Machines Make History?' *Technology and Culture* 8 (1967): 335–345.

Hughes, T. *Networks of Power: Electrification in Western Society, 1880–1930*. Baltimore and London: John Hopkins University Press, 1983.

Ingold, T. *The Perception of the Environment: Essays in Livelihood, Dwelling and Skill*. London and New York: Routledge, 2000.

Latour, B. *Science in Action – How to Follow Scientists and Engineers Through Society*. Cambridge, MA: Harvard University Press, 1987.

Latour, B, and Strum, S. 'The Meanings of the Social: From Baboons to Humans.' *Information sur les Sciences Sociales* 26 (1987): 783–802.

Lawson, C. 'Collective Learning and Epistemically Significant Moments.' In *High Technology, Networking and Collective Learning in Europe*, edited by D. Keeble and F. Wilkinson. Ashgate: Aldershot, 2000.

Lawson, C. *Artefacts, Relations and Functions: an ontology of technology*. Cambridge: Mimeo, 2006.

Lawson, T. *Economics and Reality*. London: Routledge, 1997.

Lawson, T. *Reorienting Economics*. London: Routledge, 2003.

Lynch, M. 'Going Full Circle in the Sociology of Knowledge: Comment on Lynch and Fuhrman.' *Science, Technology and Human Values* 17 (1992): 228–33.

MacKenzie, D. 'Marx and the Machine.' *Technology and Culture* 25 (1984): 473–502.

MacKenzie, D. and Wajcman J. 'Introduction: The Social Shaping of Technology.' In *The Social Shaping of Technology*, edited by D. MacKenzie and J. Wajcman. Milton Keynes, UK: Open University Press, 1985.

Marx, K. *The Poverty of Philosophy*. New York: International, 1971.

Mitcham, C. *Thinking through Technology: the Path Between Engineering and Philosophy*. Chicago and London: University of Chicago Press, 1994.

Mumford, L. *The Myth of the Machine: Technics and Human Development*. New York: Harcourt, 1967.

Pels, D. 'The Politics of Symmetry.' *Social Studies of Science* 26 (1996): 277–304.

Pickering, A., (ed). *Science as Practice and Culture*, Chicago and London: University of Chicago Press, 1992.

Pickering, A. *The Mangle of Practice: Time Agency and Science*, Chicago and London: University of Chicago Press, 1995.

Pinch, T. and Bijker, W. 'The Social Construction of Facts and Artifacts: Or How the Sociology of Science and the Sociology of Technology Might Benefit Each Other.' In *The Social Construction of Technological Systems: New Directions in the Sociology and History of Technology*, edited by W. Bijker, T. Pinch, and T. Hughes. Massachusetts: MIT Press, 1987.

Rosenberg, N. 'Marx as a Student of Technology.' *Monthly Review*, 28 (1976): 56–77.

Shapin, S. 'History of Science and Its Sociological Reconstructions.' *History of Science* 20 (1982): 157–211.

Smith, M. and Marx, L. (eds). 'Technological Determinism in American Culture.' In *Does Technology Drive History? the Dilemma of Technological Determinism*, 1–36. Massachusetts: MIT Press, 1996.

Staudenmaier, J. 'Problematic Stimulation: Historians and Sociologists Constructing Technology Studies.' In *Research in Philosophy and Technology, Vol. 15: Social and Philosophical Constructions of Technology*, edited by C. Mitcham. Greenwich, Connecticut: JAI Press, 1995.

Wajcman, J. *Feminism Confronts Technology*. University Park, PA: Pennsylvania State University Press, 1991.

Winner, L. *Autonomous Technology*. Cambridge, MA: MIT Press, 1977.

Winner, L. 'Do Artifacts Have Politics?' *Daedalus* 105 (1980): 121–36.

Winner, L. 'Upon Opening the Black Box and Finding It Empty: Social Constructivism and the Philosophy of Technology.' In *The Technology of Discovery and the Discovery of Technology*, edited by J. Pitt and E. Lugo. Blacksburg, VA: Society for Philosophy and Technology, 1991.

Woolgar, S. *Science: The Very Idea*. Chichester, UK: Ellis Horwood/London & New York: Tavistock, 1988.

Woolgar, S. 'The Turn to Technology in Social Studies of Science', *Science, Technology & Human Values*, 16 (1991): 20–50.

4 Ontological theorising and the assumptions issue in economics

Stephen Pratten

Introduction

In recent years there has been a growing recognition of the need for sustained ontological elaboration and assessment within economics. Evaluations of the ontological presuppositions of influential authors or schools of thought have become recognised and valued forms of methodological reflection. Explicitly ontological contributions examining the nature of social rules and institutions or exploring the character of humans as intentional, reflective, internally structured agents are now not uncommon within the economic methodology literature and in heterodox economics circles. However, ontological analysis in economics is far from a single, unitary endeavour. Rather a diverse range of individuals and groups pursue projects of different kinds with varied intellectual ambitions. These projects sometimes differ both in how ontology itself is conceived of and in the perception of the likely contribution of ontological theorising. If one can speak of an ontological turn in economics it is important to acknowledge that it has taken a variety of different forms. An examination of how these various projects relate to one another is likely to help clarify the contribution of each and the significance of any general shift toward ontological theorising in economic methodology.

The objective of the present chapter is to differentiate between various types of ontological project and to then situate, using the distinctions introduced, three prominent sets of contributions namely those of Uskali Mäki, Nancy Cartwright and Tony Lawson. I argue that these influential projects adopt distinctive orientations toward ontological theorising that inform the type of methodological intervention each views as fruitful. As a way of illustrating the significance of these competing orientations to ontological theorising I briefly consider the position each develops on the issue of the role of assumptions in modern economics. Despite some consensus concerning the importance of the topic, and each adopting a form of realism, they arrive at rather different interpretations and draw distinct implications from their discussions of the assumptions issue.

Ontological theorising and internal metaphysics

If ontology refers to the study of being then it is useful to remember that the word being itself has two senses. Firstly it means something that is, or exists: an entity, a thing. Secondly it refers to what all the things that are have in common (see Crane & Farkas 2004: 137). A study of being attempts to identify what is, or what exists, and also outlines what it means for something to have being. It is concerned not just about whether things of certain kinds exist but also with what it is for such things to be the kinds they are. Anything that does or could exist is describable as an entity of some sort or other and, at one level, ontology offers a kind of inventory of entities viewed as significant in some or other context. We can distinguish this question concerning the 'population' of entities from a related 'definitional' question that ontology also addresses, namely what it is for items of this or that kind to have a nature and what that nature might be (see Witt 1989 and Macdonald 2005). On this basis we may differentiate *philosophical ontology* that concerns the definitional question from *scientific ontology* that focuses on the population question. Both philosophical ontology and scientific ontology may be seen as seeking principles that are true of reality but ask different questions. Philosophical ontology typically elaborates on the properties common to all objects in a relevant domain and is exhaustive in the sense that it seeks to derive a general conception that includes 'all actual developments as special configurations' (see Lawson 2003a, p. xvi and 2004a). Philosophical ontology then identifies highly abstract and fundamental features of the world, e.g., its open, structured, differentiated character. Scientific ontology is the study of the particular types of entities and processes postulated by some substantive scientific or other theory and involves consideration of their nature, structure or mode of being.

The method adopted to address scientific ontology is likely to involve unravelling the fabrics of conceptual systems (see Bhaskar 1986: 20). One method that may be deployed in order to pursue a project in scientific ontology is to consider some conceptual field in science as reliable and then examine its ontological presuppositions. Thus one might view some theoretical account of an episode of evolutionary change as reliable, reveal its ontological commitments and then be prepared to accept the results achieved as reflecting features of the relevant domain. Or one might accept Marx's account of capitalism and ask how must the social realm be structured for this theory to be true with the entities so revealed then considered as constitutive of aspects of the social world. However, as Lawson emphasises more is involved here than unpacking the ontological commitments embodied in certain types of scientific theory: 'there is an extra conceptual step required to move from (1) identifying or recognising the presuppositions of such theories and (2) accepting the plausibility of those theories and so their ontological presuppositions' (2004a: 2). If scientific ontology involves providing an inventory of central categories that in turn may require us to unpack the ontological commitments implied by scientific theories. But the objective is to generate an account of what there is – not a list of what this or that language community says there is. Lawson suggests that as 'long as we are in possession of theories widely regarded as reliable, whose content can serve as the premises for ontological analysis, there is reason to suppose that the presuppositions uncovered can relate to reality beyond conceptions' (2004a: 8). Clearly where some conceptual scheme in science cannot be taken as reliable then if scientific ontology is to be pursued at all alternative methods need to be identified.

One method that has been deployed (e.g., by critical realists) to pursue philosophical ontology is transcendental argument using the *practices* of natural science as a reliable initiating premise. According to Bhaskar (1986:13) a first step in re-establishing ontology is to appreciate that philosophical ontology need not be dogmatic and transcendent, but may be conditional and immanent. It need not take as its subject matter a world separate from that investigated by the sciences and other disciplines. Rather it can examine the structure of the world by, for example, considering what can be established about it from transcendental argument. The claim is that we can move from generalised observations about experimental practices to inferences concerning their conditions of possibility. What must be the case for scientists to engage in experimental activity where strict event regularities are produced? It must be the case that they cannot routinely find constant conjunctions of events and empirical invariances outside the laboratory. If they could then it would not be necessary to set up a laboratory *closure* at all. Experimental activity artificially induces a closure at the level of patterns of events so as to identify the operation of a causal mechanism free from interfering forces. Reflection on certain non-contentious aspects of experimental practice reveals the relevant domain of reality to be open (allowing the possibility of experimental closure), structured (constituted in part by causal mechanisms irreducible to events and their patterns) and separable (with some parts that can be insulated from others). However, even amongst those who acknowledge the possibility of philosophical ontology there remains disagreement about its legitimate scope and consequently views vary concerning the type of intervention that one might expect from this form of ontological theorising.

If philosophical and scientific ontology can be seen as addressing different questions and using distinct techniques or methods, how do these projects interrelate? Can a scientific ontology be read off from a philosophical ontology? Many have attempted to deduce a comprehensive set of categorial principles from an initial philosophical ontology but none have succeeded (see for discussion Bhaskar 1986: 21). A philosophical ontology may inform an attempt to elaborate on some entity that is the object of scientific or substantive analysis but these projects are irreducible each to the other and the development of scientific ontology requires additional empirical insights in order to proceed.

Philosophical and scientific ontology can be seen as conforming to a traditional conception of ontology and more broadly metaphysics in so far as they seek to provide a general account of the fundamental kinds that there are and an account of what their fundamental natures are. Ontology of this type should in turn be clearly differentiated from what might be referred to as internal metaphysics (see Smith 2003). Internal metaphysics constitutes a theory of the ontological content (categories, properties, entities, etc.) implied by certain representations or implicit in certain practices. It is an exercise that concerns itself not with the world itself but rather with systems of belief. Traditional ontologists are seeking principles that are true of reality beyond our conceptions. Those engaged in internal metaphysics, in contrast, are seeking to elicit principles from theories, conceptual fields or practices. The elicited principles may or may not be true, but this, to the practitioner of internal metaphysics, is of no concern, since the significance of these principles lies elsewhere. The objective may, for example, be to accurately identify the taxonomical system used by speakers within a given language community or by the scientists working in a given research programme. To the extent that we should acknowledge that these conceptions are themselves part of being, then we can see internal metaphysics as constituting a very narrow kind of ontology. Just as a division was drawn between philosophical and scientific ontology a similar distinction can be drawn within internal metaphysics. Thus revealing the ontology presupposed by a philosophical account of science may constitute one form of internal metaphysics involving the identification of the kind of world in which that account of science would be appropriate. This can be distinguished from those projects directed toward identifying the particular types of entities and processes postulated by some substantive scientific or other theory where there is no commitment to the reliability of the theory focused on.

Note that to differentiate between ontologically orientated projects in this manner is not to say that they should be pursued independently, rather it is to suggest that by making clear the differences it may help in locating disagreements and misunderstandings. Any given project may be engaged in both philosophical and scientific ontology and also carry through various exercises in internal metaphysics. Thus at the level of internal metaphysics we may be interested in examining a contributor's ontological presuppositions and this is often likely to be a fruitful exercise. We may discover that some author has a consistent ontological position and revealing it may help us understand more clearly the nature of their substantive contributions. Equally we may find inconsistencies in individual contributor's ontological preconceptions; they may have a broad ontological vision that is found to be inconsistent with the presuppositions implied by their own theoretical framework. A project that is prepared to engage in philosophical and/or scientific ontology goes beyond the evaluation of the internal consistency of others and provides an account of the structure of reality. This may then be used as a means of commenting on the adequacy of ontological positions presupposed or advanced by others. A project might engage in a variety of different forms of ontological theorising then but equally may choose to focus more or less exclusively on one set of activities, philosophical or scientific ontology or internal metaphysics. Indeed, a project may engage in internal metaphysics while doubting the very possibility, or the fruitfulness, of philosophical and/or scientific ontology. In such cases ontological theorising is effectively being collapsed into internal metaphysics. In the remaining sections of the chapter I locate the contributions of Mäki, Cartwright and Lawson using these distinctions and show how their orientations to ontological theorising inform their distinctive positions on the assumptions issue in economics.

Minimal realism, ontological constraints and forms of fiction

A distinctive feature of Uskali Mäki's framework is the adoption of a thin or minimal notion of realism. This involves abstaining from the explicit elaboration of a sustainable social ontology, one evaluated and defended against alternatives. In this sense it seems his is not primarily a project in either philosophical or scientific social ontology as conceived and described above but rather is more or less exclusively concerned with internal metaphysics. His argument does not seem to be that such ontological elaboration is impossible but rather that it is not what is currently most urgently required in the context of contemporary debates in economic methodology.

Mäki's preferred core or minimal realism does not involve commitment to any particular social ontology. Holistic as well as atomistic social ontologies, although quite distinct and incompatible with one another, may be seen as entirely consistent with a realist position being adopted by their proponents. Mäki wishes to stress that an array of different forms of realism may be at play within a discipline such as economics and a central task for the methodologist is to provide an accurate account of the ontological presuppositions of particular economic theories and the ontological commitments of specific economists (2001a: 12). In pursuing such exercises he expresses a preference for detailed case study analysis of specific branches of economics and or particular authors. He suggests: 'One takes big risks by maintaining that economics is like this or economics is like that – for the simple reason that there is no one homogenous "economics" about which one can justifiably make straightforward claims. A more differentiated approach is advisable' (2002a: 8). Opposing any *a priori* approach to economic ontology[1] Mäki proposes an alternative in which one proceeds 'by way of empirical case studies in descriptive economic ontology so as to develop, in an *a posteriori* fashion, an accurate account of the actual ontological commitments of particular economists. By comparing these to one another and to the ontologies of other social sciences and scientists, one may then possibly end up identifying interesting mismatches and using them to develop arguments of a revisionary kind' (2001a: 12). According to Mäki unpacking the ontological presuppositions of authors and their theories is a demanding undertaking calling for subtle interpretation. He suggests that in many cases deep-rooted tensions may operate: the ontological commitments embedded in theories or models may not match up with the deeper convictions authors have about the nature of the economic system. In cases where the economic methodologist can identify and elaborate upon such tensions this may encourage further technical refinements aimed at resolving the inconsistencies (2002a: 17).

Mäki's project appears to involve rather limited critical engagement with the ontological commitments of the various theoretical and other positions examined. Mäki does not say that once different ontological positions have been identified they can never be critically evaluated – but it is not an undertaking he carries through in any sustained manner nor does his framework clearly identify how such choices could be made. He is ultimately highly cautious at the level of ontological elaboration. The project is one of clarification seemingly with the aim of facilitating greater precision in communication. Mäki suggests that an advantage of his position is that it allows for a more complete and adequate characterisation of the peculiarities of a discipline. By comparison ontologically bold projects are seen as effectively too concrete, prematurely committing themselves to a specific ontology. When such ontologically ambitious projects attempt to get to grips with the complex peculiarities of a discipline they are seen as liable to provide only a distorted account, likely to unnecessarily limit fruitful communication and even undermine pluralism (Mäki & Oinas 2004: 1772).[2]

If Mäki can be seen as primarily engaged in internal metaphysics how does this orientation influence his analysis of the assumptions issue in economics? Mäki (1992, 1994) has devoted much effort to clarifying this issue and one theme he has elaborated on at length concerns how the various ontological commitments of economists impinge on theory choice and theory development. So, for example, Mäki (1998, 2002b, 2004) has not only been concerned to reveal the implicit ontological presuppositions of economists like Coase, Richardson and Williamson, but also carefully traces through the way in which such commitments influence the stances these authors adopt toward various substantive economic theories. Mäki shows that for some economists at least the consistency of a theory with some underlying vision of the nature of the economic system remains an important criterion against which to assess those theories:

> Coase and Richardson admit that all theories are bound to be unrealistic in the trivial sense of excluding much, in being isolative. But they also think there are limits to narrowness. The appropriate isolations have to meet an ontological constraint provided by a well grounded conception of the way the economic system works. They further believe that the model of perfect competition does not meet the constraint, and therefore cannot be taken as an adequate representation of the core or essence of the competitive economy – not even as a hypothetical possibility (2002b: 42).

For Mäki all models and theories are unrealistic in the sense that they isolate[3] but what he is interested in is tracking the way in which some economists mobilise their ontological commitments as a resource when evaluating and developing theory (2001b: 383).[4] Mäki is even prepared to suggest that this is an appropriate constraint (2001b: 371). What he seems less willing to engage in, despite all his clarifications of the puzzles surrounding the assumptions issue, is an exercise whereby he sets out his own ontological commitments with regard to the social realm and deploys these as criteria to assess prevailing assumptions, models and theories.

Local realism, Galilean idealisation and false idealisation

Psillos, when reviewing Cartwright's work in the broader field of the philosophy of science, suggests that one of her major contributions has been to show how 'metaphysics can be respectable to empiricists' (2002: 1). But what type of metaphysical project does Nancy Cartwright in fact pursue and as her attention has turned to economics what if any relevance does she view ontological theorising as having? It is clear that, at times, Cartwright engages in internal metaphysics. She is interested, for example, in teasing out the ontological presuppositions of various projects in econometrics but certainly does not commit herself to the implicit picture of the world so identified (1989a: 158). It may be suggested that Cartwright engages in quite a broad project of internal metaphysics, in so far as she identifies an implicit metaphysical perspective that informs certain projects in econometrics. At other times she seems to focus in on the implicit ontological presuppositions implied by the deployment of particular categories. This latter exercise may perhaps be seen as more in line with the kind of study Mäki often favours. It is the distinction between these two kinds of study and the recognition that they may call for the deployment of rather different methods that Cartwright seems to be pointing to when she writes: 'If you want to find out how a scientific discipline pictures the world, you can study its laws, its theories, its models and its claims – you can listen to what it says about the world. But you can also consider not just what is said but what is done' (1999a: 102). Broad philosophical accounts of being may be held implicitly and it may be fruitful to focus on the practices of scientists rather than their theories if they are to be revealed effectively.

Once certain sets of ontological presuppositions have been located Cartwright appears prepared to go further and consider their validity or adequacy. Consider the way in which she expresses her concerns regarding the assumption, standardly adopted in much econometric analysis, that data can be conceived of as being drawn from an underlying probability distribution: 'You shouldn't think that the probabilistic approach [to econometrics] avoids ontology. It just chooses one ontology over another. To my mind it makes the wrong choice' (Cartwright 1995b: 72–3). Mäki recognises that the evaluation and critique of alternative ontological positions is a possibility but seems to hold back from it, judging it less than productive in present circumstances. On what basis does Cartwright proceed to evaluate between different ontological frameworks? How can she claim that a wrong choice has been made? Here it is important to recognise that Cartwright's project is not confined to internal metaphysics.

Cartwright's project can be seen as very much engaged with ontology – providing insights into the structure of reality independently of the ways we think or speak about it. But how can we possibly carry out any such project? In pursuing a project in philosophical ontology she deploys a form of transcendental argument:

> My advocacy of realism – local realism about a variety of different kinds of knowledge in a variety of different domains across a range of highly differentiated situations – is Kantian in structure. Kant frequently used a puzzling argument form to establish quite abstruse philosophical positions (Φ): We have X – perceptual knowledge, freedom of the will, whatever. But without Φ (the transcendental unity of the apperception, or the kingdom of ends) X would be impossible, or inconceivable. Hence Φ. The objectivity of local

knowledge is my Φ; X is the possibility of planning, prediction, manipulation, control and policy setting' (1999a: 23).

Note here that, as with critical realism, her initiating premises relate not to scientific theory but practice 'How then do we figure out what the world is like? ... I do not believe that there is a convenient place called "theory" where that is encoded. I also presuppose strong empiricism: it is empirical success that determines what our best available science is' (2003: 4).

Cartwright reaches the result that in order to render intelligible significant aspects of scientific activity, i.e., experimental manipulation and the application of scientific knowledge outside the experimental set up, a layered ontology is required. She commits herself to knowable deeper levels of reality and sees science as engaged in a process of identifying underlying Aristotelian natures. With regard to the significance of experimental activity she suggests that these artificially produced environments allow us to trigger a single kind of process in relative isolation, free from the interfering flux of the open world enabling us to observe its detailed workings (1999a: 86). Cartwright opposes certain entrenched conventional contemporary accounts of scientific knowledge and defends the reality and knowledge of not only surface phenomena but also of causal capacities, tendencies and natures. Without a structured ontology and if science is conceived as a search for event regularities then the absence of spontaneously occurring strict event regularities threatens to fence science off from most of the goings on in the world and restrict its applicability predominantly to artificially constructed contexts. With a structured ontology of the kind suggested by Cartwright persistence and generality can obtain at a different level. She maintains that 'the use of Aristotelian-style natures is central to the modern explanatory programme' (1999a: 83). Cartwright conceptualises laws as referring us to Aristotelian natures and introduces the idea of tendencies seeing these as signifying the continuing activity of a power or capacity that is exercised without necessarily being fully manifest (see 1999a: 82).

For Cartwright 'Galilean Idealisation' is the procedure underlying all modern experimental enquiry. It is the method by which causal capacities are revealed:

> Galileo's experiments aimed to establish what I have been calling a tendency claim. ... the experiments were designed to find out what contribution the motion due to the pull of the earth will make, with the assumption that that contribution is stable across all the different kinds of situations falling bodies will get into. How did Galileo find out what the stable contribution from the pull of the earth is? He eliminated (as far as possible) all other causes of motion on the bodies in his experiment so that he could see how they move when only the earth affects them (1999b: 5).

Cartwright is concerned to examine what it is that is ideal about these experimental circumstances. What is 'falsely' ideal within Galilean idealisation is the material isolation of the factor, such isolations are not typically immediately available to us but are hard won and laboriously achieved. But what is not falsely ideal but on the contrary quite real is the nature of the thing which is better revealed within the idealised conditions produced. She writes:

> What is an ideal situation for studying a particular factor? It is a situation in which all other 'disturbing' factors are missing. And what is special about that? *When all other disturbances are absent, the factor manifests its power explicitly in its behaviour.* When nothing else is going on, you can see what tendencies a factor has by looking at what it does. This tells you something about what will happen in very different, mixed circumstances – but only if you assume that the factor has a fixed capacity that it carries with it from situation to situation (1989a: 190–1).

Cartwright argues that we find (via philosophical ontology) that the image of the world implied by the methods used in our most successful studies of it is very different from the image of the world that we find (via the study of ontological presuppositions) implied by more conventional views of science and which may have been imported as an ideal into economics. Yet Cartwright is reticent about extending the project of philosophical ontology into the social realm and reluctant to engage in any bold programme of ontological elaboration. She writes: 'I think, in so far as we have to make bets about metaphysics, because our methodology hinges on it, they ought to be very small bets' (1995a: 214). In the context of economics it is the dogmatic belief in the existence of master regularities that Cartwright implies are the large and unnecessary metaphysical bets that are too often placed. However, if economics and social science more generally is unable to provide robust empirical successes of the kind Cartwright seeks as a starting point for her excursions into philosophical ontology then it seems likely that any ontological outline of the social realm must remain faint indeed.

The scope of philosophical ontology is limited for Cartwright particularly with respect to the social domain. Nonetheless, Cartwright's orientation to ontological theorising is clearly broader than Mäki's (or at least her interests extend further than Mäki's as those are expressed in the project he currently publicly engages in). But how does this inform her treatment of the assumptions issue in economics? Again Cartwright seems to want to go beyond Mäki. That is she is not satisfied with identifying the ontological commitments of various authors and tracing through how these in some cases act as constraints on their theorising. Cartwright wishes to identify more fundamental problems with the manner in which mainstream economists deploy unrealistic assumptions. Cartwright's concerns about the role of assumptions within the modelling project of contemporary mainstream economics are expressed in the language of Galilean and non Galilean idealisations:

> The problems I worry about arise when not all of the unrealistic assumptions required for the derivations are ones that characterise an ideal experiment. What I fear is that in general a good number of the false assumptions made with our theoretical models do not have the form of Galilean idealisations.

They do not serve first to isolate a single mechanism but are rather far stronger than this ... The need for these stronger constraints – the ones that go beyond Galilean idealisation – comes I believe, on account of the nature of economic theory itself (1999b: 6).

Cartwright emphasises the mundane or meagre nature of the key categories of mainstream models and sees this as reflecting a conscious strategy on the part of the model builders: 'Almost any principle with real content in economics is highly contentious. So we try to construct models that use as few controversial assumptions as possible' (1999b: 8). In such a context and if deductive modelling is seen as essential to the appropriate conduct of economics then a way to 'get deductivity when you do not have it in the concepts is to put enough of the right kind of structure into the model. That is the trick of building a model in contemporary economics: you have to figure out some circumstances that are constrained in just the right way that results can be derived deductively' (1999a: 3–4). The result she concludes is that:

> economics becomes exact – but at the cost of becoming exceedingly narrow. The kind of precise conclusions that are so highly valued in contemporary economics can be rigorously derived only when very special assumptions are made. But the very special assumptions do not fit very much of the contemporary economy around us' (1999a: 149).

For Cartwright the kind of idealisation that goes on in contemporary mainstream economics does not seem to correspond very closely to the method of Galilean idealisation. To the extent that mainstream modellers persist with such forms of non Galilean idealisation one question that emerges is are there any robust defences available that suggest that insights of value might still be forthcoming from the prevailing procedures? Another question implied by Cartwright's position concerns whether there are reasonable grounds for anticipating that methods that do deploy Galilean idealisation more faithfully have a legitimate field of application in the social realm? Given the faintness of Cartwright's social ontology this is an issue that it is difficult for her to address entirely satisfactorily. When considering theoretical modelling in economics Cartwright insists that 'the analogue of Galilean idealisation in a model is a good thing' (1999b: 5–6). Now there seems to be an ambiguity here, this could mean that the way in which we move through Galilean idealisation to an understanding of capacities/natures is a good thing or she may mean this *and* that the particular procedures, including the strategies of isolation, through which this is accomplished via the experimental set up is desirable, appropriate or even essential. In the context of experimental activity itself the nature of the material being studied allows for a type of isolationist intervention and the shielding of a stable causal mechanism from interference. However, at times Cartwright seems to move to the claim that the analogue of Galilean idealisation, including its isolationist aspects, in models whatever their domain is desirable or indispensable. To the extent that Galilean idealisation is tied to strategies of isolation, to propose it as a method appropriate for social science is highly problematic for those who maintain that the social realm is not only open and structured but also holistically constituted. As soon as Galilean idealisation is exported outside the context of the experimental set up then its relevance has to be assessed by reference to the nature of the material under investigation. It is here where Cartwright's reluctance to engage in social philosophical ontology appears as particularly problematic. It is quite feasible to maintain that the movement to underlying causal mechanisms/Aristotelian natures is a primary scientific objective and yet conclude that the kind of stability and separability presupposed by Galilean methods as described by Cartwright cannot be safely assumed in the social realm. Cartwright is aware of the kind of ontological presuppositions made of the social world of proceeding with a method of Galilean idealisation but at times sees little alternative (1989b: 197). Cartwright does not ultimately commit herself to the kind of atomistic, isolatable social ontology presupposed by such methods. Indeed, she is careful to highlight that others, including Keynes, have argued forcefully against such metaphysical positions. Rather, her argument seems to be that if the social world is not of a nature which facilitates the application of Galilean methods then the prospects of developing causal explanations of social phenomena may turn out to be rather limited.

Critical realism, real abstraction and contrast explanation

Like Mäki and Cartwright, critical realists such as Lawson engage in internal metaphysics. That is they are interested in unravelling the implicit ontological presuppositions of others. At times this is undertaken at a broad philosophical level where the often implicit general theory of being implied by say an account of science or an approach to economics is identified. Thus Bhaskar (1978) examines the largely implicit philosophical account of being or ontology (empirical realism) associated with Humean inspired conceptions of science. Lawson has also been concerned with internal metaphysics at this broad level. He demonstrates that underpinning, or essential to, the practices of mainstream economics is a commitment to deductivism. Here the mainstream project in economics is seen as essentially a methodologically driven one in which only arguments that take on a deductivist form are seen as legitimate contributions. Critical realists show that deductivism itself carries metaphysical implications. Those who suggest or assume that it is relevant are committing themselves to a certain account of being one that can be unravelled and set out systematically for consideration. In addition to this form of internal metaphysics critical realists also carry out more finely grained studies, Lawson (1988) for example looks at what is being presupposed about the nature of probability in the relevant contributions of Savage, Ramsey, Lucas, Knight and Keynes. Also critical realists have been concerned to examine the degree of internal consistency associated with the ontological presuppositions of particular authors or traditions. Just like Mäki, critical realists draw out the complex tensions that often exist regarding different aspects of author's ontological commitments. It has been found in a number of prominent cases that the initial project or wider vision that an author started out with turn out to be incompatible with the ontological presuppositions implied by the theoretical frameworks that they construct (see Pratten 1998).

Critical realism is not exhausted by exercises in internal metaphysics it is also concerned, like Cartwright, with ontology as traditionally conceived. Moreover, as we have seen it too uses the method of transcendental argument starting from the practices of natural science and the application of scientific knowledge outside the experimental set up to generate results about the open, structured, differentiated nature of reality. The ontology defended by critical realists helps us understand many aspects of science not least the process of abstraction. Indeed, it is the ontology of relatively enduring and transfactually active causal mechanisms that can be seen to ground abstraction in science. The concrete is the union of many determinations. In abstracting we focus on one (set of) aspect(s) of an object of investigation, whilst momentarily leaving aside others or the concrete whole. As Chalmers notes: 'We may abstract the falling of the leaf from other aspects of its motion, or the dip in the intensity of light from a laser from details concerning the absolute intensity, direction and spread of the beam' (1993: 202). Further abstraction is also at work as we identify and comprehend that aspect, or set of aspects, of reality that is essential to the phenomena that we want to explain. What is distinctive about the experiment from the angle of abstraction is that with this form of intervention it is possible to actualise abstractions in relative isolation and test them separately.

Whereas Cartwright restricts her exercises in philosophical ontology, critical realism extends its own ontological elaborations in a much more thoroughgoing way to the social realm. Proponents of critical realism, and particularly Lawson, have been prepared in the social realm, where empirical successes seem rather thin on the ground and scientific theories remain so highly contested, to move beyond the theories and practices of social science in order to find initiating premises facilitating philosophical ontological elaboration. Lawson notes:

> one fruitful approach to philosophical ontology is to seek (possibly via transcendental) arguments starting from premises concerning successful social practices. Although most of the practices of social science may not be said to be (or be recognised as being) reliable I think we can accept that we all of us engage in many successful social practices in our daily going on in life. Our practices are successful in the sense that they allow us to negotiate our way round a complex reality, an outcome intelligible only on the assumption that these practices are mostly appropriate to their objects (2004a: 14).

Thus, if we start with certain generalised features of experience – that some practices are both shared and routinised, that typical behaviour is often out of phase with behaviour regarded as legitimate, that practices are segmented, that rule-governed social routines and practices are regularly oriented towards the different practices of determinate others, practices whose occurrence they presuppose – we can then proceed to reveal their conditions of possibility. The results achieved from these kinds of exercise include the conclusion that the social realm is best characterised as structured, emergent, holistically constituted and processual.[5]

Finally here it is worth noting that critical realism seems to open up a space for social scientific ontology. The task of scientific ontology recall is to elaborate on some of the central categories and processes postulated within a substantive scientific or other theory. With regard the social realm categories such as institutions, gender, trust, markets, firms, money, technology, etc., seem obvious candidates requiring this kind of ontological elaboration and clarification. Now given the contested nature of so much social theory it seems that committing to a particular theoretical account of a social category and then unravelling its ontological presuppositions may not be the best way of proceeding with a project in social scientific ontology. What is required is a set of criteria by which the formulation of a social category may be accepted into one's ontology and then defended against alternative accounts. Lawson (2004b), in outlining such a set of criteria, suggests that one criterion be that any account of a social category (his example is the institution) cohere with the results of the exercises undertaken in social philosophical ontology: 'If we possess a sustainable ontological theory of the relevant sort, i.e., an explanatorily powerful conception of the fundamental constituents of social reality, it would be unreasonable to advance a conception of institutions that was inconsistent with it. To the contrary it makes sense to use any such theory to direct our endeavour to elaborate a conception of any important social category, such as the institution' (2004b). He suggests that in addition to this requirement an account of a social category developed within a social scientific ontology should: pick out a definite feature of reality, be consistent with historical usage and carry some theoretical and/or practical utility. Lawson accepts that this kind of work while entirely consistent with the project of critical realism has yet to be undertaken in any systematic fashion.

We can thus see that critical realism contemplates a far more extensive ontological programme than Mäki or even Cartwright. What implications follow for the treatment of the issue of assumptions in economics? The account of abstraction offered by proponents of critical realism is important to understanding their perspective on the assumptions issue. In the social realm we cannot cordon off causal mechanisms physically in the manner that is sometimes possible in certain of the natural sciences. We can choose carefully the most favourable conditions for testing a theory but this only ever eliminates some of the irrelevant factors. In the social realm where, given its holistic nature, we cannot construct physical systems which effectively isolate mechanisms we need to rely on the 'power of abstraction' to bracket off irrelevant forces in thought, recognising that when we come to apply the thought to reality, these factors will be present and affect the outcome. Concrete realities are complex wholes composed of many processes that interact to produce the outcome. These processes, however, are not immediately visible to us. We start by observing a concrete totality and analysing it to discover the many processes. The features on which we focus are aspects of more concrete realities, as well as being conditioned by, they may also be internally related to, other aspects upon which, momentarily, we are not focusing. But, as Lawson emphasises, with this interpretation of abstraction there is no reason at all to suppose that the unavoidably partial nature of the analysis necessitates our falling back on claims or conceptions we already believe to be fictitious:

> If I focus on a person's eyes in an attempt to gauge his or her reaction to what I am saying, or if I describe them in reporting my impression to others, I do not suppose that they exist in isolation; nor do I otherwise necessarily miss-represent the person's reaction in any way …. To take a partial approach is not per se to deform. (1997: 240).

When we have formed the concepts of the partial processes, we may start the process of thought that shows how they combine to form the complex whole. At the end of some cycle of investigation we may have a complex idea of the whole that hopefully expresses the real whole; but to reach such a point we have had to pass through the stage of analysis, abstracting the particular processes from their place in the whole. In the social realm it is recognised that these abstracted processes could not really have occurred apart from the whole; in other words this abstraction or separation occurs only in thought. Both the natural and social sciences are then analysing concrete structured wholes and explaining them in terms of real abstractions, but where experimental intervention is not possible the abstraction arrived at is not measurable, it cannot be actualised in relative isolation, and is testable only by its capacity to explain the minute particulars of concrete entities (see Collier 2003: 119–121).

Now just as Cartwright questioned whether the use of unrealistic assumptions in mainstream economics could be seen as corresponding to the methods of Galilean idealisation proponents of critical realism in economics question whether they can be seen as real abstractions. For Lawson the kinds of assumptions that characterise economic models are not real abstractions at all but convenient fictions that are employed so as to facilitate deductivist methods. For Lawson it is the characteristic insistence upon deductivist methods that serves to encourage the adoption of fictitious assumptions. In order for deductivist methods to be deployed it must be supposed that the items examined in the analysis exercise their own separate, independent and invariable (and so predictable) effects (relative to, or as a function of, initial conditions). Deductivist theorising of the sort pursued in modern economics ultimately has to be formulated in terms of such atoms so as to ensure that under given conditions x the same predictable or deducible outcome y always follows. However Lawson shows that the assumption of atomism is not sufficient on its own to ensure closure and facilitate deductivist explanation and prediction. For even with an atomic ontology, the total effect on an outcome of interest may be changed to almost any extent if all the other accompanying causes are different. That is why he suggests, in mainstream economic contributions, the atomic individuals tend to be treated as part of an assumed to be isolated and self-contained set or system. More specifically Lawson argues that typically the most abstract features within mainstream models refer to only the thinnest and broadest of generalisations that hardly begin to identify the nature of real causal mechanisms and possess little in the way of explanatory content. In such a context, in order to get any novel results out of a modelling exercise, a battery of additional assumptions have to be relied upon. And it is as these further 'supporting assumptions' are supplied that the *a priori* commitment to deductivist modes of explanation makes its presence felt (Lawson 1997: 233).

Cartwright's social ontology remained rather faint and as a consequence the methodological implications that followed from her analysis were ambiguous. Proponents of critical realism argue much more forcefully for a particular social ontology, one that is open, structured, processual and interconnected. A consequence of this bolder programme of ontological elaboration in the social realm has been that critical realists have been concerned to uncover explanatory methods appropriate to such conditions. One such (advanced by Lawson, 1997, 2003a) is contrast explanation. The essence of this approach is not to explain some x but rather to explain why 'x rather than y' in conditions where y was expected given that a process thought to be the same as that producing x has produced y. For example the quest is not to explain crop yield (which involves knowing all the factors responsible) but why it is much higher at one end of the field. The point here is that by asking why x rather than y, that is why at one end crop yield is higher (x) rather than the same as elsewhere (y), it can with reason be assumed that all factors affecting yield are fairly constant throughout the field over time except the one (set) making the difference to the yield. The application of the method of contrast explanation requires, then, merely that (i) over some region, referred to as the *contrast space,* good reasons are available to encourage researchers to expect that two outcomes of a certain kind have the same or a similar causal history and (ii) that *a posteriori* the researchers are surprised by outcomes that diverge from those anticipated. The controlled experiment can be seen as constituting a special case of the method of contrast explanation. However, closure is not a necessary condition for the success of projects in contrast causal explanation and those conditions that are necessary for contrast explanation can be shown to hold for the social as well as for the natural realm.

Concluding remarks

If Mäki, Cartwright and Lawson each try to reveal the metaphysical dimensions of economics they do so in quite different ways. While Mäki can be seen as engaged primarily in a project of internal metaphysics both Cartwright and Lawson pursue ontology in a more traditional sense. This is not to suggest that Cartwright and critical realists do not undertake exercises in internal metaphysics, far from it. They devote much effort to the task of unravelling the ontological presuppositions of others. However neither collapses ontology into internal metaphysics, nor do they believe that an exclusive focus upon internal metaphysics is the appropriate strategic response to the current state of the economics discipline. Where Cartwright and critical realism differ concerns the scope of their projects. Cartwright's social ontology remains faint while critical realists are prepared to provide a far bolder outline of the metaphysics of the social realm.

Distinctive orientations toward ontological theorising have been shown to inform the respective treatment offered by the three projects of the assumptions issue in economics. Mäki considers the ontological commitments of others and traces how these sometimes act as constraints allowing certain identified authors to distinguish within their own frameworks between harmless and vicious fictions. Cartwright goes further, suggesting that the role of assumptions in economics goes far beyond anything that could be safely justified on the basis of Galilean methods. However the methodological implications of her analysis ultimately remain ambiguous due to the thinness of her social ontology. Lawson expresses similar concerns about the way assumptions are deployed in economics. In particular he argues that the assumptions routinely adopted in mainstream economics are not real abstractions but convenient fictions, more or less forced on mainstream modellers by their insistence upon deductivist methods. Critical realists such as Lawson though, with their thicker account of the social realm as structured, dynamic, holistic, processual, etc., are encouraged to elaborate on methods that show that causal explanation can proceed without any need to fall back upon known fictions.

Notes

1 Mäki contrasts his own favoured 'bottom-up approach' to a 'top-down approach' that he seems to see critical realism, for example, as conforming to (see 2002c: 91). The claim that critical realism in economics constitutes a 'top-down approach' is difficult to justify and has been rejected, see Lawson 2003, Chapter 2.

2 Mäki also suggests that his approach with its roots in a variety of realist philosophical positions provides a more effective challenge to post modernist developments in economic methodology. Mäki has certainly contributed very substantially to the task of critically engaging with proponents of various forms of post modernism in economic methodology. Critical realists have also taken up that challenge (see Lawson 1994). Mäki's suggestion that his approach allows a priviledged position from which to consider the limitations of post modernist contributions can be questioned (see Sayer (2004) for a discussion of this in the context of human geography).

3 The method of isolation for Mäki is the process 'whereby a set of elements is theoretically removed from the influence of other elements in a given situation' (1992: 318). For Mäki isolation is basic and idealisation and abstraction are seen as forms of isolation.

4 According to Mäki 'All representations are partial in that they isolate small slices of the world from the rest of it' (1994: 243). Therefore 'all theories are unrealistic in a number of ways' (1994: 239). Mäki is particularly concerned to catologue the different ways in which assumptions can be held to be realistic and unrealistic. He distinguishes between realism and realisticness suggesting that: '"realism" and "non-realism" be reserved for denoting a variety of philosophical theses, and that "realisticness" and "unrealisticness" be adopted for denoting various properties of linguistic and other representations such as economic theories and their parts' (1994: 248).

5 Lawson summarising writes: 'First I accept that social reality is the domain of phenomena whose existence depends, at least in part, on us ... I find the social domain to

be *open* in the sense that reasonably strict event regularities (or correlations) are but a special (and seemingly rare) occurrence. It is also *structured* in the sense of being constituted in part by features that cannot be reduced to human activities and other events. Such features include social rules, relations, positions, powers, social mechanisms, and tendencies. Related to this, I identified the social domain as *emergent* with social structures possessing emergent powers ... The social realm, in addition, is intrinsically dynamic or *processual*; social structures such as language systems both depend on us and are continually being reproduced or transformed as we draw upon them. In other words the social world is a process ... The social realm is also highly internally related (or holistic). By this I mean numerous aspects of the social domain are what they are, and can do what they do, by virtue of the (internal) relations in which they stand to other aspects ... The social domain also consists of (internally related) *positions*. Individuals essentially 'slot' into a range of different positions, where such positions are found to have rights, obligations and prerogatives attached to them' (2003b: 121). For an extended elaboration of the social ontology outlined by critical realism see Lawson, 2003a, Chapter 2.

References

Bhaskar, R. *A Realist Theory of Science*. Harvester Wheatsheaf, London, 1978.

Bhaskar, R. *Scientific Realism and Human Emancipation*. Verso, London, 1986.

Cartwright, N. *Nature's Capacities and their Measurement*. Clarendon Press, Oxford, 1989a.

Cartwright, N. 'A Case Study in Realism: Why Econometrics is Committed to Capacities', *SA* 190–197, 1989b.

Cartwright, N. 'An Interview with Nancy Cartwright', *Cogito,* 203–215, 1995a.

Cartwright, N. 'Causal Structures in Econometrics'. In D. Little (ed), *On the Reliability of Economic Models*, Kluwer, Boston, 1995b.

Cartwright, N. *The Dappled World: A Study of the Boundaries of Science*. Cambridge University Press, Cambridge, UK, 1999a.

Cartwright, N. 'The Vanity of Rigour in Economics: Theoretical Models and Galilean Experiments'. *LSE Centre for Philosophy of Natural and Social Sciences, Discussion Paper 43*, 1999b.

Cartwright, N. '*Against the system*', Mimeograph, London School of Economics, 2003.

Chalmers, A. 'So the Laws of Physics Needn't Lie'. *Australian Journal of Philosophy*, 71 (No. 2), 196–205, 1999b.

Collier, A. *Marx*, One World, Oxford, 2003.

Crane, T. and Farkas, K. *Metaphysics: a guide and anthology*. Oxford University Press, Oxford, UK, 2004.

Lawson. T. 'Probability and Uncertainty in Economic Analysis', *Journal of Post Keynesian Economics,* 11 (No. 1), 1988.

Lawson, T. 'Why are so many economists opposed to methodology?' *Journal of Economic Methodology*, 1 (No. 1), 105–134, 1994.

Lawson, T. *Economics and Reality*. Routledge, London, 1997.

Lawson, T. *Reorienting Economics*. Routledge, London, 2003a.

Lawson, T. 'Ontology and Feminist Theorizing' *Feminist Economics*, 9 (No. 1), 119–150, 2003b.

Lawson, T. '*A Conception of Ontology*'. Mimeograph, Cambridge, UK, 2004a.

Lawson, T. '*What is an Institution*', Mimeograph, Cambridge, UK, 2004b.

Macdonald, C. *Varieties of Things: Foundations of contemporary Metaphysics*. Blackwell, Oxford, UK, 2005.

Mäki, U. 'On the method of isolation in Economics'. *Poznan Studies in the Philosophy of the Sciences and Humanities*, 26, 319–354, 1992.

Mäki, U. 'Reorienting the Assumptions Issue'. In R. Backhouse (ed), *New Directions in Economic Methodology*. Routledge, London, 1994.

Mäki, U. 'Is Coase a Realist?'. *Philosophy of the Social Sciences*, 28, (No. 1), 5–31, 1998.

Mäki, U. 'Economic ontology: what? why? how?'. In U. Mäki (ed), *The Economic World View: Studies in the Ontology of Economics*. Cambridge University Press, Cambridge, UK, 2001a.

Mäki, U. 'The way the world works (www): towards an ontology of theory choice'. In U. Mäki (ed), *The Economic World View: Studies in the Ontology of Economics*. Cambridge University Press, Cambridge, UK, 2001b.

Mäki, U, 'The dismal queen of the social sciences'. In U. Mäki (ed), *Fact and Fiction: Models, Realism and Social Construction*. Cambridge University Press, Cambridge, UK, 2002a.

Mäki, U. 'On the issue of realism in the economic of institutions and organizations: themes from Coase and Richardson'. In S. Dow and J. Hillard (eds), *Post Keynesian Econometrics, Microeconomics and the Theory of the Firm*. Edward Elgar, Cheltenham, UK, 2002b.

Maki, U. 'Some non reasons for non realism about economics'. In U. Maki (ed), *Fact and Fiction in Economics: Models, Realism and Social Construction*. Cambridge University Press, Cambridge, UK, 2002c.

Mäki, U. 'Theoretical isolation and explanatory progress: transaction cost economics and the dynamics of dispute'. *Cambridge Journal of Economics*, 28 (No. 3), 319–46, 2004.

Mäki, U. and Oinas, P. 'The narrow notion of realism in human geography'. *Environment and Planning A*, 36, 1755–1776, 1998.

Pratten, S. 'Marshall on tendencies, equilibrium and the statical method'. *History of Political Economy*, 30 (No. 1), 121–63, 1998.

Psillos, S. '*Cartwright's Realist Toil: From Entities to Capacities*'. University of Athens, Mimeograph, 2002.

Sayer, A. 'Realism through thick and thin'. *Environment and Planning A*, 36 (No. 10), 2004.

Smith, B. 'Ontology'. In L. Floridi (ed), *Blackwell Guide to the Philosophy of Computing and Information*, pp 155–166. Blackwell, Oxford, UK, 2003.

Witt, C. *Substance and Essence in Aristotle*. Cornell University Press, Ithaca, NY, 1989.

5 Wittgenstein and the ontology of the social: some Kripkean reflections on Bourdieu's 'Theory of Practice'

Lorenzo Bernasconi-Kohn

Section I

With the proposal of a 'Theory of Practice', Pierre Bourdieu sought to develop a new ontological account of the social world that transcends the most important conceptual oppositions that have burdened traditional social science.[1] Chief among these is the opposition between 'objectivism' and 'subjectivism'.[2] On Bourdieu's view, all of traditional social science falls under the scope of one of these two competing theoretical paradigms, or 'modes of knowledge' (Bourdieu 1973, p. 53).[3] These perspectives differ in their respective conceptions of human action and social order. According to subjectivist theories, all of our actions are the result of our conscious mental states. On this view, social order is explained exclusively in terms of our individual and collective intentions and beliefs. By contrast, according to objectivist theories, our mental states and actions are nothing else but a set of non-intentional mechanisms and phenomena. Social order is thus rendered as the mechanical resultant of specific structures, laws and systems of relations.[4]

Bourdieu developed his 'praxeological' account as an attempt to resist the reduction of social reality to either of these extremes. We must, he insists, abandon all

> ... theories which explicitly or implicitly treat practice as a mechanical reaction ... But rejection of mechanistic theories in no way implies that ... we should reduce the objective intentions and constituted significations of actions and works to the conscious and deliberate intentions of their authors (1977, p. 73).

According to Bourdieu, the social world has 'an intrinsically twofold reality' which any adequate social science must capture (1990b, p. 135). As highlighted by subjectivism, it is partly constituted by the everyday meanings, representations, thoughts and judgements of social agents. An understanding of agents' subjective categories of perception is therefore indispensable for a true and proper conception of the social world. As Bourdieu states:

[to] 'treat social facts as things,' according to the old Durkheimian precept … [is] to leave out everything that they owe to the fact that they are objects of knowledge, of cognition – or misrecognition – within social existence (1989, p. 14).

Thus, for instance, to understand the persistence of systems of domination, symbolic violence and class privilege, Bourdieu argues that we need to investigate the systems of representation and meaning that make these inequitable power relations seem legitimate in the eyes of the subjugated.[5] However, Bourdieu notes that no satisfactory theory of social reality can rest at the level of subjectivism. There is more to the social world than agents' representations and meanings. As objectivism rightly insists, the social world is also made up of structures and systems of relations that are irreducible to ideas and intentions. These objective phenomena 'form the basis for representations and constitute the structural constraints that bear upon interactions' (1989, p. 15). Any satisfactory social theory thus also needs to pay close attention to this second dimension of the social world. The theoretical challenge that Bourdieu therefore sets himself is that of finding a framework able to capture the 'dialectical relationship' between these two realities of the social world (1989, p. 14). To wit, his 'Theory of Practice' is an account of how objective social structures shape our mental representations and practices, and vice versa.

In developing this framework, Bourdieu acknowledges the important influence of some of Wittgenstein's writings on rules and rule-following:

Wittgenstein is probably the philosopher who has helped me most at moments of difficulty. He's a kind of saviour for times of great intellectual distress – as when you have to question such evident things as 'obeying a rule' (1990a, p. 9).

As suggested by this quote, Bourdieu takes his praxeological view to be an extension of some of the basic insights of Wittgenstein's rule-following considerations. Several commentators have concurred with this assessment and indeed one of the reasons Bourdieu's framework has received such acclaim is that it has been taken to be one of the most successful social scientific theories to integrate the insights of Wittgenstein's later thought.[6]

In this paper, I explore an interpretation of Wittgenstein's rule-following considerations that suggests a different conclusion. Rather than viewing Bourdieu's project to be an extension of the basic lessons to be learnt from Wittgenstein's rule-following considerations, this interpretation places his project at odds with them.[7] My point of reference in exploring this theme is Saul Kripke's reading of Wittgenstein in *Wittgenstein on Rules and Private Language: An Elementary Exposition*. Kripke reads Wittgenstein as marshalling reasons to be sceptical of the merits of ontological theories aimed at explaining meaning, understanding, thinking and cognate notions by appeal to our internalisation of specific rules or principles. According to Kripke's Wittgenstein (or 'Kripkenstein'), the search for such ontological accounts is fundamentally misguided – it is the result of a philosophical illusion that leads us to erroneously assume that these phenomena are in need of such metaphysical explanations. On this reading, Wittgenstein's aim is to help us to come to see that the philosophical problems that call for such explanations are not real problems in need of a 'solution', but rather that they are inventions of the intellect in need of a 'dissolution'. As Wittgenstein famously remarked: 'What is your aim in philosophy? – to show the fly the way out of the fly bottle' (*Philosophical Investigations*, §309). Heeding this suggestion, Kripkenstein carefully retraces the steps that lead us to be held captive by a certain erroneous picture of the epistemology and ontology of rule-following. The aim of this diagnosis is to free us from the presumptions that led to our captivity in the first place and accordingly to help us find a way out of the hopeless philosophical difficulties that this picture gives rise to. In what follows, I shall show that Bourdieu's 'Theory of Practice' is committed to a picture of rule-following of precisely the sort targeted by Kripkenstein's analysis. Consequently, I argue that Kripkenstein raises a number of powerful considerations that bring into question not only the coherence of Bourdieu's praxeological theory, but also the more general project of ontological theorising that fuels it.

Section II

At the heart of attempts to uncover the ontology of our practices (and social order more generally) lies the question of how *normatively constrained* areas of human thought and action are reproduced and transformed. This question arises from the fact that many of the practices which characterise the social world, and particularly those that are of most interest to social scientists, are not just repeated patterns of behaviour imposed upon us by physical necessity, but rather, are regular in virtue of responding to socially constructed norms and demands. They are, in other words, normative: i.e. in one form or another they are sustained by standards of correctness and incorrectness. Highlighting this distinctive feature, normative practices have often been characterised as involving rules. Language, morality, etiquette, religious customs, judicial systems, political institutions, economic structures are all phenomena of this sort: they are all sustained by practices that can be evaluated on the scale 'correct – incorrect'. The implication of this fact is that the existence of such normatively constrained, or rule-like practices (and *a fortiori* the phenomena and institutions that are underpinned by them) hinge on our ability to act in accordance with specific prescriptions of correctness and incorrectness.

In considering how our practices can come to possess such normativity, an intuitive assumption to make is that there must be specific *facts* that establish their relevant requirements. Take for example the following arithmetical series: 2, 4, 6, 8, 10 … It seems platitudinous that if there is objectivity to the judgement of what continuations are correct and incorrect, there has to be some *normativity-*

determining fact that establishes this objectivity, i.e. a fact must exist in virtue of which we can say that '12' fits the series correctly whereas '11' doesn't. In this case, it is the rule 'add 2' that seems to do the job: it provides an objective standard of correctness that exists independently of anyone's subjective inclinations and exists prior to any specific instance of continuing the series. Thus, when someone makes a mistake in following the series, or disputes whether a particular number fits, it is by reference to this rule that the matter is settled.

Given this picture, when I am able to follow this arithmetical series correctly, it is natural to assume that the rule 'add 2' plays some role in the generation of my thoughts and actions. When I correctly continue this series, I do not suppose that I reach a correct answer as a result of an unjustified guess, or an innate biological impulse, but in virtue of me having somehow grasped what the rule in question requires.

According to Bourdieu, social theorists have all too often fallen into the trap of taking this intuitive picture at face value and erroneously assumed that all of our normative practices can be explained in terms of us following rules in such a manner. This, for Bourdieu, is the result of an 'intellectualist bias' that tempts theoretical forms of knowledge. Social theorists, Bourdieu argues, are prone to conceptualise practice in terms of rules because of the particular nature of the relationship they hold with the object of their study. As members of the intellectual community, social theorists are endowed (or at least think of themselves as endowed) with a position of social power. This leads them to assume that they enjoy a privileged, undetermined gaze of the 'spectacle' that is the social world situated supposedly 'above and beyond' that of participants observed. Under the illusion of being equipped with such a perspective, these social theorists impose their observations and analysis of practice – stated in semi-formalised terms such as 'rules' – upon the agents observed. This results in them unwittingly falling victim to what Bourdieu refers to as the fallacy of taking 'the things of logic for the logic of things':

> Having discovered the regularities or structure in accordance with which the phenomena are organised, and having stated them in the form of more or less formalised models or theories, the social scientist tends to place these models, which belong to the order of logic, in the individual or collective consciousness of the individual agents or groups (1973, p. 305).

To avoid this 'intellectualist' trap, Bourdieu suggests that social science abandon talk of rules and instead reflect on other modes of existence that normativity-determining facts might have. Thus, as he once commented, 'all my reflection originated from this: how can behaviour be regular without being the product of obedience to rules?' (1987, p. 81). For Bourdieu, the importance of Wittgenstein's rule-following considerations lies in hinting towards an answer to this question. More concretely, Bourdieu takes Wittgenstein as pointing towards a novel way of thinking about normativity-determining facts in terms of culturally shaped dispositions that lie beyond the level of conscious rule-following.[8]

Thus, whilst Bourdieu thinks that traditional social science has badly misunderstood the nature of the factuality of our normative practices, he does not bring into question the basic fact-based model of rule-following presupposed by these theories. For Bourdieu there are incontrovertibly normativity-determining facts which 'guarantee the "correctness" of practices and their constancy over time ...' (1990b, p. 54). As he writes, there is an 'unwritten musical score according to which the actions of agents, each of whom believes she is improvising her own melody, are organised' (1980, p. 89) quoted in (Wacquant 1992, p. 8). Indeed, according to Bourdieu, our ability to engage in normative practices is a matter of the internalisation of the requirements of a store of independent principles out of which all aspects of our rule-like practices are generated. This central idea is expressed by Bourdieu in the preface to *The Logic of Practice* as follows:

> The coherence without apparent intention and the unity without an immediately visible unifying principle of all the cultural realities that are informed by a quasi-natural logic ... are the product of the age-old application of the same schemes of action and perception which, never having been constituted as explicit principles, can only produce an unwilled necessity which is therefore necessarily imperfect but also a little miraculous, and very close in this respect to a work of art (1990b, p. 13).

Delineating this same idea, Bourdieu argues that when a child successfully learns to act in accordance with the norms of her cultural community, this is the result of her grasping 'material' that is

> the product of the systematic application of a small number of principles coherent in practice ... in [their] infinite redundance, [they] suppl[y] the key to all the tangible series, their *ratio,* which will be appropriated in the form of a principle generating practices that are organised in accordance with the same rationality (1990b, p. 74).

According to Bourdieu, the greatest insight of objectivism is that it recognises that the factuality of our practices is socially constrained and that it therefore correctly treats sociology as an 'objective' science.[9] And, as he further argues, it is only by recognising this objectivity that we can 'pose the question of the mechanisms through which the relationship is established between the structures and the practice or the representations which accompany them' and in so doing go beyond a mere *description* of social order to offer instead an *explanation* that digs below the phenomenal to the deeper ontological level of the habitus (1977, p. 21). In other words, it is only by recognising this objectivity that we can come to appreciate the central problem of the 'dialectical relationship' between subjectivism and objectivism that his 'Theory of Practice' is an attempt to answer.

Section III

The conclusion that Kripke draws from Wittgenstein's rule-following considerations points in a very different direction. Against Bourdieu's supposition that Wittgenstein offers us a new way to conceive of the factuality of our normative practices, Kripke reads Wittgenstein as trying to prise us away from conceiving of them on such a model. On Kripke's reading, the critical point of Wittgenstein's rule-following considerations is to show that the assumption that our normative practices can be adequately accounted for in terms of such normativity-determining facts (whether characterised in terms of rules, principles, or some other fact) is an ontological myth, a philosophical flight of fancy. Thus, if Kripkenstein is correct, descriptions, theories and explanations of social life premised on this assumption are to be – to some extent or other – flights of fancy too.

In Kripke's exposition, Wittgenstein establishes this point via an *immanent* or *Pyrrhonian* critique of the fact-based picture of rule following. Thus, on this interpretation, Wittgenstein's aim is not to offer us a conception of the 'true' ontological nature of the social world by appeal to some privileged Archimedean standpoint, but to show that any theory premised on the assumption that our practices are underpinned by normativity-constituting facts will fail on standards that are internal to the theories themselves.

The immanent nature of Kripkenstein's sceptical challenge means that his argument begins by *accepting* the intuitive assumption that our normative practices are explained by a certain normativity-determining fact. He focuses on meaning – a *prima facie* paradigmatic example of a normative practice. Kripkenstein's challenge then consists in trying to locate a fact that fixes the normativity of meaning. In doing so, he imagines that we have unlimited epistemic access to all areas where such a fact might reside. He does so in order to consider all metaphysically possible candidate facts. Kripkenstein then introduces a sceptic who analyses each of these proposals to see whether it is able to do the job required: i.e. tell us in a novel case what the relevant meaning would require of us. Against our initial intuitions, the sceptic shows that no fact is up to the job. Kripkenstein's sceptic thus concludes that there are no normativity-determining facts: if, even under conditions of complete epistemic access the sought-after-normativity-grounding facts elude our grasp, then it follows that there simply are no such facts there to begin with. Thus Kripkenstein draws the famous sceptical conclusion that 'there can be no such thing as meaning anything by any word' (Kripke 1982, p. 54).

By this, however, Kripkenstein means only that there can be no such thing as meaning *if* we conceive of meaning as resting upon our initial assumption that our normative practices are underpinned by a certain type of fact. But, given that we clearly *do* have meaning (and other normatively constrained practices), the point of the sceptical conclusion is to argue that our initial conception must be flawed.

Section IV

With the general strategy of Kripkenstein's sceptical challenge in mind, we can now ask how these considerations relate more specifically to Bourdieu's attempt to transcend the clutches of the subjectivist/objectivist antinomy. I shall begin by looking at what Kripkenstein's arguments have to say against possible subjectivist and objectivist proposals. This will allow us, first, to better locate the axes around which Bourdieu developed his praxeological solution. Second, and more importantly however, by looking at the considerations that Kripkenstein raises against subjectivism and objectivism individually, it shall become clearer to see why Bourdieu's solution that involves a combination of these perspectives cannot work either.

As we saw above, subjectivists locate the dynamic of social life in the conscious intentions of individual agents. Whilst subjectivists differ in stressing the purported voluntaristic or autonomous nature of these intentions, all are united in the belief that the determining causes of action are ultimately thought objects. On this assumption, subjectivists account for social order in terms of us consciously following, in some form or other, the same rules. That is, we have social order because we share in our minds common rules that guide us to act in similar ways.[10]

In line with this conception, subjectivists assume that we can read off the requirements of a rule from the representation that we have of it in our mind. Put otherwise, subjectivists assume that the conscious representation of a rule that we have in our minds can serve as a normativity-determining fact. Kripkenstein's argument challenges this presupposition by showing that the normative requirements of a rule can never be fixed once and for all by an object of intellection. His argument runs roughly along the following lines.

Suppose someone by the name of Jones is presented with an addition problem that she has never encountered before. For simplicity, let us say that '68 + 57' is an example of such a problem. In response to this query, Jones answers '125'. Jones is convinced that this is the correct answer as this is the answer that accords with what in the past she always meant by the plus sign ('+').

At this point Kripke asks us to imagine a 'bizarre sceptic' who doubts whether in the past Jones in fact used the plus sign to mean the addition function. Expressing this doubt, the sceptic asks Jones to cite some fact that determines that in the past she really meant *addition* by plus and not some other function such as *quaddition*, where quaddition coincides with addition for all cases where the numbers being added are smaller than 57, but otherwise gives the result of 5. In raising this question, the sceptic challenges Jones to cite a normativity-determining fact establishing that by the plus sign Jones in the past meant addition rather than quaddition. The point of the sceptic's challenge is not therefore to question the computational abilities of Jones: the sceptic does not doubt that '125' *would be* the correct answer to the query '68 + 57' *if* in the past the plus sign had been taken to mean addition and Jones was in this instance acting consistently with this belief. As Kripke puts it, the sceptic's challenge is not arithmetical, but 'metalinguistic': it concerns what fact establishes that in the past Jones' understanding of the plus sign tracked addition rather than some other function.

Jones cannot of course appeal to the finite pool of her previous behaviour to justify that she meant addition by plus because all of her past performances are equally compatible with her having meant quaddition. She feels however compelled to rule out the sceptic's seemingly wild hypothesis and with her subjectivist hat on, seeks to justify her presupposition that she meant addition by plus and not quaddition by reference to some fact about her thought objects. Clearly – Jones supposes – there *must* be something inside her head that constitutes her understanding of addition and not quaddition by the plus sign.

Jones thus answers that she meant *addition* and not *quaddition* by plus because she has internalised in her mind a finite set of simple instructions that determines what she should answer to the question 'What is 57 + 68?'. For instance, one such algorithmic procedure might be that used in the counting of marbles. We can determine the outcome of 57 + 68 by arranging two heaps of marbles, one with 57 and the other with 68 elements, combining the two heaps into one, and counting the overall number.

Such an algorithmic procedure, Jones argues, is what she explicitly followed in guiding her counting behaviour in the past and it is what guided her in every new case thus justifying '125' as the correct answer. How does Jones' following of the basic 'counting' procedure help in satisfying the sceptic's challenge? As Kripke points out, not very much at all for the sceptic can always answer that by 'counting' Jones could have meant 'quounting' where quounting refers to the procedures by which she should give the sum 5 when one of the heaps counted exceeds 57.

Perhaps in this case Jones might appeal to a more basic linguistic rule to interpret the counting rule. The problem with this proposal is that the sceptic can again come up with a deviant interpretation for what this more basic rule demands. Given that all contentful mental states can be interpreted in any number of different ways, the point raised by this challenge can be generalised to any set of instructions meant to facilitate the understanding of a rule. Kripke takes himself here to be expounding Wittgenstein's remarks in the *Philosophical Investigations* on 'a rule for interpreting a rule':

> [A]ny interpretation still hangs in the air along with what it interprets, and cannot give it any support. Interpretations by themselves do not determine meaning (*Philosophical Investigations*, ¶198).

What flows from this analysis is that no contentful representation in the mind gives us an appropriate normativity-constituting fact.[11] By implication, no subjectivist view presupposing thought objects as the generating principle of our actions can do the job of justifying whether Jones' meant *addition* or *quaddition* by plus.

Given the problems just considered with the subjectivist approach, objectivism may appear to offer a more promising candidate fact to satisfy the sceptic's challenge. Kripke considers such an objectivist response to the sceptical challenge in the form of dispositions. Such a response simply says that it is a fact about Jones that, when faced with the query '68 + 57=?', she is disposed, *ceteris paribus*, to answer '125'. There is here no reference to intentional or representational mental content. The *prima facie* attraction of such a dispositionalist view is that Kripke's attack against subjectivism falls by the wayside. This proposal says that our intentional states are *reducible* to our dispositions, hence the infinite regress that threatens 'a rule for interpreting a rule' is immediately pre-empted.

Kripke however shows that this dispositional account cannot ultimately satisfy the sceptic either. Whilst not susceptible to the sceptic's attack against subjectivism, dispositionalist accounts are beset by a different set of problems. One that is central is that dispositions cannot perform the crucial task of drawing the conceptual borderline between correctness and incorrectness that underwrites our normative practices.[12] As Kripkenstein shows, this means that they cannot perform the crucial task of establishing whether Jones meant addition by plus.

This problem is brought out by Kripke in showing that objectivism cannot accommodate our intuition that someone can mean *addition* by '+' and yet systematically make mistakes. If, as an objectivist argues, meanings reduce to dispositions, then it should be possible to read off our meanings from our dispositions. So, for instance, if in response to the query '68 + 57=?', Jones answers '125', according to dispositionalism we can read off that what she means by '+' is the *addition* function.

Alas, consider what happens in the case where Jones systematically makes a mistake. Imagine for instance that she systematically fails to carry such that in response to the above query she gives the answer '115'. In this instance, we still want to say that Jones is an adder (albeit a faulty one). On the dispositionalist view, however, there is nothing we can appeal to in order to justify this claim. Such an appeal would presuppose what function she means independently of her dispositions. Thus, on pain of circularity, it would be impossible to tell whether Jones is simply a faulty adder who really meant addition by '+' or whether she is a competent 'skadder' where 'skaddition' has the extension generated by adding without carrying. In short, as Wittgenstein summarises the point and as quoted by Kripke: in the case of dispositionalism 'whatever is going to seem right to me is right. And that only means that here we can't talk about 'right'' (§258) (Kripke 1982, p. 24). Thus, a reductive dispositionalist account of the sort objectivism proposes cannot do the job required of a normativity determining fact either.

The upshot of Kripkenstein's analysis is that no candidate fact offered by either subjectivism or objectivism can establish whether Jones in the past meant *addition* or *quaddition*. Given the fact that the present will become past in the next moment, the sceptical argument can be reapplied to show that neither perspective can ever establish which rule or principle Jones is following in the present either. The devastating implication of Kripkenstein's paradox is thus laid bare: if there is no fact that corresponds to following rules or principles correctly or incorrectly, this result can be extended to show that we can have no such things as normative practices at all.

Section V

Given however that we clearly do have such things as normative practices, Kripkenstein's considerations against subjectivism and objectivism can be interpreted as bringing out two important insights for any account of social order. First, as Kripkenstein's challenge of subjectivism teaches us, the normativity of our practices cannot be thought of as determined by intentional or representational thought objects. And second, as Kripke's challenge against objectivism shows, our normative practices cannot simply be reduced to non-intentional dispositions either.[13]

The first question to consider then is whether Bourdieu's praxeological theory avoids the problems that confront subjectivism. It seems at first sight that it does. Although Bourdieu's reasons for rejecting subjectivism are distinct from those presented by Kripkenstein, he is emphatic that the dynamics of social life *cannot* be understood at the level of our conscious representations.[14] As Bourdieu notes:

> ... to account for the quasi-miraculous and therefore somewhat incredible necessity, without any organizing intention, that [is] revealed by analysis, one [has] to look at the incorporated dispositions, or more precisely the body schema, to find the ordering principle ... capable of orienting practices in a way that is at once unconscious and systematic (1990b, p. 10).

Bourdieu again stresses the unconscious nature of the 'ordering principle' of our practices in his description of the *habitus*, a term he introduces to refer to these 'incorporated dispositions':

> The schemes of the habitus are the primary forms of classification ... [that] ... function below the level of consciousness and language, beyond the reach of introspective scrutiny or control by the will' (1984, p. 466).

For Bourdieu conscious thoughts are in fact never the ultimate generator of our practices. Even if phenomenologically it may sometimes strike us otherwise, Bourdieu insists that this is but an illusion:

> It is, of course, never ruled out that the responses of the *habitus* may be accompanied by a strategic calculation tending to perform in a conscious mode the operation that the *habitus* performs quite differently ... (1990b, p. 53).

Recall that the problem confronting subjectivism was that any proposed normativity-determining candidate at the level of conscious representations can be variously interpreted. By specifying the ordering principle of practice in terms of embodied dispositions, this problem of multiple interpretations is avoided and Bourdieu's account is safe from this line of attack.

The further question then is whether Bourdieu avoids the central problem that confronts objectivism. To answer this question we need to consider in some more detail Bourdieu's understanding of the nature of our embodied dispositions and the role that they play in fixing the normativity of our practices. More specifically, we need to explore whether or not Bourdieu thinks that the normativity of our practices can be explained on the basis of the properties of our embodied dispositions. In short, does Bourdieu think that the normativity of our practices is *reducible* to our embodied dispositions? The reason for the importance of this question lies in the fact that Kripke's challenge against objectivism only has purchase on a reductionist picture. On such a view, the normative properties of our practices are conceived to be nothing else but the properties of our dispositions; what the normativity of our practices 'really are', as it were, is nothing else but a property of our dispositions. An identity relationship is thus assumed to exist between the two. Kripkenstein's claim against objectivism hinges on this insight: as rehearsed above, he points out that the normativity of our practices cannot be accounted for by the properties of dispositions and thus concludes that they cannot perform the task of a normativity-determining fact.

On a non-reductive model, these Kripkensteinian objections are extraneous. On this view, the normativity of our practices is an *irreducible* category – it cannot be explained in terms of the properties of more basic elements. Thus, any argument to the effect that our dispositions cannot account for the normativity of our practices causes no problems as an identity relationship between the two is denied. This does not of course mean that on such a model we cannot speak of dispositions to act in various ways, but these dispositions do not account for, or explain the normativity of, our practices. Under which of these two conceptions then does Bourdieu's theory fall?

In *Distinction*, Bourdieu suggests an answer to this question when he notes that to account for our practices we need to take into account not only the dispositions of the habitus, but also the elements of 'capital' and 'field' according to the formula: '{(Habitus) (Capital)} + Field = Practice' (1984, p. 101). As this formula highlights, it is clear that for Bourdieu *not all* of the properties of our practices can be reduced to the dispositions of the habitus. Judging from this formula alone, it is therefore unclear whether or not it is to our embodied dispositions that Bourdieu reduces the normativity of practices. However, what this formula does make clear is that for Bourdieu the normativity of our practices is *not* an irreducible category. What it tells us is that the normativity of our practices *can* in some form or other be accounted for in terms of the more basic elements of habitus, capital and field. The question then is which of these elements either individually or collectively does the job?

We seem to have already touched upon Bourdieu's answer to this question in the passages quoted above that clarified Bourdieu's view that the generation of our practices happens below the level of consciousness. In the first of these quotes, Bourdieu notes that to find the 'ordering principle ... capable of orienting practices' one has to 'look at the incorporated dispositions' and in the second, he writes that 'the schemes of the habitus are the primary forms of classification'

(1990b, p. 10), (1984, p. 466). These passages suggest that of the three arguments composing the left-hand side of the formula, it is indeed by appeal to the properties of the habitus that Bourdieu accounts for the normativity of our practices. However, to see whether it is to the habitus *alone* that normativity is reduced, we need to look at the role that the notions of field and capital play in Bourdieu's conception of the generation of practice.

Bourdieu compares the concept of field with that of a game. Just as a 'game' refers to a set of objective structures that define spheres of play (e.g. a particular pitch or board, a set of rules, scores, outcomes etc.), the term 'field' describes the patterned system of objective forces that define domains of practice.[15] Developing this analogy, Bourdieu describes capital as what is efficacious in a given game. For instance, the ace of spades is a form of capital in a particular game if it allows the possessor to win a hand. Similarly, actors who possess capital in a particular field, possess economic, social, cultural or symbolic attributes or qualities that allow them to act effectively within it (1992, p. 98). What the concepts of field and capital thus highlight is that observed practices are partly a function of the game being played, and partly the relative capital that agents playing the game possess.

With the introduction of these terms, Bourdieu points to important considerations that need to be taken into account in order to gain a proper understanding of practice. However, for our purposes, neither touches upon the crucial issue of how it is that we learn the rules of the game and play according to their requirements. Neither concept, in other words, accounts for the *generation* of practices; and by the same token, neither therefore accounts for their normativity either. This is left to the dispositions of the habitus. Seen in this light, it is clear that Bourdieu does have a reductive view in mind. This presupposition is what leads him to conclude that:

> sociology treats as identical all biological individuals who, being the products of the same objective conditions, have the same *habitus* (1990b, p. 59).

If then it is the case that the normativity of our practices can be accounted for in terms of the dispositions of the habitus (such that sociology can treat individuals who share the same habitus as 'identical'), where does this leave Bourdieu's account with respect to Kripke's challenge? There is, it would seem, a straightforward answer to this question. Kripke's case against objectivism shows that any attempt to explain the generation of our rule-like practices in terms of dispositions cannot do the job of accounting for their normativity. By arguing that our practices are reducible to our dispositions, Bourdieu – it therefore seems – overlooks this crucial point and thus falls foul of the sceptic's challenge. Unfortunately, the situation is not so simple. Whilst it is clear that Bourdieu does reduce our practices to the dispositions of the habitus, matters are complicated by the fact that he characterises the nature of these dispositions in different ways.

Sometimes Bourdieu suggests that the dispositions of the habitus are *nonintentional*, i.e. ultimately reducible to physical properties.[16] This is implied in most general terms by Bourdieu's remark that his account properly understood is a 'kind of generalised materialism' that stands opposed to the lingering 'spiritualism' of Marxist materialism (1990b, p. 17). More concretely, however, the non-intentional nature of the dispositions of the habitus is suggested by several of the descriptions that Bourdieu provides of them. For instance, he writes:

> Practical sense, social necessity turned into nature, converted into motor schemes and body automatisms, is what causes practices ... (1990b, p. 69).

> ... as Leibniz put it, 'we are automatons in three-quarters of what we do' ... the ultimate values, as they are called, are never anything other than the primitive dispositions of the body ... (1984, p. 474).

Bourdieu's characterisation of acting agents as 'body automatons' whose actions are caused by 'primitive dispositions of the body' hints at a conception of practice that is the same as, if not very near to, the (non-intentional) dispositionalist account targeted by Kripke's sceptical challenge. Interpreted in this way, the matter is settled: Bourdieu's account cannot make sense of the normativity of our practice and thus falls foul of the objectivist horn of Kripke's challenge.

However, Bourdieu also supplies us with another set of references to the habitus that suggests a different view of the matter. Whilst still maintaining that our practices are reducible to dispositions, on this second view, the dispositions of the habitus are *intentional*. That is to say, they are dispositions to engage in intentional actions, i.e. to think, to mean, to intend, etc. Thus, against the intuition that dispositions at the level of the body only involve such things as brute physical movement, Bourdieu proposes a view that makes room for unconscious, embodied dispositions to perform intentional acts. On this conception, the body is conceived not just as implementing goals we consciously frame (as per subjectivism), nor as just the locus of non-intentional causal factors (as per objectivism), but as the source of understanding and intentionality. Thus Bourdieu's claim that it is at the level of the body that 'practical understanding' or 'practical sense' resides (1990b, p. 13). This view of the intentional nature of our embodied dispositions is variously suggested by Bourdieu:

> Practical belief is not a 'state of mind', still less a kind of arbitrary adherence to a set of instituted dogmas and doctrines ('beliefs'), but rather a state of the body (1990b, p. 68).

> Bodily hexis is political mythology realised, *em-bodied,* turned into a permanent disposition, a durable way of standing, speaking, walking, and thereby of feeling and thinking (1990b, pp. 69–70).

> An institution, even an economy, is complete and fully viable only if it is durably objectified not only in things, that is, in the logic, transcending individual agents, of a particular field, but also in bodies, in durable dispositions

to recognise and comply with the demands immanent in the field (1990b, p. 58).)

The conception of dispositions as intentional is repeatedly manifested in these remarks: the first quote suggests that belief is a state of body whilst the two quotes that follow suggest that for Bourdieu the body has dispositions not just to move, but also to think and to recognise. If we interpret Bourdieu by appeal to references such as these, there is a way for him to avoid the problem that the non-intentional dispositionalist reading of his account confronted. The difficulty of drawing a conceptual borderline between correctness and incorrectness is no longer a problem: intentional dispositions by their very definition are dispositions to draw such distinctions.

On this reading, it seems that Bourdieu successfully avoids the two horns of Kripkenstein's challenge: the objectivist challenge is dismissed, and in keeping to the view that the generating principle of our practices takes place beyond the level of conscious representations of the mind, so too – it appears – Bourdieu avoids the subjectivist challenge. Seen in this light, then, it seems like Bourdieu's claim to have transcended the antagonism which opposes objectivism and subjectivism whilst retaining the insights gained by each rings true.

Section VI

What prevents us from concluding our analysis here is the danger that in specifying the dispositions of the habitus as intentional, Bourdieu's account inadvertently falls into the trap of circularity. If Bourdieu's theory is to be *explanatory* of the normativity of our practices, it cannot be so by reference to further things that already presuppose normativity. Thus, if Bourdieu is to offer us more than a mere description of our intentional states, then the burden falls upon him to provide us with a non-circular account of how it is that the dispositions of the body acquire their intentional properties.

Bourdieu fortunately proposes such an account. His suggestion is that our bodies become encoded with a certain know-how or understanding as a result of a process of *socialisation.* As he states:

> the cognitive structures which social agents implement in their practical knowledge of the world are internalised, 'embodied' social structures. (1984, p. 468).)

Bourdieu insists that this homology holds because our dispositions are 'genetically linked' to objective structures. Bourdieu elaborates what he means by this by appeal to Leibniz's discussion of possible ways to conceive of the reason why several clocks show the same time. He quotes Leibniz:

> Imagine ... two clocks or watches in perfect agreement as to the time. This may occur in one of three ways. The first consists in mutual influence; the

second is to appoint a skilful workman to correct them and synchronize constantly; the third is to construct these two clocks with such art and precision that one can be assured of their subsequent agreement (1990b, p. 59).

Bourdieu identifies his position with the third possibility highlighted by Leibniz. Those who assume that we can explain the harmonisation of our practices on the model of 'mutual influence' forget that 'the precondition not only for the co-ordination of practices but also for practices of co-ordination' is that we *already* be objectively harmonised (1990b, p. 59). As for those who argue that we are harmonised on the model of the 'skilful workman', they are 'condemned to the naïve artificialism that recognises no other unifying principle than conscious co-ordination' (1990b, p. 59). The key to understanding the harmonisation of our practices is therefore on the model of the two clocks constructed 'with such art and precision' that their mutual agreement is assured. As Bourdieu goes onto say, we are harmonised in our practices because our bodies are inscribed 'by identical histories' (1990b, p. 59).

In short, Boudieu's idea is that as a result of exposure to common experiences (particularly in early childhood), members of the same group or class come to embody the same habitus (i.e., their dispositions become encoded with the same practice-generating principles). Thus Bourdieu argues:

> … the structures characterising a determinate class of conditions of existence produce the structures of the *habitus,* which in their turn are the basis of the perception and appreciation of all subsequent experiences (1990b, p. 54).

> As an acquired system of generative schemes objectively adjusted to the particular conditions in which it is constituted, the habitus engenders all the thoughts, all the perceptions, and all the actions consistent with those conditions and no others (1977, p. 95).

In providing this account, Bourdieu does – it seems – absolve his theory of the charge of circularity: our dispositions acquire their intentional properties not by appeal to other intentional facts, but as a result of training and exposure to regularities in practice constitutive of a particular type of environment. However, Bourdieu's insistence on such a strict connection between the dispositions of the body and the social comes at a grave cost. If indeed the habitus engenders all the thoughts, all the perceptions, and all the actions consistent with those conditions and no others, as many commentators have pointed out, Bourdieu thus introduces an implausibly overly deterministic explanation of the reproduction of social order that leaves no proper room for inventive adjustments and other localised dynamics of change.[17] Along similar lines, others have argued that Bourdieu's insistence on this strict correspondence means that his account pays insufficient attention to the essential role of interaction in the constitution of social order.[18]

Whatever the merits of these criticisms, from the perspective of Kripkenstein's sceptic, there is a more fundamental problem that burdens this aspect of Bourdieu's theory. This is that Bourdieu's explanation of the homology between social structures and embodied dispositions re-introduces the same troubles as raised by the sceptic's attack against subjectivism. As a result, whether Bourdieu's theory turns out to be deterministic, individualistic and/or still something else, as far as Kripkenstein is concerned these problems are immaterial, for not even *in principle* can we accept this as a satisfactory account of the generation of our practices. The problem lies in specifying how the practice-generating principles we supposedly interiorise at the level of the body can tell us what to do at the next new case.[19] As the sceptic reminds us, nothing from the finite pool of our past experiences can specify unequivocally what the principle we purportedly grasp requires of us. Even if we all share 'identical histories' as Bourdieu suggests, any principle can be interpreted in many different ways. If we try to salvage this picture by appeal to a further principle or rule for determining the correct interpretation of the original, matters are not improved as the same problems arise again. Thus, we again face the infinite regress of a rule to interpret a rule and accordingly this interpretation of Bourdieu's account also falls foul of the sceptical challenge. It therefore appears that no matter which way we interpret Bourdieu's account, there is no way for him to escape the clutches of Kripkenstein's sceptic.

Conclusion

If Kripkenstein's sceptical challenge is sound, the upshot of Bourdieu's failure to provide an answer to it is that it is impossible to account for social order on the terms of his praxeological theory. According to Kripkenstein, this result of course generalises to *any* attempt to explain rule-following by appeal to our grasp of independent normativity-determining facts. Any such account, Kripkenstein insists, will inevitably carry with it its own set of hopeless epistemological/ontological difficulties.

We might think that if we are to give up such a view, Kripkenstein must offer an alternative explanation of our normative practices. Kripkenstein, however, offers no such alternative. His point is not to outline a philosophical response to questions about the possibility of rule-following, but to show that the demand for such accounts is based on a mistake. According to Kripkenstein, once we recognise that the demand for deep ontological explanations of social order is misplaced, we come to see that the problems that gave rise to them in the first place disappear. Thus, for instance, once we see that insofar as explanations refer to normativity-determining facts, they refer to nothing real, the problem of the dialectical relationship between subjectivism and objectivism fuelling Bourdieu's project very quickly evaporates. If there are no independent facts that fix the normativity of our practices, then understanding how we come to grasp what their requirements are no longer is a real problem. Similarly, the problem of how these independent facts are established and shaped by our subjective categories no longer even makes sense as a question. With this view, one might argue that what emerges from Kripkenstein's analysis as the essential problem with Bourdieu's account is not so much that he offers a bad solution to a good question, but that he seeks to answer a bad question.

In this vein, Kripkenstein argues that all we can offer in response to the sceptic is a 'sceptical solution'. This solution acknowledges that it is impossible to provide the kind of account that the sceptic demands. Thus, what this 'solution' aims to do is offer a *dissolution* of the assumptions that gave the sceptical challenge its initial purchase. This dissolution has two parts. The first offers a diagnosis of our urge to seek fact-based explanations of our normative practices, whilst the second consists of an argument to the effect that – contrary to appearances – our normative practices do not require for their tenability the sort of justification which the sceptic has shown to be untenable.

Why then are we led to assume that our normative practices must be underpinned by a normativity-constituting fact? According to Kripkenstein, philosophers tend to badly misconstrue the nature of rule-following as the result of a misunderstanding of our ordinary ways of talking about rule-like practices. Not dissimilar to how Bourdieu labelled his diagnosis of the reasons we fall victim of the 'intellectualist bias',[20] Wittgenstein catalogued this mistake as that of 'predicat[ing] of the thing what lies in the method of representing it' (*PI* §104). Because the words we use to describe our normative practices share a similar grammar to words used to describe physical events, philosophers commit the category mistake of assuming that conditionals that concern our normative practices are the same as conditionals about real or possible events. Martin Kusch (2004) illustrates this mistake nicely with the following example. Consider:

[1] If the brakes work then the car will (must) stop before reaching the wall.

[2] If Jones means *addition* by '+' then she will (must) reply '125' to '57 + 68'.

In the case of [1] we take it that the brakes of the car *cause* it to stop. By contrast, in the case of uttering sentences such as [2], we typically do not take this to be making claims about the physical or mental causes of Jones' thoughts or actions. Kripkenstein's point is that whilst sentences or thoughts like [2] are commonplace in our talk about normative practices, philosophers make the mistake of reading them on the model of [1]. That is, they take Jones' meaning of addition by '+' to be what *causes* her to reply '125' to '57 + 68' – the antecedent is taken to be the cause of the consequent. Interpreting our practices in this way, philosophers are easily misled into assuming that meaning and cognate normative practices are dependent upon our grasp of the antecedent (i.e. independent facts of correct usage). Under the grips of this picture, philosophers rush into formulating theories that satisfy the urge to explain how these facts come into being and how we come to grasp them under the illusion that this will provide us with a deeper understanding of the mechanisms that underpin social life.

With this diagnosis in mind, we are enjoined by Kripkenstein not to look for such metaphysical facts corresponding to our practices but rather to look at the circumstances under which ascriptions of 'correct' practice are actually made and the utility that resides in ascribing them. The principal idea behind this 'solution' is to recognise that whilst our fact based view of rule-following leads us to assume that it is rules (or principles) that explain our agreement in practice, the truth of the matter is really the other way around, it is our agreement in practice that sustains our rules and rule-governed practices. Once this is recognised, we see that there is nothing *metaphysical* to uncover about engaging correctly in normative practices. The only reality of which we can meaningfully speak about consists of interlocking patterns of actual and potential justification and explanation, actions and reactions.[21] The key then is simply to recognise that it is a basic fact about us that everyday forms of training and interaction do succeed in perpetuating practices of various kinds. Whilst this would appear easy enough, it is another matter for those of us still enthralled by the seductive promises of philosophical theorising. Summing up the matter, Wittgenstein wrote in *Remarks on the Foundations of Mathematics* (VI, §31):

> The difficult thing here is not to dig down to the ground; no, it is to recognise the ground that lies before us as the ground.

> For the ground keeps on giving us the illusory image of a greater depth, and when we seek to reach this, we keep on finding ourselves on the old level.

> Our disease is one of wanting to explain.

Notes

1 I am very grateful to Martin Kusch for discussions of the topics treated here, from which I have greatly benefited. I wish to also thank Raymond Geuss, Bill Grundy, John Latsis, Peter Lipton, Nicolas Martin, Antti Saaristo and two anonymous referees for their very helpful comments on earlier drafts.
2 As Bourdieu notes: 'Of all the oppositions that artificially divide social science, the most fundamental, and the most ruinous, is the one that is set up between subjectivism and objectivism' (Bourdieu, 1990b, p. 25).
3 All references are to Bourdieu unless otherwise stated
4 Thus Bourdieu also refers to the opposition between objectivism and subjectivism as that between 'physicalism' and 'psychologism', or that of 'structures' and 'representations' (1989, p. 14).
5 Bourdieu explores this theme most systematically in Bourdieu and Passeron (1977).
6 This is, for instance, suggested by Dreyfus and Rabinow (1993), Taylor (1995), Wacquant (1992), and Reckwitz (2002).
7 In speaking of 'Bourdieu's project', I here refer exclusively to his theoretical aim of finding a 'praxeological solution' to the subjectivism vs. objectivism antinomy. Thus, to the extent that Bourdieu's expansive writings in ethnography, education, culture and sociology can be separated from his praxeological theory, I do not think Wittgenstein's rule-following considerations necessarily tell against much of Bourdieu's impressive and insightful work in these areas.

8   Thus we can make sense of Bourdieu's choice of epigraph to *The Logic of Practice* taken from the *Philosophical Investigations* as a statement meant to point out the naivety of a view that takes conscious rule-following as primary: "'How am I able to follow a rule?' – if this is not a question about causes, then it is about the justification for my following a rule in the way I do. If I have exhausted the justifications I have reached bedrock, and my spade is turned. Then I am inclined to say: This is simply what I do' (§217).

9   See Wacquant (1992, p. 8). By the same token, according to Bourdieu the greatest drawback of subjectivism is that it fails to recognise this objectivity. Bourdieu indeed argues that what fundamentally defines subjectivism is that it excludes all interrogation about the conditions of possibility of our primary experience of the social world (1973, p. 53).

10 It is important to note here the idiosyncratic sense of rules 'guiding us to act in similar ways' for the paradigmatic examples of subjectivism identified by Bourdieu: the philosophy of action implicit in Sartre's *Being and Nothingness* and rational choice theory. As Bourdieu characterises Sartre's subjectivism, he conceives of a supra-voluntaristic agent bestowed with creative free will, able to constitute – *ex nihilo* – at every moment the meaning of the world anew (Bourdieu, 1990b, pp. 45–6) Similarly, the 'rational actor' of the subjectivism of rational choice theorists is conceived as only constrained by his/her previous unconstrained rational decisions (1990b, pp. 46–7). In these instances, social order can be said to be determined by us sharing common rules with the caveat that the subjectivist actor only ever 'follows' a rule to the extent that she 'decides to' or 'sees as rational to do so'.

11 In arguing this Kripkenstein does not of course deny that thought objects can sometimes help us clarify what we mean. What he denies is that these thought objects can have the distinct ability of fixing once and for all the normativity of our terms/practices in a way that subjectivism insists is not only possible, but necessary.

12 In addition to this problem, Kripke proposes two further arguments against dispositionalism. First, our dispositions are finite whilst rules have an infinite nature. Second, dispositions cannot provide normativity: they cannot make sense of the notion that to mean *addition* by '+' involves certain commitments to act in a certain way (and not just the disposition to act in these ways).

13 Kripkenstein of course generalises these comments to argue that there are *no* satisfactory normativity-determining candidate facts at all, be it as described by subjectivism, objectivism or any other perspective. I shall however limit myself here to a discussion of Kripkenstein's critique of subjectivist and objectivist views as it is around these alternatives that Bourdieu constructs his synthesis.

14 For a general discussion of Bourdieu's criticisms of subjectivism see Bourdieu, 1990b (especially Chapter 2).

15 Bourdieu however notes that this metaphor needs to be considered with caution for unlike a game, the regularities of a field are not the product of 'explicit and specific rules', but the product of 'a long, slow process of autonomization' (1990b, p. 67).

16 The use of the term intentional here refers to our capacity to have states of the mind or of the body that are directed upon, or at objects. In this sense, it is only tangentially related to our everyday use of the term that refers to conscious thought objects.

17 This criticism is for instance raised by Brubaker (1985), Jenkins (1982) and Thévenot (2001).

18 See Barnes (2000, p. 55); King (2000, p. 429) raises a similar point.

19 It is worth noting that this formulation of the problem is slightly different to how Kripkenstein presents it. As discussed above, the problem that Kripkenstein's sceptic raises is one of justifying at each novel case the principle which was being followed in the past. Whilst the upshot of these formulations of the challenge is the same, I here present this alternative exposition because I think it makes the problem stand out more clearly.

20 As we saw above, Bourdieu terms the 'intellectualist' error as that of taking 'the things of logic for the logic of things'.
21 This should not be read as committing Kripkenstein to a form of behaviourism. To deny that rule-following consists in the internalisation of normativity-determining facts is not to deny talk of inner states (see Kripke, 1982, p. 107). Similarly, it would be wrong to read this solution as a retreat to a form of subjectivism. As explored above, subjectivists presume that thought objects serve as normativity-determining facts, an assumption that Kripkenstein's sceptic of course denies.

References

Barnes, B. 2000 *Understanding Agency: Social Theory and Responsible Action*, London: SAGE Publications.

Barnes, B. 2001 'Practice as collective action', in T. R. Schatzki, K. D. Knorr-Cetina and E. von Savigny (eds) *The Practice Turn in Contemporary Theory*, London: Routledge.

Bloor, D. 1996 'Wittgenstein and the priority of practice', in T. R. Schatzki, K. D. Knorr Cetina and E. von Savigny (eds) *The Practice Turn in Contemporary Theory*, London: Routledge.

Bloor, D. 1997 *Wittgenstein, Rules and Institutions*, London: Routledge.

Boghossian, P. A. 2002 'The rule-following considerations', in A. Miller and C. Wright (eds) *Rule-following and Meaning*, Chesham, UK: Acumen.

Bourdieu, P. 1973 'The Three Forms of Theoretical Knowledge', *Social Science Information* 12: 53–80.

Bourdieu, P. 1977 *Outline of a Theory of Practice*, Cambridge, UK: Cambridge University Press.

Bourdieu, P. 1980 *Questions de Sociologie*, Paris: Les Éditions de Minuit.

Bourdieu, P. 1984 *Distinction: A Social Critique of the Judgement of Taste*, London: Routledge & Kegan Paul.

Bourdieu, P. 1987 *Choses dites*, Paris: Éditions de Minuit.

Bourdieu, P. 1989 'Social Space and Symbolic Power', *Sociological Theory* 7(1): 14–25.

Bourdieu, P. 1990a *In Other Words*, Cambridge, UK: Polity.

Bourdieu, P. 1990b *The Logic of Practice*, Cambridge, UK: Polity Press.

Bourdieu, P. and Passeron, J. C. 1977 *Reproduction in Education, Society and Culture*, London: Sage.

Bourdieu, P. and Wacquant, L. J. D. 1992 *An Invitation to Reflexive Sociology*, Chicago: The University of Chicago Press.

Brubaker, R. 1985 'Rethinking classical sociology: the sociological vision of Pierre Bourdieu', *Theory and Society* 14(6): 745–775.

Brubaker, R. 1993 'Social Theory as Habitus', in C. Calhoun, E. LiPuma and M. Postone (eds)

Brubaker, R. 1993 *Bourdieu: Critical Perspectives*, Cambridge, UK: Blackwell Publishers.

Butler, J. P. 1997 *Excitable speech: a politics of the performative*, New York; London: Routledge.

Calhoun, C. 1993 'Habitus, Field, and Capital: The Question of Historical Specificity', in C. Calhoun, E. LiPuma and M. Postone (eds) *Bourdieu: Critical Perspectives*, Cambridge, UK: Blackwell Publishers.

Calhoun, C. LiPuma, E. and Postone, M. 1993 *Bourdieu: Critical Perspectives*, Cambridge, UK: Blackwell Publishers.

Chauviré, C. 1995 'Des philosophes lisent Bourdieu. Bourdieu/Wittgenstein: la force de l'habitus', *Critique: Revue générale des publications françaises et étrangères* 579/580: 548–553.

Cicourel, A. V. 1993 'Aspects of Structural and Processual Theories of Knowledge', in C. Calhoun, E. LiPuma and M. Postone (eds) *Bourdieu: Critical Perspectives*, Cambridge, UK: Blackwell Publishers.

Corcuff, P. 1999 'Le collectif au défi du singulier: en partant de l'habitus', in B. Lahire (ed) *Le travail sociologique de Pierre Bourdieu: dettes et critiques*, Paris: La Découverte.

DiMaggio, P. 1979 'Review Essay on Pierre Bourdieu', *American Journal of Sociology* 84(6): 1460–1474.

Dreyfus, H. and Rabinow, P. 1993 'Can there be a Science of Existential Structure and Social Meaning?' in C. Calhoun, E. LiPuma and M. Postone (eds) *Bourdieu: Critical Perspectives*, Cambridge, UK: Blackwell Publishers.

Jenkins, R. 1982 'Pierre Bourdieu and the Reproduction of Determination', *Sociology* 16(2): 270–281.

King, A. 2000 'Thinking with Bourdieu Against Bourdieu: A 'Practical' Critique of the Habitus', *Sociological Theory* 18(3): 417–433.

Kripke, S. A. 1982 *Wittgenstein on Rules and Private Language: an Elementary Exposition*, Oxford: Blackwell.

Kusch, M. 2004 'Rule-scepticism and the Sociology of Scientific Knowledge: The Bloor-Lynch Debate Revisited', *Social Studies of Science* 34: 571–591.

Kusch, M. 2006 *A Sceptical Guide to Rule-Following and Meaning: A Defence of Kripke's Wittgenstein*, Chesham, UK: Acumen

Reckwitz, A. 2002 'Toward a Theory of Social Practices: A Development in Culturalist Theorizing', *European Journal of Social Theory* 5(2): 243–263.

Schatzki, T. R. 1996 *Social Practices: A Wittgensteinian Approach to Human Activity and the Social*, Cambridge, UK: Cambridge University Press.

Schatzki, T. R. 1997 'Practices and Actions: A Wittgensteinian Critique of Bourdieu and Giddens', *Philosophy of the Social Sciences* 27(3): 283–308.

Taylor, C. 1995 'To follow a rule,' in C. Calhoun, E. LiPuma and M. Postone (eds) *Bourdieu: Critical Perspectives*, Cambridge, UK: Blackwell Publishers.

Thévenot, L. 2001 'Pragmatic regimes governing the engagement with the world', in T. R. Schatzki, K. D. Knorr-Cetina and E. von Savigny (eds) *The Practice Turn in Contemporary Theory*, London: Routledge.

Turner, S. 1994 *The Social Theory of Practices: Tradition, Tacit Knowledge and Presuppositions*, Cambridge, UK: Polity Press.

Wacquant, L. J. D. 1992 'Toward a Social Praxeology: The Structure and Logic of Bourdieu's Sociology', in P. Bourdieu and L. J. D. Wacquant (eds) *An Invitation to Reflexive Sociology*, Chicago, IL: The University of Chicago Press.

Wittgenstein, L. 1953 *Philosophical Investigations*, 3rd Edition, Oxford: Blackwell.

Wittgenstein, L. 1956 *Remarks on the Foundations of Mathematics*, Oxford: Basil Blackwell.

Wittgenstein, L. 1958 *Blue and Brown Books*, Oxford: Basil Blackwell.

Wright, C. 2001 *Rails to Infinity: Essays on Themes from Wittgenstein's Philosophical Investigations*, Cambridge, Massachusetts: Harvard University Press.

6 Deducing natural necessity from purposive activity: the scientific realist logic of Habermas' theory of communicative action and Luhmann's systems theory

Margaret Moussa

Introduction: science, natural necessity and purposive activity

The ontology of natural necessity is defined in the following propositions: the objective world is comprised of intrinsically powerful and liable entities. An entity's essential constitution or natural *kind* is the structure of components giving rise to its distinctive powers and liabilities. The action and reaction of entities is manifest in open systems of cause and effect. If systems can be open, then the universe we happen to inhabit must be a complex of heterogeneous structures. It cannot be a single, all-embracing substance.

Scientific realists such as Roy Bhaskar claim that natural necessity is implied in the coherence of science as a body of thought. It is implied in the intelligibility of scientific language and in experimentation.[1] This argument has been challenged on the Humean grounds that natural necessity cannot be inferred from empirical facts such as the existence of science.[2] This criticism may be addressed if we consider that, whatever else it may be, science is a form of reasoning activity. It is this element of science that gives force to Bhaskar's argument. It is one thing to deduce ontological principles from just any empirical fact. It is another thing to deduce ontological principles from the very possibility of reasoning activity.

Considering this, the following paper attempts to develop the argument that natural necessity is implied in purposive or reasoning activity generally. It does so by examining the ontological basis of two major sociological theories of action. These are Habermas' theory of communicative action and Luhmann's action systems theory. Neither Habermas nor Luhmann would regard himself as a scientific realist. Indeed each attempts to solve fundamental problems within Weber's idealist theory of action. I nonetheless attempt to show that there is an element of scientific realist logic to Habermas' and Luhmann's endeavours and that this logic stems from the fact that natural necessity is implied in purposive activity.

The first section of this chapter traces the problems with Weber's idealist distinction between the given ends and systemically alterable means of action. The second section considers Habermas' dynamic theory of intersubjectivity as an attempted resolution of these problems. The third section examines Luhmann's conception of social action as a systemic response to a troublesome external environment. In tracing Habermas' and Luhmann's theories, we shall see that intersubjectivity and systemic action both presuppose the objective existence of natural powers and liabilities in open systems of cause and effect. The paper concludes that Habermas and Luhmann cannot resolve the problems of Weberianism because they do not completely reject this tradition's idealist ontological premises.

Weber's idealist theory of action

Max Weber insists that structures are essentially products of intention.[3] Like Kant, Weber posits an inherently active subject constructing an in itself formless objective world. The difference is that Kant posits a generically 'human' construction of objects, while Weber insists that intentions are individual and potentially varied.[4] For Weber each set of intentions must be some person's 'meaning-complex of action'.[5]

If intentions by definition shape an in itself disparate objective world, then each set of intentions must be an *inherent* unity. Weber therefore insists that a meaning-complex cannot be dissected or analysed according to some external principle. It can only be interpreted as the relation of its parts. This implies that different meaning-complexes of action are incommensurable. Weber therefore rejects the possibility that the various intentions of various individuals can be rationally integrated into some overarching 'social' purpose. Weber thereby rejects that a society can substantively exist, in and for itself. A Weberian social structure 'exists' only to implement an individual set of intentions. It exists only to the extent that a batch of individuals *happen* to possess the same set of intentions. Weberian sociology therefore begins with the question; 'What motives determine and lead individual members of this community to behave in such a way that the community came into being in the first place and continues to exist?'[6]

In response to this question, Weber spreads an array of possible or 'pure' types of society, each distinguished by specific constituting principles. These range from voluntary associations based on mutual self-interest to 'structures of dominancy' in which the substantive will of various individuals has been somehow subjugated to that of a ruler or ruling group. Weber observes that, in actuality, these distinctions are not so marked. For example, even a voluntary association must have some means of 'persuading' the minority with deviant wishes. However Weber believes that most social formations are essentially 'structures of dominancy'. In his view; 'The structure of dominancy and its unfolding is decisive in determining the form of social action and its orientation towards a single goal'.[7]

We must not imagine the 'structure of dominancy' as brute coercion. Weber believed that it typically arises from 'charisma'. It arises from individuals' con-

viction that a certain person possesses extraordinary, or even supernatural, qualities. 'Structures of dominancy' are constituted by the conviction that this person
was born to rule and therefore *must* be obeyed. Weber observes that;
'Psychologically, this "recognition" is a matter of complete personal devotion to
the possessor of the quality, arising out of enthusiasm, or of despair or hope'.[8] He
stresses that in each case the *actual* qualities of the 'leader' are entirely irrelevant.
In uncovering the origins of particular social formations, all that matters is how
this person is regarded by his or her disciples.

On the factors which consolidate and perpetuate 'structures of dominancy',
Weber is somewhat forked. One on hand, Weber observes that by the time
charisma is 'routinised', by the time the thrall has worn away, most individuals
are in the sheer habit of conforming to what has become the dominant intention.
He observes that the minority which might reflect upon their actions nonetheless
tend to conform for sake of convenience. In his view:

> The stability of merely customary action results essentially from the fact that
> the person who does not adapt himself to it is subject to both petty and major
> inconveniences and annoyances so long as the majority of the people he
> comes into contact with continue to uphold the custom and conform to it.[9]

Weber on the other hand stresses that the ruling group cannot take convention for
granted. He emphasises that, if they are to survive, structures of dominancy must
be continually legitimated. In his words: '... the continued exercise of every domination (in our technical sense of the word) always has the strongest need for self-
justification through appealing to the principles of legitimation.'[10] Weber believes
that primitive or traditional societies are typically glued together by affective factors such as religion and custom. By contrast, modern societies are legitimated by
appeals to the legality (to the impartiality and formal rationality) of their institutions.

Weber's emphasis on legitimation reminds us that each Weberian social system
is predicated upon a single, given set of intentions. In other words, the substantive
identity of the system is static. The system can develop only as an increasingly
specified and differentiated means of implementing the ruling intention. Weberians
in this sense depict the social development from (what they call) primitive societies
to modernity as a technically informed, progressive division of labour

Being instrumentalist, the Weberian theory of action leaves itself open to
being also technologically determinist. Having *defined* society as an enhanced
means of achieving given ends, Weberians are subsequently forced to explain
(away) ostensibly non-functionalist social behaviour as irrational. The point is
that this behaviour can only be perceived as irrational from the perspective of a
future, technically superior stage of social development. Instrumentalists are
therefore compelled to define any specific stage of social development as *constitutively* a solution to the logistical problems of its predecessors.

Weberians account for the rise of modern market societies in these terms as a
resolution of the pre-modern or 'primitive' conflation of means and ends.[11] They

argue that the ostensibly non-functionalist element of the market (the conflict of interest between producers and consumers and between producers) will in turn be ameliorated by bureaucratic planning. Indeed Weber insisted that, from a purely technical perspective, all social roads led to bureaucracy. In his view:

> The decisive reason for the advancement of bureaucratic organisation has always been its purely *technical* superiority over any other form of organisation. The fully developed bureaucratic apparatus compares with other organisations exactly as does the machine with the non-mechanical modes of production.[12]

Beginning with the absolute power of individuals' intentions and culminating in the inevitability of bureaucracy, Weberian sociology appears to have swept the ground from under its feet. Is purposive activity at all conceivable in a world where all roads lead to bureaucracy? Can Weber's theory of action avoid being technically determinist? Weber might again remind us that a social system exists to implement an intention. This means that, however inexorable it may seem, any particular course of instrumental logic becomes redundant with the expiry of *its* directing purpose. In other words, a theory of instrumental rationality presupposes the capacity to stand back from, compare and potentially change the ends of action. The double bind is that substantively differing intentions are rationally incommensurable within a Weberian framework. We could conclude that Weber's theory of action is incoherent because it presupposes and at the same time excludes the possibility of rationally scrutinising intentions themselves.

Habermas attempts to resolve this problem by contextualising instrumentalism within a dynamically rational account of subjective identity itself.

Habermas' conception of substantive action

In *The Theory of Communicative Action* Habermas depicts the rational development of intentions as an intersubjective process. This theory promises to support Habermas' earlier claim that the bureaucratic-economic 'System's' colonisation of the socio-cultural structures of identity formation is historically specific and therefore remediable.[13] By the same token, the theory of communicative action could inform the resolution of (what Habermas sees as) the contemporary tension between social institutions as they exist, on one hand, and the normative claims of such institutions to legitimacy on the other hand.[14] *The Theory of Communicative Action* in this way connects Habermas' earlier work of political economy with his relatively recent attempt to articulate a democratic basis for public life. Let us examine his argument.

Habermas insists that individuals intrinsically structure experience within a 'Lifeworld'.[15] Habermas observes that the Lifeworld is inherently unified in virtue of the intrinsic, structuring power of linguistically constituted consciousness. Like the Weberian 'meaning-complex', the Lifeworld cannot be abstracted or dissected by some principle external to it. Nor can it be assessed or refuted on empirical grounds. In Habermas' words, the Lifeworld 'forms a universe that is hermeneutically sealed'.[16]

Unlike Weberian 'meaning-complex of action,' the Lifeworld is intersubjective and therefore (according to Habermas) it is dynamic.[17] Drawing on Austen and Searle, Habermas predicates this dynamic intersubjectivity upon the successful performance of 'illocutionary acts.' As Searle defines it:

> ... the illocutionary act is the unit of *meaning* in communication. When the speaker says something and means something by what he says, and tries to communicate what he means to the hearer, he will, if successful, have performed an illocutionary act.[18]

Habermas like Searle emphasises that a successful illocutionary act presupposes the integrity of the speaker's intention. The speaker must believe that he or she is conveying something new to the listeners. Habermas observes that if individuals *typically* used language without conveying or intending to convey new meanings, then language would not be genuinely communicative.[19] It would not be *activity*. It would merely decorate an unchanging, unchangeable, pre-linguistic 'essence'.

Habermas moreover insists that an illocutionary act is successful only if its content is in principle confirmable or deniable. Given the opportunity, listeners must be at least capable of recognising *grounds* for confirmation or denial.[20] The listeners must feel that they also could experience this novel something. The intelligibility of communication in other words presupposes that speaker and listener have *at least the conception* that there is a common source of experience external to the consciousness of both. Habermas in this sense predicates dynamic intersubjectivity upon individuals' capacity to distinguish between their 'personal' world, their already shared 'social' world and the yet to be fully experienced 'objective' world.[21]

Drawing on Horton, Habermas depicts a substantively rational progression from primitive or 'mythical' societies to the modern societies in terms of the capacity to abstract these three world concepts. He observes that the members of primitive or 'mythical' societies conflate individual perspective, normative social tradition and natural events. They have consequently no ground for either personal reflection or social criticism.[22] By contrast modern individuals are at least capable of recognising their respective persons and societies as specific and therefore substantively changeable.

Habermas in these terms challenges Weber's view that the existence of substantive alternatives to an action-system entails social-systemic fragmentation. He insists that 'legitimation crises' are avoidable and resolvable given the potential to communicatively reconcile substantively differing subjective intentions. Moreover, the intersubjective dynamic of the Lifeworld makes it possible to recognise any technical-bureaucratic System of logic *as* merely the instrument of one specific set of intentions. As Habermas explains: 'The systems-theoretic perspective is relativised by the fact that a rationalisation of the Lifeworld leads to a directional variation of the structural patterns defining the maintenance of the

System'.[23] Habermas therefore insists that it is possible for a society to develop a substantially new 'System' of instrumental reasoning, given its members' capacity to critically reflect upon their personal identities and social identities, given their capacity to redefine the boundaries between 'subjective', 'social' and 'objective' in communicative action.

The critical question is how and why individuals should at all *conceive* of an independently existing objective world, given Habermas' insistence that human beings intrinsically *structure* the universe *in* consciousness. We've traced Habermas' argument that the abstraction of the three world concepts is the outcome of communicative action itself. However this is circular reasoning since Habermas predicates successful illocutionary action upon individuals already possessing a concept of the objective world. To reframe the problem, how could individuals conceive of a substantially new source of (genuinely communicable) experience if the structure of experience is completely equated with Lifeworld consciousness? It would seem that Habermas' explanation of dynamic intersubjectivity is incompatible with his argument that (at least) human reality is structured in consciousness. It would seem that the flaw in Habermas' *The Theory of Communicative Action* stems from his implicitly idealist ontological premises.

This is confirmed if we consider Rom Harre's alternative explanation of the possibility of successful illocutionary acts. Harre maintains that a speech act is successful, that is, it is sincere, novel for the listeners and potentially affirmable or refutable only if the speaker has *actually* experienced (or has been informed of another's experience) of an objectively existing something in the world.[24] If a speech act refers to the operation of some natural power (and Harre notes that this is likely, given the abundance of power predicates in our descriptions of the world) *then this natural power must objectively exist*.[25] Harre's argument can be more generally stated by observing that *reference is meaningfully about a state of affairs irreducible to the imagination of the referrer*.

Taking this, we may conclude that Habermas is ultimately unable to explain for the substantive ends of action as a rational process. Habermas is therefore unable to resolve the problems with Weber's theory of action. Rather, the problems with both theories appear to stem from their common idealist premises. To generalise, if human beings cannot empirically verify how the universe might be 'in itself', then we have as little ground for assuming that the universe is passive and formless as we have for assuming that it is active and structured. So Hegel questions Kant's epistemology in observing that: 'though the categories such as unity, cause and effect are strictly the property of thought, it by no means follows that they must be ours merely and not also characteristics of the object'.[26]

In other words, idealists cannot simply *assume* that the universe is passive and formless. In lieu of empirical evidence, this ontology is acceptable only if the universe could be conceivably structured in more than one way. The bind is that it is impossible to rationalize a plurality of worldviews within an idealist framework. By equating form with the activity of consciousness, idealists cannot explain the substantively differing forms that consciousness itself could take.

It would seem that substantive (and therefore also instrumentalist) activity pre-supposes a structured and active natural world. It is therefore significant that Habermas' critique of Weber invokes the *concept* of the objective world. However *The Theory of Communicative Action* cannot be regarded as scientific realist. If Habermas had proceeded from the ontology of natural necessity, he could not have sustained the distinction between System and Lifeworld. If human beings are part of a structured and active objective world, then they must be to some degree subject or liable to this objective activity. In which case technical-material activity could not be cordoned off from the structures of identity forma-tion. The ontology of natural necessity negates the very distinction between 'instrumentalism' and substantive self-reflection.

This becomes apparent if we consider Luhmann's attempted resolution of the problems within Weberian sociology.

Luhmann's conception of systems in time and space

Luhmann tries to imagine *how* a system could actually begin, develop, how it could *be* in time and space. Luhmann asserts that a system cannot conceivably exist without an environment external to it. In his words: 'It only becomes neces-sary (and for that matter possible) to recognise or identify a system when this sys-tem is distinguished and demarcated from its environment'.[27] Now Luhmann is not simply alluding to a system needing 'material'. He is not alluding to con-sciousness requiring a lump of 'raw matter' on which to act. He is not merely restating the Kantian view that intelligible experience presupposes a real (if utterly scattered) 'manifold' of things-in-themselves.

Luhmann specifically insists that an entity internally develops in relation to an environment that is *in itself* qualitatively determinate and active. Luhmann emphasises that the system's environment puts up a real presence. He variously describes this environment as 'hostile', 'troublesome', 'uncontrollable', 'prob-lematic', 'threatening'. The system does not construct this environment, it must 'negotiate' with it in order to survive. The system needs to develop *its* particular quality, build *its* complexity to avoid being substantively swallowed by this deter-minate-in-itself environment. Luhmann therefore defines the structural technique of differentiation as a 'matching' of external and internal complexity.[28]

Luhmann believes that the determinate qualities of the external environment help to explain the system's specificity as well as its internal dynamic. He observes that the system relates to some forces in its external world and not to others. The system therefore builds one form of complexity rather than another. The multiplicity of negotiation by the same token gives the system richness and depth.

Luhmann observes that the system's outcomes are to some extent historically contingent and uncoordinated, given this qualitative heterogeneity of the external environment. Luhmann observes that the qualitative variability of the environ-ment may indeed require strategically incompatible responses on the part of the system. As he explains:

If we conceive of systems as open-systems-in-environments, structural changes have to presuppose non-coordinated events in systems and environments. Non-coordinated events are contingencies in themselves with respect to their coincidence and their conjectural causality.[29]

In consequence of its specificity, its possible contradictions and the contingency of its outcomes, Luhmann's system is not an inexorable unfolding of a compelling technical logic. The system is *open* to multiple outcomes, given the active, qualitative heterogeneity of its external environment. Luhmann in these terms rejects Weber's linear means–end model. By the same token he rejects Habermas' argument that systems rationality presupposes a culturally homogeneous or unified substantive 'Lifeworld'. Given a system's struggle with a substantive-in-itself environment, the substantive unity of this system is a goal to be achieved. It is not an *a priori* given.

Luhmann in these terms questions classic sociology's tendency to either ignore the environment external to a system or to assume that this environment uniquely exists for the system's convenience. Indeed, Luhmann advocates replacing the classic Weberian model of strategic systems unity with a 'living organisms' analogue. As he explains:

In general the conception of systems is still defined traditionally as a network of relations that integrates parts into a whole. But underneath this idea of a purely internal ordering of parts into a whole, a different conception of systems is demanding our attention. According to this, the significance of system building lies not merely in a purely internal ordering of the parts into a whole, but instead in a system's negotiation with its environment. The problems that arise in this regard are what determine whether the internal ordering of the system will succeed and maintain itself in the face of threats posed by its environment. The guiding concept is that of living organisms.[30]

Luhmann articulates the 'living organisms' analogy, firstly, in terms of the operations of large, modern organisations.[31] Luhmann maintains that, given the extreme complexity of its environment, a large organisation cannot effectively operate as a totally cohesive unit working toward a single end. He observes that contact with the environment qualitatively varies between different levels of the organisation. The 'chief executive' often lacks detailed knowledge of and control over subordinates' various dealings with the outside world. Luhmann observes that exploitation of this knowledge cannot be simply 'commanded'. There is a decisive shift of gravity from top to bottom in consequence of the subordinates' unique negotiation with specific aspects of the external environment. As Luhmann explains; 'Commands from the blue are increasingly prompted, requested or even formulated by their recipients. As a result, the flow of information from bottom to top becomes more "interesting"'.[32]

Luhmann maintains that a large organisation can develop quite contradictory goals, given this extreme complexity of its external environment. He insists that contradiction does not in itself spell the organisation's destruction. In his words: 'The ends pursued by an organisation, even its "ultimate" and "highest" ones can be modified, reinterpreted or completely altered without the identity of the organisation having to disappear and a new one having to be founded'.[33]

Luhmann in these terms argues the Weberian chain-of-command model is incapable of explaining behaviour within corporations and state bureaucracies. In Luhmann's view:

> Simple categories of means and ends, or command and obedience, while adequate for the purposes of everyday life, fail as a means for providing a scientific account of human thought and action. Fundamentally, they are ideas of single, linear relationship. A causes B. They do not work as conceptual tools for grasping highly complex processes such as the conditions of actual behaviour in large organisations.[34]

Luhmann contextualises this 'open systems' theory of organisations within a 'living organisms' model of societal subsystems. Luhmann posits each subsystem facing a distinctive environmental cluster comprised of other subsystems within an overriding or shared social system. Each subsystem thus faces distinctive challenges which do not occur on the level of the social system as a whole. For example, the economy experiences political events in a different manner from the cultural, religious or educational subsystems. To use one of Luhmann's examples, compulsory school attendance and mass education are different environmental problems for the political system, the economic system, familial, religious and medical systems.[35] Luhmann believes that a subsystem develops its distinctive type of complexity by negotiating to meet the challenges posed by *its* unique environmental cluster. As he observes:

> Functional differentiation requires a displacement of problems from the level of society to the level of subsystems. This is not simply a process of delegation or decentralisation of responsibilities and not simply a factoring out of means for the ends of society. The displacement integrates each specific function into a new set of system/environment references and produces types of problems and solutions that would not, and could not, arise at the level of the encompassing system.[36]

Luhmann emphasises that unless we conceive of each subsystem engaging with its unique environment, the internal differentiation is simply not conceivable. Luhmann specifies this 'relative autonomy' of each subsystem in terms of three system-environment references. In terms of its *function*, a subsystem relates to the social system as a whole. It relates to the various other subsystems in terms of (what Luhmann calls) its 'input and output performances'. Finally, each subsystem has a relation to itself. A subsystem can be self-reflective. Luhmann emphasises that these three system-environment references are by no means identical or reconcilable. For example, there may be a tension between forward-looking performance and backward-looking self-reflection. There is contingency, unpredictability and change within the social system because each subsystem is not equal in its capacity to distinguish between and balance function, perform-ance and self-reflection. The economic subsystem might be highly functional, for example, while the political subsystem is highly performing and the religious and cultural systems extraordinarily self-reflective.

Luhmann believes that these 'imbalances' negate the Weberian means–end model as an explanation of complex modern societies, taken in conjunction with the distinctive problems and solutions thrown up by each subsystem's unique internal environment, Luhmann insists that:

> ... the social primacy of a specific function cannot serve as an integrative formula or minimal ethics for all system/environment relations. This is because, in a sense, the whole is less than the sum of its parts. In other words, functionally differentiated societies cannot be ruled by leading parts or elites as stratified as stratified societies (to some extent) could be. They also can-not be rationalised as by means/ends chains as a technocratic conception would suggest. Their structural complexity can be adequately formulated only by models that take into account several systems/environment refer-ences at once.[37]

Now, if the distinctive character of each subsystem arises from its unique engage-ment with other subsystems, the initial distinction between subsystems itself pre-supposes an active, qualitatively determinate environment for the social system as a whole. Luhmann's social theory therefore distinguishes two kinds of envi-ronment – the external environment common to all societal subsystems and a sep-arate, internal environment for each subsystem. As he explains: 'The signpost indicating the road to concretisation can be found only if we go back to the dis-tinction between outer and inner differentiation. Outer or primary differentiation is the general precondition for evolution as such at any level of physico-chemi-cal, organic or sociocultural evolution.'[38]

Now this external environment common to all subsystems *can only be the nat-ural world*. Even if we consider various societal or cultural systems providing environments for each other, the difference between them *must* ultimately invoke a substantive, non-human reality. A system's activity in time and space therefore presupposes this system as part of a world containing other structured, powerful entities.

Luhmann himself does not fully take this further step. In taking this further step, Luhmann would have to completely re-think his (idealist) assumption that social action systems are essentially instrumentalist and not also substantive. Failure to take this further step ultimately leaves Luhmann's systems theory float-ing in ether. Having rejected the Weberian–Habermasian argument that technical systems develop to implement individuals' intentions, Luhmann is then unable to specify essentially *what* it is that systems do, other than 'survive'. We find Luhmann nebulously positing that:

... rationality on the level of individual actions is not the same as rationality on the level of social systems – the rationality of a system cannot be ensured simply through the rational action of its participants. It presupposes new combinations of meaning, perhaps even different categories of understanding that belong to the system itself.[39]

This may well be true. However, unless we specify what and how these 'new combinations' exist in the natural world, we cannot determinately act within or upon the system.

Conclusion: deducing natural necessity from the possibility of purposive activity

I have outlined Habermas' and Luhmann's theories as reactions to problems within the Weberian or classic sociological theory of action. I have suggested that Habermas and Luhmann veer toward scientific realism because the contradictions of Weberianism stem from this theory's idealist foundations. At the same time I hope to have developed the argument that natural necessity is implied in the possibility of purposive activity. It strikes me that Luhmann and Habermas are essentially committed to the integrity of human effort – as are scientific realists such as Bhaskar and Harre. Habermas attempts to grasp language as an absorbing activity, not merely a set of symbols or a façade for the spirit. Luhmann posits systemic unity as a goal to be achieved in struggle with the environment. Bhaskar similarly depicts the 'arduous task' of day-to-day scientific hypothesising, research and experimentation as a drive to uncover new, deeper, explanatorily more basic strata of reality.[40] Each of these theories brings to mind Hegel's insistence that:

> The life of God and divine intelligence can if we like be spoken of as love disporting with itself, but this idea falls into insipidity if it lacks the seriousness, the suffering, the patience, the labour of the negative ... True scientific knowledge demands abandonment to the very life of the object, or which means the same thing, claims to have before it the inner necessity controlling the object, it forgets to take that 'general survey' which is merely a turning away from its content, back into itself.[41]

To conclude, the strengths and the problems within Habermas' and Luhmann's theories respectively suggest that purposive activity presupposes the objective existence of generative mechanisms operating in open systems of cause and effect. My analysis of these theories in this way generalizes Bhaskar's arguments regarding the possibility of that purposive activity we call 'science'.

Notes

1 Bhaskar (1978). See also Harre and Madden (1975).
2 Suchting W. (1992); Maryani-Squire E. (forthcoming).

3　Weber (1947) p. 101.
4　Kant (1934) p. 152.
5　Weber p. 118.
6　Weber (1947) p. 107.
7　Weber (1968b) p. 941.
8　Weber (1947) p. 358–359.
9　Weber (1947) p. 123.
10　Weber (1968b) p. 954.
11　Luhmann (1982) p. 297.
12　Weber (1968) p. 973.
13　Habermas (1975) p. 26ff.
14　Habermas (1996).
15　Habermas (1985) p. 112, p. 125.
16　Habermas (1984) p. 112.
17　Habermas (1985) p. 148.
18　Searle (1999) p. 137.
19　Habermas therefore argues that the manipulative use of language (the 'perlocutionary act') is parasitic upon the success of illocutionary acts. In other words, manipulation presupposes the sincerity of typical action. Habermas (1984) pp. 290–291.
20　Habermas (1984) pp. 317–318, p. 17.
21　Habermas (1984) pp. 69–70.
22　Habermas (1984) p. 51.
23　Habermas (1985) p. 148.
24　Harre (1986) pp.165 ff.
25　Harre (1986) p. 165.
26　Hegel (1892) p. 90.
27　Luhmann (1982) p. 327.
28　Luhmann (1982) p. 286.
29　Luhmann (1982) pp. 252–253.
30　Luhmann (1982) p. 37.
31　Indeed, Luhmann was inspired to reject the classic Weberian chain-of-command model after reading studies on how actual organisations operate.
32　Luhmann (1982) p. 32.
33　Luhmann (1982) p. 28.
34　Luhmann (1982) p. 36.
35　Luhmann (1982) p. 231.
36　Luhmann (1982) p. 241
37　Luhmann (1982) pp. 238–239.
38　Luhmann (1982) p. 253.
39　Luhmann (1982) p. 22.
40　Bhaskar (1978) p. 211.
41　Hegel (1970) p. 81.

References

Bhaskar, R. 1978. *A Realist Theory of Science*. The Harvester Press, Sussex, UK.

Habermas, J. 1975. *Legitimation Crisis* (trans. T. M'Carthy). Beacon Press, Boston, MA.

Habermas, J. 1984. *The Theory of Communicative Action. Volume One. Reason and the Rationalisation of Society* (trans. T. M'Carthy). Beacon Press, Boston, MA.

Habermas, J. 1985. *The Theory of Communicative Action. Volume 2: Lifeworld and Systems: A Critique of Functionalist Systems* (trans. T. M'Carthy). Beacon Press, Boston.

Habermas, J. 1996. *Between Facts and Norms* (trans. W. Retig). Polity Press, Cambridge, UK.

Harre, R. 1986. *Varieties of Realism: A Rationale for the Natural Sciences.* Basil Blackwell, Oxford.

Harre, R. and Madden, A. 1975. *Causal Powers.* Basil Blackwell, Oxford.

Hegel, G. W. F. 1970. *The Phenomenology of Mind* (trans. J. B. Baillie). George Allen and Unwin, London.

Hegel, G. W. F. 1892. *The Logic of Hegel* (translated from *The Encyclopaedia of the Philosophical Sciences* by W. Wallace). Clarendon Press, Oxford.

Kant, I. 1934. *Critique of Pure Reason* (trans. N. Kemp-Smith). Macmillan and Co, London.

Luhmann, N. 1982. *The Differentiation of Society* (trans. S. Holmes and C. Larmore). Columbia University Press, New York.

Maryani-Squire, E. 2005. 'Doubting the Transcendental Realist Solution to the Human Problem of Induction', in M. Moussa and G. Brown (eds.) *Engaging Realism: Proceedings of the International Association of Critical Realism 2005 Annual Conference,* University of Western Sydney and University of Wollongong, Australia.

Searle, J. 1999. *Mind, Language and Society.* Weidenfeld and Nicolson, London.

Suchting, W. 1992. 'Reflections on Roy Bhaskar's "Critical Realism".' *Radical Philosophy,* 61: 23–31.

Weber, M. 1964. *The Theory of Social and Economic Organisation* (trans. Talcott Parsons). The Free Press: New York.

Weber, 1968. *Economy and Society, Volume 3* (G. Roth and C. Wittich, eds.) Bedminster Press Inc., New York.

7 'Under-labouring' for ethics: Lukács' critical ontology

Mário Duayer and João Leonardo Medeiros

> The objectivity of values is based on the fact that they are moving and moved
> components of the overall social development.
>
> G. Lukács

Introduction

Over the last 30 years or so critical realism has advanced its project of elaborating an ontology that can rival the empiricist ontology implicit in both positivist and idealist traditions. The ontology resulting from this collective effort should be capable of furnishing science, whether natural or social, with an explicit philosophical foundation. As early as in his first work Bhaskar (1997: 10) employed the Lockean expression 'under-labour' to refer to the supporting role played by philosophy (particularly ontology) in scientific development.[1] According to him, in under-labouring *for* science philosophy would function as a 'second-order knowledge', insofar as the knowledge produced by it would be 'a knowledge of the necessary conditions of knowledge' (Bhaskar 1979: 10).

Obviously, a philosophy for science such as proposed by critical realism presupposes that truth makes a difference. Against most fashionable theoretical contemporary doctrines for which truth is nothing but a 'fifth wheel', critical realism seems to concentrate most of its efforts in demonstrating the relationship between knowledge and human practice as follows:

> If the fundamental norm of theoretical discourse is descriptive or representative adequacy or truth, the fundamental norm of practical discourse is the fulfilment, realisation or satisfaction of human wants, needs or purposes. If there are real grounds (causes) for belief or action, then it is possible that we are mistaken about them, and if we fail in truth we may also fail in satisfaction (Bhaskar 1986: 206).

Thus, even when stated as a philosophy for science, critical realism is actually concerned with the ability of scientific discoveries in assisting the satisfaction of human ends. Accordingly, critical realism must address *from the beginning* questions about the origin of human values and their ontological status – that is to say, with ethics. In spite of this, it seems impossible to recognise a set of propositions that could characterise a critical realist ethics with the same readiness that one could identify critical realist understanding of the ontological content of the scientific discourse, just to mention one of several points of general agreement.

An influential position on these issues, however, is that defended by Bhaskar, according to which ontology is a sort of *third*-order knowledge in relation to ethics. More specifically, ontology would serve as the basis for the scientific analysis of human nature, which, in turn, would allow the identification of those transcendentally human values (i.e. values present in any social context). This division and organisation of theoretical labour is formulated accordingly:

> ... some anthropology is the condition of any moral discourse at all. As ontology stands to epistemology, so anthropology stands to ethics. Indeed, one could say that anthropology is just the ontology of ethics. But just as a theory about the nature of the world is implicit in any cognitive claim, a theory about the nature of (wo)men is implicit in any moral one (Bhaskar 1986: 207).

In our view, a quite distinct attitude concerning the relationship between ontology and ethics can be found in Lukács' late endeavour to put forward a Marxist ethics. Its difference from the above mentioned position is due exactly to Lukács' understanding that his Marxist ethics could only be based *directly* on a Marxist ontology of social being. In other words, we would suggest that, for Lukács, it is ontology, instead of anthropology, that 'under-labours' for realist ethics. This explains why his concerns regarding ontology were delivered as an introduction to his ethics, although what many authors refer to as the 'ontological turn' of Lukács' thought can be tracked down to the early 1930s (Oldrini 2002: 54).[2]

Tertulian was right to say, in this context, that Lukács' project of developing an ontology was, from the beginning, linked to the problem of human praxis in regard to emancipation. To go beyond the aporias of *Realpolitik* it was necessary to reject, as did Lukács:

> the identification of revolutionary action with *Realpolitik* (that is, an aethical pragmatism) because, for its own objectives (human liberty and disalienation), it transcends vulgar pragmatism and utilitarianism, being directed on the contrary to the realisation of 'humankind for itself' [*Gattungsmäßigkeit für sich*] (Tertulian 1999: 131–2).[3]

This rejection entails a conception of society in which revolutionary (transformative) action could really make sense, that is, an ontology of social being in which history and law-like processes, relations and structures are not mutually exclusive. It presupposes also an immediate appraisal of ethics, since a transformative practice can only arise based on a negative valuation of existing social structures, relations, etc.

It would be possible to affirm, furthermore, that Lukács' ontology is based on a clear understanding that, on the one hand, the main philosophical traditions entirely neglected ontology and, on the other, that this attitude could only be concretely grasped if referred to a social order that seemed to deny any transcendence to itself – the order posited by capital. It is this interpretation that underlies the structure of Lukács' *Ontology*, as can be readily perceived in the way the work is organised.

In the first part, Lukács deals with philosophical traditions and authors that either disavow or affirm ontology; in the second, there is an investigation of those categories that, in his view, are the main complexes of social being, namely, labour, reproduction, the ideal and ideology, and alienation. Such an arrangement, in which the positive contribution to the ontology of the human world appears in the last part of the work, is not unintentional. For it stems necessarily from the analysis carried out in the first section, in which Lukács provides a broad picture of the fate of ontology in philosophies of the past and of the present (Lukács 1984: 325). The radical attack on ontology undertook by neopositivism,[4] its more subtle (but still radical) rejection implicit in existentialism and other idealist philosophies (neo-Kantianism) and the contradictory or insufficient character of the ontologies put forward by Hegel and Hartmann, deserved special consideration and criticism.

With regard to the first two schools of thought, neopositivism and neo-Kantianism, Lukács stresses the convergence and complementarity of traditions that are usually seen as antithetical – the convergence here refers precisely to their common dismissal of ontology. This attitude is contrasted with Hegel's and Hartmann's explicit effort to illuminate various decisive ontological questions (such as Hegel's investigations into the teleological character of labour, for example) and, not surprisingly, with Marx. In this last case, Lukács emphasises the fact that all Marx's statements 'are in the last instance intended as direct statements about being, i.e. they are specifically ontological', though paradoxically 'we find in Marx no independent treatment of ontological problems' (ibid.: 559). It is this ontological legacy that is employed by Lukács as the ground for developing a Marxist ontology of society in the second part of the work.

Given this effort to reaffirm ontology *against the current*, it is certainly astonishing that Lukács' posthumous work has received almost no attention. This could be explained by the very fact that Lukács writes in the midst of a theoretical milieu that completely repudiated any ontological inquiry: it is well-known that *postist* fashion either attracted or paralysed even Marxist circles. Yet it is more difficult to explain why Lukács' *Ontology* has gone largely unnoticed in one of the most serious recent attempts to reaffirm ontology, i.e. in critical realism.

The present chapter does not try to speculate about the reasons for this particular lack of interest,[5] but seeks to underline the obvious mutual benefits that might accrue if the insights of critical realism could be combined with those put forward by Lukács. One of these benefits relates directly to the domain of ethics. Hence, this chapter concentrates on specific moments of Lukács' *Ontology* which seem to demonstrate the importance of his contribution in general and on reference to the relationship between ontology and ethics.

One of these moments is certainly Lukács' ontological analysis of the proto-typical form of human practice (labour), which is employed, among other things, to establish the particularity of social being in comparison to organic and inorganic beings. We provide a brief account of this analysis in the first section below. A second section delineates Lukács' examination of the genesis of human consciousness in labour and its dialectical relationship with social practice. The last section attempts to indicate how Lukács defends value as a new and decisive category of social being, the genesis of which is to be found in labour.

Labour and the emergence of social being

One possible way to start an account of Lukács' ontological analysis of labour is by recalling Marx's critique of the ontological conception of human being implicit in Adam Smith's idea of labour as curse:

> 'Tranquillity' appears as the adequate state, as identical with 'freedom' and 'happiness'. It seems quite far from Smith's mind that the individual, 'in his normal state of health, strength, activity, skill, facility', also needs a normal portion of work, and of the suspension of tranquillity. ... Certainly, labour obtains its measure from the outside, through the aim to be attained and the obstacles to be overcome in attaining it. But Smith has no inkling whatever that this overcoming of obstacles is in itself a liberating activity – and that, further, the external aims become stripped of the semblance of merely external natural urgencies, and become posited as aims which the individual himself posits – hence as self-realisation, objectification of the subject, hence real freedom, whose action is, precisely, labour (Marx 1973: 610).

Apart from being a glaring illustration of Marx's ontological critique,[6] this particular formulation is relevant to us to the extent that, in sharp contrast to bourgeois scientific conceptions, it shows that human activity, especially labour, is a constitutive determination of social being. Labour, understood by Marx as 'self-realisation, objectification of the subject, hence real freedom', is thus the key to understanding the dialectical unity of necessity (law) and liberty (freedom) that distinguishes social being from organic and inorganic beings.[7]

Two things are quite clear in this critique: (1) that it illustrates Lukács' suggestion that all Marx's statements 'are in the last instance intended as direct statements about being, i.e. they are specifically ontological'; (2) that in this particular statement, Marx asserts the centrality of labour for social being.[8] The same perspective is adopted by Lukács when he underlines that the analysis of labour has to be the starting point to expound, in ontological terms, the specific categories of social being. Precisely because this exposition seeks to apprehend the peculiarity of social being, it has to clarify how these categories have their genesis in the precedent *forms of being* (inorganic, organic), how they are based upon them and connected to them, and how they differentiate themselves from them (Lukács, 1986: 7). This section intends to outline Lukács' demonstration of the necessity and fruitfulness of this point of departure. Since his reasoning unfolds in an entire chapter of his *Ontology (Labour)* – not to mention its nexus with questions raised and developments carried out throughout the whole work – only a few moments of a complex and extremely articulated analysis can be focused on here.

Lukács observes that Marx had for long understood that there is a set of determinations in the absence of which 'no being can have its ontological character concretely apprehended' (Lukács 1984: 326) These determinations make up a general ontology that simply comprise the general ontological foundations of every being. The categories of this general ontology remain as superseded moments in the more complex forms of being that emerge in reality (life, society). As an ontology of inorganic nature, this ontology is general by the 'simple' fact that there can be no being that is not ontologically based on inorganic nature. In life the categories that account for the peculiarity of its form of being can only operate with 'ontological efficacy' on the basis of those general categories and in connection with them. Similarly, in social being the categories that determine its particularity interact with organic and inorganic categories. For this reason:

> [the] Marxian inquiry on the essence and the constitution of social being can only be rationally formulated on the basis of a foundation structured in that manner. The investigation around the specificity of social being implies the confirmation of the general unity of all being and, simultaneously, the evidencing of its own specific categories (ibid.: 327).

All forms of being thus emerge from, but remain grounded, in inorganic nature. This process of genesis and development in the case of the organic world and, even more, in society, means the emergence and increasing dominance of those categories that are specific to the form of being that each time comes into reality. These specific categories constitute then a particular totality precisely because they account for the peculiar character of a new form of being. Moreover, they can only be comprehended if referred to the web of relations in which they appear. In other words, in the totality they mould together with the categories brought from other forms of being.

Under this perspective, therefore, when the aim is to understand social being there is no alternative except to admit that its specific and decisive categories – labour, language, cooperation and division of labour, consciousness, etc. – can only be properly conceived in reference to the totality they constitute. It means that they cannot be conceived in isolation. Otherwise, one would have to suppose that social being has emerged by means of a sequential incorporation of singular categories. Consequently, when Lukács defends the necessity and fruitfulness of starting with the analysis of labour, he clearly presupposes not only the totality of social being, but also the indissoluble nexus of its specific categories.

In suggesting labour as the starting point of the analysis of social being, that is to say, of an already existing totality, Lukács admittedly relies on Marx's method deployed in *Capital*. The object of the latter is obviously the mode of production ruled by capital, which is definitively a totality with multiple categories of its own. The ideal reconstruction of this complex totality had to depart from one of these categories.[9] However it is not indifferent which category is selected for this purpose. By using the Commodity as the starting point for the analysis in *Capital* it was possible to mentally reproduce that totality 'not as the chaotic conception of a whole, but as a rich totality of many determinations and relations' (Marx 1976: 36) Labour performs an analogous role in Lukács' ontology of social being.

Hence the question posed by Lukács: how to justify labour as the central category of social being? He starts by observing that all other categories (language, cooperation and division of labour, consciousness, etc.) already essentially presuppose a social character. Only labour has an intermediate character, in the sense that it is precisely labour, which is a metabolism between human being (society) and nature. In other words, it is only labour that 'characterises ... the transition in the working man himself from a purely biological being to social being' and, therefore, that eventually impels corresponding changes in other categories. (Lukács, 1986: 10) In Lukács words:

> All those determinations which we shall see to make up the essence of what is new in social being are contained *in nuce* in labour. Thus labour can be viewed as the original phenomenon, as the model for social being, and the elucidation of these determinations gives so clear a picture of the essential features of social being that it seems methodologically advantageous to begin by analysing labour (ibid.).[10]

As with the emergence of every new form of being, man's coming to be human also entails what Lukács calls an ontological leap: a set of qualitative and structural changes in being.[11] In social being, this ontological leap is noticeable in labour. Whereas in the other 'animal societies' the organisation of the species' material relation with nature is biologically fixed, i.e. has no immanent possibility of further development, in society man creates, by means of labour, his or her own conditions of reproduction. This property of labour makes expanded reproduction the typical situation in social being – as testified by the formal plasticity it shows in history.

Hence, grasping the specificity of social being means grasping the way man creates social life itself out of nature. This requires understanding the activity by means of which this process operates or, in other words, understanding the distinctive character of human labour (activity) in comparison to its merely biological counterpart.[12]

Following Marx, Lukács notes that the most distinguishable feature of labour, as an exclusively human activity, is that 'through labour, a teleological positing is realised within material being, as the rise of a new objectivity' (ibid.). This makes labour the model of any social practice to the extent that social practice is synonymous with teleological positings that, no matter how mediated, have in the end to be materially realised. Yet, although labour as the model of social practice can be used to illuminate other kinds of social positing – just because it is their original ontological form – Lukács emphasises that its prototypical character could be unduly extrapolated in two directions. First, when taken too schematically to understand other social-teleological positings, it blurs their distinctive traits. Second, when its teleological character is generalised without limit.

This generalisation can be ontologically explained by the fact that labour is experienced in everyday life as the realisation of a teleological positing, being present in myth, religion and philosophy. Even Aristotle and Hegel, authors who were able to recognise labour's teleological character, did not realise that teleology is restricted to labour (and other human practices) and raised it up to the status of a 'universal cosmological category' and 'motor of history' respectively. These conceptions illustrate, says Lukács, a 'lasting relationship of competition, an insoluble antinomy between causality and teleology' present in the entire history of philosophy derived from the latter's improper generalisation (ibid.: 13). When conceived as a universal category, teleology implies purpose both in natural and human history and, for this reason, prevents the identification of those realms in which it is actually operative.

The point then is not proving the teleological character of labour, but rather to subject this quite 'unlimited generalisation to a genuine critical ontological treatment'. In order to do this, argues Lukács, it is necessary to acknowledge, on the one hand, that causality is a principle of motion that relies on itself; and this is so even when it might have had its origin in an act of consciousness. Teleology, by contrast, is by its own nature a posited category, in the precise sense that teleological processes presuppose an end and, consequently, a positing consciousness. Therefore, assuming teleology either in nature or in history necessitates not only that both move towards an end, but also that their 'existence and motion ... must have a conscious author' (ibid.: 14).

Thus such generalisations, as attempts to find a way out of the antithetical character of teleology and causality, end up by affirming the former and doing away with the latter, or vice-versa. The correct ontological answer to this question, says Lukács, is provided by the Marxian teleology of labour. The explanatory power of Marx's solution is due, above all, to a clear comprehension of teleology as a real process, hence endowed with an ineliminable ontological character. To posit an end means in this context that consciousness gives rise to a process – the teleological process itself – through which the end becomes real. It is just in labour that this real process can be ontologically proved, that is to say, 'labour is not one of the many phenomenal forms of teleology in general, but rather the only point at which a teleological positing can be ontologically established as a real moment of material actuality'. With this explanation, concludes Lukács, teleology receives a 'simple, self-evident and real foundation' (ibid.).

To circumscribe teleology to labour (and to human practice) might give the impression that its relevance is thereby being improperly deflated. On the contrary, points out Lukács, because in so proceeding it is possible to demonstrate that teleology is exactly the distinctive and specific category of the most developed form of being, namely social being. In other words, circumscribing teleology to labour (human practice) is the only way to emphasise that it is by the 'ongoing realisation of teleological positings', presupposed in labour, that social being can be understood in 'its genesis, its elevation from its basis and its becoming autonomous' (ibid.: 16).

From this perspective, in social being teleology and causality constitute the categorical basis of reality and of its movement. Naturally, these categories remain antithetical in social being, but do so within a real and unitary process (labour, social practice) whose mobility results just from the reciprocal effects of these antitheses. To create reality from the latter, the process has to transform pure causality into posited causality, without violating the inner nature of the former.

Recalling Aristotle's examination of labour, Lukács describes how this unity is realised. Aristotle analytically divides labour in two components: *thinking* and *producing*. In the first, both the positing of an end and investigation of the means of its realisation are carried out; in the second, the realisation of the previously posited end takes place. This description is made more concrete, says Lukács, by the further division of the first moment suggested by Nicolai Hartmann. Accordingly, the two moments comprised in thinking are explicitly broken up into two acts (thinking and producing). This complement by Hartmann does not change the ontological insight of Aristotle, the essence of which consists of conceiving labour as that complex of social being in which an ideal project realises itself materially; in which an imagined positing of end modifies material reality; in which something radically and qualitatively new is brought to reality. That is to say, reality becomes something that it could never be by itself, something that could not be logically derived from the 'immanent development of its properties, of its powers and law-like processes' (ibid.: 18).

The analytical distinction between end-positing and investigation of means is, however, of enormous relevance for the ontology of social being. This is precisely the distinction that reveals the inseparable link of teleology and causality. Considering that the investigation of means is oriented towards the realisation of ends, it cannot but imply an objective knowledge of the 'causality of those objectivities and processes that have to be set in motion to materialise the posited end'. Since natural reality – a system of law-like complexes – is in itself indifferent to human projects and endeavour, the end-positing and investigation of means are not able to produce anything new unless natural causal systems are rearranged. The separation of those two moments of Aristotle's thinking shows at this point its fecundity to the extent that it allows the recognition of the two functions performed by the investigation of means. On the one hand, it discovers the causalities – that exist independently of consciousness – governing the objects related to the production of the end in question. On the other, it devises new arrangements of these causalities that constitute the end itself and that might, when set in motion, materially realise the end. Hence, this last function is crucial for transforming pure into posited causalities. Lukács illustrates this point with a rather trivial example: since a stone in itself is not even potentially a cutting-tool, its realisation as such can only happen if its immanent properties are firstly correctly apprehended and, secondly, posed in a new combination (ibid.: 19).

Therefore, conceived in this manner, the essence of the labour process reduces itself to the transformation of natural causalities into posited causalities. In this process, then, 'nature and labour, means and ends render something that is in itself homogeneous: labour process and, in the end, the product'. In this sense, labour involves the overcoming of the heterogeneity of nature as regards human ends. Nevertheless, such overcoming of heterogeneities has defined limits. These limits do not refer just to the obvious fact that the homogenisation is constrained by the 'correct knowledge of the causal connections that are not homogeneous in reality'. They concern more properly the dialectical delimiting of the correctness of knowledge. In the first place, given that any object has infinite determinations (properties and relations with other objects), correct knowledge can only mean in this context the adequate knowledge of those determinations indispensable to realise the posited end, being consequently always limited. It is the limitedness of 'correct' knowledge connected to a particular labour process that explains that a successful practice may be based on false notions or lead to false generalisations (ibid.).[13]

Secondly, the limits have to do with the fact that the subordination of means to ends is not as trivial as it appears at first sight. The positing of ends emerges from a social need and is oriented towards its satisfaction. Means, however, have a natural substratum extrinsic to those ends. This extrinsic character of means, i.e. their heterogeneity, argues Lukács, induces the autonomy of the investigation of means. In contrast to what happens in the concrete singular labour processes, in which the end regulates and governs the means and sets the criterion of correctness of their investigation, in this autonomisation the process is reversed: the investigation of means becomes an end in itself. The way this autonomy gained by the investigation of means results from the enlargement of human practice is formulated as follows:

> We have already indicated the principle of the new, which even the most primitive labour teleology contains. Now we can add that the continuous production of the new, which is how we could call the regional category of the social appears in labour ... This has the result that the end commands and governs the means in every concrete individual labour process. Yet in speaking of labour processes in their historical continuity and development within the real complexes of social being, we see the rise of a certain reversal of this hierarchical relationship – certainly not an absolute and total reversal, but one that is for all that of the utmost importance for the development of society and human kind. For since the investigation of nature that is indispensable for labour is concentrated above all on the elaboration of means, these means are the principal vehicle of social guarantee that the results of the labour processes are established, the experience of labour continued and particularly further developed (ibid.: 21).

The emphasis here is that, on the one hand, the investigation of means can never dispense with the repertoire acquired in real causalities previously posed. On the other, it continuously accumulates the acquisitions derived from the ongoing positings. In brief, Lukács describes thereby the constitution, conservation, transmission and expansion of past, materialised, dead labour as the ever increasing condition of living labour. The identification of this relative autonomy of the investigation of means in labour, in which the correct apprehension of concrete causalities becomes for social being more important than the realisation of any singular end, illuminates the ontological foundation of science. In other words, the genesis and development of scientifically oriented thought derives from the immanent tendency of the investigation of means to become autonomous in labour process. This is a tendency that, in science, finally converts truth (the comprehension of the ontological constitution of things) into an end in itself.

This autonomisation, though giving rise to social practices and corresponding forms of consciousness whose connections with labour are complexly mediated, can never be absolute, that is, completely severed from the material production and reproduction of life. Thus, for Lukács, no matter how subtle and far removed from labour and immediate practice forms of consciousness might be, there does not follow any duality between social existence and social consciousness, between necessity (law) and liberty (freedom).

In sharp contrast to idealist conceptions, in which there is an unbridgeable abyss between 'the (apparently) purely spiritual functions of human consciousness ... and the world of mere material being', Marx's theory is able to clarify their 'genetic linkage as well as their essential difference and antithesis'. That is why labour – understood by him, as already indicated, as 'self-realisation, objectification of the subject, hence real freedom' – was said to be the key to understanding the dialectical unity of necessity (law) and liberty (freedom) that distinguishes social being from organic and inorganic beings. In short, Marx's analysis of labour demonstrates that there is a qualitatively new category in the ontology of social being: realisation as the effective fulfilment of a teleological positing. The central character of labour as an intermediary category is shown then by the fact that 'the activity of man as a natural being gives rise, on the basis of inorganic and organic being, and proceeding from them, to a specifically new, more complicated and complex level of being, i.e. social being' (ibid.: 26).

Human consciousness as the condition of possibility of labour

We are now in position to deal with some aspects of Lukács' account of human consciousness in connection to the complex of labour and its ontological relationship to reality. In analysing human consciousness he emphasises, once again, the mediating character of labour and the relevance of the category of realisation just mentioned. He notes that before dealing with human consciousness it is necessary to distinguish it from the consciousness of other animals, especially the higher ones. The consciousness of the latter, despite the fact that it already expresses their more complex and developed relation to the environment, has still an epiphenomenal character. It is true that consciousness in this case is essential to the reproduction of the singular, but its role is confined to a reproduction of the species that is ultimately biologically regulated. By contrast, human consciousness goes far beyond this role of being instrumental to mere adaptive interaction to the environment.

Having established that teleology is a category exclusive to social being and that it implies a subject who posits ends, it seems easy to understand that we are dealing here with a kind of activity of the singulars that has no parallel with the 'activities' of the singulars of other species. The radically different character of human reproduction is due precisely to the purposeful activities of the singulars on which it is based. For this reason, the ontological analysis of the complex of labour makes it possible to show that human reproduction is a reproduction which posits its own conditions, instead of a passive reaction (adaptation) to changes of the environment. Thus, from the concrete existence of labour it can be assured that consciousness is one of its necessary presuppositions, and that this consciousness cannot be epiphenomenal.[14]

Now, this new consciousness that emerges in labour as its necessary condition transcends the epiphenomenal character only when it posits an end and the means of its realisation, i.e. with the teleological positing as a self-guided act. So its distinction lies precisely in its deliberative or intentional nature, which is missing in the 'activities' and, consequently, in the consciousness of other animals. In other words:

> from the moment that a realisation of an end becomes a transmuting and new-forming principle of nature, consciousness that gave the impulse and direction to the process can no longer be ontologically an epiphenomenon (ibid.: 27).[15]

After examining this specificity of human consciousness, particularly its role in the emergence of a new form of reality, Lukács seeks to investigate its concrete modes of manifestation and its concrete mode of existence. With this purpose in mind, he recalls initially the two acts that constitute the 'true existing complex of labour': the exactest possible reflection [Widerspieglung][16] of the realm of reality relevant to the end at hand and the associated positing of the causal series necessary to its realisation. Even an abstract description indicates that these two acts, indissociable in labour, are reciprocally heterogeneous and, in consequence, represent two modes of considering reality. Modes that are heterogeneous because, as already pointed out, they involve both the apprehension of the world as it is in itself and the world viewed from the particular standpoint of the end. It is just this new ontological connection of acts that are heterogeneous in themselves that, besides building the existing true complex of labour, can be shown to constitute the ontological foundation of social practice.

Furthermore, the two heterogeneous modes of considering reality entailed by those acts form the basis of the ontological specificity of social being. The distinction of the two acts, it is necessary to repeat, is merely analytical, since in reality they are internally related, which means that their heterogeneity can be shown by the analysis of any of them. Taking the first, the reflection, its inspection immediately reveals the unequivocal separation between objects that exist independently of the subject and subjects that, by acts of consciousness, are able to reproduce objects more or less accurately – hence subjects that turn the objects into their *spiritual possession*. This separation is the presupposition and the result of the teleological positing itself, in that it simultaneously requires those two heterogeneous considerations of reality just mentioned (ibid.: 29).

For the sake of emphasis, it is worth reiterating that given the presence of ends and means in labour, it follows that labour presupposes the reflection of reality. Neither the end could be conceived nor could the means to its realisation be prepared without knowledge of reality, viz. without a reflection. Now this reflection produces (and presupposes) a separation and detachment of human being from its environment which is manifested in the confrontation of object and subject. Clearly, Lukács' contention here is that the subject of the reflection has in this very act not only to reproduce reality as her/his spiritual possession, but also that she/he can only do this by conceiving her/himself as distinct from the reality that is being reproduced. That is to say, a subject that turns both the external reality as well as herself into her spiritual possession. The ontologically necessary character of this separation is expressed by Lukács as follows:

> Turned conscious, this separation of subject and object is a necessary product of the labour process, and at the same time the basis of the specifically human mode of existence. If the subject, separated from the object world as it is in consciousness, were unable to consider this object world and reproduce it in its inherent being, the positing of ends that underlies even the most primitive labour could not come about at all (ibid.).

The analysis of the reflection also discloses that a new form of objectivity comes into being. Actually, in reflection, consciousness converts the reproduced reality into a 'reality' of its own. Despite being an objectivity, the reproduced 'reality', as a content of consciousness, is not a reality. As a reproduction in consciousness it cannot have the same ontological nature as that which it reproduces, let alone be identical with it. Hence from the ontological distinction between reality and 'reality' – resulting from those two diverse modes of considering reality in reflection – stem the two heterogeneous moments into which social being divides itself: being and its reflection in consciousness.[17] From the point of view of being, emphasises Lukács, they confront each other as things that are not only heterogeneous, but absolutely antithetical (ibid.: 30).

This heterogeneity between reflection ('reality') and reality, according to Lukács, constitutes the fundamental fact of social being. Fundamental because it represents the circumstance that the subject is in a position to consider reality from the angle of the end in view, which, as said, is heterogeneous to reality as it is in itself. In other words, the heterogeneity between reflection ('reality') and reality expresses a distancing of human being from reality. And the continuing interaction of these two heterogeneous moments – being and its reflection – is presupposed in the *creation* of a reality that is specifically human. This is what Lukács meant when he observed that, with the referred duality, human being elevates itself from the animal world (ibid.: 30).

The duality represented by this heterogeneity is not suppressed by the permanent relationship of being and reflection. It is not eliminated even considering that the reflection has already in labour an effect upon being and, conversely, is determined by its object. As a matter of fact, Lukács gives an account of the way this duality is reproduced in the interaction of two tendencies. Firstly, the reflection of reality demands systems of mediation that are more and more complicated (such as mathematics, geometry, logic, etc.) in order to reproduce as accurately as possible reality as an independent objectivity. As mentioned above, this reproduction represents an objectification of reality in thought and, as such, a further distancing. Lukács is referring here to the obvious fact that ever more detailed knowledge of reality presupposes an increasing distancing between subject and object that enlarges (extensively and intensively) the 'range of vision'. This ever more deep and extensive knowledge of reality does not naturally exclude the possibility of mistakes. The more you know, the greater your chances of being mistaken – taken for granted that the mistakes grow in complexity. Consequently, even if this process involves a deepening of reflection, the distancing rules out any idea of 'a quasi-photographic and mechanically true copy of reality' (ibid.: 31).

Secondly, the reproductions are always determined by the end-positings, i.e. they are genetically linked to the social reproduction of life. It is the concrete teleological orientation of this reflection (determined by the end) that is responsible for its fruitfulness, since it is the source of the new in social being. Hence operating here are two opposing tendencies: the concrete teleological orientation of reflection and the tendency of objectification (i.e. of reality as spiritual possession), working as a corrective. The reflection, thereby, has a 'peculiar contradictory position':

> One the one hand, it is the strict antithesis of any being, it is not being exactly because it is a reflection; on the other and simultaneously it is the vehicle for the rise of new objectivity in social being, for its reproduction at the same or higher level. In this way the consciousness that reflects reality acquires a certain possibilistic character (ibid.).

This possibilistic character of human practice is, according to Lukács, decisive to understanding the ontological relationship between reflection and reality. What is decisive in this case, of course, is not the fact that the reflection is not reality, but *that it might be*. Being different from reality, reflection expresses a possibility precisely because it might or might not be concretely realised. Since human practice is always teleologically oriented this potential nature of reflection endows it with an insuppressible alternative character. Furthermore, this alternative character must be based on concrete and correct apprehension of causal structures of reality, as a necessary condition for the transformation of causal structures into posited structures. In this sense, the alternative is ontologically founded on the structure of reality itself. Besides, as reality does not produce the end in question by itself, its capacity of being other – i.e. its plasticity – is realised in labour (human practice). The possibility entailed by the posited end in reflection is, thus, always referred to a concrete possibility.

Lukács points out that Aristotle's *dynamis* and Hartmann's *lability* are categories intended to denote precisely the possibilistic character of human praxis (ibid.: 31–2). Both categories capture the idea that labour is endowed with the power of transforming non-being into a concrete realisation. Now, as the concrete alternatives of labour characterise both the determination of ends and all phases of the working process itself, the complex of labour entails countless acts of judgement. The 'locus' and 'organ' of such judgements, decisions, selections, valuations is human consciousness. Since the results of such judgements become a new reality – a humanly produced reality – values are ontologically constitutive of social being. It should not be a surprise that in the chapter on labour in his *Ontology* Lukács fruitfully explores several aspects related to ethics. The next section focuses upon these arguments.

Under-labouring for ethics

Before moving to a discussion of Lukács' attempts to ground ethics in ontology, however, it is helpful to recall several features of Lukacs' account of labour. First, it was shown that social consciousness has its genesis and development in practice. Secondly, the ontological interaction between social consciousness and social being was established. Particular emphasis was given to the fact that social consciousness constitutes a new type of objectivity. Thirdly, having explained the heterogeneity between reflection and reality it was possible to argue that the dynamics of social being derives precisely from their relationship. Fourthly, reflection, though determined by reality, can give rise to new forms of reality by virtue of its relative autonomy. Finally and consequently, the alternative character of human practice can be demonstrated.

Although emphasising repeatedly that the complex of problems regarding values could only be properly dealt with in the framework of his projected *Ethics*, Lukács suggests that the ontological genesis of values is to be looked for in labour. Such an account of values is relevant chiefly because it is able to demonstrate the origin of values in the production and reproduction of social life itself – i.e. their ontological status – instead of construing them in a reified manner. Unfortunately, as already mentioned, Lukács' *Ethics* remained an unaccomplished project. Therefore, the intention here is just to explore some of the connections he establishes between human praxis and values in his analysis of labour examined above. In this regard, it should be recalled that Lukács' analysis, though focusing mainly on labour, in no way presupposes the homogenisation of the various human practices or their reduction to labour, as the author expressly emphasises.

Indeed, when analysing the particular kind of value – use-value – that emerges in labour, viz. in the metabolism between human being (society) and nature,

Lukács is not presuming its identity with values that are characteristic of other spheres of social being, as might be thought at first glance. On the contrary, his intention is precisely to shed light on the emergence of a form of being in which value is an ontologically constitutive category distinct from others in which there is no value at all. That is to say, as a model, use-value is to other values exactly as labour is to other socio-teleological practices.

The arguments by means of which Lukács maintains labour as the central category of social being have already been presented. This centrality has to do, among other things, with the fact that labour, for its teleological nature, cannot be merely taken as an activity towards the satisfaction of needs. Satisfaction of needs as such is a common trait to both human and other animals. What distinguishes labour is rather that it is a mediating category, which, in its development, establishes an ever increasing distance between needs and their satisfaction. This distance is due to the increasing chain of alternatives entailed in labour from the positing of ends to the continuous monitoring of the whole process up to their actual realisation. Along this process the working subject is faced with the necessity to judge whether instruments and materials are suitable for the realisation of the ends in view. The same applies even to the ends and to the attitudes of the working subject her- or himself.

Since what is at stake in labour is the metabolism between human being and nature, the ends in question are use-values. Relying again on Aristotle's notion of *dynamis*, Lukács argues, radically against the conventional wisdom, for the objectivity of use-values: to become something adequate for the satisfaction of a particular human need, an object must have inscribed in its inner constitution the possibility of being (or not) transformed in a determined way. Hence, alternatives refer to values objectively given in things themselves, viz. to the objective possibilities things are endowed with of being converted from potential into realised values. Under this perspective, use-value is nothing but the human recognition of the utility (value) of things themselves.

If observed from the point of view of the working subject the same process shows that this distancing between needs and satisfaction also presuppose a lability of human beings, i.e. the possibility of being other. The concrete realisation of a posited end by means of labour requires considerable transformations of the working subject, whose affects, emotions, instincts, etc. must be put on hold for two reasons: first, satisfaction is no longer immediate; second, the working process involves self-controlled behaviours and attitudes. It is quite clear that such conditions of possibility of labour, as described by Lukács, are exactly those highlighted by Marx when he says that men, by transforming external nature, transform themselves.

For our argument, however, what is important to stress is that Lukács devises in the possibilistic character of that double transformation (of things and of human beings) the objective foundation of both ethics and morality. Ethics are founded on the objective character of values (the possibility of becoming other of things); morality is founded on the objective possibility of 'becoming other' of human behaviour, hence of the 'becoming other' of human being.

In order to deal with these problems raised by Lukács one should depart from the alternative character of labour. The concrete alternatives of labour always involve in the last instance the choice between trueness and falseness, just because the realisation of the posited end rests on this ability of discerning the true constitution of things, relations, etc. This implies that the alternatives of labour have an insuppressible cognitive character. Now that which, in the process of labour, is recognised as correct or incorrect, true or false, useful or useless, etc., by an act of consciousness is naturally related to the end of the process. It is related, thus, to a use-value. This means that, for Lukács, human consciousness emerges as an 'organ' of judgement that, stretching out the metaphor, secretes valuations. Lukács synthesises these ideas as follows:

> The alternative thus gives rise to a bifurcation of the objective world effected by the subject on the basis of the known properties of the object related to the reactions which the interactions with the world induce. This series runs from the opposition of the useful and non-useful, beneficial and harmful, by way of many social mediations, up to the 'highest values' such as good and evil (Lukács, 1984: 502).

Yet to understand the role performed by consciousness in human practice and its relation to values, it is necessary to notice that the direction of the determination of action is inverted by it. Taking for granted that the decisive act of the subject is the teleological positing and its actualisation, it becomes clear that 'the categorically determining moment of this act comprises the emergence of a praxis determined by the "ought"'' (Lukács, 1986: 61). Hence, whenever intention intervenes, the envisaged future governs the present in the form of an 'ought' that simultaneously impels and constrains action. The radical inversion involved here can be clearly grasped if we consider that in biology:

> the normal causal determinability, in men as well as in animals, emerges as a causal process in which the past inevitably determines the present. Even the adaptation of the living being to a changed environment takes place with causal necessity, as far as the organism, on the basis of its properties produced by the past, reacts on such a change in assimilative or destructive way. The end-positing ... reverses this relationship: the end exists (in consciousness) prior to its actualisation, and in the process that leads to this actualisation each step and each movement is governed by the posited end (by the future) (ibid.).

What is governed by the future, then, is a series of causal chains that, when selected, rearranged, put into movement and continuously monitored in an adequate way, brings about the posited end. The regulation of the whole process by the future takes the form of a new category of social being – the 'ought' – which is the determining factor of the subjective praxis. This new category is indissolubly bounded to value, but it is not identical to it. On the one hand, the 'ought' can only perform that specific function in practice because what is intended is a value to human beings. On the other, the value cannot be realised unless it imprints on the working subject the 'ought' of its realisation as a criterion of practice (ibid: 68).

From this perspective the 'ought' is understood as the social objectivity of values reacting back on subjects as the internal criterion of adequacy of practices. The fact that this criterion of adequacy, which operates along a complex chain of alternatives, is always predicated on a desired end (on a value) demonstrates both the unity and the difference of the 'ought' and value. By acknowledging this difference in unity Lukács could illuminate the process by which the crystallisations of human practice (realised values) appear to human beings in practice as reasons to act (the 'ought'). Reasons to act do not emerge out of nothing, but are grounded on those crystallisations, which are conserved, developed or transformed in and by practice. Therefore, the values implicit in those reasons to act, no matter how contradictory they might appear to individuals, are always antecedent given to them. Similarly to social production, relations, structures, etc. that are outcomes of individual acts, but not their external and *post festum* aggregation – as pretended in the fairytales about the superlative isolated individual – values are alternative outcomes of individual acts, but not synthesis of individual teleological positings.[18]

For this reason, says Lukács, it is possible to affirm that: 'Every genuine value is then an important moment in every fundamental complex of social being that we denote as practice'. Actually, production and reproduction of social life is a complex process carried through by innumerable and distinct teleological acts that in practice are concretely linked to the acceptance or rejection of a value. Such a process is just the condition of realisation of values and should not be confused with their ontological genesis (ibid.: 83). On the contrary:

> The genuine source of the genesis is rather the uninterruptable structural change in social being itself, from which the value-realising positings directly arise. It is a basic truth of the Marxian conception ... that men make their own history, but not under circumstances they can choose. Men rather respond – more or less consciously, more or less correctly – to those concrete alternatives that the possibilities of social development place before them at the time. But value is already implicitly involved in it. ... [Value] is a moment of social being, and is therefore really existent and effective even if it is not conscious, or only incompletely so (ibid.: 83–4).

With this, Lukács is able to vindicate, in his analysis of labour, the social objectivity of both values (ethics) and the 'ought' (morality). Nevertheless, it should not be inferred from this that Lukács is reducing all the complexity of the question of values to those that were treated when examining the complex of labour. The purpose of the latter, as already mentioned, was 'simply' to establish that the specificity of social being is based, among other things, on the fact that the activity by means of which human beings elevate themselves out of nature – labour – already presupposes values.

In our opinion, the fecundity of Lukács' analysis rests precisely on the fact that the role of subjectivity is objectively connected already in labour to the recognition that this new form of being creates the conditions of its own reproduction. The peculiarity of the development of social being, therefore, consists in its being an open, non-teleological process that comes about by means of socio-teleological positings. Such a development amounts to a process of structural differentiation in which new spheres, categories, relations, etc. emerge, conforming social being as a totality of relatively autonomous complexes. This complexification involves obviously the multiplication and diversification of the alternatives ever facing human beings, together with the specific values of each complex. The development of social being then brings about a differentiation within the complex of values that do not prevent the opposition or even the antagonism among values of different spheres.

Despite the differentiation of spheres and the possibly contradictory character of their values, Lukács emphasises the ultimate unity of the totality of social being. All values, no matter their mutual contradiction, are connected in a more or less mediated way to the reproduction of social being, in the last analysis, to its material reproduction. In opposition to Max Weber who, according to Lukács, wants to derive a relativist conception of values from those contradictions or from the fact that it is impossible to abstractly rank the different values, he asserts the contradictory nature of the constitution and development of social being (ibid.: 85). For him, the fact that, for instance, economic values might be in contradiction to other values, say, aesthetical, legal, everyday life values, just expresses the semi-autonomy of the complexes of social being with their corresponding values, and their complex interactions.

In class societies this contradictory character of values within and between distinct complexes is self-evident. Admitting that the first truly universal society is that posed by capital in a movement that tends to abolish and/or turn irrelevant all but social differences,[19] it is understandable that this very objective development of social being may give rise to conflicting values. Values such as solidarity, identity (in difference), equality, etc. emerge as a result of the same process of universalisation that prevents their realisation. This is exactly the case in which, according to Lukács, economic values are in direct contradiction to the values that might be objectively held in other domains.

Concluding remarks

In these concluding remarks it is worth repeating that most of the arguments presented here were directly derived by Lukács' inspection of labour. Therefore, when the problem of correctness of reflection was first raised and discussed, it referred mainly to natural reality. Nothing was said as regards the objectivity of reflection when what is society itself is at stake. Nevertheless, it should not be forgotten that one of the main tenets of Lukács' conceptions is that there is no such thing as a general teleology, either in nature or society. Now, even if it is impossible here to pursue any further the reasoning of Lukács, it follows from this recognition that society is, like nature, an objective and structured totality in process. Hence, as far as reflection is concerned, there is no need for any substantial change in the analysis provided by Lukács when its objects are the causal structures of society, except by the fact that these structures are posited, that is to say, they are at the same time the conditions and results of the interaction of a myriad of individual (and social) teleological positings.

Society as nature has to be reproduced in thought, it has to become the spiritual possession of individuals. In the objectification of the reflection both nature and society are means and objects of the positing of ends: both have to be apprehended as they really are and have to be thought differently from what they actually are. That is the way human beings, in and through practice, mould the world to satisfy their needs, aspirations and desires. But that which is desirable about society is quite different from that which is desirable about nature. Desirability in nature involves inscribing in nature something that it would never have by itself. Desirability in society means inscribing in it some possibility that it can only have by itself. In both cases, the decision about what is to be inscribed is determined by social reality itself. But in society such objectifications have an ulterior determination, since the concrete alternatives are opened up by social evolution itself. In Lukács' words:

> Human social and economic action releases forces, tendencies, objectivities, structures, etc. that arise exclusively as a result of human practice, even though their nature may remain completely or in large part incomprehensible to those who make it (Lukács, 1984: 592).

If therefore society is conceived as a 'complex of complexes'[20] and if from the interaction of these complexes result tendencies that govern its evolution, then the two heterogeneous acts involved in the reflection also apply to society. In the first, the point is to reproduce as exactly as possible these existing tendencies. In the second, the point is to posit social ends (values) that, despite their objectivity, might or might not be compatible with existing social structures. Now the possibility of realising these ends, as we have seen, depends ultimately on the first act. Considering emancipation as the realisation of such values generated by the evolution of social being itself, its accomplishment presupposes a true knowledge of tendencies and of the possibilities they concretely offer to human action.

In this regard, what is relevant in Lukács' analysis is not his claim that everything that pertains to so-called human nature is a product of the development of social being in practice and by practice, since this is a common ground within the Marxist tradition. What is most fundamental is the connection he establishes between the values that emerge in this very progress of social being and the 'ought' as socially posited values that regulate social practice – both the most elevated values cherished by humanity, even when expressed in an idealised form, and the most humanly repulsive values belong to social being. Their antagonism expresses the contradictory nature of the social structures, relations, tendencies, etc. that foster or hinder the realisation of social values.

Within the Marxist tradition, the conception of human praxis in regard to emancipation can be traced back to Marx himself as the realisation of 'free individuality, based on the universal development of individuals and on their subordination of their communal, social productivity as their social wealth' (Marx 1973: 158). More concretely, it is conceived as the realisation of

> the universality of individual needs, capacities, pleasures, productive forces etc., [...] the absolute working-out of his creative potentialities, with no presupposition other than the previous historic development, which makes this totality of development, i.e. the development of all human powers as such the end in itself, not as measured on a *predetermined yardstick*, [... a development in which] he does not reproduce himself in one specificity, but produces his totality; [...] strives not to remain something he has become, but is in the absolute movement of becoming (ibid.: 488).

Thus, if emancipation can be ultimately synthesised in Marx's aphorism that 'the free development of each is the condition of the free development of all', as repeatedly stressed by Bhaskar, then it can be understood as the process by means of which the development of social being is carried out by socio-teleological practices governed by the future. A future that, in straight analogy to the 'ought' operating in labour, represents the objective possible developments discernible from today's conditions.

From this perspective, it is reasonable to claim that 'human nature' lies in the future rather than in a past that could be either presupposed or discovered by anthropology. Human nature is rather a future that human consciousness has to figure out from the present circumstances. But it has always to be figured out in the midst of socially determined ontological representations that often crystallise themselves into a social power. These ontological representations, nevertheless, might be in contradiction with the very cognitive act of conceiving a possible future. Under certain social conditions such ontological representations might in fact disallow the future. Or, what amounts to the same thing, render it the perennial reproduction of the same, consequently reducing social-teleological positings to mere practical manipulation of present conditions (institutions, knowledge, productive forces, etc.) in order to accomplish their corresponding goals. For Lukács, these are conditions presently facing humanity. The manipulation of all spheres of social life as the ever-increasing condition of the reproduction of capitalism can proceed indefinitely and uninterruptedly, exempt as it is from a scientific consciousness that voluntarily gives up or nominally refuses to talk about a scientifically founded ontology. It is against this false ontological consciousness, based on dominant social necessities, that Lukács emphasises the need for an ontological critique that could not only show that a rational ontological conception of the world is possible, but that in a social world so conceived there are alternatives – concrete alternatives.

Notes

1 The term 'under-labour' was employed first by John Locke (1689) to describe the process of 'clearing the ground a little, and removing some of the rubbish that lies in the way to knowledge'.

2 Lukács set out this project of writing a Marxist ethics just by the beginning of the 1960s, after the publication of the first two volumes of his (unfinished) *Aesthetics*, though he had been collecting a huge amount of material since the late 1940s for this purpose. His voluminous work, *The Ontology of Social Being*, published in German after the author's death in 1971, was actually meant as a prolegomenon of his projected *Ethics*.

3 In the jargon of critical realism, one could say that Lukács is obviously dealing here with the problem of reproductive and transformative activity. In proper Marxian terms, the question here is to understand political praxis and politics not as an *end* in itself (praxis designed to accommodated irreconcilable interests of *civil society*) but as a *means* to change society. For an illustration of Marx's thought on this question, see for instance Marx (1994).

4 Neopositivism is the term employed by Lukács to denote the late theoretical avatars of the positivist tradition.

5 It could be argued, for instance, that the fragmentary English edition of Lukács' *Ontology* represents a considerable obstacle to its worldwide diffusion. Actually, just three chapters out of ten were published in English. In addition to that, it should be mentioned that the translation has various shortcomings.

6 The ontological critique is accomplished to the extent that Marx, in what follows, gives an account of the social objectivity of such ideas, despite their falseness: 'He is right, of course, that, in its historic forms as slave-labour, serf-labour, and wage-labour, labour always appears as repulsive, always as *external forced labour; and not-labour*, by contrast, as "freedom, and happiness"' (Marx: op. cit.).

7 As it will be seen below in this section.

8 It should be noted that the word 'labour' is taken here from the English edition of Lukács' *Ontology* as the translation of the German word 'Arbeit'.

9 For Lukács' defence that, for Marx, society is a totality that is always already immediately given, see Lukács (1984: 579).

10 Exactly in opposition to the argument of Karlsson (2001), Lukács calls attention to the fact that, though being analysed in isolation, labour does not actually exist isolated. So the analysis consists of an abstraction *sui generis*, methodologically similar to that made by Marx in *Capital*, as above mentioned.

11 Ontological leap refers to a process of emergence of a new form of being out of precedent conditions that, nevertheless, cannot be deduced from them.

12 In the examination of the specific nature of labour, it could be said that Lukács comes close to what is named retroductive analysis in the terminology of critical realism.

13 This is the foundation of Lukács' ontological critique of neopositivism and other philosophical traditions that, after reducing practice to immediate practice, cannot but identify truth with empirical adequacy.

14 Lukács' procedure here illustrates once again the type of inference called 'retroduction' by critical realism.

15 It is right at this point, notes Lukács, that dialectical materialism differentiates itself from mechanical materialism. While the latter admits only nature and its law-like processes as objective reality, the former is able to demonstrate that the realised ends resulting from human practice, from labour, become part of the world of reality, constitute new forms of objectivity that, though not 'derived' from nature, are no less real. (ibid.: 28).

16 Though Lukács employs here the term 'reflection' it is obvious from the whole conception of the author that it has absolutely nothing to do with the idea of a mechanical mental reproduction of reality. Actually, it will be seen below that for him mental reproductions can never be a photographic and mechanically true copy of reality.

17 Needless to say that Lukács' *retroductive* analysis of labour makes clear the ontological genesis of those two domains of social reality correctly put forward in the ontology of critical realism: the intransitive and the transitive.
18 Though obvious, it is worth emphasising the parallel between this formulation and Bhaskar's conceptions as presented in his critique of methodological individualism and in the chapter entitled Societies (Bhaskar: 1979).
19 In this sense, it is perhaps justifiable to say of capital what Marx says about money: '[...] money ... like the radical leveller that it is, does away with all distinctions'. (Marx, 1992: Sec. 3.A).
20 Society as a totality of interacting structures is conceived by Lukács as follows: 'a complex constituted of complexes, the reproduction of which interacts in a multiple and manifold manner with the process of reproduction of the relatively autonomous partial complexes, though the totality presents itself as the predominant influence of these interactions' (Lukács, 1986: 227).

References

Bhaskar, R. (1986). *Scientific Realism and Human Emancipation*. London: Verso.

Bhaskar, R. (1979). *The Possibility of Naturalism*. Brighton, UK: The Harvester Press.

Bhaskar, R. (1997). *A Realist Theory of Science*. New York: Verso.

Bhaskar, R. (2002). *From Science to Emancipation*. New Delhi, India: Sage Publications.

Borges, J. L. (1999). *Selected Non-Fictions*. London: Penguin.

Collier, A. (1994). *Critical Realism: An Introduction to Roy Bhaskar's Philosophy*. London: Verso.

Collier, A. (1999). *Being and Worth*. London: Routledge.

James, W. J. (1907). *Pragmatism: A New Name for Some Old Ways of Thinking*. New York: Longman Green and Co.

Karlsson, J. (2001). 'The Ontology of Work: Social Relations and Doing in the Sphere of Necessity'. 5th Annual International IACR Conference. Roskilde University, Denmark, August 2001.

Locke, J. (1689). *Essay Concerning Human Understanding*, Epistle to the Reader. On line version: http://humanum.arts.cuhk.edu.hk/Philosophy/Locke/echu/.

Lukács, G. (1984). *Zur Ontologie des gesellschaftlichen Seins*. Erster Halbband. Luchterhand: Darmstadt.

Lukács, G. (1986). *Zur Ontologie des gesellschaftlichen Seins*. Zweiter Halbband. Luchterhand: Darmstadt.

Marx, K. (1992). *Capital: a Critique of Political Economy*, I. London: Penguin Books.

Marx, K. (1973). *Grundrisse*. London: Penguin.

Marx, K. (1976). *Ökonomische Manuskripte 1857–1858 (Grundrisse)*, MEGA, Band 1. Berlin: Dietz Verlag.

Marx, K. (1994). 'Critical Marginal Notes on the Article: 'The King of Prussia and Social Reform. By a Prussian'', in J. O'Malley (ed.), *Early Political Writings*. Cambridge, UK: Cambridge University Press.

Marx, K. and Engels, F. (1970). *The German Ideology*. London: Lawrence & Wishart Ltd.

Oldrini, G. (2002). 'Em Busca das Raízes da Ontologia (Marxista) de Lukács' in M. O. Pinassi *et al.* (eds.) *Lukács e a Atualidade do Marxismo*. São Paulo, Brazil: Boitempo.

Searle, J. R. (1998). *Mind, Language and Society: Philosophy in the Real World*. New York: Basic Books.

Tertulian, N. (1999). 'O Grande Projeto da *Ética*'. *Ad Hominen* 1, I. São Paulo.

Part II
Ontology and philosophy

8 Quine and the ontological turn in economics

*John Latsis**

Introduction

Contemporary social theory (Archer 1995; Lawson 2003; Fleetwood & Ackroyd 2004) and philosophy of social science (Bhaskar 1979; Cartwright 1989; Maki 2001) make frequent reference to ontology, often stressing the central importance of ontic considerations in the construction and criticism of both theory and empirical approaches. This 'ontological turn' within the social sciences is a mixed bag, incorporating a number of different and occasionally conflicting points of view (for more detail on this see Chapter 4). This chapter will focus on one strand within ontologically orientated social theorising: critical realism. More specifically, I will focus on Tony Lawson's contributions to the development of critical realism in economics in relation to similar developments in analytic philosophy.

The connections between traditional analytic philosophy and critical realism are limited and their respective literatures seem to evolve in parallel, rarely recognising each other. My aim in this chapter is to contribute to a potential dialogue by showing that critical realism is addressing a series of problems that have only recently been re-opened for debate within philosophy in general. Whilst Bhaskar is responsible for this re-awakening within critical realism and the philosophy of the social sciences more generally, Willard Quine re-introduced the study of ontology within analytic philosophy. Quine's impact was revolutionary and, according to my arguments, he raised many of the fundamental questions that need to be addressed by *any* form of ontological research. This is of particular interest to social scientists and philosophers of social science because much of Quine's extended discussion centred around 'abstract objects', a subject that is crucial to the elaboration of modern socio-ontological systems. Moreover, an investigation of Quine's views on ontology raises another important issue for modern social ontology: the diversity of ontological perspectives. In the case of Quine and Lawson, we can see that two authors with similar motivations and styles of argument come to radically different conclusions about the

* I am grateful to Lorenzo Bernasconi, Clive Lawson, Nuno Martins and Catherine Meldrum for comments on an earlier draft of this paper.

constitution of the world. Common agreement on the importance of *ontology as a discipline* is not sufficient for the common acceptance of *an ontology* (a world-view).

This chapter will begin with a brief exegesis of Quine's early contributions to ontology. I will then argue that there are significant parallels between Lawson's ontological turn in economics and Quine's seminal arguments set out in his 1953 book *From a Logical Point of View*. Having demonstrated that Quine and contemporary social theorists such as Lawson are grappling with the same problems, I will show where the contrast sets in. A common focus on renewing ontological research does not lead in one pre-ordained direction. The conclusions of ontological research and the methodological advice it may generate can take divergent, even conflicting, forms. In the final part of this essay the full implications of Quine's ontology are drawn out. His approach is found to present a distinct set of challenges to Lawson's social-ontological project.

Quine's ontological turn

Ontology, normally understood, is the science of being, the systematic study of the fundamental structure of reality. Philosophers of the early twentieth century had distanced themselves from any ability to partake in such an activity. So discussions of ontology were both uncommon and unfashionable when Quine began writing in the 1930s.[1] The logical positivists and empiricists who dominated analytic philosophy tended to regard it as obscure and outdated and references to ontology or metaphysics were usually pejorative. One of the dominant figures of this early period was Rudolf Carnap, who was both the inspiration for, and the target of, Quine's writings.

Carnap believed that philosophers did not engage in substantive debates. Philosophical arguments were mistakenly carried out in the 'material mode' (the mode used to discuss substantive problems) when they should have been carried out in the 'formal mode' reflecting their status as issues about linguistic expression. Thus, according to Carnap, the traditional philosophical disputes about the existence of objects, properties and universals were actually discussions about language. For example the philosophical question 'Are there properties?' could be translated as 'Should we adopt a linguistic framework which employs "– is a property" as one of its fundamental general terms?'. Questions of ontology ultimately turned on which linguistic frameworks a given community settled on. Moreover, according to this view, the adoption of linguistic frameworks was the result of pragmatic considerations rather than correspondence to reality, so the ontological import of philosophical debate disappeared completely. Philosophers could safely multiply their usage of abstract categories without having to justify them on traditional empiricist grounds because these categories made no claims about the constitution of the world.

Quine's rejection of the dominant orthodoxy was based on a refusal to truncate philosophy and scientific thought in this manner. In a series of essays published in 1953 as *From a Logical Point of View*, Quine provided the basis for a new research programme in analytic philosophy. Quine believed that the natural sciences were the most successful area of human knowledge production and that philosophy was continuous and interconnected with them. The ideas that he explored were intended to demonstrate this posited continuity. One important argument involved showing that both philosophical and scientific questions, unlike his predecessors had maintained, turn on ontological issues.

However, Quine did acknowledge what he regarded as an obvious reason for the belief that ontology didn't matter. He realised that the existence claims of any theory are so basic to it that they can become virtually transparent to the theorist, allowing philosophers to ignore them.

> One who regards a statement on this subject [ontology] as true at all must regard it as trivially true (Quine 1953: 10).

Thus, for Quine, any discussion of being is parasitic on a set of sentences that are implicitly accepted as *true*. These 'observation sentences' are the source of human knowledge and any theory can ultimately be reduced to them.[2] It is only once some such set of sentences have been accepted as truths that questions of existence can be raised. This is why Quine concentrates his attention on the ontological commitments of theories. The objects which any given theory is about must be those objects that are claimed to exist if the theory is to be true.

Quine addressed a number of philosophical disputes using these insights.[3] In so doing, he accentuated the parallels between philosophical problems and scientific ones by likening philosophical ontologies to sets of theoretical entities:

> Our acceptance of an ontology is, I think, similar in principle to our acceptance of a scientific theory, say a system of physics: we adopt at least insofar as we are reasonable, the simplest conceptual scheme into which the disordered fragments of raw experience can be fitted and arranged (Quine 1953: 16).

While he did not associate ontological speculation with an ability to intuit the 'real' structure of the universe, Quine was determined to show that philosophers and scientists alike were committed (through their conceptual schemes) to the existence of the entities they discussed: they could not shy away from ontology. In this sense, different theories were describing different worlds, and those who posited apparently fictitious theoretical entities in order to achieve their theoretical goals would have to admit that they held those entities to *exist* and hence presumably to empirically investigate these existence claims.

But ontology had been neglected in philosophy precisely because the ontic commitments of theories were usually implicit and unstated. In order to draw attention to these commitments, Quine proposed a departure from the dominant Russellian theory of reference.[4] In principle, this would allow him to show the ontological commitments of any given theory. He avoided the pitfalls of the riddle of non-being by insisting that a name does not require objective reference in order for it to have meaning. Instead, the conveyors of meaning are what modern logicians call *bound variables*, these can be expressed as sentences beginning with 'there is', and variables of quantification such as 'something', 'nothing' and 'everything'. Bound variables do not work like names, they possess a generality and intrinsic ambiguity that allows them to refer to entities broadly, without denoting specific, pre-assigned objects. So, according to Quine, 'To be is to be the value of a variable' (1953: 15). In other words, we commit ourselves to an ontology containing a centaur when we say that '*there is something* that is a centaur', but we can still safely say '*there are not* centaurs' without invoking their existence.

Both scientists and philosophers make ontological commitments in their usage of bound variables and they become committed to entities through linguistic performance. The resort to the canonical notation of first-order logic allowed Quine to determine the ontic commitments of theories.[5] These commitments are made explicit through formalisation and cannot be admitted unless they can be translated as the value of a bound variable.

By introducing the study of ontic commitments, Quine recognised that there is basic ontological inconsistency between competing theories. As we shall see later, he suggested that pragmatic criteria such as simplicity would decide between competing conceptual schemes. His discussions of ontology gave renewed credence to the notion that different theories can indeed propose different accounts of the world and conflicts between these accounts are important to the development of human knowledge.

Lawson's ontological turn

Echoes of Quine's work have recently appeared in the writings of some critical realists interested in the social sciences. A recent example of this is Tony Lawson's critique of economics (1997, 2003). For Lawson the critique of mainstream economics must be ontological:

> ... for a central aim of my project is to indicate the significance of ontological enquiry, of facing up to ontological issues *explicitly* (Lawson 1997: 33).

Accordingly, the widespread disarray in economics is due to a generalised neglect of social ontology. Much like Quine, Lawson claims that economists *do* make ontic commitments in their models, yet these commitments are difficult to uncover. Economists are usually quick to deny that the assumptions of their models are supposed to reflect reality, so Lawson investigates explicit commitments in order to uncover implicit ontological *presuppositions*. This leads him to investigate what he sees as the defining feature of modern mainstream economics: *method*.

Through his research into social ontology, Lawson provides a twist on the Quineian dictum that all theories presuppose an ontology, he argues that all methods presuppose one too:

Now, all methods have ontological presuppositions or preconditions, that is conditions under which their usage is appropriate. To use any research method is immediately to presuppose a worldview of sorts (Lawson 2003: 12).

The argument is simple. In order for a particular method to generate explanations and predictions it must presuppose a world with certain features. Few economists state or recognise the type of worldview they rely on in their theories. However, their methods do not lie: they are only appropriate for a certain type of world. The lack of appreciation for this relationship between method and ontology is the leading cause of what Lawson perceives to be a systematic lack of fit between economic theories and the social world.

More precisely, Lawson contends that the methods of economics commit economists to a world with certain key characteristics. For example, one important ontological presupposition is a direct consequence of the attempt to deduce predictions in terms of regularities in events:

> ... any presumption of the universal relevance of mathematical modelling methods in economics ultimately presupposes a ubiquity of (strict) event regularities (Lawson 2003: 13).

In the language of critical realism, the presuppositions of mainstream economics include the view that the social world is a closed system.[6] In addition to this, economists rely on a number of other implicit ontic commitments. In modelling the social world as a closed system, they are compelled to treat the units of their analysis (individuals) as social atoms devoid of intrinsic structure and only activated by the impingement of external forces and stimuli. Furthermore, in order to be able to aggregate successfully, individuals must also be conceived of as isolates. Their actions must be unresponsive to all conditions not explicitly set out in the model.

Yet, according to Lawson, the lack of observable patterns in events is evidence that social scientists are not dealing with a system with these characteristics. The social system that economists study does not display event-regularities of the sort 'whenever *x* then *y*' in the form of a closure of causal sequence. Economic agents are not atomistic or isolated. For Lawson, this realisation is the crucial step in the formulation of an alternative ontology for economics, one that is both explicitly stated and studied in its own right. He elaborates a specific vision of the social world inspired by Bhaskar's transcendental realism: the 'transformational model of social activity' (Lawson 1997: 157–188; 2003: 3–62). According to this alternative worldview, the social world is an open system populated by active intentional agents with their own aims, plans and goals. These agents are not isolated but evolve in an environment characterised by emergent social structures inherited from prior generations. Individuals live in large networks of internally related social positions, their actions are influenced by rules and conventions. The dynamic and processual nature of social life is recognised by the transformational model. Change is incorporated as new generations of agents adopt, reject or trans-form the structure inherited from their predecessors.

It is not the purpose of this chapter to fully develop or defend the ontological reforms suggested by the Lawsonian critique of economics. Instead I describe it in order to show that, like Quine, Lawson has demonstrated a desire to take ontol-ogy seriously. This attitude contrasts with the majority of economists who, licensed by the positivistic disdain for ontology, ignore the implications of their ontic commitments. Theoretical assumptions are widely acknowledged by econ-omists not to be descriptive of the social world and are openly adopted in order to facilitate the construction of axiomatic-deductive models which are the typical output of the profession. Thus, the ontic commitments of economics are disguised by both a complex method and a neo-positivist rhetoric, leaving them obscure and implicit. Like Quine before him, Lawson draws attention to the intrinsic problems of this strategy and demands that economists face up to the ontological commitments that their theories necessarily make.

Common ground?

A number of features undeniably figure in both Quine's critique of positivist phi-losophy and Lawson's critique of neoclassical economics. Both writers were reacting against a dominant mainstream that is disdainful of ontological enquiry by emphasising the fact that their opponents cannot avoid ontic commitments. Indeed the revolution in philosophy that was facilitated by Quine's arguments laid the groundwork for many of the modern developments in social ontology. The criticism of positivist philosophy of science encouraged those who favoured a much more metaphysics-heavy approach, hence the increasing dominance of realist philosophies of science within the academic mainstream. The demise of positivism in economic methodology was also in large part due to the transplan-tation of these critical arguments. Some commentators have explicitly drawn attention to this, linking the development of realism in the philosophy of the social sciences with the philosophies of the leading critics of positivism, Quine and Thomas Kuhn (Hands 2001: 116–117).

It is also clear that both Quine and Lawson are interested in what some com-mentators have referred to as traditional metaphysics or ontology (Lowe 1998: 2; Smith 2003: 8–9). They are both defending a view of ontology that is directed at the world, not at the arguments or ideas of other philosophers or economists. In emphasising the importance of ontological commitment, Quine was pointing out that any theory had to range over some set of entities, and that scepticism or con-firmation of the theories should result in the belief or denial of those entities. As a direct result, many of his arguments were negative, directed against the prolif-eration of philosophical and logical categories that had followed in the wake of logical positivism. Lawson makes a similar point about the structure of the social world. His criticism of economics is premised on the argument that economists must recognise the world that their models purport to describe. By investigating the ontological presuppositions of economic theory, Lawson teases out economists' ontic commitments and suggests an alternative. Even though one talks of the explicit ontic commitments of theory and the other of the implicit ontic presuppositions of method, both Quine and Lawson defend the view that the existence claims of any scientific approach are crucial to our understanding of it.

In addition, both Quine and Lawson share a radical and revisionist approach to ontological theorising. Historically, one of the important functions of ontology has been to uncover and describe the ontological commitments of theological or scientific doctrines. This taxonomic function persists in the work of modern ontologists and is even seen by some as the primary goal of ontology.[7] It is therefore common to emphasise the importance of a taxonomy of existing theory and remain reticent about pursuing an explicitly revisionist programme. Neither Quine nor Lawson hesitate to use ontological arguments for critical purposes. Quine used his ontological insights to problematise a number of empiricist categories that were widely accepted by his contemporaries. By showing what philosophical theories made existence claims about, Quine was able to propose revisions that were consistent with his preferred physicalistic ontology and naturalised epistemology. In the same vein, Lawson proposes a radical overhaul of economic theory by examining its ontology and contrasting it with the transformational model.

The status of 'abstract entities'

There is strong evidence that the arguments of Quine and Lawson bear a family resemblance, but the philosophical background to these arguments is significantly different. While they agree on the importance of recognising and studying ontology they disagree on which ontic commitments one should adopt and why. The locus of the disagreement can be drawn out by investigating the Quinian category of 'abstract entities'.

Quine emphasises simplicity as the guiding principle in the choice of ontological and conceptual frameworks. Conceptual frameworks are at the service of research practices. If they increase the organisation and efficiency of scientific procedure, the entities they assume can be admitted. On this reading not all ontic commitments are equal, they are justified by their utility within a productive scientific enterprise. This Quinian take on ontic commitment is usually referred to as 'pragmatic'.[8]

Quine suggests that, given these pragmatic considerations, physical objects are to be generally preferred to abstract ones. There are two overriding reasons for having such confidence in an ontology of physical objects: physical objects are accepted as the basis of common linguistic communication; and they are also accepted as the termini for scientific explanations (Quine 1960: 238). According to Quine, this makes them a good bet for ontic commitment. But there is no grand philosophical argument for this view; Quine rejects philosophical arguments that justify the reification of physical objects in light of their closeness to sense experience.[9] Neither logic nor scientific practice rule out a nonphysicalist ontology.

Thus an ontology containing 'abstract entities' is in principle acceptable to Quine, provided that those entities fulfil an indispensable role in simplifying and expediting scientific enquiry. He gives the example of real numbers and classes as possible candidates for this ontological status on the grounds that they can be successfully employed in mathematical and scientific problem-solving (Quine 1960: 237).

Nevertheless, though Quine's pragmatism rules out an outright rejection of non-physicalistic ontologies, he tries to minimise their invocation. Speaking of his imaginary opponent Wyman, Quine expresses this desire eloquently:

> Wyman's overpopulated universe is in many ways unlovely. It offends the aesthetic sense of us who have a taste for desert landscapes ... (Quine 1953: 4).

There is an obvious tension between the recognition of abstract entities and Quine's desire to limit the range of entities and promote the simplicity and efficacy of theory.

A major theme of the early Quine's writings was the discussion of ways to control the proliferation of ontic commitments and prevent 'disorderly ontic slums'. Though his discussions tend to focus on the philosophical categories prevalent at the time of his writing, he still gives a good idea of how this control could be achieved. Drawing on contemporary philosophical disputes, Quine suggests a criterion for abstract entities to be recognised: *discernible identity conditions*[10]:

> Still the lack of a standard of identity for attributes and propositions can be viewed as a case of defectiveness on the part of 'attribute' and 'proposition'. Philosophers undertook, however unsuccessfully, to supply this defect by devising a standard of identity, because they were persuaded of the advantages, in systematic utility or whatever, of taking 'attribute' and 'proposition' as full-fledged terms and so admitting attributes and propositions to the universe of discourse (Quine 1960: 244).

So, not only must a prospective abstract entity play some important role in increasing the simplicity and power of our theories about the world, it must also have a clearly defined standard of identity. Quine defends physicalistic ontologies by appeal to the body of scientific research that (allegedly) proposes clear and discernible conditions under which any given entity x persists over space and time.

This means that, for Quine, our common-sense vocabulary of material objects is fundamentally anchored in physical theory which ascribes spatio-temporal continuity to objects. Similarly, the advocates of abstract entities must show that these too have discernible identity conditions. According to Quine these identity conditions would then provide more or less definite standards for individuating one abstract entity from another and could therefore play an important role in the development of theory.

At first glance this might seem a significant challenge to a research programme that has principally concerned itself with the elaboration of abstract categories in social ontology. Critical realists use the transcendental method to infer the existence of abstract categories, however few if any attempts to ascribe clear identity conditions to the elements of the transformational model of social activity have been made so far. It appears that ideas such as emergence, social structure, or macroscopic causal powers might be difficult to accommodate within Quine's framework. It is also questionable whether critical realism would be able to subscribe to the Quinian insistence on strict identity conditions.

Reality, identity and physicalism

In the case of the transformational model of social activity ontic commitments tend to proliferate. Abstract entities and categories are essential to the attempt to theorise the social world along Lawsonian critical realist lines. So whilst Quine's parsimonious taste does not rule out social ontology, it presents a challenge to those who would regularly appeal to non-physical entities and processes in their analyses of the social world.[11] But before considering how Quine might challenge the Lawsonian approach to economics, we must address an initial objection that could be raised against any juxtaposition of these two authors whatsoever.

A serious question over the validity of any comparison between Lawson and Quine arises out of the status each confers to theoretical language. For Quine, the study of ontic commitment involves the study of the basic observational statements of a scientific language. Thus, his claim that ontology should be taken seriously can be re-interpreted as a simple plea for linguistic clarity in scientific theory. On this view, the specific content of a set of ontological claims is not central to the Quinian project, whereas the logical structure of arguments and the rigour of existential statements is.

It might be objected that in contrast to this Quinian approach, the project of critical realism in economics has a very different purpose. Critical realist ontology is often understood as the study of being itself and, particularly in the case of the social sciences, this activity is not necessarily mediated by existing theory. The introduction of theory as a wedge between ontological elaboration and experience of the world might be seen as a crucial step in the Quinian argument and one which the critical realists are unwilling to take. Thus, it could be objected that Quine commits an epistemic fallacy: he takes the subject of ontology to be talk about the world as opposed to the world itself.

While this objection does help to focus attention onto some of the important distinctions between Quine's and Lawson's projects, it does not undermine our ability to draw significant parallels. At the root of the objection is the argument that Quine's emphasis on theoretical entities removes ontological discourse from the realm of entities and places it in the realm of concepts and ideas. The ontologists' concern is thus deflected from questions of being to questions of meaning and reference. But this interpretation of Quine, at least in his early writings, is simplistic. The insistence on the use of existential quantifiers to articulate clear theoretical entities *does* reflect a concern with the concepts we use in order to make existence claims. However this is an unremarkable observation: ontological analysis is always mediated through concepts. Studying the thing-in-itself and the concept by which we delineate the thing cannot be neatly separated. This applies to Lawson in the same way as Quine: neither can transcend language, and so conceptual analysis remains a crucial part of ontology for both.

At this point an objector might change tack. The crucial difference between Lawson and Quine is one of motivation, the former is concerned with describing the world while the latter is simply concerned with describing the presuppositions of scientists. But this objection involves a further misunderstanding of Quine's position. He was interested in making more precise the 'internal metaphysics' of the scientific community (particularly physicists), but this was not an arbitrary choice, it reflected an ontological commitment to physicalism.[12] Physicalism amounts to the belief that the ultimate constituents of the universe are described by physical theory and that, given this, the termini of explanations should attempt to reflect or at least be consistent with that theory.[13] This, paired with Quine's advocacy of a holistic understanding of science, led to a belief that physical theory held a privileged position in the web of human knowledge.[14] By elucidating the ontological presuppositions of physical theory, Quine believed that we could get the best available purchase on the world around us.

It is in this overriding commitment to physicalism that the first serious divergence between Lawson and Quine arises. In his later writings such as *Word and Object* (1960), Quine's position is very specific in limiting the legitimate scope of ontology. He distinguishes 'top rate' and 'second grade' conceptual systems, conferring epistemological priority to the former and refusing to acknowledge that the latter might help us elucidate anything about the world. So while the Quinian focus on the presuppositions of natural scientific theory is perfectly in line with the traditional approach to ontology advocated by Lawson and other critical realists, the substance of his ontological position and his advocacy of physicalism is not.

For Lawson the ontological turn in economics involves a form of transcendental argument from practices to their conditions of possibility:

> That is, it is accepted that all actual practices, whether or not scientific, and whether or not successful on their own terms, have explanations. There are conditions which render practices actually carried out (and their results) possible. Let me refer to this supposition as the *intelligibility principle* (Lawson 2003: 33).

> The form of reasoning that takes us from widespread features of experience (including here conceptions of generalised human practices, or aspects of them) to grounds or conditions of possibility, is the *transcendental argument* (ibid.: 34).

In further characterising his argument as *retroductive*, Lawson shows how the strategy he adopts involves a move from the phenomena of experience to their underlying causes. Herein lies a development characteristic of recent philosophy of social science within the critical realist tradition: underlying causes are not restricted (as they would be by Quine) to the microphysical level and hence physicalism is rejected. For Lawson the ontic commitments of a successful economics might include (amongst other things), social relations, positions, rules and conventions. These aspects of social structure are seen as causally implicated in the conditioning of human behaviour and the production of human practices and Lawson makes no attempt to reduce them to the facts of biology or physics. This critical realist perspective sees the restriction of ontology to the domain of the posits of the natural or experimental sciences as arbitrary and unjustified, a relic of scientism.

This brings us to a second major divergence. Quine tends to restrict discussion to ontic commitments to 'entities' of some sort or other. This, of course, fits with his own emphasis on the natural sciences and with the empiricist tradition of modern analytic philosophy. Even when he discusses abstract categories such as real numbers and logical operators, the discussion is still couched in terms of entities.[15] Yet Lawson and other critical realists appear not to restrict their discussions to entities. More specifically, in the case of social ontology the metaphor of entities seems particularly inappropriate. Social categories do not represent 'things' with the phenomenological characteristics of the medium-sized objects so beloved of philosophers. This bears importantly on the difficult Quinian question of identity conditions. If social phenomena are not characterised as entities at all, then how can they be assigned stable conditions of identity?

There is little in the critical realist literature that can settle this issue. However, the extensive reference to social structure as a central mechanism of the transformational model of social activity shows where the difficulties are likely to arise. Social structures, if they are to exist and persist over time, would have to accommodate the possibility of changing membership. If their temporal continuity is to be preserved, they cannot be reduced to the sum of their physical parts (individuals). Thus one traditional candidate (individuals) for a strict reductionist criterion of identity in the case of social structures is ruled out from the onset. In fact, much of what Lawson writes suggests that the analogy of entities and the accompanying quest for stable conditions of identity might be impossible. For example his discussion of society as an 'ontology of process' appears to rule out a sufficiently strict set of such conditions:

> What about the idea that society is a process? According to the conception sustained, social structures such as households, markets, universities, schools, hospitals and systems of industrial relations do not independently exist (and often endure over significant periods of space–time) and undergo change. Rather, change is essential to what they are, their mode of being. They exist as a process of becoming (and decline) (Lawson 2003: 44).

Of course, the discourse of critical realism has not been developed in conjunction with older discussions of ontology within analytic philosophy, and so the import of these two Quinian challenges is difficult to assess. My brief discussion of the difficulties of establishing stable criteria of identity within a critical realist ontology of the social world does not rule out the possibility that they might be discoverable.[16] However it does point to a fundamental divergence in practice between Quine's ontological turn and the one proposed by Lawson and the project of critical realism in economics. Quine's desert landscape is in stark contrast to Lawson's rich and complex social reality.

Concluding note

The task of this chapter has been to develop a critical comparison between new developments in critical realist-inspired social ontology and older debates within analytic philosophy. Quine is the main figure in the re-introduction of ontology as a respectable discipline within twentieth century analytic philosophy and as such his position provides an interesting contrast case. Both Quine and Lawson undertake self-conscious ontological challenges to the assumptions of their respective disciplines. Both deny the ability of practicing theorists to shy away from ontic commitments and demand that those commitments be explicitly stated. We can go further by claiming that Quine and Lawson share a traditional ontological perspective that goes beyond the simple enumeration of scientific presuppositions. The presuppositions of science are relevant to ontology inasmuch as they give us a better purchase on the structure of the world around us.

The real divergences emerge when Quine's ontological prescriptions are put into practice. The physicalist perspective that he defends and his scepticism about abstract entities challenge the content of the critical realist transformational model of social activity. Social phenomena are rarely characterised as entities in the latter framework, and our ability to discover clear and stable identity conditions for them is thrown into doubt. These insights suggest a set of issues that could be developed within the literature on social ontology. Are Quine's demands for strict identity conditions legitimate in the case of social objects? If so, can the processual nature of those social objects be accommodated? Future research in social ontology would benefit from attempting to answer the Quinian challenge and adding greater depth and detail to the transformational model in the process.

Notes

1 In discussing Quine's contribution I will concentrate on early publications that were crucial to the reintroduction of ontology into modern philosophical debate. His later work on 'ontological relativity' (Quine 1969) marks a development of these ideas that has also generated a great deal of discussion. I shall not discuss these later views in this chapter as they represent a departure from his initial position.

2 Observation sentences are uncontroversial statements such as 'it's blue', 'there's a car' and 'it's dark'. These sentences must fulfil three criteria: they must be complete utterances whose truth value changes according to the occasion on which they are uttered;

they must be directly tied to the stimulation of the uttering individual's sensory system; there must be general acceptance of the conditions under which these utterances are acceptable from the point of view of the linguistic community.

3 Most famous perhaps was the 'riddle of non-being' (Quine 1953: 1–16). In an early article, he contrasts his position with the views of two fictitious philosophers (McX and Wyman). These philosophers contend that there is something that Quine does not recognise. However, in order to formulate the disagreement between them, Quine cannot admit the disputed entity without contradicting his prior rejection of it. This riddle of non-being stubbornly resists Occam's razor because a non-entity must be 'something' in some sense, otherwise what is it that we claim there is not?

4 Russell's theory of descriptions translates names into singular descriptions that affirm the uniqueness that is implicit in the use of 'the' in a given sentence. This approach implies that the name acts as an incomplete symbol that can be paraphrased out in context to give a meaningful description.

5 Theories were never completely isolated, however. Echoing Pierre Duhem, Quine argued that scientific theories were interconnected, theories in the biological sciences, for example, are related to and supplemented by theories in the other sciences as well as the theorems of logic and mathematics.

6 According to Lawson, a closed system is one in which the triggering of real causal mechanisms results in the production of predictable empirical patterns expressed as regularities of the form 'whenever x then y', where x and y are two events in a causal sequence. The latter proviso is intended to cover the possibility of event regularities where x and y are simultaneously caused by a third variable. Closures of this type are referred to as 'closures of concomitance'. These systems involving closures of causal sequence are rare even in the natural world and critical realists have argued that they only infrequently occur outside the laboratory.

7 See the work of Uskali Maki for an example of this. His definition of economic ontology highlights the taxonomic character of ontology: 'The study of economic ontology is concerned with what may be called "the economic realm": the economic realm consists of those parts or aspects of the universe which are set apart as constituting the subject matter of economics' (Maki 2001: 4).

8 A reference to the American pragmatist tradition of Dewey and James.

9 For a discussion of the possible conflict between the physicalistic and phenomenological conceptual schemes see Quine (1953: 17–19).

10 This is consistent with his discussion of ontic commitment because clearly stated conditions of identity make terms accessible to variables of quantification.

11 The only recent attempt to introduce Quine into the methodology of economics is notable for its quietist attitude towards social ontology and its criticism of 'Lawsonian Realism' (Boylan & O'Gorman 1995: 171–177).

12 Ironically, Quine's overriding physicalism eventually affected his attitude towards ontology in general. In a later piece he carried out a systematic deconstruction of the very concept of a physical object motivated by his (updated) understanding of contemporary physical theory (Quine 1976). Quine concluded that, as physicalists, our ontology of the world must reduce to pure set theory, yet he recognised that theories and systems of knowledge cannot be so reduced (ibid: 502–503). This move permeated his writings in the seventies and eighties, bringing them much closer to the caricature alluded to above. Quine's radical shift towards internal metaphysics is stated unambiguously in the final lines of the 1976 paper: 'We might most naturally react to this state of affairs by attaching less importance to mere ontological considerations than we used to do. We might come to look to pure mathematics as the locus of ontology as a matter of course, and consider rather that the lexicon of natural science, not the ontology, is where the metaphysical action is' (ibid: 503–504).

13 In a more recent contribution Quine refers to naturalism as fundamental to his position: 'Naturalism looks only to natural science, however fallible, for an account of

what there is and what there is does. Science ventures its own tentative answers in man made concepts, perforce, couched in man-made language, but we can ask no better' (Quine 1992: 9). This has been recognised as a return to a more explicitly ontological project on his part (Georgialis 1999).

14 Quine's views on the interlinked nature of human knowledge are discussed in a later publication, *The Web of Belief* (Quine & Ullian 1970).

15 This position changed in his later writings as the 'entities' physicalist philosophers liked to invoke came to be undermined by physical theory itself (see for example Quine 1976; and footnote 12 in this essay).

16 A critical realist response could, of course, take a completely different tack in responding to the demand for identity criteria. Quine's later writings on ontology suggest that stable identity conditions for physical objects are highly problematic themselves (1976: 497–499). With the development of physics through the latter part of the twentieth century, it could be argued that physical objects have begun to take on many of the problematic features of their social counterparts. Thus, for example, one potential account of what physical objects views them as spatio-temporally scattered and lacking the neat boundaries that the early Quine required.

References

Archer, M. 1995. *Realist Social Theory: the Morphogenetic Approach*. Cambridge, UK: Cambridge University Press.

Bhaskar, R. 1979 [1998]. *The Possibility of Naturalism: A Philosophical Critique of the Contemporary Human Sciences* (3rd ed.). London: Routledge.

Boylan, T. and O'Gorman, P. 1995. *Beyond Rhetoric and Realism in Economics*. London: Routledge.

Cartwright, N. 1989. *Nature's Capacities and Their Measurement*. Oxford: Oxford University Press.

Fleetwood, S. and Ackroyd, S. 2004. *Critical Realist Applications in Organisation and Management Studies*. London: Routledge.

Hands, D. W. 2001. *Reflection without Rules*. Cambridge, UK: Cambridge University Press.

Hookway, C. 1988. *Quine*. Cambridge, UK: Polity Press.

Georgalis, N. 1999. 'Ontology Downgraded All The Way', *Pacific Philosophical Quarterly*, Vol. 80: 3, pp. 238–256.

Gibson, R. F. (ed.) 2004. *The Cambridge Companion to Quine*. Cambridge, UK: Cambridge University Press.

Lawson, T. 1997. *Economics and Reality*. London: Routledge.

Lawson, T. 2003. *Reorienting Economics*. London: Routledge.

Lowe, E. J. 1998. *The Possibility of Metaphysics*. Oxford: Clarendon Press.

Maki, U. (ed.) 2001. *The Economic World View*. Cambridge, UK: Cambridge University Press.

Quine, W. V. O. 1960. *Word and Object*. Cambridge, UK: The MIT Press.

Quine, W. V. O. 1969. *Ontological Relativity and Other Essays*. New York: Columbia University Press.

Quine, W. V. O. 1976. 'Wither Physical Objects' in R. S. Cohen *et al.* (eds.), *Essays in Memory of Imre Lakatos*, pp. 497–504. Dordrecht: D. Reidel Publishing Company.

Quine, W. V. O. 1980 [1953]. *From a Logical Point of View* [2nd ed.]. Cambridge, MA: Harvard University Press.

Quine, W. V. O. 1981. *Theories and Things*. Cambridge, Massachusetts: Harvard University Press.

Quine, W. V. O. 1992. *Structure and Nature*, Journal of Philosophy, Vol. 89, No. 1 (Jan.), pp. 5–9.

Quine, W. V. O. and Ullian, J. 1970. *The Web of Belief*. New York: Random Nord.

Romanos, G. D. 1983. *Quine and Analytic Philosophy*. Cambridge, MA: The MIT Press.

Smith, B. 2003. 'Ontology', in Floridi, L. (ed.) *Blackwell Guide to the Philosophy of Computing and Information*, pp. 155–166. Oxford: Blackwell.

9 Tracking down the transcendental argument and the synthetic *a priori*: chasing fairies or serious ontological business?

David Tyfield

Introduction

Ontology is now widely recognised to be of central importance to science, philosophy and the interaction between the two. Yet there is no clear agreement on how it should be done or even what the term means. This paper is concerned with only one form of such theorising, namely the transcendental argument (henceforth 'TA'). For this mode of realist theorising has attracted significant criticism and misunderstanding such that many continue to deny it any validity at all.[1]

Two issues in particular have aroused such criticism, namely: (1) the nature of the argument, in respect of (a) the nature of its premises and status of its conclusions and (b) the validity of its inference, as one of 'necessity'; and (2) the connection between the examination of conceptual presuppositions and the uncovering of knowledge concerning the nature of being, that is the ontological purchase of the TA.

Now, any discussion of these issues immediately opens up huge philosophical questions, most evidently the relation between (the theory of) meaning – i.e. as regards conceptual presuppositions – and ontology, for which there is evidently insufficient space here. The aim of this chapter is limited to providing a preliminary examination of research regarding the nature of the TA in order to defend it against various critics working in the empiricist tradition. In particular, this paper has three aims:

(i) To establish the synthetic *a priori*, which the TA deduces, as the conclusion of a form of reasoned necessity that is non-logical but nevertheless valid, against the denials of empiricist philosophers, by showing it to be a question of the necessary conditions of intelligibility of the premiss;
(ii) To examine the nature of the ontological commitment of the synthetic *a priori*; and
(iii) To establish that the TA, so formulated, remains sufficiently Kantian to merit the Kantian title of 'transcendental argument', even if it differs from Kant in respect of its lack of commitment to transcendental idealism.

In doing so, the strategy is to examine the implications of theories of meaning and reference for the TA, the synthetic *a priori*, and ontological commitment, as regards both their existence and their sense, with particular regard to a seminal debate in 20th century empiricist philosophy of meaning between Quine and Strawson. Thus three interlinked themes are discussed, and while this makes matters complex, their very interlinking does not allow any other way to discuss them. The three are: (1) the theories of meaning and reference and the relations between these notions; (2) the resultant conceptualisations of the nature of 'ontological commitment' and thus the 'transcendental argument' and the 'synthetic *a priori*'; and (3) the problem of meaningful but referentless (MR) statements. The latter is not merely a dry question of purely scholastic interest but is the crucial test for any theory of meaning/reference, with the very possibility of knowledge at stake. For, given that our point of departure is the verificationist identification of meaning and reference and that we are ontologically committed to that which our beliefs presuppose, it follows that, because we can only meaningfully state that which refers, we are thrown into the paradoxical situation that anything we believe to be false we must also believe to be true, and this would immediately render knowledge impossible. In other words, ontological commitment (2) compels us, on pain of the impossibility of knowledge, to examine our theory of meaning and reference (1), in order to resolve (3), i.e. to show how we are *not* committed to the truth of that which we believe to be false.

It will be argued that following this debate takes us to a position where, if we are to make any further progress towards its solution, we must abandon the empiricist way of thinking about the problems altogether, and turn our attention to ontological issues, i.e. issues about the nature of being *per se* and not about *what* exists. But if we do this, we also transform our theory of meaning and reference and thus, derivatively, our understanding of the sense of the terms 'transcendental argument', 'synthetic *a priori*' and 'ontological commitment' itself, so that the whole problem changes. Once thus changed, however, the original problems with which we were presented in our theory of meaning and reference are seen to be resolved. In short, in trying to *clarify* the nature of these various terms, we also *transform* our understanding of them, the whole way we think about the issues, the result being an overall conception that vindicates the valid and *sui generis* status of both the TA and the synthetic *a priori*. Alternatively, if we think of the TA as a tool employed in addressing the problem of MR statements, we see that attempts to resolve the problem lead not only to redefinition of our theory of meaning, but also, thereby, to a transformation of both the problem itself *and* the tools with which to tackle it, i.e. the TA, the synthetic *a priori* and ontological commitment.

What is the transcendental argument?

The conception of the TA at (i) above is not original, but follows the work of Bhaskar, Lawson and other critical realists, who are quite clear that they view the

TA and the synthetic *a priori* to be intimately linked. Lawson (1997: 50–51) writes, for instance, that on his 'account of transcendental analysis' the TA seeks to 'establish synthetic *a priori* knowledge (of the sort we are hoping to achieve).'[2] Similarly, Bhaskar (1998: 5) writes, rather more obliquely, that 'if philosophy is to be possible (and I want to contend that it is in practice indispensable) then it must follow the Kantian road' which is then, implicitly, connected with the synthetic *a priori*: e.g. 'It is only in this relative or conditional sense that philosophy can establish synthetic *a priori* truths'.

Furthermore, I take it as evident from the works of Bhaskar and Lawson that they interpret the TA to have the following characteristics:

1   It proceeds not by stating 'X is', *nor* by reasoning 'if Y is then X is' but rather 'given Y, X must be the case (in the world)', where the nature of the necessity in the 'must' (and hence the inferential step of the argument) is neither logical nor analytical but such as to yield synthetic a *priori* truths (if they exist).[3]
2   It proceeds from fallible premises chosen with regard to the particular comparative perspective of present interest and to which there is prior ontological commitment (hence providing a 'critical' philosophy in the Kantian sense) and thus gives rise to conclusions that are conditional on those premises.[4] As such, nothing is 'proven' with complete certainty or to be absolutely true or necessary.
3   Finally, *contra* Kant, the TA investigates necessary conditions of *intelligibility* of its premises and not (just) conditions of the *possibility of experience*.[5]

Regardless of the merits of these claims, this formulation does, I would argue, capture one crucial element of the TA. For, as I understand it, in order to be a 'transcendental argument' at all, it must accord in some way with Kantian specifications. The crucial Kantian innovation in this regard, I would argue, is the recognition of the synthetic *a priori* as a distinct form of truth claim, the means of deriving such claims then being labelled a 'transcendental argument'. Thus a 'transcendental argument' that does not result in synthetic *a priori* truths is not a TA at all and the validity of the TA as a distinct form of argument stands or falls with the validity of the synthetic *a priori*.

What, then, is the synthetic *a priori*? Unfortunately, there is relatively little discussion of the nature of the synthetic *a priori* in critical realism, and even less that attempts to connect it with the voluminous debate on the notion elsewhere in philosophy. This chapter is just such an attempt. But the first stop is to contextualise the question by setting it against those common empiricist objections to the TA, alluded to above, regarding the nature of the argument. For it is my argument that these empiricist objections are best understood as revolving around the central debate of the nature of the synthetic *a priori*. Without this framing, such criticisms of the critical realist TA, for example, appear to be almost deliberate in their misreading of Bhaskar's and Lawson's work.

Thus, objections that the TA is both hubristic or arrogant and unsuccessful in its claims of proof or certainty are evidently undercut by the explicit and repeated affirmation of the conditionality of its results.[6] Similarly, arguments that the transcendental argument (and any example thereof) is neither logically nor analytically valid may be conceded without compunction, for the arguments are not intended to be valid in this way, but as the derivation of synthetic *a priori* truths.[7]

Conversely, when one recognizes the general suspicion with which the notion of the synthetic *a priori* is viewed amongst philosophers of the empiricist or analytic tradition and their scientific followers, then one can easily see that the debate cannot progress while this glaring disagreement remains unaddressed. Indeed, I think it no exaggeration to say that just what is at issue between critical realists and empiricists is the validity and nature of the synthetic *a priori*, which goes some way to explain the apparent incommensurability of the two programmes for there does not appear to be any middle ground between affirming and denying its validity. To date, no attempt has been made (that I know of) to tackle this issue. It is the aim of this paper to start that process.

Philosophical debate on the synthetic *a priori* and ontological commitment

How, then, has the synthetic *a priori* been interpreted? The first thing anyone will notice on considering the history of the notion is that it is highly contentious and, indeed, has always been ever since its initial proposal by Kant. And, indeed, both the notorious difficulty of Kant's prose and the absence, if not self-affirmed impossibility,[8] of any clear definition of its status does little to assist his readership to track down this elusive – possibly mythical? – beast, as is noted by various eminent trackers.[9]

We may say, however, at the very least that the synthetic *a priori* is a notion which lies within the intensional theory of meaning, according to which meaning is explained *as* a purely intensional concept and so can only be explained *by and in terms of* other already accepted meanings. But it immediately follows from this that it is impossible to present a step-by-step account of the synthetic *a priori* going from mutually acceptable premises to novel conclusions. Rather, in a sort of inversion of Wittgenstein's ladder analogy, any argument or explanation concerning the synthetic *a priori* and the TA must, as it were, already have these notions accepted and can only clarify their sense (though this can result in a radical shift in our understanding). Thus any such exposition is not taking us up a ladder that we then discard, or notice to be fictitious, but must be from a position already 'up' and can only make sense of this new position by pointing out where we have come from and how we got here (perhaps taking us further 'up' in the process). The present chapter is no exception to this, and it will have been noticed that I have already made 'assumptions' in my explication. All I can say in defence is that this is quite unavoidable: the various notions at issue here do not admit of explanation in any other way.

It also follows that if I am to present a full and fair account of all three of the theories of meaning I examine in the paper, including the critical realist conception elaborated, I must 'take sides', for the argument just is that the latter offers a perspective that is simply not available to the empiricist. Consistency, rather than question-begging, therefore, demands that the arguments presented regarding the critical realist conception are in terms not accessible to empiricist thought but *not vice versa*; in short, the critical realist conception transcends and encompasses the empiricist paradigm or it does not make sense at all, even on its own terms.

Now we can see immediately that *if* the synthetic *a priori*, and meaning more generally, is intensional, then any attempt to explain these notions in extensional terms and logical step-by-step argument must necessarily find them to be bogus. But this goes right to the heart of the matter, for the impossibility of explaining intensional terms other than by way of other intensional terms is just what so annoys the empiricist. Surely this just shows false, question-begging reasoning at work? The question then is, 'how can we have valid reasoning regarding and making use of intensional concepts?' In short, we must turn our attention to theories of meaning.

In doing so, let us consider among the strongest arguments against the synthetic *a priori* from a seminal debate in 20th century philosophy of meaning. For there are two types of naysayers of the synthetic *a priori*: the disillusioned trackers, who have laboured and suffered in its pursuit, catching occasional glimpses, but ultimately in vain; and those who never even looked but dismissed the whole enterprise as chasing fairies. This difference is nowhere more evident, and their disagreements nowhere more eloquently argued, than in the writings of Willard Quine and Peter Strawson, representing a naturalised logical empiricism (or hard-headed scoffers) and a linguistic analytic tradition (or valiant grail-seekers) respectively.

Both parties accept the Kantian definition of the synthetic *a priori* as a matter of presuppositions and ontological commitment:

> **TA₁**: 'A transcendental argument is one in which the ontological presuppositions of a premiss are examined, the conclusion of which is a synthetic *a priori* truth to which the believer of the premiss is (also) ontologically committed'.[10]

For Quine and Strawson, however, this formulation merely reveals that the so-called 'synthetic *a priori*' conclusions are nothing but logical or analytical truths respectively, as we shall see. For both of them, therefore, the TA is not a *sui generis* form of reasoning and the synthetic *a priori* does not exist at all. Hence, the argument is not about the relation amongst these notions, which is accepted from Kant, but how each of the relata are themselves understood and, thus, whether they are to be considered philosophically valid or not.

My argument is that these twin notions (synthetic *a priori* and ontological commitment) can be best articulated by treating them as a matter of intelligibility, whereupon the synthetic *a priori* is revealed to be not only legitimate (or existent) but necessary for there to be any thought at all. Let us consider first the case of the hard-headed scoffers.

Quine and logical necessity: meaning eliminated in favour of reference

Quine's project was to construct a philosophically rigorous logical language that dispensed with the fuzzy ambiguities of everyday language and employed purely extensional terms, this being understood to be the structure provided by the exemplar of knowledge that is natural science.[11] Drawing a strict distinction between the 'theory of reference' and the 'theory of meaning', Quine (1953c: 130 and 1953a: 11) argued that the parlous, i.e. logically shambolic, state of the latter, which included all intensional concepts, was to be avoided at all costs while the former was a valuable contributor to knowledge. Quine thus completely excluded meaning from his account, eliminating it altogether as a philosophical object of interest, and focused on reference alone. It followed that neither the synthetic nor indeed the analytic, being intensional concepts, was acceptable to Quine (1953b) and their distinction was accordingly dismissed as 'dogma', distinguishing between two types of nonsense.

Quine points out, however, that the strict distinction between meaning and reference is needed on pain of insoluble paradox. This follows from his definition of ontological commitment as purely a question of logic, thus:

TA_Q: 'X presupposes P if and only if P $must_L$ be true if X is <u>true</u>.'[12]

Given this definition of ontological commitment, Quine asks how, if the meaning of a term or proposition is its reference (as it is in the verificationism of logical positivism), one can meaningfully deny the existence of something (X), for in order to be able to understand what it is we are denying, X must 'exist' in some way in order to be an object of reference. In other words, the meaningfulness of the statement about X apparently *logically* commits us to the *existence* of X, i.e. *onto-logically* commits us to X.[13] Yet such 'existence' offends the empirical sensibilities of those who argue that meaning is reference; sensibilities, moreover, that Quine shares. Alternatively, consider the related problem of how the following statement:

S: 'The King of France is wise.'

can be meaningful? We know that there is no King of France, yet I expect that we would also concede that S makes sense to us. But if S is meaningful, it must be referring to something. So, Quine points out, we must say either that we are deluding ourselves and S does not make sense as a proposition, or that there must *be* a King of France in some way, say as an abstract entity or counterfactual, but this then offends his empiricism.

Given his evolved (naturalised, pragmatised) logical empiricism, Quine attempted to resolve this problem in purely logical and empirical terms by employing the seminal developments in logic at the turn of the 20th century, in particular Russell's theory of descriptions. The strategy is to parse such statements into their logical constituents and then redraft them in logical notation, thereby limiting the existential assertions of the statement to the bound variables, such as 'some', 'all' or 'none', hence excluding the need for the predicates or descriptions themselves to refer, i.e. effectively stipulating that 'to be is to be the value of a variable'.[14]

This then solves the problem with S by showing that the premiss of the TA that 'X is true' is not satisfied in that case, because we do not believe there is an X such that X is a King of France, and so we are not ontologically committed to anything unpleasant. Conversely, if we take another example, say 'the dog is white', and this is believed to be true then we are committed simply to the truth of all that this truth itself entails, e.g. the dog is not black.

Thus, we can say that S is meaningful as a statement but *all* meaning is ultimately of no philosophical interest, bearing no relation to epistemological concerns. True and false propositions, and indeed utter nonsense, can all take the same appearance as 'meaningful' but what matters epistemically is whether or not the statement *refers*, its truth or falsity. As Quine (1953: 11) puts it: 'I feel no reluctance toward refusing to admit meanings, for I do not thereby deny that words and statements are meaningful … I remain free to maintain that the fact that a given linguistic utterance is meaningful … is an ultimate and irreducible matter of fact'.

In summary, then, let us consider how Quine understands the various notions at issue. Following from his theory of meaning, which consigns meaning itself to philosophical irrelevance while maintaining reference as the relevant criterion for knowledge, the transcendental argument is merely interpreted as one species of logical argument and the 'synthetic *a priori*' is simply unnecessary, superfluous jargon for describing a conclusion from an empirical premiss. Finally, ontological commitment is understood as commitment to the truth of conclusions logically entailed by our express beliefs.

Strawson and analytical necessity: meaning separate from reference

For philosophers of the analytic tradition, such as Strawson, Quine's proposed abolition of the analytic/synthetic distinction was clearly a direct challenge to which they had to respond. There followed, therefore, a series of essays by Strawson and others subjecting Quine's argument to immanent critique.[15] By examining the various possible interpretations of Quine's theory, Strawson shows that Quine can only deny the need for intensional concepts by making use of them. Thus, for instance, one cannot even begin to apply logic to a proposition unless its terms have an analytic (or defined) meaning – yet this is one of the intensional notions prohibited by Quine.[16] Quine is forced, therefore, either to admit analytic meaning into his schema, and so his argument against intensionality collapses, or to continue denying the analytic, but then also to deny logic (and/or logical *necessity*) and be left equally empty-handed. Given then that Quine's theory of meaning is wrong, he has not resolved the problem of S nor can we accept his formulation of the TA. What, though, is Strawson's solution?

Following his critique of Quine, Strawson resurrects some notion of meaning, or 'significance', and shows that reasoned necessity is not only logical but can also be analytical. This is demonstrated, for instance, in a discussion (1950) of the notion of presupposition as an *analytical*, and not a logical, relation between concepts, highlighting the difference between presupposition and implication. So, for instance, denying a presupposition of a statement is not logically contradicting the statement. Thus in response to the statement 'that is a fine red butterfly', denying its presupposition would be 'but there is no butterfly at all', while logical contradiction is 'that is not a fine red butterfly'.[17] Strawson therefore shows that Quine was wrong in explicating presupposition as a logical relation. But he argues further that Quine was also wrong about the relation between meaning and reference, for there *is* such a relation in that we cannot have reference without meaning.

Consider again our example statement S. Strawson (1950) argues that there is a relation between meaning and reference, as shown by the distinction between a statement and its use: a *statement* in itself makes no reference but only refers when it is *used* to do so. Thus S *per se* refers to nothing in particular (as can be seen by its possible use across the centuries with varying truth values) but is *meaningful* regardless, meaning being a separate matter dependent on the rules or conventions of language.

Conversely, if put to concrete use, S analytically presupposes the truth of the phrase 'there exists the King of France' and in the absence of that truth is neither true *nor false*. Thus, the truth of 'the dog is white' does not *logically* presuppose the truth of 'there exists a dog', but rather its truth *or falsity* presupposes this *analytically*. Otherwise, stating 'the dog is white' while pointing to a chair is merely false, rather than nonsensical. In this respect, the ontological commitment of the proposition is to that empirical truth that is presupposed. Hence Strawson's definition of the TA can be summarised:

TA_S: 'X presupposes P if and only if P $must_A$ be true if X is <u>true *or false*</u>.'[18]

But because the conclusion, that the King of France exists, is a straightforward empirical truth, given Strawson's (Grice & Strawson 1956) identification of the analytic/synthetic and *a priori*/empirical distinctions, on this conception there is nothing special about the 'synthetic' or empirical conclusion of the TA.[19]

Consider, though, the nature of Strawsonian ontological commitment. Its 'commitment' rests on the prior commitment to the empirical truth or falsity (i.e. the having of a truth value) of the premiss. Yet, as Strawson (1954) notes, we can, of course, choose not to make that prior commitment, as when we say 'there has been no summer in Narnia for hundreds of years', or we can lie (i.e. make meaningful assertions presupposing truths we know to be false) or we can just make honest mistakes concerning the truth of our presupposition. Thus, the ontological commitment here is merely what must be believed to be the case *if* the proposition is believed to be empirically true or false and leaves open the question whether or not it *is* so believed, let alone whether or not the presupposition is in fact empirically true.

The problem of Strawson's account: turning to ontological issues

Strawson's account of the synthetic *a priori*, however, is inadequate and ultimately unsustainable. First, as Kitcher (1995) and others have argued, his subsequent attempt to employ his arguments in order to redraft Kant in terms of analytical TAs is a substantial misreading of Kant's work that renders it patently absurd.[20] This may be a merely exegetical point, but it should put us on guard.

But Strawson's greatest weakness arises from his determination to completely separate questions of meaning from questions of reference, as he does in his distinction between statements and their use.[21] The plausibility of this distinction rests on the observation that one statement can be used in many different contexts to refer to many different things, just as 'the King of France' can refer to Charles the Bold or Louis XIV, etc. ... Therefore, while we cannot have reference without meaning (for the statement must precede its use), we can have meaning without reference.

But further investigation of the statement/use distinction shows it to be quite untenable. For the idea that abstract statements are first constructed according the rules of language and are then applied to concrete uses raises the question: 'but whence the rules of language?' For Strawson to maintain that the meaning resides in the rules of language, therefore, he must either concede that these rules themselves arise from use of the language, in which case his distinction collapses, or he must maintain that meaning arises before use, in which case he is committed to a mysterious Platonic realm of meaningful statements which are then plucked and used in concrete instances.

Furthermore, if we recall that the reference of a statement is what it is about, it is clear that a statement without any reference at all (because it is not yet in *use*, when reference comes into play) is not about anything at all. It follows that it can be used to refer to *anything*. But then it is quite meaningless. In other words, we cannot have meaning alone, as *per* Strawson, for the only way that the use (or reference) of statements can be limited, and hence the statement be meaningful, is if the statement itself 'refers' in some way. So we cannot accept Strawson's theory of meaning, nor the formulation of the TA that arises from it.

But why does Strawson feel compelled to separate meaning from reference so strictly? I believe that in order to understand this point, we must return to the original problem of MR statements. For it is clear from the very fact that this is perceived as a problem that the paradigm upon which Strawson was building included certain crucial assumptions, in particular:

(a) the difficulty of distinguishing meaning and reference; and

(b) the limitation, as much as possible, of the possible objects of reference to empirical, concrete particulars, i.e. an empirical realist ontology.[22]

Otherwise, respectively, (a) statements can be meaningful without committing us to the existence of their referents, or (b) they can be meaningful by having non-empirical referents, such as a counterfactual or abstract King of France. Seen in this light, it is clear that Strawson's argument with Quine concerns the difference between reference and meaning, i.e. is limited to (a). He does not, however, challenge (b) at all. Given (b) and the consequent epistemic priority of reference to meaning, however, there are only a limited number of options with (a): that meaning equals reference (*per* verificationism); that meaning does not equal reference but only the latter is of concern (*per* Quine); or that meaning does not equal reference and we are concerned with them both (*per* Strawson).

Yet we have seen that each of these alternatives leads to a dead-end, so it is clear that resolution to this problem cannot lie in (a) and that there must be underlying assumptions that are false. In other words we must move to examination of assumption (b). It is the argument of this paper that assumption (b) must be challenged in particular by changing the definition of reference along two dimensions: (1) we must expand it from *actual* reference (X does or does not refer) alone to *possible* reference (X can or cannot refer); and (2) we must change the possible objects of reference, i.e. shift from an empiricist to a wider ontology. Why? First, as regards (1) let us compare S with a similar statement:

T: 'The King of Pope is wise'.

Both S and T are without actual referent, but T is different, in that it is also without *possible* referent – it cannot refer to the world, that is, it is unintelligible. So the intelligibility of a statement is its possibility of reference.

But this takes us immediately to (2), the ontological question, because in order to be able to have *possible* reference, we must directly address and expand our ontology, i.e. our theory of the nature of reality *per se* and *not just* its constituents, as 'ontology' is understood by Quine and Strawson. That is we must challenge the limitation of the possible objects of reference to the empirical. In order to see why this is the case, consider the nature of reference: there is a referring expression, a referent and the relation of reference between them (as well as the referrer, of course). As with all relations, the nature of the *relatum* of the permissible objects of reference, i.e. our ontology, necessarily determines the nature of the *relation* of reference. So, in the case of the empiricist, if we have empirical facts and then words, it is clear that the only conceivable relation between these two relata is one of names or labels; *per* Quine (1960), there is the 'word' and the 'object' and that is all. So an empirical realist ontology necessarily sets reference as a naming relation. But it follows that reference is limited to the actual, excluding 'possible reference', because labels either do or do not (actually) name things: if a 'label' does not name something it is not a label at all. So long as our ontology is empiricist, therefore, we cannot make sense of 'possible reference', and the MR problem remains unresolved.

It follows that in order to be able to resolve the original problem of how statement S is intelligible (i.e. take step 1 from actual to possible reference), we actually have to go one step further (i.e. step 2) and challenge our *ontology* so that it affords the possibility of possible reference. To do this is to ask outright the ontological question of 'what must reality be like if the phenomenon of possible reference is itself possible?' It follows that S itself is not an appropriate *type* of premiss for a TA at all. Rather, such a premiss should be, for instance (the statement describing) the *phenomenon* of which S is an example and which we *do in fact* believe to be true:

Y: 'There are propositions that *can*, but actually *do* not, refer (e.g. S).'

So it is not S itself (a statement, *ex hypothesi*, we do not take to be true) that challenges our ontology, as Quine and Strawson see it, but that *phenomenon* of which S is an example, and which we *do* believe is true, that does so. And, of course, this must be the case, for how can any ontological conclusions arise from a premise we do not believe to be true? That Quine and Strawson do not ask the ontological question, however, shows that they are putting the cart before the horse, for the problem of MR statements can be addressed in two ways (*Cf* (a) and (b) above) and only one of these is legitimate. On the one hand, we can seek to show that MR statements do not commit us to the existence of things which offend our ontology (here conceptualised as our theory of what exists), in which case the problem is to construct a theory of meaning and reference which shows how ontological commitment does not arise in these cases. On this approach, therefore, we change our theory of meaning in an attempt to fit our ontology, thereby taking the nature of reality itself as evident and the nature of the human phenomenon of meaning as problematic, even though the latter is clearly more accessible to us.

Alternatively, instead of begging the question as regards the ontological implications of MR statements, we can accept that MR statements exist (as empiricists also do) and actually ask 'what are the implications of the existence of MR statements for our ontology?' Clearly, given their unquestioning acceptance of (b) and the consequent exclusive focus on (a), Quine and Strawson take the former route, but this is to make the unwarranted – and, as we have seen, self-defeating – assumption that their ontology is beyond question.

Bhaskar and 'intellective' necessity: meaning and reference as mutual conditions of possibility

So the step beyond Strawson, which the failure of *his own* programme forces us to take, demands in fact *two* steps. But what are the implications of these two steps for our formulation of the TA? Our proximal goal is to answer the question of the conditions of intelligibility of S, that is 'what is *presupposed* by S being possibly true or false?' This gives us the TA formulation (step 1):

TA_{CRS}: 'X presupposes P if and only if P must$_s$ be true if X is *possibly* true or false'.[23]

where the relevant type of necessity is what I suggest we call, in an unavoidable neologism, 'semantic necessity'. This semantic necessity demands, for instance, that:

P_{S1}: '"King of France" *means* something that *can possibly* be "wise"'.[24]

The conclusions of this TA, therefore, are merely truths concerning the (current) *meanings* of various words or propositions. But if S, or any other given proposition, is possibly true or false, this demands not only that certain conditions be met within meaning itself but also (step 2) that reality is such that it can be expressed in propositions. That is, reality itself must be intelligible. For if reality is unintelligible, true or false statements are *a priori* impossible. It follows that believing *any* statement to be true (or false) immediately ontologically commits us to the intelligibility of reality. Furthermore, given that meaning is the possibility of reference (i.e. the possibility of truth or falsity), it follows that meaning presupposes the possibility of believing propositions to be true or false and so that *understanding* (the meaning of) any proposition, that is propositional thought itself, ontologically commits us to the intelligibility of reality.[25]

But if reality is intelligible, then all that exists is intelligible, and all that we believe to exist (i.e. the referents of all the propositions that we believe to be true) is intelligible *qua phenomenon* (as in the unfolding of science). Furthermore, if it is an intelligible entity, then it can be said to *exist* only insofar as it is intelligible, for in asserting something is an 'X' we are thereby asserting that – if we don't already – we can, in time, come to understand just what an 'X' is. So in this case its conditions of intelligibility are its conditions of possibility.[26] Accordingly to examine the conditions of intelligibility of that which we believe to be true is to examine its ontological conditions of possibility. This gives us the formulation:

TA_{CRO}: 'Y presupposes P if and only if P must$_I$ be true if Y is *intelligible*'.[27]

Here, the relevant type of necessity is that P is a necessary condition of the intelligibility of the premiss. This differs from TA_{CRS} above in that the necessity is related to the intelligibility of the *phenomenon* described not just the statement describing it, i.e. that, with sufficient conceptual elaboration, we could scientifically explain the phenomenon. I therefore propose the further (but again unavoidable) neologism of 'intellective' necessity, as 'relating to intelligibility'. But this is merely Bhaskar's formulation of the TA. So on the one hand, step 1 here depends on or leads inexorably to step 2, hence my tentative tribute of step 1 to Bhaskar in the 'CRS' subscript nomenclature I am using. But on the other hand, the resolution of the empiricist debate of Quine and Strawson, and its connection with the critical realist argument in step 2, is dependent on step 1, which is what I have outlined in this chapter.

So, returning to our earlier comments, we have seen that in order to be able to make the step of resolving the problem of MR statements in terms of their *possible* reference, we must go further and ask the ontological question of 'what are the conditions of possibility of this *phenomenon*?' (in this case, the problematic phenomenon of meaning being possible reference, which in turn explains the problematic phenomenon of MR statements). Now it may legitimately be asked what is it for a phenomenon to be the premiss of an argument? And how do we investigate its conditions of possibility?

But the answers to these questions are immediately forthcoming from the description above. For, first, to be the premiss the phenomenon must be expressed under a particular description in an intelligible proposition that we also take to be true. But if we take it to be true, we have seen above that we believe that the statement is not only intelligible as a proposition (as is S) but that it is also intelligible as a description of reality, i.e. that the described phenomenon can itself be understood. And we have seen that if the phenomenon is intelligible, then we can examine its conditions of possibility for these are its conditions of intelligibility. But it follows, further, that we can show the relation between meaning and reference is one of mutual conditions of possibility. For, as we saw above, there cannot be meaning unless there is reference, while for reference to be possible, there must be a meaningful proposition that refers. Strawson is thus seen to be halfway there, with the latter insight.

How does this alternative CRO conception of the TA work? The classic example to hand is Bhaskar's (1978) TA from experimental practice. The premiss is that the event regularities needed to test natural scientific hypotheses are only forthcoming in the special and closed conditions of the laboratory, and yet we employ the resultant knowledge of laws of nature outside those conditions where the event regularities do not occur. If we then apply the TA to this premiss, we are examining the necessary conditions of intelligibility of this practice (as thus described), which include that the laws thus discovered in the laboratory cannot themselves be of the form of regularities of events, but must refer to tendencies that exist not at the level of events at all. For if laws refer to events, they only hold in the laboratory. In other words, reality must be stratified. And this is a synthetic *a priori* truth to which anybody who assents to the intelligibility of laboratory science producing knowledge of reality is ontologically committed, *regardless of whether or not they explicitly agree with the conclusion*. Note also that, for reasons I cannot expand upon here, this form of argument is applicable to any social practice, i.e. any practice that depends on intentional agency, including, as herein, the employment of meaning in discourse.

Now if we compare the nature of the so-called 'synthetic *a priori*' conclusion in this case, we see that it is the conclusion of a form of reasoned necessity (hence '*a priori*'), as for Quine and Strawson, but also that this is an *intellective*, and not a logical or analytical, inference, so that it is of quite a different type to the conclusions of their respective TAs. It follows that it stands vindicated as a *sui generis* form of reasoning; one, moreover, that this dialectic of immanent critique from Quine and Strawson reveals to be necessary for *their* conceptual frameworks as well. Finally, I note that I have used this TA in the very process of explicating it, but I refer the reader back to my earlier comments on intensionality. For there is simply no way to present these notions other than to demonstrate them and show their reflexive consistency.

What though is the nature of ontological commitment in this case? Unfortunately, I can offer here only a few of the most obvious differences between this conceptualisation and that of Quine and Strawson. First, let us attend to the sense of the individual terms. For 'ontological' no longer refers to a theory of what (kinds of) things exist but to a theory of the nature of existence *per se*. Similarly, 'commitment' is no longer something that it is *always* possible to alter by revising our explicit beliefs. For while we can, of course, change our beliefs and so alter some of our ontological commitments (as, for instance, when we repudiate those beliefs that commit us to an empirical realist ontology), we cannot renounce *all* our ontological commitments for, as we have seen, some of them arise as the necessary presupposition of the very act of thinking. In other words, some of our ontological commitments are inexorable. It follows that there is not the permanent deferral to a separate empirical investigation as regards these ontological commitments, contrary to Quine and Strawson.

We have also seen that to believe any statement to be true is to believe that the phenomenon described therein is itself intelligible. But this is just to be ontologically committed to the intelligibility of the phenomenon. In other words, the difference between believing a statement to be intelligible *qua* statement (as S is) and true (as S is not) *just is* that in the latter case we are ontologically committed to the intelligibility of the statement's referent. It follows that the ontological conclusions we derive using the TA are ontological commitments precisely because we are *already* ontologically committed, in this new sense, to the premiss, just as we would expect. But, *contra* Quine and Strawson, this prior commitment is sometimes *itself* inexorable given that we think at all.

Finally, then, how do we understand S? Consider our new theory of meaning. The meaningfulness of the statement is a question of the intensional web of meaning in the speaker/auditor's mind in which the necessary conceptual resources exist *already* and are such that they can be combined in a propositional form that renders the resulting statement sensical. This latter criterion is fulfilled when the pre-existing concepts *are really believed to* have real referents (i.e. we are ontologically committed to them) and ones that allow their conjunction, as 'king' and 'pope' in T do not. S thus has reference but only *indirect* reference via the conceptual resources put together to constitute the new statement, and this is merely *possible* reference because whether or not the statement *does* refer can only be ascertained separately and empirically, or rather scientifically, thus including *both* empirical and theoretical moments.[28] Like Strawson, therefore, we are not in any way committed to the existence of an abstract or counterfactual King of France by the meaningfulness of S but, *contra* Strawson, S is believed to have reference, albeit only indirect and possible, and so we can explain its meaningfulness despite our believing that it is without *actual* referent.[29]

Is the TA sufficiently Kantian (to merit the label)?

Finally, let us turn briefly to the third question, *viz*. 'is the 'synthetic *a priori*' thus articulated sufficiently Kantian to merit the title?'[30] Given that the '*a priori*' element refers to necessity, our focus here is on the label 'synthetic' and Kant's reasons for its use.[31] A consideration of the literature on this point reveals that the synthetic has two pre-eminent meanings for Kant. The first reflects the active participation of the mind in the (ontic) construction of the premiss, hence 'synthesis'.[32] But we may also ask, what is being conjoined by the synthesis and hence what is created? I suggest that this is best explained by the formation of connections between meanings or senses (while analysis is the severing of (fallacious) links, as its etymology suggests), which thereby reveal further meanings or senses.

Does the condition of intelligibility formulation of the synthetic *a priori* satisfy these definitions? It is clear that it does. Thus, on the one hand, intelligibility is evidently a notion that involves the active participation of mind,[33] while on the other, proposition P is intelligible just in the case that the meaning of P can be explicated by conceptual links with other meanings. The condition of intelligibility formulation, therefore, does fit the crucial characteristics of Kant's synthetic, and hence the title 'synthetic' is correctly attributed to this explication of the synthetic *a priori*.

Conclusions

We have investigated the arguments concerning the existence of the synthetic *a priori* and thereby connected the arguments of empiricist critics of the notion with those of one of its foremost, if understated, champions, Roy Bhaskar. Furthermore, we have found it to be not such an exotic creature after all. Rather, as though it has been in our back garden all along, it is a perfectly ordinary and, indeed, invaluable element of our thinking toolkit such that the naysayers can only deny its existence while riding on its back.

Whence, then, the feverish anxiety about the synthetic *a priori*? It is clear that this derives more from the Procrustean bed of an empiricist ontology ((b) above) into which its critics have forced it, and thus from those critics themselves, than from any property of its own. Thus abused, it is not surprising in the least that it should transform into some sort of bogeyman; one, moreover, that as inalienable will always be there to haunt its empiricist detractors. Once admitted, however, we see that the synthetic *a priori*, and the TA with which to derive it, poses no threat to the logical (and analytical) necessities beloved of the empiricist. Rather, it can be seen to ground and complement, but not substitute for, these forms of reasoning. I have not argued, thus, that Quine and Strawson were completely wrong but that, by setting their investigations within an empirical realist ontology, they ruled out *ex ante* the only possible route to develop fully the implications of their genuine insights. In short, the present argument is not for the wrong-headedness of empiricism, but for its harmful incompleteness. The acceptance of the synthetic *a priori* is a crucial step towards rectifying this.[34]

Notes

1 One common non-realist interpretation of the TA is as a primarily anti-sceptical device (e.g. Brueckner (1996) and Stroud (1968)).
2 See also Lawson's (2003: 33) 'intelligibility principle'.
3 Compare, for example, the argument of Ross Harrison (1974), of a similar vintage to Bhaskar's (1978) original exposition of the realist TA in *A Realist Theory of Science*. See also e.g. Wilkerson (1970), Kitcher (1995), and Cassam (1987).
4 See, for example, Lawson (1997: 49–50) and Bhaskar (1998: 5).
5 Where the italics compare the mode of inference, and the underlinings compare the premisses.
6 See e.g. Parsons (1999a).
7 See e.g. Guala (2002), Parsons (1999b).
8 See Kant (1781/1953) at B755.
9 See e.g. Strawson (1966) and Walsh (1975).
10 'Also' because we are also ontologically committed to the premiss.
11 See Quine (1980) generally and Quine (1953a, b, c, d) in particular.
12 Where the subscript 'L' denotes logical necessity and the underlining is there to highlight a feature of the definition that merits comparison with other formulations. Note that Quine actually repudiates the concept of logical necessity, as Strawson (1957) notes. Nevertheless, I employ 'must$_L$' if only for the ease of comparison with the subsequent formulations.
13 For example: (1) If P(X) is meaningful and meaning is reference, then P(X) refers. (2) P(X) is meaningful. Therefore (3) P(X) refers. Therefore (4) X exists. And this holds even if P(X), that is the proposition that includes mention of X, states '~X'.
14 Quine (1953a) p. 15. Compare also (p. 13) 'to be assumed as an entity is, purely and simply, to be reckoned as the value of a variable' and (p. 13) 'to be is to be in the range of reference of a pronoun'.
15 See e.g. Grice and Strawson (1956), Strawson (1956), Strawson (1957) and Cartwright (1954).
16 Grice and Strawson (1956) p. 146.
17 Strawson (1950) p. 333.
18 Where the subscript 'A' denotes analytical necessity.
19 There is, of course, a great deal more to say about Strawson's conception of the synthetic *a priori*. See e.g. Stroud (2000). While not affecting the account greatly, my focus here is rather on his conception of presupposition and ontological commitment.
20 For Strawson's analytical account of Kant see Strawson (1966). For arguments against such analytical treatment see e.g. Kitcher (1995), Beck (1967) and Wilkerson (1970).
21 See, e.g., Strawson (1950) p. 329, where meaning and reference are described as 'quite independent'.
22 I note that even Quine admitted sets, which are abstract objects, into his ontology. The point is rather that he does so with great reluctance.
23 Where the subscript 'CRS' is an abbreviation for 'critical realist statement' TA or 'critical realist semantic' TA, and the subscript 'S' denotes semantic necessity.
24 That is, given the presently understood senses of these phrases. Thus statement T above could easily *become* intelligible upon the discovery or invention of a country called 'Pope', as in a children's game. Nevertheless, until that semantic move is made (one, moreover, that is perfectly compatible with this intensional theory of meaning), T is unintelligible.
25 This does *not* mean that reality *is* in fact intelligible, only that we are committed to it being so *if* we believe propositional thought is meaningful and sometimes true.
26 It is in this way that the epistemic and ontic domains, which must generally be kept separate, are connected – itself a necessary condition of the epistemic, for if it is *completely* separated from reality, knowledge cannot be *of* reality and so cannot be *knowl-*

edge at all. While ontic conditions of possibility simply are what they are, regardless of our thoughts about them, it is only insofar as conditions of possibility are conditions of intelligibility that *we can come to know them.*

27   Where 'CRO' stands for 'critical realist ontological' TA and the subscript 'I' denotes intellective necessity. Note also that the premiss in this case has changed from X to Y. For the example of S used throughout this paper, Y might also be denoted 'Y(X)' to illustrate the fact that the premiss is the phenomenon of which statement X is an example.

28   The relevant type of possibility here is 'semantic', i.e. concerned with the meaningfulness of a statement. For the important difference between 'empirical' and 'scientific', see Bhaskar (1978).

29   Note that this is *not* equivalent to actual reference to possible worlds as in the work of David Lewis or Leibniz (see Rescher (1997), Chapters 5 and 7). In that case, statements are taken to *actually* refer to a *possible or counterfactual* reality. The present argument, however, is that statements *possibly* refer to the *one and only* reality, without any need for such hypothetical realities.

30   Compare Viskovatoff (2002).

31   As John Dupré has reminded me, I accept that Kripke (1980) has argued that the *a priori* is not synonymous with necessity. I cannot answer this point in detail here, but I note merely that it seems that Kripke, like Quine, has limited necessity to logical necessity and so is quite correct, on those terms, to point out the existence of contingent *a priori* truths. This, however, poses no threat to the present argument and so I will continue to use the terms interchangeably.

32   See, for example, Hintikka (1972) and Machina (1972).

33   The term 'intelligible' is preferable to 'meaningful' for this reason, in that the former term highlights the fact the meaning resides in the mind.

34   I am particularly grateful to Francesco Guala, John Dupré, Adrian Haddock, the participants of the 2004 IACR conference in Cambridge and two anonymous referees for comments and questions. Any errors that remain are mine alone.

References

Beck, L. W. (1967) 'Can Kant's Synthetic Judgments be Made Analytic?' in *Kant*, R. P. Wolff (ed.), pp. 3–22, New York: Doubleday.

Bhaskar, R. (1978) *A Realist Theory of Science*, Hassocks, UK: Harvester Press.

Bhaskar, R. (1998) *The Possibility of Naturalism*, London and New York: Routledge.

Brueckner, A. L. (1996) 'Modest Transcendental Arguments', *Noûs* Vol. 30, Supplement: Philosophical Perspectives, 10, Metaphysics: 265–280.

Cartwright, R. L. (1954) 'Ontology and the Theory of Meaning', *Philosophy of Science* 21(4):316–325.

Cassam, Q. (1987) 'Transcendental Arguments, Transcendental Synthesis and Transcendental Idealism', *The Philosophical Quarterly* 37(149):355–378.

Grice, H. P. and Strawson, P.F. (1956) 'In Defense of a Dogma', *The Philosophical Review* 65(2):141–158.

Guala, F. (2002) 'Talking About Structures: the 'Transcendental' Argument', unpublished paper delivered to INEM Conference, Stirling, Scotland.

Harrison, R. (1974) *On What There Must Be*, Oxford: Clarendon Press.

Hintikka, J. (1972) 'Transcendental Arguments: Genuine and Spurious', *Noûs* 6(3):274–281.

Kant, I. (1781/1953) *The Critique of Pure Reason*, translated by Norman Kemp Smith, London: Macmillan.

Kitcher, P. (1995) 'Revisiting Kant's Epistemology: Skepticism, Apriority, and Psychologism', *Noûs* 29(3):285–315.

Kripke, S. (1980) *Naming and Necessity*, Oxford: Blackwell.

Lawson, T. (1997) *Economics & Reality*, London and New York: Routledge.

Lawson, T. (2003) *Reorienting Economics*, London and New York: Routledge.

Machina, K. F. (1972) 'Kant, Quine and Human Experience', *The Philosophical Review* 81(4):484-497.

Parsons, S. D. (1999a) 'Why the 'transcendental' in transcendental realism?' in *Critical Realism in Economics*, S. Fleetwood (ed.), pp. 151–168, London and New York: Routledge.

Parsons, S. D. (1999b) 'Economics and Reality: a Philosophical Critique of Transcendental realism', *Review of Political Economy* 11(4):455–466.

Quine W. V. O. (1953a) 'On What There Is', in Quine (1980).

Quine W. V. O. (1953b) 'Two Dogmas of Empiricism', in Quine (1980).

Quine W. V. O. (1953c) 'Notes on the Theory of Reference', in Quine (1980).

Quine W. V. O. (1953d) 'Logic and the Reification of Universals', in Quine (1980).

Quine W. V. O. (1960) *Word and Object*, Cambridge, Massachusetts: Harvard University Press.

Quine, W. V. O. (1980) *From a Logical Point of View* (2nd Edition), Cambridge, Massachusetts and London: Harvard University Press.

Rescher, N. (1997) *Profitable Speculations*, Lanham, Maryland: Rowman & Littlefield Publishers, Inc.

Strawson, P. F. (1950) 'On Referring', *Mind* 59(235):320–344.

Strawson, P. F. (1954) 'A Reply to Mr. Sellars', *The Philosophical Review* 63(2):216–231.

Strawson, P. F. (1956) 'Singular Terms, Ontology and Identity', *Mind* 65(260):433–454.

Strawson, P. F. (1957) 'Propositions, Concepts and Logical Truths', *The Philosophical Quarterly* 7(26) 15–25.

Strawson, P. F. (1966) *The Bounds of Sense*, London: Methuen.

Stroud, B. (1968) 'Transcendental Arguments', *The Journal of Philosophy* 65(9):241–256.

Stroud, B. (2000) 'The Synthetic A Priori in Strawson's Kantianism', in *Understanding Human Knowledge*, pp. 224–243, Oxford: Oxford University Press.

Viskovatoff, A. (2002) 'Critical Realism and Kantian Transcendental Arguments', *Cambridge Journal of Economics* 26:697-708.

Walsh, W. H. (1975) *Kant's Criticism of Metaphysics*, Edinburgh: Edinburgh University Press.

Wilkerson, T. E. (1970) 'Transcendental Arguments', *The Philosophical Quarterly* 20(80) Special Review Number: 200–212.

10 Re-examining Bhaskar's three ontological domains: the lessons from emergence

Dave Elder-Vass

Introduction[1]

Although Roy Bhaskar's ontology in *A Realist Theory of Science* (Bhaskar 1978) is explicitly stratified into a hierarchy of levels, he makes relatively little attempt to examine the basis of this stratification, or its implications for his three domains of the empirical, the actual and the real (Collier 1994: 130). This chapter attempts to remedy that deficiency, by investigating the nature of a stratified reality based on emergence, and considering how this impacts our understanding of experiences, events, entities, and causes. Bhaskar uses 'stratification' to indicate two quite different ontological schemes: the stratification of the world into emergent explanatory levels, which I shall call *level stratification*, and the division of ontology into domains, which I shall call *domain stratification*. It is the relation between these two different schemes that is the central theme of this chapter.

I hasten to emphasise that my objective here is primarily to refine Bhaskar's argument, and to repackage it in a form that provides greater clarity, rather than to undermine or contest its essential content. My argument in no way conflicts, for example, with claims for the existence of level stratification, or with the need to separate causal powers from actual causation and both from empirical experience. What this chapter does seek to do, on the other hand, is to add some depth to the characterisation of experiences, events and entities, and to examine their relationship to Bhaskar's ontological domains. Ultimately this will lead it to question the nature of Bhaskar's distinction between the domains of the actual and the real, and to consider an alternative way of looking at this distinction.

The chapter will begin by introducing the key terms: Bhaskar's three domains, the concept of emergence, and two different ways of looking at multilayered entities and events. It will then move on in turn to discuss the implications of level stratification for events, entities, causes and experiences. Finally it will bring together the threads of the argument to re-evaluate Bhaskar's three domains.

Bhaskar's three domains

In *A Realist Theory of Science*, Bhaskar argues from the intelligibility of experimental activity to the conclusion that 'there is an *ontological* distinction between scientific laws and patterns of events' (Bhaskar 1978: 12). Such laws depend upon the existence of 'natural mechanisms', and 'it is only if we make the assumption of the real independence of such mechanisms from the events they generate that we are justified in assuming that they endure and go on acting in their normal way outside the experimentally closed conditions that enable us to empirically identify them' (p. 13). Similarly, 'events must occur independently of the experiences in which they are apprehended. Structures and mechanisms then are real and distinct from the patterns of events that they generate; just as events are real and distinct from the experiences in which they are apprehended. Mechanisms, events and experiences thus constitute three overlapping domains of reality, viz. the domains of the *real*, the *actual* and the *empirical*' (p. 56). The relationship between these domains is summarised in a table, reproduced below as Figure 10.1.

Bhaskar clearly intends the domain of the empirical to be a subset of the domain of the actual, which in turn is a subset of the domain of the real (Bhaskar 1978: Note to Table 1, p. 56; Bhaskar 1993: 207). We can represent these inclusion relations in a Venn diagram (see Figure 10.2).

Emergence and its basis

The second element of Bhaskar's ontology with which this chapter will engage is the stratification of the intransitive world into levels – the atomic, the molecular, the biological and the like. This level stratification depends upon the phenomenon of emergence, which is most simply described as the relationship which makes it possible for a whole to be more than the sum of its parts. Bhaskar himself defines emergence as 'the relationship between two terms such that one diachronically, or perhaps synchronically, arises out of the other, but is capable of reacting back on the first and is in any event causally and taxonomically irreducible to it, as society is to nature or mind to matter' (Bhaskar 1994: 73).

To put it more simply, emergence occurs when a whole has properties or powers that are not possessed by its parts. In this sense, the concept of emergence is inherently compositional, in the sense that higher-level entities always emerge from collections of lower-level entities that are their components or parts.[3, 4]

	Domain of Real	Domain of Actual	Domain of Empirical
Mechanisms	X		
Events	X	X	
Experiences	X	X	X

Figure 10.1 Bhasker's three domains: populating entities (Bhaskar 1978: p. 130).

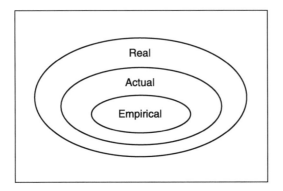

Figure 10.2   Bhaskar's three domains: inclusion relations.

But how is emergence possible? If we accept that emergent wholes have properties that are not possessed by their parts, then where do those properties come from?

Like many others, I argue that they come from the organisation of the parts, from the maintenance of a stable set of relations between the parts that constitute them into a particular kind of whole (Archer 1982: 475; Cilliers 1998: 43; Cunningham 2001: S68; Emmeche *et al.*, 1997: 106; Lloyd Morgan 1923: 64; Sawyer 2001: 560; Sperry 1986: 266).[5] Thus it is the fact that a higher-level entity is composed of a *particular stable organisation* of lower-level entities that gives it the possibility of exerting causal influence in its own right. In other words, it is the set of relations between the lower-level entities that makes them 'more than the sum of their parts'. Only when this particular kind of part is present in this particular set of relations to each other does the higher level entity exist, and only when this particular kind of part is present in this particular set of relations to each other do they have the causal impacts that are characteristic of the higher-level entity. As Archer puts it, 'Emergent properties are therefore relational: they are not contained in the elements themselves, but could not exist apart from them' (Archer 1982: 475). Note that a higher-level entity is only emergent when it just so happens that, when a set of lower level entities is so organised as to create it, the resulting entity has a consistent causal impact that is not a simple summation of the impacts of its components. Now, the particular causal influences that any particular entity type may exert, and the way in which the presence of its parts in the required relations produce these higher-level effects, are a matter for the particular science of the case – we cannot go any further at the philosophical level in explaining why particular cases of emergence work.

We can go further, however, in identifying another general prerequisite for emergence. As the existence of the whole is inseparable from the continuing presence of the required parts in the required arrangement, then emergence itself depends upon the set of causes that maintain a set of such parts in just such an arrangement. Bhaskar has commented on the dual aspect of emergence as a synchronic and diachronic relation; but the diachronic aspect of his account seems to relate to the original creation of the new level of reality. While this original creation is clearly necessary, the maintenance of the particular entities that constitute that new level is equally important. There is not only a set of causes that brings the entity about, but also a further (possibly overlapping) set that maintains its continuing existence – what I will call, after Buckley, its *morphostatic causes* (Archer 1982: 480, n8; Buckley 1998: 53). It is these causes that are responsible for the stability or persistence of the entity.

The role of these morphostatic explanations of continuity of structure is critical to emergence. Any number of accidental combinations of lower-level entities may be brought about by a vast range of morphogenetic causes over the course of time, but it is only those combinations that have continuity of structure that persist. At any time, it is possible that a more powerful morphogenetic cause may overcome the morphostatic causes for any given entity. At this point, the emergence of the higher level entity is dissolved. It is the ability of morphostatic causes to resist such effects that sustains the existence of higher-level entities and hence any emergent properties they may have. But this continuing existence is always dependent upon the uncertain outcome of the ongoing tension between these different types of cause.[6]

Emergence, then, is the outcome of a process by which a set of morphostatic causes, which may be both internal and external, sustain a set of lower-level entities in relationships that constitute them into a stably organised higher-level entity that can as a result exercise powers that are not possessed by its component entities either in isolation or in an unstructured aggregation.

Level abstracted and downwardly inclusive views

One implication of emergence is that entities with emergent properties or powers are themselves composed of other such entities, which are in turn so composed, and so on.[7] A plant, for example, consists of cells, the cells consist of molecules, the molecules consist of atoms, and so on. Any given entity, then, can be seen as internally stratified into many different levels or layers, each level representing sets of parts that are combined into the entities at the next level up.

Now, for most purposes, when we discuss any given entity we are in the habit of ignoring the role of its parts. To treat an entity in this way is to take what I propose to call a *level abstracted* view of it – i.e. a view that considers the effects of the whole entity in isolation from the existence or effects of its parts. I will argue in this chapter, however, that for other purposes we sometimes need to treat a whole entity quite explicitly as a stratified ensemble of parts at various ontological levels. This is to take what I call a *downwardly inclusive* view of the entity. These two terms are illustrated in Figure 10.3.

Here, L1 represents the highest level of a whole – to continue the example, a plant. L2 represents the first decomposition of the whole into its parts – in this case, perhaps, the cells of the plant, and the relations between them that consti-

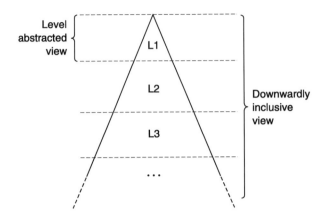

Figure 10.3 Internal stratification.

tute them into a whole plant. L3 represents the next decomposition – here, the molecules that make up the cells and the relevant relations between them. And the pyramid may continue downwards, until its base is lost in the mists of our limited understanding of sub-quantum science. Of course, a plant is not made up of the whole plant *plus* its cells *plus* its molecules, and so on; each of these levels represents a different decomposition of the same whole; it is only our view of the plant that must sometimes encompass the recognition that the whole plant is simultaneously each of these different decompositions.

With these preliminaries completed, we can now turn to examining the nature of the elements that inhabit Bhaskar's three domains in a level stratified world.

Experiences

Let me begin with experiences. There are two key factors that influence the shape of our experiences.

First, as Bhaskar tells us, 'Experiences, and the facts they ground, are social products' (Bhaskar 1978: 57). Experiences are social products because our experiences are not simply a set of sense-data, but rather the result of our application of a socially influenced conceptual framework to the interpretation of that sense-data. Our eyes may detect a pattern of colours; but what we experience is 'seeing' a set of meaningful objects behaving in meaningful ways. It is in this interpolation of our conceptual frameworks between sense data and 'experience' that experiences become 'social products'. Hence 'experiences' are no longer purely the outcome of the events they might appear to reflect, but rather a product of the combination of those events with our prior knowledge.

Second, our experiences, despite being interpreted, are constructed on the basis of our sense perceptions. Those sense perceptions are inevitably limited to impressions of those segments of reality that we are capable of perceiving with the senses we possess, as augmented by any artificial tools that are available.

Now, the combined effect of this process of interpretation and our restricted perceptual (and perhaps cognitive) abilities is that we generally perceive reality as 'flat' in the sense that our experiences are interpreted as impressions of entities at a single level of stratification. When we perceive the human being, we do not simultaneously and inseparably perceive the organs, the cells, the molecules that make them up. If we perceive the cells of a living tissue under a microscope, we do not simultaneously and inseparably perceive the organ or the organism to which they belong.

Thus, our experiences are already, through the process of abstraction that is inherent to perception, and as a result of the limited slice of reality to which our senses give us access, level abstracted views of what is in actuality an inherently multi-levelled occurrence.

Events

Now, because of the nature of our experiences, our everyday (empirical) concept of an 'event', which we take to be the naturally given subject of any explanation in science, is itself an abstraction from reality. Thus, when we say, for example, 'the pen fell on the floor', we are already, in framing our reportage of the event, making an assumption about which abstraction from what was happening in a multi-level stream of interconnected happenings is the one that is relevant and requires explanation. We could have looked at the same happenings and chosen to explain the behaviour of the molecules or atoms involved, or the writing process or the world-historical events or the social history of which the falling of the pen formed a part. But in selecting out one of these happenings from the rest as the thing to be explained, we have already created the illusion that this is an event that can be given an explanation in its own right, independently of its component events and of the larger events of which it forms a part: here we have a *level abstracted view of the event*.

In seeing events as level abstracted, we implicitly frame the (retroductive) question of how they are caused in a way that demands explanations of a particular form – in a way that pushes us into thinking in terms only of a particular stratum or level of organisation.[8] But any causal account of an event seen in level abstracted terms forms only part of a larger picture. A more complete explanation can always be provided by re-integrating the event into the larger stratified picture of which it forms a part, and relating its explanation to the explanations of the other events in which it is inextricably implicated, either as subset or superset.

Now, I suggest that the way to make sense of causal explanations of individual events in this context, where an event is defined as the behaviour of a given entity at a given time, is to allow that every event inescapably includes the behaviour of the composing lower level entities as well (Lloyd Morgan 1923: 15). To view an event in these terms is to see it in *downwardly inclusive* terms. It might seem that we could also look at the event in *upwardly inclusive terms*, in which sense it would also include the behaviour of all the higher level entities of which the first entity is a part. But this seems inherently infeasible, given the indeterminate (and indeterminately large) range of higher-level entities that may be part of this set, all the way up to the universe itself. There is no apparent reason why our interest in the falling of a pen, for example, should also require us to be interested in that complete set of higher level events, even for metaphysical purposes. We may, of course, be interested in some *particular* higher-level event of which the falling of the pen is part, but if that is so we can take a downwardly inclusive view of that higher level event, which will include the behaviour of the pen. As a general rule, then, we need not take an upwardly inclusive view of an entity or event.

Hence, in explaining a downwardly inclusively conceived event, we recognise, for example, that when a pen drops, it is inseparably part of this event that the components composing the pen remain in a set of relationships through which they constitute the pen, and behave in whatever ways are required for the pen to drop. This is the inevitable consequence of the set of morphostatic causes whose operation must be present for the pen to exist as such through the entire course of this event. Thus, the various material parts of the pen go through a set of events that forms part of the higher (downwardly inclusively conceived) event, the molecules that compose those parts go through another set that also forms part of the higher events, and so on through the atoms, subatomic particles, and so forth. Given that we do not have fully adequate understandings of the lower end of this spectrum, we must accept that only partial descriptions and hence only partial explanations are possible of the lower-level set of events that composes the higher level event. For most practical purposes we can and indeed must ignore the lower levels of this hierarchy, but for the purpose of understanding the ontology of events and causation we must recognise their significance.

If we wish to understand the role of emergence in individual events, and the relations between causes at different emergent levels, then, the correct (downwardly inclusive) account of individual events is inherently level stratified. We need to recognise that the events which populate Bhaskar's 'domain of the actual' are downwardly inclusive and multi-levelled. This clearly corresponds to Bhaskar's conception of the actual as that domain of reality in which a vast range of particular causes interact to cause events. And on my account the actual includes not only events that are unobserved by virtue of the absence of an observer, but also those levels of multi-levelled events that are unobserved by virtue of operating below (or above) the perceived levels of reality.

Entities

Now, events involve the behaviour of things, or entities. Like events, entities are inherently and inclusively multi-levelled, but when we label them in empirical experience, and also when we employ them in causal statements, we typically abstract from most of those levels.

Where do entities fit in Bhaskar's three domains? If events are constituted by the behaviour of entities, and if (downwardly inclusive) events belong in the domain of the actual, then it would seem clear that (downwardly inclusive) entities must also belong in the actual. Indeed, at one point Bhaskar indicates that 'the domain of actualities ... may be extended to include things as well as events' (Bhaskar 1978: 32). The claim that what we experience is a subset of the actual would also seem to support this argument – clearly we can experience things as well as events,[9] and hence the portrayal of the empirical domain as a subset of the actual domain would be incoherent if things were considered real but not actual.

However, Bhaskar also identifies causation with 'relatively enduring structures and mechanisms' that are 'nothing other than the ways of acting of things' (Bhaskar 1978: 14); or to put it in other words, 'the generative mechanisms of nature exist as the causal powers of things' (Bhaskar 1978: 50) (Lawson 1997: 21). Now for Bhaskar, causal powers and generative mechanisms exist in the domain of the real, but not in the actual, and this could be taken to imply that the same is true of entities. Since causal powers exist *only* as emergent features of entities, it is hard to see how these causal powers could exist in a different ontological domain from the entities of which they are features.

Fleetwood seems to imply something similar when he argues that 'when ... one writes that *a mechanism has a tendency to x*, one is, in reality, referring to the ensemble of structures, powers, and relations: it is, strictly speaking, the ensemble that has a tendency to *x*. Once understood, however, there is no harm in shortening the phrase by omitting reference to structures, powers and relations' (Fleetwood 2001: 211). We can translate this into the language of emergence by equating 'ensembles' with higher-level entities whose components are lower-level entities and the relations between them. Fleetwood's argument thus translates into the claim that mechanisms are simply a level abstracted view of a multi-levelled entity. If a mechanism simply *is* an ensemble of structures, powers and relations, then it *is* an entity – and it becomes yet clearer that if mechanisms are real but not actual, then so must be entities.

This, however, would seem to lead to a contradiction: one part of the argument entails that entities exist in the domain of the actual, whereas another seems to imply that they exist in the domain of the real but not in the domain of the actual. There are several possible responses to this contradiction; this chapter will only discuss what seems to me the most plausible interpretation of Bhaskar's intention.[10]

This response is to insist that *actual* entities *do* possess *real* (but *non actual*) causal powers – in other words, that a thing's 'way of acting' can exist in a different ontological domain from the thing itself. This would require a repudiation of Fleetwood's direct identification of mechanisms with ensembles, but could potentially be made consistent with Bhaskar's looser formulation. Given that the three domains of Bhaskar's ontology describe classes of what *exists*, this also rests on causal powers 'existing' in a somewhat different sense than entities, events and experiences. I shall return critically to evaluate this way of resolving the contradiction in a later section, but first it is necessary to discuss in a little more detail the relation between the real and the actual in the critical realist account of cause.

Real causes and actual causation

Bhaskar's account of cause in *A Realist Theory of Science* is focused on the role of causal mechanisms, which he identifies as part of the domain of the real (Bhaskar 1978: 13). As we have seen, these mechanisms 'exist as the causal powers of things' (Bhaskar 1978: 50). In such situations, we can, as Fleetwood suggests, work successfully with an abstracted ontology that ignores the fact that each entity or thing is composed of a variety of levels of lower entities, and simply sees it as existing at a specific level of organisation. The composition of the entities we seek to explain (or use as causal factors) is simply one of the many things that we abstract from in formulating laws. It therefore seems in the resulting generalisations that the entities which 'cause' and whose behaviour is 'caused' are free-floating level abstracted entities that are autonomous of their component parts, and that can be treated in those causal accounts as if they had no component parts at all.

Such a level-abstracted conception of cause is perfectly usable and indeed positively desirable in the process of formulating theoretical laws. It also works quite reliably in many practical applications, both everyday and scientific, when level abstracted views of causation often seem to reflect what is going on well enough to provide us with reliable explanations and hence expectations. However, as Bhaskar himself recognises in more recent work, it is quite inappropriate for the discussion of what is happening over multiple levels when we turn to causation at the level of individual instances:

> unlike theoretical explanation in at least many of the natural sciences, viz. from explanatory significant structures to their higher-order structural explanation, applied explanation of concrete singulars, like changes in a particular [entity], are a much messier affair … An event e at a level L is as likely to be (multiply) explained by elements at the same and lower-order levels in addition to higher-order (deeper) ones, and/or even laterally, diagonally, tangentially (Bhaskar 1993: 133).

Let me now use an example to show why level abstracted causal accounts are inadequate to the causal explanation of individual events over multiple levels. Consider the case of photosynthesis by a plant. In certain circumstances which need not detain us here, many plants 'convert' carbon dioxide from the atmosphere into oxygen. At the highest level of the event (i.e. a case of photosynthesis) we may simply say that it was caused by the power the plant has to photosynthesise. Many useful explanations may indeed rest on this power, and a scientist could investigate, for example, the differential rates at which plants produce oxygen in different contexts without worrying about how photosynthesis worked at the cellular or molecular level.

But there are some parts of the event concerned that would inevitably remain unexplained by such an account. At another level (the molecular), the process of photosynthesis is a chemical reaction, and we could not explain either *how* photosynthesis works or *which* lower level parts of the entities involved are affected, and in what way, without looking at this process at the molecular level. This would not be an account of a different event, but a different account of the same event – one that is abstracted at a different level from the whole event.

And yet, the lower-level account still gives us only a partial account of the causal process at work here, because any explanation at only the molecular level will miss the key *higher-level* causal factors which are also necessary for the event to occur. Thus, these molecules would not have been brought into an arrangement that made this chemical reaction possible unless they had been organised into the form of the plant in the first place (with organisation into cells as an equally essential middle level). Furthermore, the same molecules blended into a soup would no longer have the causal power of photosynthesis, which arises from their organisation into the form of a plant. The causal power of photosynthesis thus belongs to the plant and not to the molecules, but to provide a complete causal explanation of what happens when photosynthesis occurs we need a causal account that operates at multiple levels simultaneously, invoking both the causal powers of the plant and the causal powers of its molecules.

In other words, it is impossible to explain fully the causation of the event except as the outcome of a causal interaction between the whole 'pyramids' – between the entities concerned, viewed in downwardly inclusive terms – and not just the single points at the top – the same entities viewed in level abstracted terms.[11]

We can see why this is a useful way to look at causation if we consider the problem posed to level abstracted accounts by multiple realisability, i.e. in cases where the higher-level outcome is consistent with a variety of different lower-level configurations. Such accounts are underdetermined, in that they can provide an account of the change that occurred at a higher-level, but not an account of how the implicit lower-level changes occurred, thus leaving the higher level change floating unsecured without any confidence in how its components could have been brought to a state consistent with it. Downwardly inclusive accounts, by contrast, resolve this underdetermination since the whole range of states of all the component entities and sub-entities involved in the multi-levelled event are available to contribute to the causation of the lower-level changes.

Of course, each of the interactions at the lower levels can also be considered as inclusive events in their own right, so the higher-level event is at least partially composed of a whole set of smaller pyramidal events. Now as a result of this, a reductionist might argue that the inclusive account suffers from the opposite problem to that discussed in the previous paragraph: it may seem to be overdetermined,[12] if we believe that the higher-level entities are no more than the sum of their parts, and lower-level explanations are available for the behaviour of each of those parts. In this case, it would seem that causes at the higher-level are redundant to the explanation of the event, since the lower level causes do all the causing that is needed to produce it.

But there are a number of problems with this reductionist claim. First, the meanings of some of the terms that describe the events to be explained may be incoherent at a lower level. Many animals can 'see' things, for example, but the concept of 'seeing' is meaningless when reduced to the behaviour of organs or cells. It is hard to see how lower-level explanations of a concept that is meaningless at the lower level can be complete. Second, there will generally be features of the higher-level entity that are contingent on the relations between its components, and not just their separate presences summed; and it is the addition of these relations as an ongoing feature that distinguishes the higher-level entity from the mere collection of lower-level ones. A causal account of the lower-level entities will not explain the higher-level entity unless we go beyond that causal account to explain the set of relations between them too, and when we do this we have reintroduced the higher-level entity into the explanation. Third, even the separate presences of those component entities in a particular situation are often difficult to account for except as the consequence of their being part of the higher-level entity concerned. Why do we find this particular collection of lower-level entities or events present in the first place, and not some other, perhaps random, collection? Why, because it is precisely this collection that constitutes the higher-level entity and is held together by its morphostatic causes.

The causation of events thus operates across the whole pyramid of entities and sub-entities involved, not at a single level of it. Events, in all their multi-levelled glory, are the products of a combination of a variety of causal mechanisms operating on the prior state of the set of entities involved in the event. In Bhaskar's account, this 'individual instance causation' (which is of course interlinked with other individual instances of causation) occurs within the domain of the actual, but it is the consequence of the interaction of the real (but not actual) causal mechanisms or powers of the entities involved.

These causal powers exist as emergent properties of the entities that possess them. Because they emerge at a specific level (e.g. the ability to photosynthesise belongs only to the plant as a whole; the molecules or cells of the plant couldn't photosynthesise if they were not organised into the form of a plant), then it is entirely reasonable to think of them in level abstracted terms. Nevertheless, they can only lead to actual events when they are combined with a multiplicity of causal mechanisms from other levels of the ontological strata. Thus 'real' causal powers can be described in a level-abstracted form, while 'actual' causation always occurs in the form of multi-levelled events. We may for some purposes be able to provide perfectly adequate explanations of these events that neglect many of the levels involved – perhaps even all but one. But when we wish to discuss questions concerning the relationship between different levels – such as the questions of emergence and reduction – we cannot do so in purely level-abstracted terms, but must recognise the *inherent* inter-relatedness of the different levels.

Multiple determination

Bhaskar himself addresses this question of the contribution of causes operating at different levels through a concept which he calls 'dual control', 'multiple control' or 'multiple determination'. In considering actual natural and social events, he argues, we must accept that different causal mechanisms and the interactions between them account for different aspects of the events concerned, and that no single law 'determines' the whole result:

> Laws leave the field of the ordinary phenomena of life at least partially open … To say that laws situate limits but do not dictate what happens within them does not mean that it is not possible to completely explain what happens within them. The question 'how is constraint without determination possible' is equivalent to the question how 'can a thing, event or process be controlled by several different kinds of principle at once?' To completely account for an event would be to describe all the different principles involved in its generation. A complete explanation in this sense is clearly a limit concept. In an historical explanation of an event, for example, we are not normally interested in (or capable of giving an account of) its physical structure (Bhaskar 1978: 110–111).

This is not just a statement about the relationship between different levels of stratification, but rather a more general discussion of the nature of actual causation. But Bhaskar makes the link to level stratification explicit in a more recent work: 'Emergence makes possible the important phenomena of *dual* and *multiple control*' (Bhaskar 1994: 75). It is precisely because 'the [actual] ordinary phenomena of the world' are inherently multi-layered, that we need to bring to bear different (real) single-layered causal mechanisms to explain different aspects of them. Thus explanation at each level, in the 'area of autonomy' left by the incomplete explanations at other levels, requires a 'putatively independent science' of that level (Bhaskar 1978: 114). And it is in combining all these level-specific explanations of the different levels of a particular multi-layered event that we 'completely account for an event'. Although, of course, because we do not have viable sciences of every level, we can only produce incomplete subsets of the 'complete' multi-layered account, which is why such a complete account can be seen only as 'a limit concept'.

To put this in my terms: in decomposing the behaviour of a downwardly inclusive entity across its ontological levels, it is the organisation that appears at each level, the set of relations between the relevant lower-level entities, that is the 'extra' piece of explanatory information that appears at that level; and this is what makes the 'multiple determination' approach viable. We attribute a portion of the causal influence on a particular event to the set of relations between parts that constitute the organisation of the topmost level, a portion to the set at the next level down, and so on. This allows us to construct causal accounts of multi-levelled single instance causation in which all the levels of the prior situation can have an appropriate influence on the various levels of the outcome. In this model, any insistence on 'explanatory priority' for any particular level becomes nothing more than a metaphysical prejudice.

It is worth noting that this conception of multiple determination is also required by the transcendental argument from the nature of experimental science.

The most obvious causal regularity in experimental situations is the causal impact that the intervention of the experimenter has on the results of the experiment. Clearly there is a sense in which the experimenter 'causes' the results of the experiment (Bhaskar 1978: 33). It is only when we have a concept like 'multiple determination' that allows different mechanisms at different levels to contribute to the determination of a multi-layered event that there is room for any other sort of cause to operate in experimental conditions as well as the causal input of the experimenter. Since experimental science works on the assumption that such other causes are in fact at work in experimental situations it also assumes that multiple determination is a feature of the world.

Multi-levelled causation of the actual, then, is an unavoidable feature of Bhaskar's ontology.

The consequences for Bhaskar's three domains

Let me now pull together and round out the implications of the foregoing for the three domains of Bhaskar's ontology.

There is relatively little to be said here about the empirical domain. In the context of level stratification, it is important to recognise that our experiences take the form of level abstracted views of a multi-levelled reality. This is the result of the combination of two factors: the inherent limitations of our perceptual tools, and the interpretive habits that are integrated into the very process of perception. Now, it is of course true that this form of perception is enormously effective in practical situations, or it would not have been favoured by biological evolution. And this effectiveness in turn derives from the fact that in many practical situations we can afford to ignore levels of stratification other than those we are in the habit of perceiving. Level-abstracted perception and indeed level-abstracted approaches to the causation of everyday behaviour work well for normal human purposes.

But science seeks to go beyond this type of understanding of the world we live in, and in delving into other layers of our level stratified world it reveals that there is more to events than meets the eye. An event at any given level is inseparably also made up of a set of events at lower levels (and may be a part of other events at higher levels). The theory of emergence enables us to see that if we want to explain a multi-levelled event then there will be a whole set of causal mechanisms involved, all operating simultaneously at multiple levels. If we wish to understand the relations between causes at different emergent levels we need to re-integrate these partial explanations with the other levels that are inseparably part of the same event, in what I have called a downwardly inclusive causal account. These multi-levelled events are the inhabitants of Bhaskar's domain of the actual. Other than qualifying the treatment of level stratification, then, the consideration of events here has no significant consequences for Bhaskar's three domains.

When we come to consider entities, however, the consequences are more significant. As we have seen above, there are good reasons to believe that entities belong in Bhaskar's domain of the actual – but there are also good reasons to believe that they belong in the non-actual portion of his domain of the real. Earlier, I introduced one possible approach to resolving this apparent contradiction, which seems in keeping with Bhaskar's intention. I will argue below, however, that this approach can not succeed.

The strategy adopted in this approach is to argue that entities belong unambiguously in the domain of the actual, but that actual entities can and do possess real causal powers. Here, the causal powers of an entity exist in a different domain from the entity itself. Since Bhaskar clearly locates the 'mechanisms' underlying causal powers in the non-actual real, he must mean something different than Fleetwood by the term mechanism. Rather than identifying 'mechanism' with the ensemble of parts and relations that constitute the (actual) entity possessing the powers, which would be incoherent if mechanisms are not in the actual, he must mean to identify 'mechanism' with something like 'the way in which the relations between the parts produce the causal powers of the whole'. This is indeed a useful description of the concept of mechanism, and exactly the sort of description we would expect in an emergent account of level-stratified reality.

Nevertheless it is clear that such a mechanism is not a separate thing from the entity that possesses it, but rather a consequence of how it is put together. Furthermore, it is also clear that this conception of *real* mechanism is closely analogous to the process of *actual* causation.[13] In actual causation, any given event is the outcome of the actual interaction between the real causal powers of those entities causally involved in it, and the net outcome of these interactions depends upon the (purely temporary) relations in which these entities stand to each other at the time. This is directly analogous to the generation of the causal powers of a particular type of entity, which is the outcome of the interaction between the causal powers of its parts. The primary difference is that in the first case, the relations between the entities concerned are contingent and temporary, whereas in the second, the same set of significant relations is maintained over time as a result of the operation of morphostatic causes that maintain the structural stability of the entity, and hence there is a level of consistency in these causal powers over time.

Real and actual causation both therefore appear to be consequences of the same generic type of structural relation: the (diachronic) causal consequences that flow from a given set of entities existing (synchronically) in a given set of relations to each other. Real causal powers, on this account, are distinguished from ordinary instances of actual causation because (a) they provide only part of the explanation of any given event; (b) they may not be active in any given case; and (c) they are present consistently in all instances of the type of entity that possesses them.

The first and third of these differences, however, provide no obvious basis for declaring causal powers non-actual. In the first case, if the causation of an event occurs in the domain of the actual, we might reasonably expect the parts that combine to produce it to occur in the same domain. In the third, a consistent feature of an actual entity would seem at first sight to be actual too. It is the second difference upon which Bhaskar's argument rests: that causal powers constitute a separate ontological domain from actual causation because causal powers may be unexercised or unrealised in any particular actual case, and hence have an existence that is independent of actual *events*.

But once we recognise that entities are also part of the domain of the actual, as is done in the 'actual entities with real causal powers' argument under discussion, it is clear that the existence of a causal power can *not* be independent of the existence of an actual *entity*.[14] It is not the existence but only the *operation* of a causal power that is distinct from its instantiation in a particular actual entity. This suggests that the attribution of causal powers to a separate ontological domain overstates the separation between causal powers on the one hand, and the domain of actual entities, causation, and events on the other. Causal powers, like actual causation, are the consequence of the interaction of actual entities, and both are intimately tied to the existence of particular sets of entities.

The distinction between the two, however, is still important and useful. The identification of causal powers that can be combined in cases of actual causation becomes a technique for breaking down the analysis of causation into manageable chunks that can be separately investigated by scientists. This is indeed the obvious application of Bhaskar's analysis of cause, and I continue to believe that it is a very valuable one, but it is hard to see how this justifies the treatment of causal powers as existing in a separate ontological domain from the actual entities that possess them or from the closely analogous process of actual causation.

My argument therefore suggests a methodological as opposed to an ontological division of actual causation from causal powers. This division still enables us to analyse cases of actual causation by identifying the entities involved and their characteristic emergent causal powers, then investigating how those powers combined to produce multi-levelled actual events. This may, after all, be all that Bhaskar hoped to achieve from the domain stratification of his ontology.[15]

Conclusion

I believe that many of the difficulties of existing approaches to emergence and reduction stem from the inappropriate application of a level-abstracted ontology. I have sought to demonstrate that Bhaskar's depth ontology, as enhanced and, I hope, clarified in this chapter, offers part of the solution to this problem. Conversely, I have also sought to show that the careful study of emergence can enrich Bhaskar's ontology.

On the one hand, depth ontology's division of actual events from emergent causal powers is an essential prerequisite for the understanding of causation in a multi-levelled world. On the other, when we need to take full account of the level stratification of the world, it seems that we need to see *actual* events and entities as inherently multi-levelled, whereas it is appropriated to see *real* causal powers (as well as *empirical* experiences) in level abstracted terms. It is thus only by combining causal mechanisms from a number of different levels that we can provide an adequate causal account of a downwardly inclusive event. This seems consistent with what Bhaskar anticipates in his account of multiple determination.

Having said this, it seems to me that there is still much more work to be done on this question of the relationships between and among levels in causal accounts, a question which is fundamental to understanding emergence and causation. Having understood that emergence is important, we need to examine in more detail just how it works, following in a tangential sense Bhaskar's own advice: 'When a stratum of reality has been adequately described the next step consists in the discovery of the mechanisms responsible for behaviour at that level' (Bhaskar 1978: 169). The outcome of such an exercise may well lead us to conclude that the higher stratum had not been adequately described in the first place. In a similar way, examination of the mechanisms of emergence may alter our perception of the nature of emergence itself and its ontological role, as I hope I have already demonstrated in this chapter.

Notes

1 I would like to thank Jason Edwards, the participants at the IACR 2004 conference, and three anonymous referees for their useful comments on earlier drafts of this chapter.

2 I assume the reader has a certain degree of familiarity with some of Bhaskar's concepts, notably the transitive/intransitive distinction.

3 Bhaskar sometimes uses 'higher' and 'lower' in the opposite sense to this, but I shall maintain the usage that 'lower' entities are components of 'higher' entities for the sake of consistency with most other work on emergence.

4 Although sometimes critical realists seem to adopt a compositional definition of emergence (see, for example, Collier 1998: 264) at other times this is denied (e.g. Bhaskar 1978: 169; Collier 1994: 116). I defend the compositional approach against Collier's argument in Elder-Vass (2005). The compositional approach is implicit in virtually all of the non-critical-realist literature cited in this paper.

5 Useful histories of the concept of emergence can be found in McLaughlin (1992) and Blitz (1992).

6 There is a useful role in the explanation of morphostasis for concepts like 'negative feedback' from cybernetics and 'strange attractors' from complexity theory. Some realists have sought to explain morphostasis in terms of the necessity of 'internal relations' (e.g. Archer 1995: 173; Sayer 1992: 119). This is useful where it is taken to mean that certain combinations of parts tend by *natural* necessity to hold together; but not when it is read as a claim for the *logical* necessity of certain relations. I intend to discuss this question in more depth elsewhere.

7 It is not clear in the current state of science whether this nesting proceeds indefinitely or whether there is some lowest level of entity that will eventually be reached in this series of progressive decompositions. We can ignore this question for the purposes of the argument presented here.

8 On retroduction, see Lawson (1997: 24).

9 My thanks to an anonymous referee for reminding me of this point. (Also see Bhaskar, 1978: 31–32.)

10 The version of this paper presented at the IACR 2004 conference offered a different resolution of this problem, which I no longer find plausible.

11 This is a sub-case of the determination of events in the actual by a mix of many causes; and also a case of what Bhaskar calls multiple determination, which will be discussed below.

12 I use 'overdetermined' here, not in Althusser's sense, but rather to indicate a logically impossible case – i.e. where the set of causally effective factors exceeds those required to explain the set of outcomes, with the result that they appear to mandate a set of outcomes that may be inconsistent with each other.
13 I develop the argument made here and in the remainder of this section in more detail in Elder-Vass (2005).
14 Unless a 'real causal power' is an abstract universal. Although this is the approach I investigated in the version of this paper presented at the IACR conference, I now believe that this was not Bhaskar's intention, as is revealed by a careful reading of Bhaskar (1978: 45–52). Bhaskar treats causal laws as universals, but not causal mechanisms.
15 Although his argument is clearly also motivated by a desire to underpin his critique of positivism; I have not considered the implications of my proposed revision for that critique, but at first sight it would not seem to affect it.

References

Archer, M. (1982). 'Morphogenesis versus Structuration'. *British Journal of Sociology*, 33, 455–483.
Archer, M. (1995). *Realist Social Theory: The Morphogenetic Approach*. Cambridge, UK: Cambridge University Press.
Bhaskar, R. (1978). *A Realist Theory of Science*. Hassocks, UK: Harvester Press.
Bhaskar, R. (1993). *Dialectic : the Pulse of Freedom*. London, New York: Verso.
Bhaskar, R. (1994). *Plato etc*. London: Verso.
Blitz, D. (1992). *Emergent Evolution*. Dordrecht, London: Kluwer Academic Publishers.
Buckley, W. (1998). *Society – a Complex Adaptive System*. Amsterdam: Gordon and Breach.
Cilliers, P. (1998). *Complexity and Postmodernism*. London: Routledge.
Collier, A. (1994). *Critical Realism*. London: Verso.
Collier, A. (1998). 'Stratified explanation and Marx's conception of history'. In M. Archer, R. Bhaskar, A. Collier, T. Lawson and A. Norrie (Eds.), *Critical Realism: Essential Readings* (pp. 258–281). London: Routledge.
Cunningham, B. (2001). 'The Reemergence of "Emergence"'. *Philosophy of Science*, 68, S62–S75.
Elder-Vass, D. (2005). 'Emergence and the Realist Account of Cause'. *Journal of Critical Realism*, 4, 315–338.
Emmeche, C. Koppe, S. and Stjernfelt, F. (1997). 'Explaining Emergence: Towards an Ontology of Levels'. *Journal for General Philosophy of Science*, 28, 83–119.
Fleetwood, S. (2001). 'Causal Laws, Functional Relations and Tendencies'. *Review of Political Economy*, 13, 201–220.
Lawson, T. (1997). *Economics and Reality*. London, New York: Routledge.
Lloyd Morgan, C. (1923). *Emergent Evolution*. London: Williams and Norgate.
McLaughlin, B. P. (1992). 'The Rise and Fall of British Emergentism'. In A. Beckermann, H. Flohr and J. Kim (Eds.), *Emergence or Reduction?* (pp. 49–93). Berlin: de Gruyter.
Sawyer, R. K. (2001). 'Emergence in Sociology'. *American Journal of Sociology*, 107, 551–585.
Sayer, A. (1992). *Method in Social Science*. London: Routledge.
Sperry, R. W. (1986). 'Macro- versus Micro-Determinism'. *Philosophy of Science*, 53, 265–270.

11 Real, invented or applied? Some reflections on scientific objectivity and social ontology[1]

Eleonora Montuschi

Some preliminaries

A philosophical distinction is normally referred to between two concepts of objectivity: an ontological concept (to be objective is to exist independently of any knowledge, perception or conception we may have about what exists), and an epistemological concept (objectivity is a property of the content of mental states and acts).[2]

The question which is normally asked as regards this distinction is the following: does epistemological objectivity require ontological objectivity (does the objectivity of, say, a belief, depend on the objectivity of the entities this belief is purportedly about)?

For the realist, epistemological objectivity depends on ontological objectivity, namely for our beliefs to be objective we ought to assume the independent existence of determinate facts, objects, properties, events, etc. (i.e., an 'objective' ontology).[3] For the anti-realist, epistemological objectivity can be assessed in its own terms, that is the objectivity of our beliefs can be established by reference to other beliefs which may provide justifiable, coherent, intelligible, rational support to the beliefs the objectivity of which is in question. It is indeed on the basis of notions such as 'the way reality appears to us', or 'the evidence which is available at this present moment in time', or 'the criteria we apply', etc. that epistemological objectivity can be at all ascertained. This goes clearly against what the realist believes, namely that epistemological objectivity without ontological objectivity is simply 'invented'.[4]

This debate translates well when we turn to discussing scientific objectivity, that is objectivity as produced and pursued by science (as an institution and as an epistemic enterprise). In the philosophy of science the distinction (and the relation) between the two concepts of objectivity becomes one of the points of contention between scientific realists and social constructivists. Objective scientific theories 'discover' real objects, for the scientific realist (E-objectivity requires O-objectivity); they rather 'invent' those very objects, for the constructivist (O-objectivity is not required; in fact, it is itself a 'construction').

What format does a constructivist argument take? Here is a possible reconstruction:[5] To argue that 'X is constructed' we ought to assume:

1. X, or X as it is at present, is not determined by the nature of things
2. X is the product of *intentional human activity* (theories, actions, inquiries, history)
3. Human activity, although necessary for the existence of X, is not itself necessary

From here we conclude: X need not have existed, or need not be at all as it is (the non-inevitability of intentional human activity is responsible for the non-inevitability of X).[6]

So, if X is 'constructed', X is what it is because X is the *product* of a contingent activity or *process*, and not of any objectively existing state of affairs, nor of any given and transcendent order of things.[7] However, assumption (1), although a necessary condition for the truth-value of 'X is constructed', is not sufficient.[8] What needs to be specified is that for X to be not inevitable, it must be possible that, say, a scientist can make other choices, and that these choices are then reflected in a world-view consistent with them. In other words, what needs to be specified is that the non-inevitability of X is due to the fact that X is the product of *intentional human activity*. It is our theories, our actions, our inquiries, or our history, which make X what it is. But the theories, actions, inquiries, history which make X what it is, although necessary for the existence of X, are not themselves necessary. The non-inevitability of intentional human activity is ultimately responsible for the non-inevitability of X.

Having specified both the necessary and the sufficient conditions, the actual argument from construction can be framed at different levels: ontological (the level of the facts of the world we live in); epistemological (the level of what we can know of those facts); and semantic (the level of what can be said about those facts and about what we know about them).[9]

The ontological level seems to entail the most demanding form of constructivism. To say that X is constructed is to say that its very objectivity depends on human action. However, if we look at the C-argument above, we should ask: When we say 'X is constructed', what is the 'X' we are referring to? Hacking reminds us of a useful distinction: the one between *object* (something 'in the world', so to speak), and *idea* (a conception, a belief, a theory, a classification or a kind).[10]

One way of interpreting the social constructivist claim is to say that X is the object, and the object is socially constructed (by the idea). In other words, what we refer to as objects are actually ideas of objects, in the sense that objects are constructed by ideas and do not exist as separate entities. Another way of interpreting the claim is to say that there is a distinction to be made between the object and the idea: X is an idea, and the idea is constructed, it is used to refer to objects, but the objects it refers to are not themselves constructed (an idea of object). So, paradoxically, in both cases X is an idea – but what this means is rather different in each case. In the former interpretation, X is the idea because there are no objects to refer to other than ideas of objects. In the latter interpretation, X is the idea because the objects exist 'in the world', and the world cannot be constructed – only the ideas (beliefs, theories, classifications, etc.) we have of it can.

By looking at these two interpretations, we come to realise why a constructivist argument might be perceived as a threat to objectivity. In the first interpretation, a suggestion is made to the effect that what we take to be real is in actual fact 'only a construction' (an idea of 'real'). From here, we might well go all the way and come to say that reality is a fiction, and socially constructed fictions cannot be objective (in the sense of O-objectivity). This interpretation would result in an underestimation of ontological objectivity and a parallel overestimation of epistemological objectivity – an actual limitation, in my view.

However, the first interpretation might also have a merit. It somehow fences off the idea that assuming the existence of a world of independent objects should be taken to mean that the classes of objects a science investigates (its extension) are always ready-made, simply 'given'. The objects questioned by a science are (in some sense to be qualified) objects of some 'scientific' inquiry. To become a referent for scientific inquiry is a complex procedure, which involves different techniques of classification, representation, experimental and conceptual design, etc.

This is something that the constructivist argument specifically takes on board, but to the extreme of claiming (its possible 'vice') that, at the very end, nothing exists beyond or behind these classifications, representations, etc. The ontological status of the referents of scientific inquiries is then said to be invented by the theoretical and practical procedures of knowledge acquisition. It is not itself an object of scientific discovery. The constructivist argument completely reverses the direction of dependence between O-objectivity and E-objectivity: the former depends entirely on the latter, to the extent that the former is 'absorbed' by the latter, and shaped by it – there included its existence.

This is how the debate between scientific realists and constructivists is normally reported to have developed. Scientific objects are either discovered or invented. If they are invented they cannot be real (ontologically speaking). If they are discovered, they must be more than an epistemological construction. Of course framed along these lines, scientific referents cannot at the same time belong to an independent ontology (order of reality) and be constructed as having a specifically devised ontology (order of a man-concocted reality).

Hacking – who does not so much care about taking sides as he rather tries to understand the actual terms of the debate – clarifies two important points. Firstly, we ought to eliminate the confusion between objects and ideas in the constructivist-argument. Secondly, and as a consequence, reversing the direction of the relation of dependence between O-objectivity and E-objectivity (as done by the constructivist-argument) does not necessarily result in deleting O-objectivity.

As a matter of fact, in the history of the debate between realists and constructivists the oppositions, although often radically framed, prove less rigid than it is suggested above. What we often perceive is instead a difference in emphasis as regards the perspective from which the issue of objectivity is questioned by each side in the debate (i.e., it is either a matter of questioning the ontological/extensional from an epistemological/intensional point of view, or vice versa).

Attempts have then been made to attenuate the divide between the real and the invented projected by this debate. For example, an interesting perspective has been recently named 'applied metaphysics' (or historical ontology) and is intended to advocate that scientific ontological objectivity can be at the same time real and invented, and therefore any concept of either ontological or epistemological objectivity has to take this into account.[11]

Applied metaphysics

A preliminary clarification of the very expression 'applied metaphysics' is in order. Unlike pure metaphysics, which deals with 'the ethereal world of what is always and everywhere from a God-eye-viewpoint', applied metaphysics – Daston points out – is concerned with what constitutes the world studied by working scientists.[12] This does not mean that the latter reduces to epistemology, to what is 'dimly known' (as opposed to 'what is really real'). Rather, it includes those special categories of phenomena which constitute the referents of scientific investigations (more epistemologically complex than everyday 'things', and yet not less real, as we will see).

Having specified the background of investigation, there are three significant steps which are taken from within an applied metaphysics, in view of re-framing the meaning and scope of scientific objectivity. First of all, and most importantly, an applied metaphysics clarifies what the object of a science is. Rather than taking its cue from ideals, models, definitions of objectivity, it questions directly what it is that we are (are meant to be) objective about in scientific inquiry. Indeed, the term 'object' is ambiguous. Its root meaning (as in *objectus*, *Gegestand*, *oggetto*, *objet*) is that of a 'throwing before', 'putting against' (standing opposite). So objects in this sense are the 'solid, obvious, sharply outlined things of quotidian experience'; 'they possess the self-evidence of a slap in the face'. [13] However, the objects of *science* are a different matter.

Unlike quotidian objects, scientific objects are elusive, hard-won. Historians, philosophers and sociologists of science, says Daston, do not confuse the quotidian with the scientific. And yet, as exemplified by the realism/constructivism debates, arguments are drawn and put forward on the acceptance of an implicit ontology of quotidian objects. These arguments take the opposition real/invented for granted, a metaphysical axiom, and they quarrel over which of the two categories objects like 'race' or 'quarks' better fit into. They do not question the opposition itself, which – Daston reminds us – got established only at some point, in the eighteenth century, and after a period in which the two terms of the opposition (at least 'invention' and 'discovery') were synonyms – as we can infer, for example, simply from consulting the Oxford English Dictionary. It was only at some stage that one of the possible meanings of the term 'invention' (i.e. fabrication or contrivance) became prevalent, triggering a whole series of negative consequences as regards its use. There is a long story to recount about this opposition, which is largely still to be explored. Nonetheless, the step Daston is taking here is clear: let's see whether a 'good' meaning of invention can be restored and reinserted as an analytical tool to describe the nature of the objects of science, where no doubt 'invention' has a part to play.

The second important step, in the context of an applied metaphysics, is then to appraise what the world that science refers to consists of. The world of science is not a static reservoir of given objects, but rather, says Daston, is a dynamic world – a world made up of objects which 'come into being' or 'fade away' as referents of epistemic inquiry, depending on how epistemic inquiry develops. Objects become referents of a science depending on the scientists' interests, lines of questioning and techniques of salience and embededness in research practice. This does not mean that scientific objects are entirely a creation of the scientist, and therefore that they are not real (not objective, in the sense of ontological objectivity). The step Daston takes here is instead to claim that, in an applied metaphysics, 'reality is a matter of degrees'.[14] Phenomena which are undoubtedly 'real' (in the colloquial sense that they 'exist') can become 'more or less' real depending on how much and how deeply they are embedded with scientific practices.

Daston uses, as her example of scientific object, the case of 'preternatural objects'.[15] Preternatural objects, as the term suggests (*preter naturam*), are natural and yet irregular, extraordinary, deviating, rare objects: images found in agates or marbles, comets presaging the deaths of kings, a Medusa's head found in a hen's egg in Bordeaux, the power of flax seeds to inspire prophetic dreams, etc. They came into being as scientific objects by means of preternatural philosophy in the 16th–17th centuries, and then faded away when preternatural philosophy was supplanted by natural philosophy in the late 17th and 18th centuries. When scientific interest abandoned these objects, agates or marbles with strange images, comets, flax seeds, etc. stayed where they were. They only ceased to be *scientific* objects.

The final, interesting step taken from within this perspective is to claim that an applied metaphysics is 'catholic' in scope. All sorts of scientific objects – dreams, atoms, monsters, culture, mortality, centers of gravity, value, cytoplasmatic particles, the self, tuberculosis – belong to the same metaphysics. So, the widely discussed differences between the objects of inquiry in natural science and those in social science (the former are real and independent of human existence, the latter are not; the former can be dealt with by scientific methods, the latter cannot; etc.) become less crucial. Both types of objects share the same ontological framework (applied metaphysics), and can be subjected to similar forms of questioning and investigation (i.e., scientific inquiry, and historical/epistemological reconstruction). Admittedly, Daston is able to reach this 'catholic' result as she works with a wider notion of science (*Wissenschaft*)[16] than the one normally suggested by the English meaning of the word, namely the one belonging to the empirical/experimental tradition. By doing this, she is able to avoid some of the confusions and ambiguities which are found sometimes in certain classifications of scientific objects.[17]

Though I am overall sympathetic with Daston's approach, I have some queries concerning its third step. I question whether accepting that all scientific objects belongs in the same metaphysics does indeed do justice to the understanding of what the objects of different sciences actually amounts to. In particular, I wonder whether blurring the distinction between invention and discovery vis à vis scientific objects also leads us inevitably and ipso facto to blurring the distinction between natural and social scientific objects.

In order to substantiate my doubts, a further and more accurate reflection on the meaning of reality, which Daston seems to rely on, is called for (second step). Namely, we should explore whether Daston's idea of 'degrees of reality' made dependent on scientific inquiry is a suitable ontological device to describe the applied metaphysics of the objects of both natural and social science. But before this, a few words on the real/invented divide as applied to social scientific objects are in order.

The case of social scientific objects

In what follows I will question whether an applied metaphysics à la Daston really equally 'applies' to the objects of the social or human sciences. What does/can such metaphysics say of objects such as: 'productivity growth', or 'racially motivated crimes', or 'rate of inflation', or 'child abuse' – or, to go for more general abstract objects, 'society' and 'culture' (the social-science objects discussed in Daston's book *Biographies of Scientific Objects*)?

Daston makes two qualifications about the notion of invention (or novelty) vis à vis scientific objects which have interesting repercussions on social scientific objects. First, by including 'invention' into the meaning of scientific object we do not only refer to interpretations or descriptions of the world, she claims. We also refer to the practical and material conditions and contexts for the coming into being of these objects (social epistemological meaning of invention), such as, she writes, 'the stacking of atoms and the profits of insurance companies'. So in this sense, she continues, 'the objects of the human sciences do not appear to be more ephemeral than those of the natural sciences'.

Secondly, by using invention as the vehicle for the 'coming into being' of scientific objects (ontological meaning of invention), a series of connotations for the idea of novelty come to the fore. By means of scientific inquiry, 'quotidian' objects become *salient* (they come to 'rivet scientific attention'), *embedded* in scientific practices (they are entrenched in institutional networks), and *productive* (they offer results, allow manipulations, etc.). Novelty, however, might also endorse a more radical connotation: objects can be said to be *emergent*, in the sense that science, as Daston puts it, does not always silhouette extant objects, but sometimes creates them 'ex nihilo'. To use the words of a supporter of his own brand of applied metaphysics (or historical ontology, as he calls it): 'the very objects or their effects (…) do not exist in any recognizable form until they are objects of scientific study'.[18] That is to say, they become recognisable as those objects only when a certain descriptive practice (classification, institutional identification and support, etc.) is put in place.

Having made these two qualifications, Daston admits (and Hacking to some extent concurs) that social scientific objects have no 'quotidian prehistory'; and also that they constitute 'the most clear cut cases for the emergence [coming into being] of scientific objects' (radical sense of novelty).[19]

Both in Daston and in Hacking it seems that social objects are more easily identifiable by science (or maybe this is their actual difficulty) without pre-recourse to extensional definitions. Does this single them out as special types of scientific objects, within Daston's catholic approach? Social scientific objects seem to pose the following ontological challenge to Daston's catholic view. Given that, according to an applied metaphysics, scientific objects are both real and invented, and that their reality is as a consequence a matter of degrees, what does it mean for social scientific objects to be 'more or less real', if there is no reality check point for these objects? Do they exist at all before science makes them 'emerge'? In other words, we are left with the question of how objects which lack quotidian prehistory (colloquial sense that they do not exist) can count as real, and become more or less real when subjected to scientific scrutiny

That this is an actual problem with social-science objects is proved by the fact that several of the debates concerning these objects are indeed about their very existence. Take the example of 'society'. Peter Wagner interestingly shows that from the start, that is from when 'society' came into being as the object of a science (sociology, social science, science of society), the case for its existence had to be argued for.[20] For example in one of the early debates (mid 19th century), Robert von Mohl was confident that something entirely new had come into being in the last 50 years, the 'particular being' of society; whereas his opponent Heinrick von Treitschke rejected all together the idea that 'society' existed as an independent entity. For him, all the relations and elements purportedly constituting this 'new object' had essential links to the State, making the case for the existence of society as a separate entity totally redundant. And so the debate developed, Does society exist as separate from the State? Does it exist as separate from individuals (citizens)? Does society have specific causal effects which can prove its existence? Does it exist as an organism? etc.

It is interesting to see the terms in which T. Parson and R. MacIver reconstruct their far-reaching genealogy for the entry 'society' in the 1934 *Encyclopaedia of the Social Sciences*. First they look at the time when '[Plato's and Aristotle's] thought on society never takes the specific sociological form'; and then move on to the much later period when society does indeed become a specific focus of study, gradually acquiring the status of an 'independent reality'. However, Wagner remarks, this might 'underestimate the importance of changes in social practices that go along with terminological shifts: if there was neither "word" nor "thought" in the proper form, could it be that "society" [the scientific object of sociology] did not really exist before sociology?'

More examples come to mind. Does alcoholism exist before it becomes the phenomenon studied by a certain sociology? Or does suicide exist before the nineteenth century emergence of a certain 'medicine of insanity'? Do inflation or productivity growth exist before a particular machinery for measuring them is put in place? Do cultural representations as studied by certain anthropologists exist before causal chains from individual to social representations are identified by cognitive science and account for the former? Questions of this sort, I believe, rightly deserve inconclusive answers – of a yes-but-no type. Did the French

Revolution really exist? Of course it did. And yet without the description offered by the term 'revolution' and the practice of historical inquiry we can't really say that it existed. Or else, to claim that the existence of drunken people makes alcoholism a real scientific object seems far too simplistic. As it is misleading to say that alcoholism as described by certain sociological studies is the entire creation of those studies. However, we might also want to resist to say, as Daston's alternative seems to advocate, that the scientific object 'alcoholism' (partly invented by, say, sociology) makes the reality of drunken people 'more real'.

There seems to be something constraining, or at least to be further explored and qualified, in the idea of 'degrees of reality', which finally affects the thrust of applied metaphysics as a way out of the strictures of the real/invented divide. Let us go back to Daston once more.

Scientific reality and social objects

In her approach Daston works with two categories of 'real', and – partly due to the nature of the approach she advocates – she often oscillates between the two. One is the everyday category: quotidian objects which are either material (flowers, comets, chairs) or immaterial (dreams, personal identity). The other is the scientific category of 'real': scientific objects alter the reality of everyday objects by turning the latter into an inclusive (or exclusive), observable, stable, rich in implication, etc. category of objects. In other words, familiar (and sometimes unfamiliar) features of phenomena become objects of expert scrutiny, elaborate theories and cultural significance. Daston's metaphor here is that in a scientific object, reality (everyday reality) is 'intensified'. Intensity comes in degrees and from here it is a short step to claim that the reality of a scientific object is a matter of degrees (of intensity). Is Daston's 'intensified reality' something in between scientific reality and everyday reality, and if so at what level do we locate intensity (i.e., is it an ontological property, or rather an epistemological/historical connotation)? Daston quotes from Rheinberger: 'scientific objects, not things per se, (...) are targets of epistemic activity. (...) It is not that there is no materiality there before such objects come into being, or that they would vanish altogether and shrink to nothing on their way into the future'.[21] It is rather that science makes them either central or marginal, depending on what science sees in them. Against the two-valued metaphysics that forces upon us the choice of either 'it exists' or 'it does not exist', in an applied metaphysics reality 'expands in a continuum'[22] (from everyday to scientific, and sometimes back to everyday). It is 'processual', it comes and goes: it (scientific reality) is reality 'in motion'.

On the other hand, Daston also quotes Latour, who makes bolder claims.[23] Like Daston, Latour argues for a homogeneous ontology, which includes both human and non-human objects. However, Latour claims, in the case of scientific objects, reality itself becomes a 'relative property', dependent on the degree of its involvement with institutionalised scientific practices. Scientific facts cannot escape their local (historical) conditions of production. This means, at least for Latour, that what we take to be historical is not only the 'discovery' of scientific objects, but those objects themselves. In other words, it is not so much a matter of adding history (and practice) to reality, as Daston seems to say; it is rather, for him, a matter of finding history in reality. Scientific reality entails 'relative existence',[24] since history, so to speak, 'makes up' the reality science deals with.

How does Daston position herself between a Kantian (post-Kantian), epistemically conscious ontology à la Rheinberger, and an all inclusive, ontologised epistemology à la Latour? Which of the two perspectives better fits the frame and purpose of her catholic approach? To answer these questions, let us reflect on what features an ontology of social objects might bring to the fore, and then wonder how social reality can be included in a scientific ontology which is partly invented and partly real.

Purportedly, the problem with the objects that social science deals with is that, despite sharing the same ontological framework as natural objects, they have some specific ontological connotations which ultimately distinguish them ontologically from natural-science objects. True, like natural scientific objects, they are partly real and partly invented, but it is (1) the role that invention plays in their ontological identification, (2) the specific mechanism by which they get identified, and (3) the identifying features of so-called social kinds, which makes a difference.

As to the first aspect, and as Searle, among others, once put it: the objects of the material world (nature) do not need human intervention in order to be where they are, social objects exist precisely because they are represented by humans.

As to the second aspect, and as Hacking pointed out, the mechanism of representation – which admittedly intervenes in classifying both natural and social objects – is itself different when we shift from the former to the latter.

As to the third aspect, and as Michael Root suggested, it is the constitutive features of social kinds that determine in what specific sense social kinds are 'real'. Let's see what each aspect amounts to.

As to the first, Searle came up with a formula which describes the underlying logic of social reality: X counts as Y in C, that is social objects belong to natural reality (X) and yet they exist only as a consequence of a collectively sustained attribution of social functions and meanings to that reality (Y, or X represented as Y).[25] The difference from natural objects is that social objects can exist only if they are represented. So their dependence on representation (the invented part in Daston's terminological distinction) is total. This makes in a sense the term 'representation' misleading in the social context. An X becomes a Y not just in the sense that it is represented as a Y. Instead, Y allows X to exist as Y. This partly shows why a metaphysics of degrees of reality à la Daston does not seem to hit the target in the case of social objects. The invented part of social objects (the Y) does not make them be 'more or less' real (the X part); it rather makes them real all together, or better it makes them exist at a specific 'level' or 'order' of reality (the Y level).

But there is more, and here is where the second aspect becomes relevant. The mechanism of representation itself is different in the two cases. In describing the objects of the natural and the social world, Hacking famously made a distinction between 'indifferent' and 'interactive' kinds.[26] 'The classification 'quark' is indifferent', he explains, 'in the sense that calling a quark a quark makes no difference to the quark'. With social or human kinds, the situation changes. People are the subject matter of these kinds, and when people become an object of study (e.g. child TV viewers, criminals, women refugees, black and white people, etc.), they 'interact' (accordingly or contrastively) with the ways they are classified, described, represented, and they also often experience themselves in the world according to ongoing classifications, descriptions, etc. There is a feedback, or 'looping' effect involved with classifying people, which does not occur in the case of natural kinds, and which typifies the representational mechanism of social-kind making. *Kinds* of people may change, because the *people* classified as being of certain kinds might themselves change, as a consequence of being so classified. To say that humans are 'social objects' must specifically take into account the fact that their relation to representation cannot be 'indifferent' – even, and particularly, as referents of social scientific inquiries. They are, so to speak, constantly on the move.

The social sciences, Hacking reminds us, are constantly under pressure to emulate the natural sciences and produce/refer to real natural kinds. But for this to be possible they should adopt an ontology and an epistemology which do not comply with the objects or referents they deal with. This does not mean that the objects social science refers to cannot ever be classified as indifferent. For example, an autistic child can be classified both interactively and indifferently, that is a social classification of autism does not exclude the possibility that some child is indeed the bearer of a certain pathology (autism can be a scientific concept). It does though rule out that an ontology built exclusively on indifferent kinds might be adequate in the case of social referents.

What effects does the way we classify social kinds have on their reality? Where should we look for their reality, if they owe their existence to the way we represent them? Michael Root argues that the reality of social kinds should be assessed at the level of the specific categories which the social order proceeds from, and not by comparison with natural-kind categories. In the social sciences, he claims, 'real taxonomy is less about generalization and more about regulations: we divide ourselves not by discovering our differences but by requiring ourselves to be different'.[27] Social categories, in other words, are normative: 'extrapolation across all instances is not possible, but normalization is', in the sense that social categories may prescribe not so much how whatever is classified by means of a certain category is, but rather how it ought to be. This is why these categories are 'well made for social regulation'.[28]

This does not mean that social categories are 'less real' than natural categories. The social world, just as the natural one, is ordered, but the source of such order is different: as Elster once pointed out,[29] it is an order based on norms and regulations. Root discusses the example of race. Race, he claims, is like crime. If we had not invented appropriate laws or drawn certain property distinctions, nobody would be guilty of theft. Yet, given that we did, social scientists can classify us along certain categories, provide descriptions and explanations by making use of them, and even try to predict or explain phenomena and trends by means of those categories. Race is biologically real (to be black is to be black, not just to be perceived as being black, or to be believed to be black). And yet, the reality of race as a social category depends 'on what we (collectively) have made of race, and (...) whether we regulate or discipline each other by race. Should we divide but not regulate by race, we would retain the races but not conserve their reality'.[30] Root concludes: 'Laws of nature do not make race real, we do'.[31] As in Searle, we add categories to the world, and make 'new things' exist in the world.

If we now compare the three aspects of social ontology, as have just been described, with the claims made in the context of Daston's approach, we come to realise what the limits of the latter might be.

Working our way back from the last aspect, to say that all scientific objects are real (shared ontology), and can be more or less real depending on how science approaches them, hides the fact that the category of reality as applied to the objects of social science is based on different foundations (e.g. norms, and not laws of nature). As a consequence, social science should aim less at being a generalising science than at being a regulation-conscious type of inquiry.

Secondly, to say that invention is part of both types of objects hides the way in which invention actually achieves its ontological objective (the identification of each type of object). Social scientific objects are 'interactive' and normative in a specific sense, and the social sciences cannot investigate them in the same way as if they were natural objects (though this does not mean that the social sciences cannot investigate natural, or indifferent, kinds).

Finally, to say that all scientific objects are both invented and real hides the fact that without invention (there included scientific invention), the objects of social science, unlike those of natural science, would not so much exist 'less', they would not exist at all. The world does not come with all the categories we use to refer to it – and in some cases man-made categories are essential to identify referents at all. This is not to deny existence to social ontology, but to offer a more in-depth understanding of what such existence amounts to.

By means of the 'more-or-less-real' device, Daston, as I take it, resists the Latourian turn (she somehow preserves a notion of independent reality); but, at the same time, she seems to overlook that 'being real', especially in the case of scientific reality, is not so much a quality of entities than it is a predicate; and that as such, it can be predicated at, or of, different levels, or be conceptualised in terms of different orders of reality.[32]

Both Daston and Latour think of their approaches as wide-ranging, and make them applicable across the spectrum of both natural and social objects. In Daston's catholic approach, social scientific objects are not substantially different from natural scientific ones, in that invention plays a part on the undoubted reality of both. In Latour's view, it is rather the other way around: human and non-human objects are all historical (invented). A 'homogeneous ontology' applies to both natural and social objects, as in both types of objects their reality is relative to their history. However, neither approach significantly shows that a shared ontology should not necessarily treat all types of objects identically: it should rather find ways to include and promote plurality and diversity of existence even within a shared background of reality.

Conclusions

To return then to the suggestions of applied metaphysics, and to the claims of scientific objectivity in a revisited framework of the debate between realism and constructivism. On the real/invented divide, Daston is right: it is time to dismantle some of the myths and ghosts which have been unduly created about it, and seriously explore the ways the two poles of the opposition come together in the concrete cases and instances science practices upon.

On the quotidian/scientific divide, I find Daston less convincing. On one side, she advocates the necessity of not conflating the two in the case of scientific objects (to avoid all the problems which, for example, haunted the realism/constructivism debates). On the other, she seems to rely on the existence of quotidian objects to show how science operates in transforming them into scientific objects. This specifically creates problems in the case of social scientific objects, and more generally for her applied metaphysics which she wants to be catholic in scope (embracing all scientific objects, natural and human). The 'more or less real' device does not seem to offer the right solution to connect the real and the invented part in both the natural and social ontology. We should not take a pre-existing ontology of quotidian (not necessarily familiar) objects as being more or less real depending on scientific inquiry, but rather look at how different levels, orders, dimensions, or – to use a critical realist term, 'strata' – of reality become recognisable and identified as 'existent' by means of scientific inquiry.

To return to where we started: what effects does this way of framing social objects and social ontology have on the issue of scientific objectivity? Once reconceptualised in a revised perspective of applied metaphysics, scientific objectivity cannot be taken as being derivative of some given or pre-determined 'way that things are'. It is rather strictly interdependent with the practical as well as conceptual ways we (the scientists) frame things in our inquiries. It is because of these ways (practices, procedures, etc.) that the objects scientific inquiries deal with become real, at various and different degrees and levels. Indeed, it seems that objectivity becomes an issue only in relation to specific systems of reference, that is in relation to objects embedded in those practical, theoretical, historical procedures of description, classification, conceptualisation and questioning, which allow them to become possible objects of specific inquiries.[33]

This has at least two important corollaries, or consequences. First, objectivity is not a fixed ideal, with a fixed meaning, applying in a fixed way across disciplines and their histories. Objectivity is rather a practice. Designing objects for scientific inquiry depends on available techniques, technologies, methods and methodologies, quantitative and qualitative, which are as much means to an end (the shaping of scientific objects) as they are themselves subject to scrutiny in terms of objective reliability (the use of methods for attaining objectivity).

Secondly, objectivity is not the exclusive task or achievement of scientific method as applied to natural objects (taken as a paradigm of objective knowledge). Saying that objectivity is a practice should not obfuscate the differences in practice pursued and developed by different sciences in their fields of inquiry.

Exploring how a specific category of scientific objects (social objects) is identified and works in the context of an applied metaphysics stands as a useful reminder of the complexity and multifaceted nature not only of scientific objectivity, but also of scientific reality.

Notes

1 Previous versions of this paper were presented to the 'British Society for the Philosophy of Science', London (February 2004), and to the 'History, Philosophy and Sociology of Science' Symposium, Assos, Turkey (June 2004). I am grateful to the participants in both meetings for their questions and their useful criticism.

2 For this distinction and the relation between O-objectivity and E-objectivity, as well as the way the latter informs the debate between realists and anti-realists, see Bell (1994).

3 The realist also assumes that ontological objectivity can be 'captured' by epistemological objectivity, in that the latter can represent, at different degrees of accuracy, 'the way things are'. Crucially instrumental to this task is the idea of method which, ever since the natural philosophers of the 17th century, was conceived as a consistent series of rules not only for good reasoning, but also for 'extracting' truth from facts (rules for the 'direction of the mind', as, for example, Descartes defined them).

4 The forerunner of epistemological objectivity is normally considered to be Kant. He is certainly the first to have made use of the term and of the concept in a specific sense and for a specific purpose in philosophy. Objectivity for Kant is a property of human understanding, not a feature of the external world. The latter would appear to us as a disconnected manifold of heterogeneous experiences if it were not for the ordering attitude of the human mind, which organizes the world by objects. The ordering itself is objective because it does not depend on individual intellects. The mind has a structure which is shared by everybody, and works by producing categories and imposing rules which are the same for everybody. Kant is not then an anti-realist, in that he does not deny that an external world is needed in objectivity talks; but he is not a full-fledged realist, as he does not claim that objectivity depends plainly on the existence of an external world.

5 Such a reconstruction takes hints from both Ian Hacking (1999: 6) and Andrè Kukla (2000: 1–3).

6 An example of this argument is offered by A. Pickering's discussion of quarks. Quarks are what they are because physics evolved the way it did, and elicited certain phenomena construed as evidence for the existence of quarks. However, physics could have evolved differently. According to Pickering, its evolution was contingent, and contrary to what many scientists would claim, it was not inevitable (Pickering 1984). Often the idea of non inevitability is associated with a negative connotation of a constructed X. As Hacking points out, 'most people who use the social construction idea enthusiastically want to criticize, change, or destroy some X that they dislike in the established order of things'. (Hacking 1999: 7). A typical example is the feminist critique of the notion of gender.

7 For the distinction between product and process, see Hacking (ibid.: 36–38).

8 See (Kukla 2000: Ch. 1).

9 For the distinction between these three levels, or 'theses' concerning the social constructivist argument see Kukla (ibid: 4–6).

10 X can also be an *elevator word* (a word used to say something about the objects, or about what we say about them). See Hacking (ibid: 22–24).
11 See Daston (2000: 3).
12 Daston (2000: 1).
13 Daston (2000: 2).
14 Daston (2000: 1).
15 See Daston (2000: 15ff).
16 Daston (2000: 5).
17 See for example Kukla's classification (2000: 24–25). He presents four main categories of facts:
    (1) scientific facts: only the facts discovered or invented by the institution of science/only the facts of the (putatively) natural sciences/the non-social facts produced (discovered/ invented) by any special epistemic enterprise that goes beyond the practice of common sense
    (2) social facts: the facts of the social sciences
    (3) everyday facts: facts whose discovery or invention takes place outside the institutional boundaries of science or any other professional epistemic enterprise
    (4) noumenal facts: facts about the world which are inaccessible by any method available to human beings.
    Immediately we see a discrepancy between (1) and (2). If scientific facts are the facts produced by any special epistemic enterprise that goes beyond the practice of common sense, then the facts of social science qualify for this category. However, category (1) is rather confused. It seems to imply, and far too quickly, that the only science is natural science; that the institution of science has nothing to do with the social; that natural science provides for a paradigm of what a 'special epistemic enterprise' should amount to.
    Kukla's classification is conceived having in mind the debate on constructivism, which appears to be particularly harsh (from both sides of the divide) when the constructed nature of *natural* facts is at stake. In order to identify the natural with non-social facts, Kukla must deny scientific status to the subject matter of the social domain. But by so doing, he ends up assuming that the social sciences are not sciences; and – at least at the stage of his argument where he is laying out this classification of objects – it is not clear by what process social objects are brought about and investigated, or ultimately how they exist.
18 Hacking (2002: 11)
19 Daston (2000: 9). Also in Hacking the examples offered of objects of this latter sort are somehow objects of study belonging to the human realm (psychic trauma, child development, multiple personality disorder, suicide, child abuse, etc.). The coming into being which occurs in science labs does not *create* objects for Hacking (facts, entities, phenomena), or – as he famously put it – labelling an atom 'atom' does not make any difference for the existence of the atom. See Hacking (2002: 14–15). However, Daston also points out that social objects share the type of novelty called 'emergency' with the objects of mathematical physics. This, among other things, is her way to show how the difference between natural and social objects is not after all so crucial, and that they can all comfortably accommodate within the same metaphysics (Daston 2000: 9).
20 See Wagner (2000).
21 Daston (2000: 12).
22 Daston (2000: 13).
23 In fact, Daston takes the expression 'more or less real' from Latour himself. In discussing the debates between Pasteur and Pouchet on spontaneous generation, Latour claims that existence is not an all-or-nothing property, but a relative property. Entities gain or lose in reality, depending on whether and how they are associated with other entities which either sustain or degrade their existence. He illustrates this by means of

a graph which shows how 'Pouchet's spontaneous generation becomes *less and less real*, and Pasteur's culture method become *more and more real*'. [my italics] (Latour 2000: 256–257).

24 Latour (2000: 251).
25 Searle (1995: 28).
26 Hacking (1999: 103–106).
27 Root (1998: 633).
28 Ibid.: 633.
29 Elster (1989: 287) quoted in Root (1998: 635).
30 Root (1998: 635).
31 Root (Ibid.: 638).
32 Latour appears to be more sensitive to the ontological nuances of the category of 'reality'. Still, by being specifically interested in showing that reality is relative in all and any scientific object, and that natural objects are no exception, he does not offer us sufficient tools to explore what a socio-historical ontology consists of in the case of social (or human) objects. Besides, and as already noted, he seems to shift far too quickly from the historicisation of the discovery of scientific objects to the historicisation of the reality of those objects themselves.
33 I argue for this view of objectivity in Montuschi (2003).

References

Bell, D. (1994) 'Objectivity', *A Companion to Epistemology*, ed. by J. Dancy and E. Sosa, Oxford: Blackwell, pp. 310–313.

Daston, L. [ed.] (2000) *Biographies of Scientific Objects*, Chicago, IL: University of Chicago.

Elster, J. (1989) *The Cement of Society: A Study of Social Order*, Cambridge, UK: Cambridge University Press.

Hacking, I. (1999) *The Social Construction of What*? Cambridge, Massachusetts: Harvard University Press.

Hacking, I. (2002) *Historical Ontology*, Cambridge Massachusetts: Harvard University Press

Kukla, A. (2000) *Social Constructivism and the Philosophy of Science*, London: Routledge.

Latour, B. (2000) 'On the partial existence of existing and nonexisting objects', in L. Daston, *Biographies of Scientific Objects*.

Montuschi, E. (2003) *The Objects of Social Science*, London/New York: Continuum Press.

Pickering, A. (1984) *Constructing Quarks: A Sociological History of Particle Physics*, Edinburgh: Edinburgh University Press.

Root, M. (1998) 'How We Divide the World', *Philosophy of Science*, 2000, Supplement to vol. 67.

Searle, J. (1995) *The Construction of Social Reality*, London: Penguin Press.

Wagner, P. (2000) 'An entirely new object of consciousness, of volition, of thought', in L. Daston, *Biographies of Scientific Objects*.

12 Theorising ontology

Roy Bhaskar

At the time of writing my first book, *A Realist Theory of Science* (1975), ontology was a taboo subject. It would have been impossible for ontology to have been the central theme for a respectable conference. In fact if someone talked about ontology there would be a certain *frisson*: it was not the sort of thing that nice people talked about. Thirty years on it seems that everyone is talking about ontology. I wouldn't want to say this is entirely due to critical realism but I think perhaps that critical realism has played some role in it. However, much of what I wish to say here will be an attempt to deflate ontology. I shall argue that although ontology is important, we also have to pay attention to other features of the intellectual landscape, including epistemology and issues to do with judgemental rationality – issues that have been of secondary importance for critical realists until recently. To get my corrective in at the start, I would say that we need to rebalance critical realism by paying more attention to the transitive and intrinsic alongside the intransitive, and the epistemological and axiological within ontology, than we have done.

The ontology of critical realism

Let us start with a discussion of ontology before turning to more normative issues. How did it come about that ontology was a virtually taboo subject? What was it that made ontology so difficult or even impossible? Although the philosophical doctrines of, say, Hume and Kant are familiar, it is important to appreciate a phenomenological or practical basis for them. This is in a kind of natural attitude to the world in which we do not distinguish between knowledge and objects, in which we don't distinguish ontology from epistemology, or the transitive and intransitive domains, in which we just talk about a *known world*. When science is doing normal science, when things are going well, epistemically it is natural to adopt what I call this '*natural attitude*' in which you don't posit ontology on the one side and epistemology on the other: you just have knowledge and you take it that that knowledge is of the world. Ontology really only becomes relevant when you are not satisfied with knowledge, when what passes for knowledge is patently wrong or absurd. Thus when I came to understand the necessity to argue for ontology *explicitly* and to revindicate it as a subject, it was because I was then very dissatisfied with the *implicit* ontologies in social science and in the philosophy of social science.

These implicit ontologies were underpinned by the Humean theory of causal laws. And it seemed obvious to me that the Humean theory of causal laws, the theory that the world is based on constant conjunctions of invariant events, which presupposes that the world is unstructured and undifferentiated and unchanging, must be wrong. My problem was how to say this, because talking about the world was taboo. I had to develop an argument which allowed me both to establish – or re-establish – ontology as a discipline and to establish a new ontology. That is what I tried to do in *A Realist Theory of Science* – by taking, in an immanent critique, the empiricist epistemological starting point that we have experimental science and arguing to its ontological and non-empirical conditions of possibility. So I argued that for experimentation to be possible the world had to be structured and differentiated. There had to be, indeed science is essentially concerned with, a level of order beyond the constant conjunction of events and a level of order that is not necessarily in phase with the patterns of events at all. So I distinguished the domains of the *real* and the *actual* and two types of system – *open* and *closed systems*. The fallacy of supposing that you couldn't do ontology was what I called the *epistemic fallacy*.

A critic might respond that although it may be necessary to change our assumptions about the fundamental nature of the world, i.e. ontology is required, surely Kant and Hume showed that ontology is an impossible project; in other words, they showed that one cannot do ontology rationally. And the critic might inquire as to how you could ever establish an ontological conclusion, because this would involve making a claim about the world which in some way you have removed from its ground, its epistemological premises. You can't talk about things in themselves apart from our modes of knowing them. This is a very insidious line of reasoning and it is very important to see what is wrong with it – because if you can't establish any conclusion, about anything, apart from our way of proving it or establishing it, then you can't have any local or separate or particular knowledge, the only knowledge you can have is of the whole, and indeed the process of the whole. So if we are going to have knowledge of subtotalities, if we are going to have knowledge of particular things, you must be able to detach the conclusions of some epistemic investigation from the epistemic investigation, and of course this is what we do in science. If we couldn't do it then whenever we wanted to say something (about the world) we would have to repeat all our supporting procedures, that is, our whole method of establishing it. So if we are going to have any separable knowledge, we are going to have to allow ontological conclusions from epistemological premises or assumptions and say that they are *sui generis* valid.

A similar misconception about ontology stems from the idea that the whole of society is required in any particular analysis. This is the fallacy of the sociologists of scientific knowledge who say that it is impossible to talk about a natural ontology because scientists are always in some social context, without which this ontology might, at least arguably, have been different. This is of course to confuse what a claim is about with all the conditions without which it might have been different. It is false to suppose that because people are in a social context they cannot have knowledge about a natural and non-social world. Otherwise again you are going to have everything which is presupposed by any item of knowledge coming in to the conclusion and you are not going to be able to establish anything in science. It is very important to see this and it is very important to see that if you do not accept this *detachment of conclusions* you are not going to have any science. Rather what you are going to have is a totality in which everything is interconnected with everything else and in which we can never come to establish anything particular, specific or discrete at all. So we are never in a position to temporally terminate an inquiry, to put something on one side as established and to be learnt and another as under investigation and yet another as false, for example, to say 'OK, that is false, there are no witches, end of story'. We are never going to be in a position to say that, we are never going to have piecemeal progress or incremental development, because the totality is always going to be involved in any statement that we make.

I am arguing that what we have, in contrast, is a process within the culture of science in which the normal naturalisation of beliefs about the world, is suspended for the ontological investigation. A culture in which we can make genuine ontological arguments by detaching the conclusion of those arguments from their epistemological grounds when they are well justified. This is of course perfectly consistent with the easiest argument to grasp for ontology: when we refer to an object what we do in that moment in which we refer to it is detach it from the subjectivity that investigates, posits, observes. This is what I call 'referential detachment' and it is what we do when we talk about the world, detaching things (including totalities) from their evidential and supporting context. So we have the motifs here of: the *suspension* of the natural attitude; the attitude which epistemologizes or normalizes ontology; and the procedure of *detachment*.

The question, in this case, is what is ontology or what is the subject matter of ontology? If it is just things that are real, if it is just beings, then surely it must include everything. In principle everything falls within the subject matter of ontology. So what is it that gives determinacy to an ontological investigation? How can we have a discipline that will talk about some but not all aspects of being as properly 'ontological'? What is the contrast that would separate some aspects of reality from others? One might want to distinguish *philosophical* from *scientific* or substantive ontologies and say that philosophical ontologies are of greater significance. Or one might want to say that we are talking about ontology as distinct from *epistemology*, so epistemology is not part of an ontology, in other words our beliefs and everything to do with our beliefs are not part of ontology for that investigation. Or the ontological might be distinguished from the *ethical*, or the axiological. Or alternatively one might simply want to say that ontology is what you make *explicit*. These are all useful contrasts that might help to demarcate a specific ontological topic, and which can, I shall argue, all be made consistent and coherent. Now we are seeing the subject matter of ontology as itself *differentiated*.

A historical digression: Kant, Heidegger and Marx

Let us now compare what I have said with what other philosophers have said about being. I want to look in particular at Kant, Heidegger and Marx, all immensely important and influential philosophers.

When Kant referred to ontology he had the metaphysics of the scholastics in mind. The erstwhile metaphysicians of his time had come to separate their onto-logical conclusions altogether from any sort of epistemological premises, so that the original evidential and argumentative context of these conclusions was alto-gether in danger of being lost. In the meantime, in the seventeenth century Descartes, Bacon and the other early philosophers of modernity had engaged once more in a kind of reflection on specific epistemological premises, drawn now from the new experimental sciences of physics and chemistry, instantiating and reflect-ing a very different cosmology from that of the scholastics. And from the stand-point of the new mechanistic philosophers, the scholastic metaphysics seemed like a lot of bad old science. But, of course, the scholastic metaphysics was good sci-ence if located in the context of medieval times. And what we have to do, whilst accepting the justice of many of the criticisms of Bacon and Locke and Descartes of scholasticism, criticisms that Kant took over and developed, is to appreciate that what the advocates of the new science were doing reflected their understanding of only one specific form of science; and that actually there had been scientific meth-ods and scientific reasoning not only in the middle ages but from at least about half way through the first millennium before the common epoch.

Not only Plato and Pythagoras, but the Buddha and Lao Tze were all involved in systematic reflections about the way in which certain structures in human soci-ety or nature, such as maybe the sun or the tides, appear in phenomenally differ-ent forms. Now the idea of the same structure manifesting in different forms is perhaps the central insight of science. You have a difference, you are not just sat-isfied to record the difference, you want to see if there is a structure at work underpinning that difference, and to identify the mechanisms that generate it.

Kant's strictures against ontology can then be understood as being a continu-ation of the polemic against the scholastic metaphysics and for the new experi-mentally based sciences of physics and chemistry, and partly as a warning that ontological reflection in science should never become too severed from epistemo-logical considerations. But it is also important to appreciate that, if you take his argument literally, you are not going to be able to say anything about the world at all. When you look at his philosophy in that light it is an extraordinarily incon-sistent – or inoperable – system because it is a system in which it is impossible to say that the categories are real. It is not possible to say that the transcendental ego is real, because it is included in ontology and ontology for Kant is impermis-sible. It is prohibited by the critical philosophy. Now we have already seen that the mistake here is to assume that because one has a conclusion about the real world, one cannot detach it from its method of investigation. Of course substan-tively that actually reflects the problem that the empiricist scientists would find themselves in, they would be confronted by an interminably insoluble problem of induction because they don't have the concept of ontological structure. There is a level of deeper structure, containing a generative mechanism, which will allow us to explain why the empirical result *must* be so, and it is this level of structure that we scientists now need to identify. Or now we have got to the alethic reason, so that we want to go on and describe the reason for that alethic reason and look at what it is that explains that. From the point of view of critical realism, saying 'That is it, eureka!, I have got to the ontological level of structure in the case at hand!', is of course primarily a way of signalling that we are stepping on to a new round of inquiry, a new level of investigation. It is not a dogmatic claim of infallibility or the closure of knowledge, but rather the opposite.

Heidegger makes a distinction between the ontological and the ontic, he points out correctly that the intercourse of human beings is one that has an interior, so that when I look at someone over there and I see a frown on his face or he says 'I don't understand' then I need to relate to that interior. That intersubjectivity is just as important an aspect of language as referential detachment. Heidegger of course was wont to contrast his rich internal totalities of the human world with the cut and dried world that he assumed operated in science. But of course the scientist is engaged in hermeneutics as well, a hermeneutic of understanding other beliefs and indeed other sciences, including importantly as necessary means of their own innovative activity, unravelling new and deeper structures, the knowledge of which will in turn be potentially critical of beliefs and actions uninformed by them.

Nevertheless it is part of critical realist orthodoxy that there is a major difference between natural and social objects in that social objects have this interior and you can't collapse it. This is part of our substantive ontology when we go into the social domain. We need not make the chronic mistake of the sociology of knowledge, which reasons in line with the epistemic fallacy, from the fact that all *knowledge is social* to the fact that all *knowledge must be about society*. That is a major mistake that again comes from assuming that we can't have specific conclusions about the world, knowledge of particular aspects of being. So we can make a balanced judgement on Heidegger. Natural science also involves intersubjectivity, hermeneutics of inquiry and communication and critiques of beliefs and actions, so that social knowledge is involved in our knowledge of the natural realm. But this transitive implication of the social for our knowledge of the natural realm should not obscure the intransitive differences between them. The major difference is that natural structures do not depend on human agency and so intentionality and conceptuality in the way that social structures do.

Marx was what I call a material object realist. He also had a proto-critical realist view of science as involving movement from appearances to deeper structures that would explain them, but he never actually theorised this and so Marx's innovations have always seemed to most Marxist philosophers and social scientists to be epistemological with the central epistemological category now becoming that of labour, with labour replacing Hegel's category of spirit. That is fine as far as it goes: it is not a criticism of Marx that he had to concentrate on certain aspects of the totality. But where we could go wrong is if we assumed there was no need for ontology. Elsewhere I have argued that the rational development of Marxism does require something like a critical realist ontology – an ontology that it actually presupposes but does not itself theorise.

The stratification of ontology

The last point to make about the general features of the subject matter of ontology is that it is not only differentiated, but it is *stratified*. As such the world can be characterised as being structured and differentiated. At a further level it can be characterised as changing or involving process, and then at a further level as being bound into totalities, and then in a yet further level as incorporating transformative agency. One can build ever more refined concepts of being within the basic structural concepts. At the same time, it is possible to take some philosophical concepts like structure and differentiation and talk about these concepts as instantiated in electricity or in magnetism or the nuclear family and look at particular forms of structures. And so it is necessary to understand being as itself structured, and structured in a way that allows the subject matter of ontology to have multiple characteristic stratifications. Indeed my own work, and its various 'turns', is probably best characterised as a progressive deepening of our understanding of being. That is, a progressive deepening of our understanding of the categories that are manifest in the natural and social world.

Thus let us take the system that I deployed in *Dialectic: The Pulse of Freedom* (1993), what Alan Norrie has characterized as the 'MELD system'. This involves four levels of categorisation: the first, which I called the prime moment (1M) and can be nominated as the level of ontology itself, sees being as structured, then once you have an idea of being as structured you can see being as in process and so you have the second edge (2E), seeing being as processual. The third level (3L) is to see being as a whole, and the fourth level or dimension (4D) is to see being as incorporating transformative agency and reflexivity. A fifth aspect or level, from about the time of *From East To West* (2000), involves seeing being as incorporating a spiritual element understood as embodying deep assumptions about human nature and the affinity of human beings with the rest of nature. A sixth realm or field, which is quite recent, is one in which being is seen as enchanted or re-enchanted, that is as immediately meaningful and valuable. A seventh zone or domain – from my works on meta-reality – consists in seeing being as nondual. So you can see these different categories as embedded within each other. Indeed in this way you can understand my work to date as being a progressive deepening of our attempt to understand ontology, or, at a categorial level, the nature of being. I will now explore some of the aspects of this progressive stratification in greater depth.

As noted, the argument for ontology in *A Realist Theory of Science* was an argument for a new ontology. The most striking feature of the argument for ontology was insistence on the distinction between the transitive and intransitive dimensions that allowed the identification of the epistemic fallacy. This was the way in which empiricism and traditional epistemologies always analysed or reduced being to our knowledge of being. As you will remember Wittgenstein said in a famous phrase that it is sufficient to talk only about the network, we do not have to talk about what the network describes. What my argument did was show that this was a fallacy. In showing that it was a fallacy I opened the way for rational arguments about ontology including the new ontology that I argued was necessary for science in *A Realist Theory of Science*.

Once epistemology is separated from ontology in this way, of course you easily run into a problem, i.e. what about beliefs? Are they a part of the world? Of course they are. Beliefs must be included within ontology, knowledge must be included within being, the referent of epistemology included within the referent of ontology. And epistemology and the whole of philosophy then can be seen in an ontological light. You would still want to have the difference between beliefs and what they are about, so you still have to smuggle back something like a concept of epistemology there. It is still important to know how beliefs are justified, which requires a concept of the intrinsic aspect of science along with some notion of judgemental rationality. So we come back to what I called the holy trinity of critical realism (ontological realism, epistemological relativism and judgemental rationality), their *embeddedness* (judgemental rationalism within epistemic relativism within ontological realism) and their *mutual compatibility*.

In an interesting new book, Archer, Collier and Porpora (2004) use this trinity to show how it allows us to redefine contemporary debates in theology about the existence of god. For to the believer, god is always going to be the sort of thing that must be real in some way, and can not just be fashionably parsed as a metaphorical re-description of our beliefs, values or community, on which the whole project of theology makes no sense. This holy trinity, then, has many implications.

The basic argument from ontology should make clear the idea of the inexorability of ontology. One does not have to make it explicit unless challenged or unless a dominant conception is thought to be wrong. If it is thought to be wrong, then ontology has to be made explicit, thematised and critiqued. But ontology is still inexorable. It is impossible to talk about a known world, one can't talk about objects of knowledge, without presupposing a certain way of being, an ontology for the world known. So that is the first theme, the theme of the *inexorability of ontology*. A second theme is that of the *all-inclusiveness of ontology*, which basically includes everything and therefore obviously we need to make a lot of important self-distinctions within ontology.

From what I have said so far it should be pretty clear that the argument for ontology is really the same as that for realism. It is the argument for referential detachment, for existential intransitivity. Critical realism's importance lies in involving realism about new kinds of things such as structures, systems, processes, wholes, agency, social structure, social relations, ideologies. Of course one could say that the great scientists already knew there were structures, and it is true much of what was involved was bringing out their rational intuitions. But if you look at it as being a set of arguments, if you look at arguments, setting arguments for ontology and arguments for realism side by side makes it possible to see that looking at the world from an explicitly ontological point of view deepens our feel for what realism is and might be.

It is possible, for example, to talk of *dispositional realism* in which possibilities are seen as just as real as, in a sense more real than, the instances that actualise them. How is it possible to have an actualisation that is not based on a real possibility? In this case a domain of real possibilities exists which should include the implicit, the enfolded and much more. Furthermore, we have a thesis that I call *categorial realism*. This is the idea, which I think is a very important idea, that the categories are not just subjective classifications of the world, they are objective features of it. So it is not just that Ohms law is real, it is that causality or nomic lawfulness as such is real, they are real features of the world. And then of course we must allow not just for Ohms law to be real generically, so to say for one instance of it to be real, but for all particular instances to be real. Moreover we must allow for Ohms law not only to be ranged under more basic structures of electro-magnetism, but also to instantiate more basic philosophical categories such as causality; and also to have ranged below it, particular groups or networks of instances of Ohms law, and then those instances in their contexts, furnishing in total a complex mosaic of differentiated (kinds of) stratifications, so that we see the whole field of ontology as being a multi-faceted configuration in its own right.

In other words, the idea of categorial realism is that philosophy has real referents. Causality, space, time, process, emergence, absence, the presence of the past, totality, holistic causality are real features in the world. They don't stand in a more problematic relationship to the world because they designate more abstract features of the world than the features designated by the referents of substantive theories, be they theories of electricity or class structure. Just as the mechanisms those theories posit are not ontologically more problematic than their instances, such as particular electrical phenomena, like the flash lightning that ravaged parts of Cornwall yesterday, or like the threatened strike by BA workers next week, all these are part of the same world. We should be able to talk about categories, mechanisms and their instances in the same breath philosophically, as part of a unified ontology, whilst realising that they occupy different levels of abstraction, or analysis in science. This is categorial realism.

A further distinction, which I have discussed, for example in *Reflections on Meta-Reality*, includes *alethic realism* (and also moral alethic realism). In this context I have also discussed the importance of *tina formations*. The idea of a tina formation is the idea of a necessity that must manifest itself even through a falsity. Actually I think this opens up an extraordinary arena for ontological investigations, looking at how particular ideological constructs, particular ways in which false and superficial theories, actually must presuppose the true and real to work, to keep going – truths which need only be brought out to show the lies, moral absurdities and performative contradictions in virtue of which oppression (including self-oppression) sustains itself. We can in fact make use of axial rationality, which I shall discuss presently, to show how theories deconstruct themselves. We can show this to those who ideologically believe in them. Of course this has to be done within the context of open rational inquiry, in which we must be equally prepared to look at our own ideological baggage.

So far my comments have been restricted to 1M, the domain of being as structured. But in this sort of way one could go through the tropes and possibilities, implications and critiques pertaining to all my seven categorial levels of being. Of course that classification, those seven levels, is just my own classification. Others may prove just as important and just as valid. In any event I think there are really important explanations and explorations in ontology to be achieved and that this is an extremely fertile, if barely broached field for critical realists to work in.

Judgemental rationality and the problem of the 'other'

Let us return to the critical realist 'holy trinity' of *ontological realism, epistemological relativism* and *judgemental rationality*. Critical realism claims to make the reality of objects, structures and so forth consistent with the ideas of the multiplicity and the relativity of our beliefs about them – in what I called the *intransitive* and *transitive dimensions* respectively of science. Moreover it also claims to be able to make both ontological realism and epistemological relativism consistent with judgemental rationality, that is the idea that there are better or worse grounds for our beliefs. As I have suggested above, a great deal of progress has been made within the critical realist literature in discussing the first two elements of the trinity. Unfortunately, it seems that we do not yet have good or convincing ways of resolving the great epistemological and moral problems of our social order.

It is helpful now to consider the concept of four-planar social being (introduced in *Scientific Realism and Human Emancipation* (1986) and extended in *Dialectic: The Pulse of Freedom* (1993)). These are the plane of our material transactions with nature, the plane of social interactions with others, the plane of social structure and the plane of the stratification of the personality. It is not difficult to see that we are in fact in crisis at all of these four levels. It is clear that we are living in a world in which there are great ills, great injustices, great asymmetries of power. It is also clear that we lack a rational organon, or a way in which we can render intelligible to ourselves and each other how we are to engage in the task of persuading people into a better social order and form of social existence, and a better mode of working and being with nature. This is a profound crisis of rationality. Again, if you look at some of the cultural conflicts, conflicts at the face of the 'social cube' which describes the plane of social interactions with others, and which reflects the conflicts between belief systems today, a continual motif is what seems to be the impossibility of understanding and reconciliation. Many Europeans have a problem with President Bush and the American leadership, the American leadership has a problem with the other in the form of the Iraqi other, western civilisation it is said has a problem with the Islamist other, the Islamist other has a problem with the west. We seem to be faced with profound problems of moral and epistemological incommensurability.

Moreover we do not have any idea of a meta-logic in terms of which we could calibrate and resolve the incommensurabilities we have in the world today.

These are all problems of judgemental rationality. What I want to argue is that we do actually have a form of judgemental rationality that is implicit in science and implicit in all cultures, which I shall call 'axial rationality'. This is a form of reasoning, based on the principle that there must be explanations for differences. This is the basic pattern of reasoning in science. If you operate with material objects and they break down, you need to posit an explanation or generative difference for that. If you want to make any progress in mathematics, or if you want to operate a computer, you will need to search for and identify the relevant generative differences that account for manifest differences in behaviour and the similarities or identities that persist through them. This primitive axial rationality is there in all cultures. I am currently writing a book in which I try to show how we can resolve our differences rationally through a method which is continuous with science but which does not beg any one form of scientific knowledge.

I would like to suggest that we are, as a species, bound by two transcendental capacities. One is the transcendental capacity to identify with others, which forms the basis of *universal solidarity* and the second is a transcendental capacity not only to identify and understand others but to reconcile with them, *axial rationality*. These are the themes that I want to stress within the context of the sort of ontology I discussed above.

Let me just motivate this approach a little further. Take the case of understanding the other. Understanding the other is clearly an essential pre-requisite for any kind of sustained communication. Of course it depends on who the other is. But in our society today we have a kind of demonisation of certain selected others. What happens if we don't understand the other and the other is a human being who nevertheless acts intentionally for reasons or motives and regards them as being grounded? The other thinks that they are right, that they have good reasons for what they are doing and that these reasons are grounded. Criteriologically, there is no difference between us and the other. Now suppose we don't like what the other is doing. The important point is that unless we actually get to what is going on in the head of the other, we are not going to change their behaviour. We will not be able to change their behaviour because we do not know what it is that is making them do what they do. If we do not understand what makes a person a terrorist, we are not going to have any effect on terrorism. Understanding the other, then, is tremendously important. Once we start to understand the other then it is necessary to think about how it might be possible to get the other to change. This will involve questions of normative justice and reconciliation. Getting the other to change will not only be easier, but actually depends upon, the extent to which we can put ourselves in the place of the other. It is not only that we must feel *as if* we could have been the other, but that actually we *could have been* the other.[1]

If I had been born into an Arab family, as I could have been, if I had been taken into an Arab context and raised in an Arab household, I would have come to have Arab beliefs. And even if from those Arab beliefs I may have perhaps now come to my actual positions, the positions that I feel I can rationally justify now, my itinerary would have been very different. There is a transcendental capacity to identify with others in virtue of the fact that we could have been other – for in virtue of the fact that we could have been any other, we must have the equipment to identify and understand the other's point of view. So there are going to be no insuperable problems of understanding.

Let us take the case of justification. If it is admitted that there is a kind of base-level rationality, which is central to the idea of axial rationality, then once a conversation is started it can be developed. Moreover once it is understood that the conversation is linked in to praxis, to material transformations of nature and society, and that the conversation is always more than a simple exchange of views, involving commitments to act, then we can gradually work our way towards mutual understanding *and* reconciliation. And then we would have a position in which we had ontological realism, epistemological relativism and judgemental rationality for the social world, based on these transcendental capacities to identify and to achieve reconciliation with others.

These capacities would be based on an ontology of universal solidarity stemming from our common humanity and the contingency of the particular circumstances of our birth; and an epistemology, or axial rationality, which is actually but imperfectly operative in all our different epistemic contexts, in virtue of which we can indeed reach agreement, or transcend differences with others, overcome alienation, conflict and social aporia generally. This is to say, in virtue of axial rationality it *is* possible to work our way through different epistemological and cultural *milieux* until we come to see how it is possible to have an agreement with others. Be that as it may, I think that it is these kinds of issues that critical realism has to address today.

How is it possible for us to talk to people in a different ideological or cultural context, which is interdependent with ours? Talk includes dialogue as well as discourse. In dialogue we imaginatively suspend the context of transformative action – of material practices, struggles and solidarity, but also music, song and dance, which are also based on particular social relations and express our four-planar social being as well – in order to better become (one with) – strange as it may be to say – the other, to achieve transcendental identity with them.

Here I think we can go back to Heidegger, or at least my take on Heidegger, and talk about subject–subject relations. Clearly if I have a relation with this table it is a subject–object relation, if I have a relation with another human being it is going to be a subject–subject one. I want to know what is going on inside, I want to understand his or her feelings, attitudes, experience, etc., I want to be able to talk to that person. This is not the same as talking to a body, and to do this I have to constitute the other person as an epistemological subject in his or her own right just as I am when I investigate nature. When I investigate the table I am an epistemological subject investigating this object. When I talk to another human being I have to see him or her as just such an epistemological subject. And understanding that person as an epistemological subject is itself a necessary condition for seeing him or her as a moral agent. This in turn is a necessary condition for seeing another person as a member of a polity that may or may not be democratic, as it is a precondition for seeing them as a rational interlocutor in a dialogue or a participant in a discourse. Treating another person as an epistemological subject is of course also a precondition for treating him or her as a human being. If I don't constitute him as an epistemological subject then someone may degrade him in a way that the British and American soldiers degraded Iraqi prisoners. It is a short step from not understanding your enemy as an epistemological subject to treating them in that degraded way; and what happens when somebody treats people in that degraded, inhuman, reified way is that they themselves become inhuman. When somebody talks or acts in that way they become inhuman, because they are not able to relate in a human way, they are not *relating as* a human being. By treating the other as an object, they dehumanize, reify and objectify themselves.

So the idea of subject–subject relations is one that should be taken very seriously, bearing in mind particularly the contingency of our own birth, our own incarnation – once we see we could have been the other. This kind of protracted or extended *subject–subject relation* is one that involves practical transformative action as well as imaginative or symbolic action, discourse as well as dialogue, material transformation and conceptual transcendence. We transform the world with the other, particularly we transform our own social structures as well as being able to operate on the social structures of the other and those social, natural and cosmic structures that connect us all. It is my claim, although I can't possibly justify it fully here, that whatever the other was doing before, we should constitute him or her as an epistemic subject and see them as ultimately governed by the logic of axial rationality. This is the same logic that governed the Buddha, Socrates and Jesus. I don't believe there is an effective culture in the world that doesn't observe this way of learning and explaining things. This is of course quite apart from the fact that we are in one globe and that some of the allegedly incommensurable cultures, such as the culture of Islam and the culture of Christianity or Judaism, are so closely connected geo-historically.

When I have a new insight about my own or somebody else's condition this will be an insight about ontology, so ontology still plays the key role. But it is ontology from the point of view of living in a better world, an ontology that includes the call for social justice without which it is unlikely that we can have peace. And unless we have social justice and peace we are not going to have a sustainable future. Indeed, we are not going to have any future at all. These other epistemological and axiological concerns need to be borne in mind then at the same time as we deepen and enjoy our ontological explorations.

Note

1 If you or I had been born in Japan we would have learnt Japanese, and would have been encultured into a Japanese way of life and even if we had come to arrive at exactly our own present beliefs and present attitudes, and as a result of purely rational processes, we would have arrived at them via a different route or itinerary.

References

Archer, M., Collier, A. and Popora, D. V. (2004). *Transcendence: Critical Realism and God*. London: Routledge.

Bhaskar, R. A. (1975). *A Realist Theory of Science*. London: Verso.

Bhaskar, R. A. (1986). *Scientific Realism and Human Emancipation*. London: Verso.

Bhaskar, R. A. (1993). *Dialectic: The Pulse of Freedom*. London: Verso.

Bhaskar, R. A. (2000). *From East to West: Odyssey of a Soul*. London, New York: Routledge.

Bhaskar, R. A. (2002). *Reflections on Meta-Reality: Transcendence, Emancipation, and Everyday Life*. New Delhi, Thousand Oaks, Calif.: Sage Publications.

Part III

Ontology and applied research

13 Freedom, possibility and ontology: rethinking the problem of 'competitive ascent' in the Caribbean[1]

Patricia Northover and Michaeline Crichlow

Introduction

Under contemporary pressures of globalisation the Caribbean Community (CARICOM)[2] seems threatened by increasing global and regional insecurity, vulnerability and marginalisation as they are seemingly once again carried across another 'middle passage rite' in the turbulent waves of a neo-liberal globalization. How can the region find safe passage in this contemporary cross roads marking yet another chapter in their struggle for 'survival and beyond'? What are the imperatives for successfully navigating globalisation, or negotiating a space – if there is little to none – in order to cross-over? Do contemporary analyses and policies for regional development provide an improved or even relevant basis for small and vulnerable states to achieve competitiveness? What exactly are the preconditions for CARICOM's success? In this paper, we explore these questions and point towards elements of an answer, which prioritises analyses about ontology, through a critical engagement of some of the existing approaches to these issues.

In particular, we argue that current perspectives for competitiveness are either still rooted on positivistic modernisation theories of development in addressing how to promote competitive performance in small states and/or they continue to bypass systematic analysis and related empirical examination of the political and social ontological conditions (inclusive of social structural, institutional or social power states) for strategic transformation or regional competitive ascent. Accordingly, there is a failure to substantively explore the complex ontological structuring of social power or the 'state of the state system' in Caribbean societies[3] and correspondingly a failure to provide analyses capable of helping one to elicit a better grasp of the complex forces shaping/challenging the state of dynamically and complexly constituted 'state systems' and 'creole societies'.[4] Yet, without this research and analysis on the 'ontology and dynamics of creole social power'[5] in the Caribbean there is little, we argue, to act on as a basis for *cogently* articulating on the region's *possibilities* to sustain contemporary local or global success in a modern world system of neo-liberal capitalist sway.

Moreover, if the region's search for success is to be tied to its long standing pre-occupation with notions of freedom and sovereignty,[6] and if one is to take by freedom (1) being 'free', 'namely … knowing, possessing the power and the disposition to act in or towards one's real interests'; and (2) being 'liberated'… 'consisting of the transformation of unneeded, unwanted and oppressive to needed, wanted and empowering *sources* of determination';[7] then success in the region, as metered by a progressive politics for emancipation and hence subject empowerment, 'depends on the transformation of structures and not just the amelioration of states of affairs'.[8] Yet, we argue again, without research and analysis on the 'ontology and dynamics of creole social power' there is little to act on as a basis for *cogently* articulating on the region's transformational *possibilities* or '*emancipatory necessities*' to sustain contemporary local or global success. In brief, as argued by Bhaskar (1989) 'emancipation is necessarily informed by explanatory social theory',[9] which in turn calls for, at a minimum, critical realist philosophical commitments.[10]

This chapter thus attempts to develop a more adequate model of social power which can address the possibilities and limits of progressive social change in the context of the Caribbean and their states' attempts to negotiate spaces of freedom through discourses on 'competitive ascent' in the global capitalist system. It is divided into three sections. In the first section we begin with a critical overview of prevailing approaches to the problem of development or progressive social change in the Caribbean. Two strands of analysis are identified. The first conceives of development as a process of Modernisation which prioritises the state (or the 'developmental state') as the main macro-institutional actor, or rather agent, in directing and managing social change. The second approach, described as 'pragmatic', is centred in a bottom-up orientation that stresses a micro-actor and culture embedded rationality in approaching the issue of national or regional progress. Both approaches are argued to be deficient in the analysis of the state–society relationship, or more precisely the problem of the relationship between modern 'power and its subjects', in processes of social change. We argue therefore that an alternative approach is required, which rests on more adequate methodological, theoretical and empirical analyses of the ontology and dynamics of social power – the relationship between 'power and its subjects'. This model is theorised in section 2 of this chapter. In the final section, we argue that this model can be used to help shed critical light on a central process involved in the historical transitions from 'feudalisms' to 'capitalisms': the process of 'rural othering'. These processes of 'rural othering' or the political negotiation over the imagining of identities and possibilities in emergent capitalism, we argue continue to play a pivotal role in the wrestling for the making of history, as may be exemplified in the politics of negotiations over international trade in agriculture, in the context of the World Trade Organisation (WTO). Some concluding comments are then provided.

Section 1: Conditions of possibility for 'achieving ascent' in the Caribbean?

The countries of CARICOM have experienced complex and diversified social histories which have been shaped by divergent geographies and geopolitics. These histories and geographies have led to variegated processes of socio-

Table 13.1 Vulnerability of Caribbean States and Per Capita GDP

	Low vulnerability	Medium vulnerability	High vulnerability	Total
Low per capita[2] income	Guatemala	Honduras Haiti[3] Nicaragua Cuba (estimated)	Guyana	6
Medium per capita income	Venezuela Colombia	Costa Rica Panama Jamaica Dominican Republic El Salvador	St. Kitts & Nevis St Lucia St. Vincent & Grenadines Grenada Dominica Belize Suriname	14
High per capita income	Mexico	Barbados Trinidad & Tobago	Bahamas Antigua & Barbuda	5
Total	**4**	**11**	**10**	**25**

Source: Association of Caribbean States (ACS) – Small economies of the Greater Caribbean, July 2001, p. 45, http://www.acs-aec.org/small_econ_eng.htm
[1] High, medium and low vulnerability are as estimated by the Commonwealth Vulnerability Index scores.
[2] High per capita income is >US$5000.
Medium per capita income is US$2000–5000.
Low per capita income is <US$2000.
[3] Haiti is the only Least Developed Country (LDC) amongst all the ACS countries.

economic change, reflected in the patterns of economic structure and performance, with some states regarded as 'out performing' others, but all today remain, by and large, vulnerable small states, see Table 13.1.[11] Furthermore, all face increasing *insecurity* at the national, regional and global level given the complex socio-economic, environmental and political effects of globalization processes,[12] deepening *vulnerability* as small or small island developing states[13] and threatened *marginalisation* in the competitive circuits of global capital.[14]

The Caribbean Regional Negotiation Machinery (CRNM), set up by CARICOM has been given the complex task of negotiating 'reciprocity' in the 'cross currents of globalization and regionalization', in order to facilitate 'strategic global repositioning' for the competitive viability of its members.[15] But what are the regional and/or national socio-political constraints and conditions of possibility for 'achieving ascent in the next century'?

Roughly, two broad types of argument on the 'conditions of possibility' or 'necessary' social and institutional forms and processes for achieving ascent can be detected in the Caribbean development literature. They are either: (a) prescriptive top down and single exit explanatory perspectives on modernization calling for national and/or 'supra-national' 'state autonomy' (the latter premised on political union within the Caribbean Single Market and Economy CSME), as *the* necessary institutional form, for enabling ascent as 'modernized capitalism'; or (b) pragmatic perspectives on modernisation that have evolved and revolve around the need for more fine grained actor perspectives on the nature of Caribbean 'identity', ideology and cultural forms and on the distinctive socio-economic and moral institutions that will sustain local endogenous transformation processes.

The first perspective expresses a vision of an essentially top-down national and/or regional type of *'Developmental State'*, that is strategically engaged in the political engineering of the conditions for modern economic change,[16] *viz.* modern industrialisation, whether manufacturing or agricultural (or both) based (Thomas 1974, 1988; Marshall 1998; Karagiannis 2002; Karagiannis & Alleyne 2003). In this approach, however, there is a failure to go beyond a broad brush and essentialising method in the analysis of complex processes. Thus, despite the introduction of historical categories, such as class or culture, into the discussion of Caribbean state–society relationships, a systematic empirical interrogation of these analytical constructs is absent, reflecting the avoidance of a deeper engagement with the nature of the social processes and practices underpinning this relationship and the Caribbean social reality. Accordingly, the conclusions remain ultimately rooted in a form of *aprioristic* reasoning that offers to deductively generalise possibilities given premises of *institutional political development* 'laws' that have been abstracted as the conditions for national or regional success. In this case, we have the implied 'law' that – strong states, idealised as those with (somehow generated) 'embedded autonomy',[17] will (somehow) effect the right mixture of repression and incentives, and thereby produce the trajectory of 'ascent'.

The second perspective points to the need for fine-grained actor perspectives on the nature of Caribbean 'identity', ideology and cultural forms and on the distinctive socio-economic and moral institutions that will sustain local endogenous transformation processes (Lewis 1955; Nettleford, 1997; Hall, 2001; C. Y. Thomas 2001,[18] 2003). In other words, this approach is more 'pragmatic' or less driven by 'formulaic' institutional prescriptions and more centred in a bottom-up, or micro-actor-orientated and culture embedded rationality approach to modernisation. This type of analysis is in turn expected to more adequately inform and shape the building of a Caribbean regional ideology and regional development process (Boxill 1997). The tendency in this approach is thus to try to focus on social, socio-economic and cultural conditions required for achieving ascent in the form of an embedded, indigenous or creole, Caribbean modernisation process. The second perspective lends support to a more *a posteriori* approach and thus tends to call attention to the issues of particular social and/or cultural histories, or particular constructions and readings of these, that are seen as shaping distinctive paths to national and regional development. But what is the relationship between the society, economy and the State, that is implied in this more pragmatic creole envisioning of creatively 'achieving ascent' under contemporary globalisation? Indeed, if a key recognition within the pragmatic approach is that the viability of the Caribbean State and society in a global capitalist system depends on its creole subversion of the process of modernisation through creole flexible creative engagement, then the practical political questions to be addressed for this approach are these. Can such desirable outcomes be achieved without, as Migdal would say, a 'State-in-society' acting, strategically, and not merely functionally, to enhance domestic capabilities through specific political processes? And, more pointedly, what is the nature of the concrete political processes or dynamics shaping this unfolding potential for the emergence of an emancipatory creole social power?

Silence on these questions would tend to support a position of functionalist political agnosticism on the strategic role of the State–society relationship, which we argue would hinder the subversive and transformational interests of the specific social powers of groups which have been at the root of the creative creole subversions of, and cultural struggles with, the experienced paradoxes of modernisation such as growth without equity, or modern change without higher or better social powers or rising productivity. The imperative here in order to support the theme of creole social empowerment in the pragmatic approach is thus to pursue an investigation of the nature of the ongoing political processes shaping the 'state of the state system' in creole social life worlds and hence the potentials and probabilities for emergent *Caribbean creole social capabilities, powers and state capacities*. In particular, what is *absent* is a specific understanding of *C/creolisation processes* which could enable a better probing of Caribbean state, society and economy relationships in order to better understand (analytically and empirically) the basis for a transformational relationship to be forged between the State and society in the making of history.[19] This would also help one to better determine or judge the possibilities for a strategising 'State-in-society' acting to link and build 'social capital'[20] and indeed acting or engaging *with* 'social movements'[21] *for* a positively enhanced Caribbean regional development.

Now, while issues of 'power' seem more foregrounded in the first perspective given the ostensive linking of state and society in attempting to grasp the basis for transformational processes, it relies on an *ultimately* deterministic and 'aprioristic' reasoning reflecting an inadequate attention to the nature of the (sociocultural and political) 'C/creolisation' processes entailed in them. The systematic examination of processes germane to institutional development trajectories are accordingly either assumed not to causally matter much for extrapolating this institutional policy formula mix for success, or the relevant mix of repression and freedom associated with 'embedded state autonomy', is apparently to be determined through class categories, or is left as an unexamined socio-political C/creolisation process, that may somehow produce the right outcomes. More generally, despite the fact that modern capitalist states are undoubtedly 'doubly embedded' in global and local social structural processes, this approach glosses over the ways in which generic real interests acting on the state are translated into particular *imagined necessities*. In so doing the complex and open-endedness of the dynamic path conditions embedding states seeking economic viability within the circuits of global competitive capital is analytically brushed aside.

In other words, the issue, as highlighted by Migdal (2001), of *how* particular *imagined necessities*, or *its form of political expression are constantly being negotiated* with *diverse* social groups given that interests pursued by the state must command/attract a level of legitimacy and public trust, within and without its shifting borders of sovereignty is left unattended. Yet these constraints on the ways that states concretely work out particular interests, or specific forms of 'embedded autonomy', as shaped by particular C/creolisation processes, in turn act to *shape* the 'state of the state system' – social powers and subject capabilities – and consequently the technological dynamism in the society. The outcomes of these political processes furthermore cannot be read deterministically.

Overall, the presence of a tendency to aprioristic reasoning leads to two major weakness in this approach as a guide to development policy. First, insufficient depth of empirical analysis, as seen for example in the absence of a study of *the processes and forms of* Caribbean creole empowerments means that there is little to substantiate and guide the *'how'* of politically acting for the claimed transformational 'necessities' to sustain local or regional success. Second, there is a tendency to oscillate between a *deterministic* pessimism on the weakness of existing states and an *unjustifiable* optimism that such weak states could execute the changes for the 'developmental state' project prescribed, given the penchant for 'aprioristic' reasoning again reflecting an inadequate attention to the nature of processes of social development.[22] On the whole then, both perspectives are insufficient for formulating an approach to regional ascent because of inadequate methodological bases for the analysis of processes of social development, which in turn engenders a failure to sufficiently or more concretely examine and analyse the institutional and socio-political *'how possible'* process and agency conditions for producing and shaping the probabilities for ascent.

The above discussion reinforces Bhaskar's reflections on the relation between explanation and emancipation, as it is clear that securing the regions' survival and beyond, requires an escape from positivistic, functionalist, aprioristic and deterministic analytical methodologies, in order to properly explore the paths for regional ascent, and the nature of the relationship between society, economy and the state, as articulated through specific C/creolisation processes. At a minimum, we argue that a reliance on critical realist methodologies that can accommodate process and complex open systems analysis, will be required to pursue the needed research into the particularities of the social and political processes shaping the 'state of the state system' in creole social life worlds and the complexity of real interests influencing the State in its unfolding role in relating to the society, to enable a Caribbean creole development.

In the next section, we seek to overcome the aforementioned analytical deficiencies by suggesting a model for grasping the ontology and dynamics of powers in our modern societies. We develop the arguments for this model by moving through a brief critical review of recent discussions examining the nature of the relationship between the state, society and history.

Section 2: 'Imagining state systems': critical reflections and new directions

Recent approaches seeking to understand the processes and politics of development and change, reflect divergent views on the State's significance to history making and have varied conceptualisations of its mode of articulation with society. The strengths and limits of these efforts however seem correlated with the extent to which they have effectively redressed the weaknesses in the perspectives on the State that have been developed out of the modernisation paradigm. One approach in particular that represents an effort to pull together the most important contributions on thinking about the state–society relationship is Migdal's (2001) 'State in Society' approach. We believe our approach represents an advance on this and also escapes the modernisation paradigm. We begin the discussion with a brief look at this dominant paradigm's treatment of the issue of the state–society–history relationship, drawing on the discussion in Migdal (2001), and then introduce our model of the relation between 'Power and its Subjects'.

In Migdal's (2001) discussion of the dominant modernisation perspective informing the study of development and change, he notes that the accomplishment of modernisation has been constantly associated with the presence of a Modern Nation State (MNS). In introducing the State as actor, these modernisation-orientated development discourses tended to rely on the Weberian tradition of defining the State as a bureaucratic organisation with a monopoly over legitimate violence, and with a *modus operandi* of bureaucratised *scientific* rationality. The effect of this characterisation is to focalise social power as being embedded within the institutionalised bounds of the MNS and thus restrict an analysis of political power in societies to this organisation's ontology and its managerial dynamics for executing power. With the ontology and dynamics of social power neatly packed into the MNS as 'representational political power', the State becomes *the 'representative' locus of authority and power in the modern society and the world*. The MNS is constructed as *the centre* for the acting of the modern subject, *the representative author* of modern change.

Unsurprisingly then, given this scripted entrance onto the modern world stage, the MNS quickly assumes, at least on stage, its 'representative' authorship over the process of modern history making, and submerges all history into its history of *the acting subject* or *the critical prime mover in society and mover of society*, with the latter, i.e. society, to be 'represented,' acted upon, and transformed by the representative holder of Modern Subject–Sovereignty, the MNS. In abstracting power in this way, and in this 'imagining' of the State, the path was thus prepared for both the crafting of sterile dichotomies along old analytical axes of centre–periphery and subjects–objects, and the engendering of critical dissent, in theory and practice. For example, from the equation core=subject=State and periphery=other/object=society we engender the State/society dichotomy and the image of *verticality* which is interpreted as the State being 'outside' and 'above' society.[23]

Criticisms of such analytical dichotomies with their implied separations between the state, society and culture, and its *gifting* of the State with *autonomous* history making powers, in virtue of its claimed '*autonomy*' have of course been made. For example, one has Geertz's (1980) inversion perspective of 'Power serving Pomp'; or the ordering powers ascribed to the State become 'State effects' according to Mitchell (1991), an appearance or spontaneous illusion, produced because of the pervasive extension of Foucauldian disciplinary technologies or governmentalities of which the State is *but a part*, rather than *apart,* standing above like some reified structure; or the ordering powers of the State become complicated, as Migdal (1988) argues, by powerful societies which produce weak states; or by class struggle in wars of position to establish hegemony according to Gramsci (1971).

Migdal's objective in his 2001 text is to critically weave these critiques against the image of verticality into his 'State in Society' approach in order to argue that the practices and *experiences* of the State – as organisations with certain powers and capabilities, whether 'weak' or 'strong' – are embedded and meaningfully constituted in society/groups/civil society, and are negotiated through culture/representations. Through this critical synthesis, Migdal attempts to break new ground or to critically develop on the analytics of the ontology and dynamics of power in society. Indeed, Migdal's critical shifts have wide appeal in the contemporary literature on the state, which as Hansen and Stepputat (2001) argue, is now more concerned to 'explore the local and historically embedded ideas of normality, order, intelligible authority and other languages of stateness'.[24] Accordingly, as Ferguson and Gupta (2002) comment, 'states are not simply functional bureaucratic apparatuses, but powerful sites of symbolic and cultural production that are themselves always culturally represented and understood in particular ways. It is here that it becomes possible to speak of states, and not only ... nations as "imagined" – that is, as constructed entities that are conceptualised and made socially effective through particular imaginative and symbolic devices that require study'.[25] And indeed they do require study, but what sorts of questions should we be asking in this more culturally and conflict sensitive investigation of the State in society/culture?

Thus, despite the breakthroughs being made here, we submit that much of what is going on in these contemporary discussions may still be reflecting a *prioritisation of the way in which the problem of order has been previously framed and solved* in the study and practice of domination and change in society.

Towards imagining 'state systems in social life worlds'

Our main concern here is to try to go beyond Migdal's study in his tendency to focus on *securing order*. As Migdal states, 'the challenge for political leaders has been how to remain apart from society – the state as the ultimate authority – while somehow still benefiting from people's "collective self-consciousness", their sense of belonging to something bigger than themselves of which they are an integral part'.[26] Thus, we note Migdal's preferences to appeal to Shil's notion of the 'image' of the State as a powerful *normative social centre,* imagined to produce the social whole, and thus can broker the peace between its individual elements in the world. Ultimately then, Migdal's study is characterised by the tendency to define the problem of order, not only in organisational terms as guided by the MNS construct, but primarily in terms of a problem of adhesiveness and the lack of adhesiveness.

What is being set up here, we suggest, is a framing of the problem of social power, or the state–society relationship, in terms of the Hobbesian problem of order which premises atomistic human beings in extrinsic relations with others.[27] This reinforces a focus on inter-actional conflict and uncertainty as the heart of the problem of social order. With this methodological/ontological frame, the relations between power and the subject are fundamentally contingent and external, a relation of force and domination. Given the above a tradition is established for oscillating these two models of social order, namely the under-socialized man (rational economic modern man living solely through contracts or markets, *Homo Economicus*) and the over-socialised man (traditional man living by rule following, *Homo sociologicus*). In both the problem conceptualisation remains the same, that is, deviation or conflict is to be addressed by finding a superstructural adhesive, e.g. state or culture as superglue, and thus legitimacy of order problems is addressed through rituals and negotiations for producing this glue.

To go beyond this level of analysis it is necessary to break with the framework for discussing order and shaping discourse on the state and power in society. To do this three ontological departures will be made based on alternative analysis of 'human subject being' in the world, which paves the way for establishing a different view of the ontological structure of 'social being in the world', and from there a conceptualisation of 'social power in social life worlds' or 'State systems in social life worlds', which is the model that we wish to set out in contrast to the approaches briefly analysed above.

We wish to begin our discussion by arguing that instead of asking the question guiding the existing approaches to the study of power and change in society, 'how is order possible?' which implicates an oscillation between rationalistic and functionalistic accounts of social order and impoverishes our understanding of dynamics, we should instead begin by asking *how does disorder, or processes of separation or even alienation, emerge*? This feeds into the related problem, *how does that experience of disordering productions shape the dynamics of process*?

This problem re-focusing requires empirical support by examining the nature of human being's social life in the world. Tim Ingold provides a very detailed examination of this very issue in his text, *Evolution and Social Life* (1986). In that text, he argues for a model of the human being as 'a conscious subject, whose life is a trajectory as entwined with those of others around him as the lives of the latter are with his [and] whose conscious life … is a movement that adopts culture as its vehicle'.[28] Social life thus 'exists in the intertwining … it is the process by which we constitute one another as persons'. Indeed he argues that our social relations are produced in the '*movement*' of this intertwining process of social life.[29] Drawing on Mauss's analysis of the exchange of gifts, he goes on to argue that the production of the social relationship is achieved through the mutual giving of oneselves, thus creating an inter-subjective bond between persons, a mutual subjectivity production. Accordingly, social order reflects processes of interpenetrative and constitutive dependence, and the experience of social order is constituted in and from these social relationships that reflect 'the temporal unfolding of consciousness through the *instrumentality* of cultural forms'.[30] As Archer (1995) succinctly states, 'social identity is an emergent from personal identity'.[31]

From this perspective of human being in the world the problem facing persons in the mutual constitution of their social lives and selves is *not how to glue together* separated beings, but rather *how to transform* the inescapable internal relations of 'being together' and 'becoming together', at both the personal and social levels, in a way that seems to offer the enhancement of personal or subject being in the world. Since this subjectivity is formed through the inter-subjective experiences of social life, the search for a better expression of person being is simultaneously a self-interested and altruistic choice for the sustaining of social life. Taking this human subjectivity and its internally related constitution of person being as the vital agents in history, the question thus becomes, how do these agents engender change? Or, as Archer (1995) would say, how do they engender the *morphogenesis* of their social worlds and consequently the state of social and subject powers?

In order to explore the analytics of this morphogenetics of power, we thus wish to briefly turn to Archer's (1985), *Realist Social Theory,* where she has argued, drawing on the philosophical orientation of critical realism, that in order to address the question of articulation between *the people* (the subjects) and *the parts* (the given conditions of social power for agents' social formation) it is necessary to maintain the notion of emergent properties at the level of agency and structure and hence subscribe to a model of complex ontological stratification of social life worlds. In her text, she elaborates on models that explain the morphogenetics of structure, culture and agency, by taking time to link, structure and agency and unpack the critical realist's Transformational Model of Social Activity (TMSA), elaborated by Bhaskar (1989).

In brief, this model of social ontology holds that structure and agency are ontologically separate yet mutually constitutive or determining of each other. But not in a mode of 'instantiation' as argued in Gidden's structuration theory, but by a process of morphogenetics, which allows for the complex time-structure mediated, *ontological interplay* between the parts (which she analytically separates into the Structural Emergent Powers (SEPs)[32] of cultural and structural systems), and the people. This allows for a study of their dynamics of transformation and avoids collapsing into models of individualism or holism for explaining social process. As she explains, 'the morphogenetic task is to supply an account of how the powers of the "parts" condition the projects of the "people" – involuntaristically but also non-deterministically, yet none the less with directionality'.[33] While one may still wish to engage Archer on her substantive arguments about the theories of the world and the nodes and modes of articulation taking place between, persons, agents, collectivities and structurally emergent properties that she has developed, we believe her contributions are critical for thinking through the dynamic of the relations between power and the subject. In particular, Archer's social models, along with Ingold's arguments on social life, allow us *to begin to pose vital questions* as to *how* our vital agents, human subjects personally, relationally and collectively *co-produce and change* their complex world, drawing on structural resources, or as constrained/enabled by structurally emergent powers (SEPs).

Thus far, by beginning with Ingold's 'constitutive' model of social life, and personal identity, we are led to support a view of the ontological stratification of human beings in an ontologically stratified world. That is, the human being is (at least) a doubly emergent person, which is to say that our person being is ontologically dependent on our relations with nature and with social conditions that predate person being in the world, but this person being is irreducible to neither.[34] There is thus an ontological articulation between social being in place/space, via the positions that we encounter in life, and the person being/human body in place/space, as mediated by the conscious subject.[35] The possibility for disorder now emerges given the inter-generational, time dated, co-evolution of our complex social life in the world. That is, this disorder emerges if, and in so far as the structural emergent socio-cultural conditions shaping social being and action *negatively* shape/constrain the subject's experiences of inter-subjectivity and their interactive exploration of themselves in the mutual shaping processes of social life production.

In the next section we will be highlighting one such process of disordering, namely 'rural othering', that emerged with modernity, but in general potential examples of 'disordering' social life may be *uncovered* in what Foucault described as 'modes of objectification which transform human beings into subjects'.[36] The first two modes of this objectification process are (a) the production of 'subjects of *scientific* study' through the formation of discourse systems or fields, such as 'political economy', that are 'the set of rules which at a given period and for a given society define the limits and forms of the sayable … conservation … memory … reactivation [and] … appropriation';[37] and (b) 'dividing practices' where 'the subject is divided inside himself or divided from others', as exemplified in sane/mad, modern/traditional, good/bad or sacred and profane dividing practices.[38] These twinned processes are *implemented with* disciplinary technologies, highlighting the embedding of body politics in all discursive regime formations, *but,* as Foucault was to later emphasise,[39] which were also *always exercised through* processes of *governmentality* – neatly described by Foucault (1983, 1991b) as 'the conduct of conduct'.

However, it is important to emphasise here that these two processes of 'objectification' or 'othering'[40] are necessarily articulated with a third form of 'objectification', which is 'the way in which a person turns him- or herself into a subject'.[41] This last process is internally but non-determinately linked to the other forms of objectification through governmentality – which is Foucault's structure–agency point of articulating contact – and it is more concerned with the work of self or subject expression or how we form ourselves into meaning giving subjects. Accordingly, the first two modes of objectification are mediated by a person's sense or consciousness of themselves in the world and so *experiences* of disorder will be subject sensitive. *If* there *is an experience (in the subjective sense indicating awareness) of disorder* this implies the engendering of a disturbance in relations of reciprocity-sustaining social relationships, that is, a disturbance in the process of *inter-subjective bonding between persons in their mutual subjectivity production*. This disorder or disturbance will then form the basis for a person's inter-subjective and ontological insecurity in social relationships, and lay the ground for the presence of fundamental uncertainty and conflict in negotiating interests and managing uncertainty in social life. Finally, this disorder or disturbance, given its (ontological and epistemological) impacts on person or subject being via social being, will also form the conditions for the subject-driven social processes of the politics of identity (or meaning) in the world, as can be seen, for example, in the complex dynamics in post colonial and gender identity politics.

Given the above, if one examines Foucault's (1983) analysis of power one now more clearly sees that Foucault's treatment of power is consistent with a treatment of power as a Structural Emergent Property (SEP). That is, as a condition for the actions of the *subject* – which Foucault also treats as a *person*, that is 'someone … tied to his own identity by a conscience or self'.[42] In particular, Foucault in speaking to power, states that:

> In itself, the exercise of power is not violence: nor is it consent which, implicitly is renewable. It is *a total structure of actions* brought to bear upon possible actions: it incites, it induces, it makes easier or more difficult; in its extreme it constrains or forbids absolutely; it is nevertheless *a way of acting upon an acting subject or acting subjects* by virtue of their acting or being capable of action. A set of actions upon other actions'[43] (our emphasis).

After which Foucault is quick to make the deliberate link back to conduct, when he argues that 'perhaps the equivocal nature of the term *conduct* is one of the best aids for coming to terms with the specificity of power relations. For to 'conduct' is at the same time to 'lead' others (according to mechanisms of coercion that are to varying degrees, strict) and a way of behaving within a more or less open field of possibilities. The exercise of power consists in guiding the possibility of conduct and putting in order the possible outcome'.[44]

The point we wish to suggest here is that Foucault is seeking, through the concept of governmentality, to elaborate on what may be termed a *State system*, defined very broadly, in the first instance, as an *irreducible social power shaping (that is, constraining/enabling) the social life worlds of persons*. We argue that this view of governmentality as expressive of a 'state system in social life worlds' is consistent with Foucault's emphases in explaining how in 'modern governmentality' 'one governs things … government is the right disposition of things, arranged so as to lead to a convenient end'.[45] Here 'things' have to do 'not with territory but rather a sort of complex composed of men and things. The things … are in fact men, *but men in their relations, links, imbrication with those other things* …'.[46] And finally in Foucault's contention that (iii) governmentality, 'is at once internal and external to the state'.[47] Foucault's comments above, we believe, are thus clearly signalling modern governmentality as the concrete expression of modern social power, a move which then enables him to shift the focus in the analysis of modern social power from the institutional–organisational level to the structural–institutional level.

By making a creative analogical extension drawing on Durkheim's *Elementary Forms of Religion* (EFOR), we wish to elaborate on the definition of a *State System, that is, as a representational system for the collective expression of positional political identities or cosmologies of social being in the world that turn on sacred and profane identity relations.*[48] We argue further that modern governmentality articulates the sacred and the profane generally along the cultural axis of *modern power rationalities.* However, the nature of the specific sacred/profane positional identities associated with a concrete state system will be dependent on the nature of the specific **agents** (adaptive and governmentality engineering tactics) culturally adapting modern governmental ensembles.[49] This leads to complexly structured politics of identity struggles within social or C/creolisation processes which are the basis for the making and the morphing of both modern P/power and modern S/subjects, and relatedly governmentality or state systems.[50]

Now, in virtue of experiencing social power within – as a representative and governor of 'biopolitics' in a city–citizen game – and without – as Representative Subject and Agent of modern social Power in a shepherd–flock game – the modern state-qua institution holds a strategic role *not just* in the *mediation* of the relationship between P/power and its S/subjects given these two games, it *also* holds a strategic role in *the transformation* of that relationship and hence the nature of these two games.[51] In particular, the experience of the state in terms of 'its survival and its limits on the basis of the general tactics of governmentality',[52] will set in train changes in states of consciousness, or states of subject experiences which will disturb the nature of the 'governmentalisation of the state' and create tendencies for the reconfiguration of social Power *in the very processes of the* state's governmentality tactics. Thus, only by engaging in an analysis that addresses *all the ontological layers of the state system* (structural, institutional and inter-subjective social powers) will one be able to identify the set of political conditions important to strategically guiding the transformation of conditions needed for deepening the experiences of subjects' empowerment in the Caribbean or elsewhere. We suggest that the following model below of 'State systems in social life worlds' provides one with such a framework for the analysis of the relationship between P/power and its S/subjects (see Figure 13.1).

Finally, to reinforce the value of our model in sustaining a shift in thinking about power and the subjects in the Caribbean or elsewhere, we want to use our model to elaborate on the *morphogenetics of power*[53] by introducing the concepts of *vertical demands* (VD) and *horizontal necessities (HN)* which together combine to constitute and produce the *politics of the cross.* Thus, from our model we have that the vertical demands on person-being in the world are produced through cultures of power (COP) which are *Representations of social Power* for the expression of social reality. While these vertical demands reinstate the verticality effect of Power being above and yet apart of the body politic, they seek concrete realisation in social relationships and thus the horizontal processes of

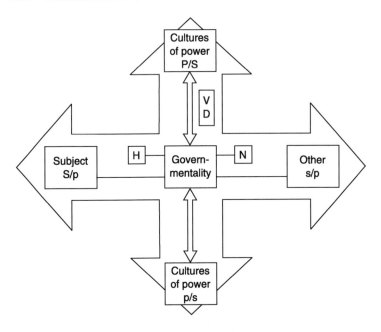

Figure 13.1 State systems in social life worlds.

*We use capitalised P to refer to social power and lower case p to refer to the agents' powers (state institutions as well as persons). Capitalised S refers to *The* Subject, sacred political identities, and lower case s refers to 'the others', represented as 'population', citizens and/or 'subjects'. The internal relations between P/S and p/s engender the cultural politics of the cross shaping the morphing of social power, culture–state systems or modern governmentality.

othering/disordering. But since social relations reflect a 'process by which we constitute one another as persons' then vertical demands will stimulate the 'horizontal necessity' of a '*struggle for meaning*;'[54] a '*cultural politics*' *that is exercised through* processes of *governmentality* – 'the conduct of conduct'.[55] Such a '*cultural politics*' engendered from the intersecting vertical demands and horizontal necessities, producing the cross, is thus implicated in the routine productions of social life.

Section 3: 'Rural othering' within modernity and its significance

As we have argued in the previous section, the open ended dynamics of processes of history making are driven by the morphing, or morphogenetics, of social political power embedded in 'State systems in social life worlds', which in turn takes place through the cultural politics of, so to speak, the 'cross'. From this perspective, we wish to emphasise that the emergence of 'capitalisms' out of 'feudalisms', given the latter's rootedness in land embedded relations between 'power and its subjects', meant that the cultural ascension of the former – a contingent social political power – would be marked by an architectural constraint channeling/expressing the reconfiguration/reconstitution of land and social labour processes around new relations of political identity.[56] Thus, in light of these transformational processes, the imagining of 'modernity' and 'modern power' was achieved largely through a politics of identity *differance*[57] with 'feudal' social political power.

Accordingly, the cultural struggles over meaning emergent out of the 'modern' vertical demands for archetyping 'modern social life' would have been orientated around what we wish to describe as a 'process of rural othering'. This term is thus used to describe the transition from 'feudalism' to 'capitalism' as it relates to the reconfiguration of social power in relation to the land. This process involves new constructions of relations of political identity/difference, and thus entails struggle and negotiation over political identity which arises as a result of or through the contested reconfiguration of relations between 'land' (or 'nature'), 'labour' (or 'subjectivity') and 'capital' (or 'modern social power').

This complex phenomena of 'rural othering' associated with the rise of the modern world economy, is a phenomenon that has been recognised from an early stage, and thus an evolving consciousness of it is threaded through the many critical and analytical reflections on the unfolding of the capitalist process. Thus from Marx's polemics in the *Communist Manifesto* (1848), which presents a picture of the inexorable logic and dominance of capitalist society in which, 'the bourgeoisie has subjected the country to the rule of the towns', and creates 'a world after its own image'; to Kautsky's critical reflections in 1899 on the 'Agrarian Question', which focused on the issues of the nature of the transformations taking place in the social relations of production with the industrialisation of agrarian societies;[58] to Karl Polanyi's 1957 critique of the 'Great Transformation', which examines the transition process in terms of the rise of the 'market society' and its limit points in its tendencies to the commodification of land and labour, which would invoke 'double movements' and reactive forms of governmentalities; and more recently, we observe that Polanyi's concerns find contemporary resonance in the anxieties expressed in U. Beck's thesis of the 'Risk society', which points to the breaching of the limits from the extension of 'market society' given the 'ageing of industrial modernity' where 'the social political, ecological and individual risks created by the momentum of innovation increasingly elude the control and protective institutions of industrial society'.[59]

These aforementioned discourses underline the fact that the ascension of modern state systems has led to processes of 'rural othering', forming and being read as a central symbolic motif for politically fixing/reifying or resisting/unsettling the sacred identity categories, or relations, that are invested in 'capital' as a modern social power. This remains the case, even as these modern social identity relations orientating capitalism are being transformed from the dynamic effects of its complexly articulated socio-cultural exercises of social power.

This can been seen in the Caribbean, for example, in terms of the efforts and impact of development economists like Arthur Lewis in promoting, through his famous dual-economy model of economic growth, an alternative and modern imagining of Caribbean societies which was different from colonial governments' construal of them as naturally 'agrarian colonial societies'.[60] Lewis's model provoked a new twist to the processes of rural othering, by creating a new identity of 'unproductive labour' in virtue of its location in 'traditional space' in the dual developing economy. The postulation of this 'traditional space' (by and large attached to the land and thus also associated with the rural/agrarian–urban dichotomy), calls for a 'development policy' to be geared to fostering growth by the replacement of this 'traditional' or 'rural', 'unproductive' space by 'modern' or 'urban' 'capitalist' enterprise, through the exploitation of this 'unlimited' pool of 'unproductive labour'. This development strategy which rests on this creative re-configuration of rural othering along traditional–modern or dual economy dichotomies suffered from sharp limitations however as the new 'non-sacred' others, marginalised from a greater inclusion in cultures of power given 'traditional political identities' experienced a worsening of conditions of social life, partly manifested in deepening rural poverty, which in turn deepened conflicts and cleavages within post-colonial nation states engaged in these development policies for modernising or catching up with modernity. The 'development crises' ineluctably produced by these innovations on rural othering processes of course also engendered counter-conducts to secure new experiences of subjectivity by playing/deconstructing, appropriating and as far as possible reshaping, the new modern nation states with its centred actors and projects of 'development' executed through that special species of post colonial governmentality.[61] The strategies of modern nation making have thus symbolically proceeded through a variety of strategies of 'rural othering', reshaping land–labour–capital and society– economy-state-system reconfigurations in response to ostensible 'failings' of the 'modernisation or development project'.

To recap then, we have argued that the *visible* expression of the 'legitimate power and authority' of the modern state system has been *symbolically located* not just in the institution of the 'modern nation-state', but also, and of equal or perhaps greater importance, in the *subordinate identities* produced in 'creating the countryside,'[62] or in *imagining* 'rural spaces' and expressed in a cultural politics of 'rural othering'. This kind of interpretive schema we believe can in this post colonial neo-modern era of WTO engagements and trans-nationalising forces, help to illuminate or direct the forging of new strategies that are needed by States–qua institutions in order to legitimise their claims to authority and rule.[63] But it is not states–qua institutions that drive the making of history, but rather the complex processes relating P/power to the S/subjects, hence, states and citizens, non-states and non-citizens, Subjects and others in the world must and will enter into different kinds of relationships with each other as they seek to reposition themselves within the global economy and reassert themselves *glocally (i.e. within and without the local and the global)*. Conjunctural and structural dynamics in the global processes of space and place making require however different strategies and processes of negotiation from within and outside states. These negotiations will thus entail complex elaborations of power 'within the social networks at the local scale and between the local and non-local (or global) scales'.[64] Critically, these negotiations may result in an unsettling of the processes of rural othering, however this potential will be dependent on the ongoing cultural struggles and C/creolisation processes associated with morphing modern social powers and state systems and thus also reflective of the real wrestlings taking place among the contesting modern state systems in social life worlds in defence of the sovereignty of the imagination.

Conclusion

In the absence of adequate analysis of the ontology and dynamics of power in the Caribbean, the existing analyses on the possibilities and processes for development in the region perpetuate an insidious bias against endogenous social transformation. In so doing they continue to ignore the lessons from Lloyd Best's observations on the complexity of Caribbean ontology – emergent from unique yet systemic 'global and local', 'structural and institutional' 'plantation and post-colonial' 'processes and forces' – and his related critiques of Caribbean's epistemology. Moreover, by continuing to fail to integrate critical observations on the nuanced character and strengths (or weaknesses) of Caribbean creolity – culture, society, polity, economy – into 'adjustment' and 'adaptation' paradigms and strategies for 'ascent', these current approaches and paradigms for 'competitive success' threaten to leave the rich depth of the Caribbean's potentials and values in a state of endogenous peripheralisation, despite the recurrent rhetorical praise for the creative spirit and ethic of the peoples of the region. Moreover as the Caribbean struggles with neoliberalisation which has generated a set of conflicts that throw into relief the issues of sovereignty and autonomy, we have sought to go beyond the customary discussion of whether states–qua institutions are being weakened or not to focus rather on the reconfiguration of states systems in societies, drawing on our model of the relationship between 'Power and its Subjects'.

Notes

1 We wish to acknowledge our debt to the anonymous referees of this paper whose comments were invaluable in helping to reshape this chapter. The paper also benefited from the comments of the participants at the 2004 Annual IACR conference.
2 The CARICOM member states are Jamaica, Trinidad and Tobago, Barbados, Dominica, St. Lucia, St.Vincent, Grenada, Bahamas, Haiti, Guyana, St. Kitts/Nevis, Antigua and Barbuda, Suriname, Belize and Monsterrat. It represents 15 million people and has an aggregate GDP of approximately US$ 36 billion (2003).
3 The modern Caribbean, or those group of countries linked by the Caribbean sea which includes more than just the CARICOM group, was shaped as a socio-economic and cultural political space through the geo-historical structure of 'the Atlantic', defined by Tomich (2001) as a 'historical region of the capitalist world economy' which is distinguished by its particular complexes of production and exchange rooted on the infamous Atlantic triangular trade, see Dale Tomich (2004). This trade entailed taking peoples from Africa to the 'New World', transforming them from freedom to slavery

in their middle passage journey to the plantation colonies of 'the Americas', and thereby financing the growth of industry and empire across the Atlantic.

4 There is of course a large literature debating the utility, politics and meaning of the term 'creole' and its derivatives, such as creolization, créolité etc., see, for example, the essays by Boland (2002) Hintzen (2002), or Nettleford's (1997) reflections on Caribbean culture and the recent text by Thomas (2004).

5 We wish to adopt the concept of 'creole' to bring attention to the dynamic ambiguity and discursive dialectic embedded in 'being-in-the-Caribbean-world'. Thus, as Stewart (1999) notes, 'creole' has a double meaning as it has been used to refer to both a racialised objectification process and to the emergent 'syncretic' creative outcomes from processes of social relationships among persons in the 'New World'. We use the term 'creole' here to highlight that given these contradictions and ambiguities in 'creole being in the Caribbean world', Caribbean societies are embedded in an ongoing C/creolisation process that is driven by human subjects seeking, as Foucault (1983: 212) says, 'to be tied to their own identity by a conscience or self knowledge'. In short we wish to argue that these societies are 'creole' in so far as they are being shaped by a complex process of C/creolization as 'cultural morphogenetics', as has been argued in our recent conference paper, 'Making Modern S/subjects – A Sketch of a method for theorising 'C/creolisation' in Atlantic History in under-labouring for a progressive politics of 'Fleeing the Plantation', submitted at the 6th Sir Arthur Lewis Institute Conference, on 'Governance, Institutions and Economic Growth: Reflections on Arthur Lewis theory of Economic growth', Jamaica, March 17–18, 2005. Our new writing of the term 'C/creolisation' is meant to, at the outset, signal our intention to disturb and complicate its meaning as a way to provoke a new reading and analysis of Caribbean creole societies.

6 See, for example in this regard the essays by Best (1967), Bogues (1998), Lamming (2004) and Scott (2001).

7 Bhaskar (1989: 178).

8 Bhaskar (1989: 178).

9 Bhaskar (1989: 198).

10 It may be noted here that Bhaskar has dealt very deeply with the issue of the relation between critical realist philosophy, explanatory social science and human emancipation in the 1986 text, 'Scientific realism and Human Emancipation'. An attempt to discuss Bhaskar's views articulated there is presented by Collier (1998). For a post'ist view on the gaps in critical realism in promoting a process of human emancipation, see Kaul (2002). In our own engagement with the issues of the relation between explanation and emancipation, as presented in this chapter, we have found it necessary to draw upon the insights of both critical realism and post-structuralism. This provoked one referee reader to draw a cautious comment on the possible 'inconsistencies' at the level of method between the ontologically bold and epistemologically cautious stance of 'critical realists' and the ontologically cautious and epistemologically radical deconstructive stance of post'ists (post structuralists, post modernists, etc.). In partial response to this readers' comment, we wish only to note that at the level of specific methodological differences, in the work of one key post'ist figure, Foucault, from whom we draw heavily in this essay, we find no necessary inconsistency between poststructuralist perspectives at the level of method and that of critical realism. This has also been argued in a recent reading of Foucault by Al Amoudi (2004).

11 For an overview of the economic performance trends of the CARICOM Caribbean countries under globalisation, see ECLAC (2002) Globalization and Development, Chapter 11.

12 See Griffiths (1997, 2004).

13 See Ocampo (2002); UWICED (2001); and Ramsaran (2002).

14 See ECLAC, *Foreign Investment in Latin America and the Caribbean. 2003 Report* http://www.eclac.cl/.

15 Bernal (2003).

16 This perspective is akin to that expressed in the classic 1985 text 'Bringing the State back in' edited by Evans, Rueschemeyer and Skocpol, which set off a storm of criticism on the seeming 'apartness' required between the state and society in explaining the successful state. For a review of these issues see Migdal (2001).

17 The concept of 'embedded autonomy' was introduced by Evans (1995), to help explain the role of the state in promoting industrial transformation, and the success of the East Asian newly industrial countries (NICS), by examining the ways in which states are organized and related to society.

18 Thomas (2001) explains the shift in his approach for a suitable political economy, as an attempt to 'elaborate on the meaning and content of political democracy, the state … as well as state–civil society relations [in order to allow for] … relaxing the [earlier] assumptions in regard to political and social conditions'. See Thomas (2001, 2003).

19 As noted before we have tried to put forward a view on C/creolisation processes as the morphogenetics of modern cultures of power, this work will be forthcoming in Chapter One of the forthcoming book, *Globalization and the Post Creole Imagination: Notes in Fleeing the Plantation*' by Crichlow with Northover.

20 Social capital – defined as norms, networks and trust – has become an important variable in explaining comparative economic performance based on its effects on reducing conflict and supporting cooperation in firms, among firms or between the state and the civil society. This view on the role of social capital is analytically linked with discussions that focus on the relationship between the economy, civil society and the state, stimulated by Putman (1992). For a discussion of the role of social capital in the relationship between the state and society, see Evans (1996). The social capital literature though blooming, reflects various treatments of this concept, causing some to question the theoretical value of the concept, and instead flag its political and rhetorical use value, see Baron *et al.* (2000).

21 The literature on social movements is also blooming, and is also defined or methodologically treated in various ways as emphasised in Escobar and Alvarez (1992). The notion seeks to capture the phenomena of the overlapping and contesting interests articulated in diverse social responses and practices that have been and continue to negotiate political and cultural space in social life/society. Given the focus on agents and their 'coming together' relationships, this idea is conceptually linked to the concept of social capital but the literatures on these two phenomenon are not linked, and tend to express divergent political concerns. The former concept, social movements, is mainly concerned with correctives to the existing status quo of rights and recognitions; while the latter is more functionalist in pre-occupation and thus tends to oscillate around a concern for social integration or social order and the attainment of common social goals. The two concepts in their own way seek to grapple with the problem of 'making history', or constructing processes, but are mired in difficult methodological issues precisely regarding the nature of the relationship between society, culture, economy, state and the subject. It is our hope that our discussions on theorising C/creolisation in the forthcoming text, *Globalization and the Post Creole Imagination: Notes on Fleeing the Plantation* will make a useful contribution to untangling the methodological knots for deeper analytical studies of modern social processes.

22 For a similar critique on aprioristic reasoning related to the behaviour of states in Africa, see Mkandawire (1998).

23 This concept of 'verticality' was adopted in Ferguson & Gupta (2002).

24 Hansen & Stepputat (*eds.*) (2001, p. 9).

25 Ferguson and Gupta (2002, p. 981).

26 See Migdal (2001: 257).

27 This schema of methodological individualism is of course also in keeping with a Cartesian dualism of Subject being standing independently of relations with Object being/the natural and social world.

28 Ingold (1986: 222, 293).
29 Ingold (1986: 222).
30 Ingold (1986: 293).
31 Archer (1995: 284).
32 Archer (1995) defines SEPs as being ' irreducible to people and relatively enduring …
     and are specifically defined as those internal and necessary relationships which entail
     material resources, whether physical or human, and which generate causal powers
     proper to the relation itself' (p. 177). In other words then, a structural power is a social
     power that is exercised through social being and acts with a certain intensity in a cer-
     tain direction in constraining or enabling the action/experiences of the subject in their
     social relationships.
33 Archer (1995: 201).
34 One could also argue, in line with Archer (1995), that this person being is a triple
     emergent, if one locates the creative properties of person being as emergent from some
     non-natural, non-social creative source.
35 Of course, this social process itself is a co-emergent from the human being's evolution
     of practical and discursive consciousness in the world, see Ingold (1985).
36 See Foucault (1983: 208).
37 See Foucault (1991a: 59–60).
38 Foucault (1983: 208).
39 Lemke (2000: 2–3), 'Foucault, Governmentality and Critique'. Paper presented at
     Rethinking Marxism Conference, Univeristy of Amherst (MA) Sept 21–24, 2000,
     accessed July 2004. http://www.thomaslemkeweb.de/publikationen/Foucault,%20
     Governmentality,%20and%20Critique%20IV-2.pdf.
40 It is these first two objectification processes that have been given intensive examina-
     tion in post-structuralist approaches which in general have been reconceptualised in
     terms of the politics of 'othering' or Derrida's concept of 'difference'.
41 Foucault (1983: 208).
42 Foucault (1983: 212).
43 Foucault (1983: 220).
44 Foucault (1983: 220–221).
45 Foucault (1991a: 93).
46 Foucault (1991a: 93).
47 Foucault (1991b: 103).
48 Durkheim in his introduction to his text, described Religion as ' … something emi-
     nently social. Religious representations are collective representations which *express*
     collective realities: the rites are a manner of acting which take rise in the midst of the
     assembled groups and which are destined to excite, maintain, or recreate certain men-
     tal states in these groups'. Quoted in Thompson (1982: 125) *Emile Durkheim*, London:
     Routledge (our emphasis). It should be noted here that given our conception of social
     life as guided by Ingold, an appeal to Durkheim's insights in no way implies treating
     human as mere actors on the social stage driven by a social script.
49 For some recent interpretations of how modern governmentality shapes Caribbean
     power relations see Scott (1999) and Persram (2001).
50 We use capitalised P to refer to social power and lower case p to refer to the agents'
     powers–state–institutions as well as persons and capitalised S to refer to *The* Subject,
     sacred political identities, and lower case s to refer to 'the others', represented as 'pop-
     ulation', citizens and/or 'subjects'.
51 Mitchell Dean (2001) argues for an interpretation of Foucault's comment on the
     demonic coupling of these two games as the attempt to combine 'sovereignty and
     biopolitics', (p. 45) where 'biopolitics refers to the relationship between the govern-
     ment and the population' (p. 47), see Dean (op cit.). We wish to suggest that the games
     also imply that the state is seeking to serve, so to speak, two masters, one the
     citizen–subject–population and the second The Subject–Power–SEP, The Sacred being

identified in the modern cosmology of social life. These two games are used by Foucault to illustrate the tension in modern systems of trying to manage power relationships through the coupling of individualisation and totalitarian strategies. See Gordon (1991).

52 Foucault (1991b: 103).

53 We follow Archer (1985: 5) here in adopting the term 'morphogenetics' to allude to two points in change processes. First that social power has no preset form or inherent natural state of equilibrium – the morph element of the term, and also that changes are like a morphing, a transformation of one image into another. Second that social power takes its shape from and is formed by, agents qua persons, and thus originate from their activities, relationships and all the intended and unintended consequences flowing from those – this is the second part of the term 'the genetics'. The whole term together implies a focus on the processes of change and transformation of social power, state systems, in social life worlds, societies.

54 We were inspired to use this phrase by Hountondji (2002).

55 We adopt the definition of cultural politics put forward for Alvarez *et al.* (1998) as follows: '… cultural politics as the process enacted when sets of social actors shaped by, and embodying, different cultural meanings and practices come into conflict with each other' in Alvarez *et al.* (1998) 'Cultures of Politics and Politics of Cultures' (p. 7).

56 Such transformations will of course be part and parcel of the complex cultural and dialectical co-evolution of 'modern governmentalities' and 'modern states' – qua institutions; see for example, Corrigan & Sayer (1985).

57 We wish to draw attention to the idea that the differences being set up, being two socio-cultural systems, seems to invoke the Derridian sense of '*différance*' which, as highlighted by one writer, remains suspended two French verbs, to 'differ' and to 'defer', thus capturing for us the inevitable mixture of structural power with cultural politics.

58 The Agrarian Question has acted as a central concern in examining the dynamics of capitalist society, and has been taken up in different ways by contemporary analysts in seminal contributions like Goodman & Watts (eds.) (1997), McMichael (ed.) (1995).

59 Beck (1996: 27).

60 The Manchester School has recently published a journal collection reviewing the impact of this model, for which Arthur Lewis was awarded in 1979 the Nobel prize in Economics, see *The Manchester School*, 72: 6, December 2004.

61 Crichlow (2005).

62 We take this apt phrase from the 1996 text 'Creating the Countryside: The Politics of Rural and Environmental Discourse', edited by Dupois & Vandergeest, Philadelphia, PA: Temple University Press.

63 We have sought to highlight these politics of rural othering in Crichlow & Northover (2004) 'Power and its subjects: Development dilemmas, Post-colonial re-structuring of rural spaces/places/identities and State reconfigurations in contemporary globalization processes', XI World Congress of Rural Sociology, Globalization, Risks and Resistance, Trondheim, Norway, July 25–30th 2004.

64 Page (1997: 145).

References

Al Amoudi, I. (2004), *Redrawing Foucault's Social Ontology: Towards a Critical realist reading of Michel Foucault*. Mimeo.

Alvarez, S., Dagnino, E. and Escobar, A. (1998), *Cultures of Politics, Politics of Cultures: Revisioning Latin American Social Movements*. Boulder, Colorado: Westview Press.

Archer, M. (1995), *Realist Social Theory: A Morphogentic Approach*. Cambridge, UK: Cambridge University Press

Baron, S., Field, J. and Schuller, T. (2000), *Social Capital: Critical Perspectives*. Oxford: Oxford University Press.

Beck, U. (1996), 'Risk Society and the Provident State' in S. Lash, B. Szerszynski B. Wynne (eds.) *Risk, Environment and Modernity: Towards a New Ecology*. London, Thousand Oaks, CA , New Delhi, India: Sage Publications, pp. 27–43.

Bernal, R. (2003), 'The Caribbean's future is not what it was'. *Social and Economic Studies*, Vol. 52, No. 1, March, pp. 185–217.

Best, L. (1967), 'Independent Thought and Caribbean Freedom'. *New World Quarterly* 3(4), pp. 13–34.

Bhaskar, R. (1989), 'Rorty, Realism and the Idea of Freedom', in R. Bhaskar (ed.) *Reclaiming Reality: A Critical Introduction to Contemporary Philosophy*, London: Verso, pp. 146–179.

Bogues, A. (1998), 'Investigating the Radical Caribbean Intellectual Tradition'. *Small Axe*, 4, September, pp. 29–45.

Boland, O. N. (2002), 'Creolization and Creole Societies: A Cultural Nationalist View of Caribbean Social History' in V. Shepherd and G. Richards (eds.) *Questioning Creole: Creolizing Discourses in Caribbean Culture*, Kingston, Jamaica: Ian Randle and Oxford. James Currey.

Boxill, I. (1997), *Ideology and Caribbean Integration*, Consortium Graduate School of Social Sciences, Mona: University of the West Indies.

Collier, A. (1998), 'Explanation and Emancipation', in M. Archer *et al*. (eds.) *Critical Realism: Essential Readings*. London: Routledge, pp. 444–472.

Corrigan, P. and Sayer, D. (1985), *The Great Arch: English State Formation as Cultural Revolution*. New York: Basil Blackwell.

Crichlow, M, (2005), *Negotiating Caribbean Freedom: Peasants and the State in Development*. Lanham, Maryland; Boulder, Colorado; New York, Toronto, Canada; Oxford: Lexington Books.

Dean, M. (2001), 'Demonic Societies': Liberalism, Biopolitics, and Sovereignty, in Thomas Blom Hansen and Finn Stepputat, eds. States of Imagination: Ethnographic Explorations of the Postcolonial State. Durham: Duke University Press, pp. 41–64.

Dreyfus, H. and Rabinow, P. (1983), *Michel Foucault: Beyond Structuralism and Hermeneutics*, 2nd edition. Chicago: University of Chicago Press.

Dupuis, E. M. and Vandergeest, P. (eds.) (1996), *Creating the Countryside: the Politics of Rural and Environmental Discourse*. Philadelphia: Temple University Press.

Escobar, A. and Alvarez, S. (1992), *The Making of Social Movements in Latin America*. Boulder, Colorado: Westview Press.

Evans, P, (1995), *Embedded Autonomy: States and Industrial Transformation*. Princeton, New Jersey: Princeton University Press.

Evans, P. (1996), Government Action, Social Capital and Development: Reviewing the Evidence on Synergy. *World Development*, Vol. 24, No. 6, pp. 1119–1132.

Evans, P., Rueschemeyer, D. and Skocpol, T. (eds.) (1985), *Bringing the State Back In*. Cambridge: Cambridge University Press.

Ferguson, J, and Gupta, A. (2002) Spatializing States: Toward an Ethnography of Neoliberal Governmentality. *American Ethnologist*, 29, 4, November, pp. 981–1002.

Foucault, M. (1983), 'The Subject and Power', in H. Dreyfus and P. Rabinow (1983), *Michel Foucault: Beyond Structuralism and Hermeneutics*, 2nd edition. Chicago, IL: University of Chicago Press, pp. 208–226.

Foucault, M. (1991a), ' Politics and the study of discourse', in G. Burchell, C. Gordon and P. Miller (eds.) *The Foucault Effect: Studies in Governmentality*. Chicago, IL: University of Chicago Press.

Foucault, M. (1991b), 'Governmentality', in G. Burchell, C. Gordon and P. Miller (eds.) *The Foucault Effect: Studies in Governmentality*. Chicago, IL: University of Chicago Press.

Geertz, C. (1980), *Negara: The Theatre State in 19th Century Bali*. Princeton, New Jersey: Princeton University Press.

Goodman, D. and Watts, M. (eds.) (1997), *Globalizing Food: Agrarian Questions and Global Restructuring*. London and New York: Routledge.

Gordon, C. (1991), 'Governmental rationality : An introduction', in G. Burchell, C. Gordon and P. Miller (eds.) *The Foucault Effect: Studies in Governmentality*. Chicago, IL: University of Chicago Press.

Gramsci, A. (1971), *Selections from Prison Notebooks*, edited and translated by Quinton Hoare and Geoffrey Smith. New York: International Publishers.

Griffiths, I. (1997), *Drugs and Security in the Caribbean: Sovereignty Under Siege*. University Park, Pennsylvania: Pennsylvania State University Press.

Griffiths, I. (ed.) (2004), *Caribbean Security in the Age of Terror: Challenge and Change*. Kingston, Jamaica: Ian Randle Publishers.

Hall, S. (2001), 'Negotiating Caribbean Identities', in B. Meeks and F. Lindahl, (eds.) *New Caribbean Thought: A Reader*. Mona: University of the West Indies Press, pp. 24–39.

Hansen, T. and Stepputat, F. (eds.) (2001), *States of Imagination: Ethnographic Explorations of the Post Colonial State*. Durham and London: Duke University Press.

Hintzen, P. (2002), 'Race and Creole Ethnicity in the Caribbean', in V. Shepherd and G. Richards (eds.) *Questioning Creole: Creolizing Discourses in Caribbean Culture*, Kingston, Jamaica: Ian Randle and Oxford: James Currey.

Hountondji, P. J. (2002), *The Struggle for Meaning: Reflections on Philosophy, Culture and Democracy in Africa*. Athens, Ohio: Ohio University Press.

Ingold, T. (1986) *Evolution and Social Life*. Cambridge, UK: Cambridge University Press.

Karagiannis, N. (2002), *A New Economic Strategy for the Bahamas: With Special Consideration of International Competition and the FTAA*. Kingston, Jamaica: UWI Printers.

Karagiannis, N and Alleyne, D. (2003), *A New Economic Strategy for Jamaica: With Special Consideration of International Competition and the FTAA*. Kingston, Jamaica: Arawak Publications.

Kaul, N. (2002), A Critical Post to Critical Realism. *Cambridge Journal of Economics*, 26 (6), pp. 709–726.

Lamming, G. (2004), *The Sovereignty of the Imagination*. Kingston, Jamaica: Arawak Publications.

Lemke, T. (2000), 'Foucault, Governmentality and Critique'. Paper presented at *Rethinking Marxism* Conference, University of Amherst (Massachusetts), Sept. 21–24, 2000. Available online at: http://www.thomaslemkeweb.de

Lewis, A. (1955), *Theory of Economic Growth*. London: George Allen and Unwin.

McMichael, P. (ed.) (1995), *Food and Agrarian Orders in the World Economy*. Connecticut; Westport, CT: Greenwood Press.

Marshall, D. (1998), *Caribbean Political Economy at the Crossroads: NAFTA and Regional Developmentalism*. Basingstoke, UK & London: Macmillan.

Migdal, J. (1988), *Strong Societies and Weak States: State–Society Relationships and State Capabilities in the Third World*. Princeton, New Jersey: Princeton University Press.

Migdal, J. (2001), *State in Society: Studying how States and Societies Transform and Constitute One Another*. Cambridge, UK: Cambridge University Press.

Mitchell, T. (1991), The Limits of the State: Beyond Statist Approaches and their Critics. *American Political Science Review*, 85; 1, pp. 77–96.

Mkandawire, T. (1998), Thinking about Development States in Africa. http://www.unu.edu/africa/00sps-global.html, and published in *Cambridge Journal of Economics* 25: 289–314 (2001).

Nettleford, R. (1997), 'Caribbean Culture: Paradoxes of the 1990's' in J. Braveboy-Wagner and D. Gayle (eds.) *Caribbean Public Policy: Regional Cultural and Socio-economic Issues for the 21st Century*. Boulder, Colorado: West View Press.

Ocampo, J. (2002), Small Economies in the Face of Globalization. http://www.revistainterforum.com/english/articles/052702arteco_en.html

Page, B. (1997), 'Restructuring Pork Production, Remaking Rural Iowa,' in D. Goodman and M. J. Watts (eds.) *Globalizing Food: Agrarian Questions and Global Restructuring*. New York: Routledge, pp. 133–157.

Persram, N. (2001), Guerrillas, Games and Governmentality. *Small Axe* 10, September, pp. 21–40.

Putman, R. (1992), *Making Democracy Work: Civic Traditions in Modern Italy*. Princeton: Princeton University Press.

Ramsaran, R. ed. (2002), *Caribbean Survival and the Global Challenge*. Kingston, Jamaica: Ian Randle Press.

Scott, D. (1999), *Refashioning Futures: Criticism after Postcoloniality*. Princeton, New Jersey: Princeton University Press.

Scott, D. (2001), 'The Government of Freedom' in B. Meeks and F. Lindahl, (eds.) *New Caribbean Thought: A Reader*. Mona, Jamaica: University of the West Indies Press.

Stewart, C. (1999), Syncretism and its Synonyms: Reflections on Cultural Mixture. *Diacritics*, 29; 3, 40–62.

Thomas, C. (2001), 'On Reconstructing a Political Economy of the Caribbean', in B. Meeks and F. Lindahl, (eds.) *New Caribbean Thought: A Reader*. Jamaica, Barbados and Trinidad and Tobago: University of the West Indies Press.

Thomas, C. Y. (2003), 'Designing and Implementing Development Policy' in K. Hall and D. Benn (eds.), *Governance in an Age of Globalization: Caribbean Perspectives*, Kingston, Jamaica: Ian Randle Press.

Thomas, C. Y. (1974), *Dependence and Transformation*. New York and London: Monthly Review Press.

Thomas, C. Y. (1988), *The Poor and the Powerless: Economic Policy and Change in the Caribbean*. London: Latin American Bureau.

Thomas, D. (2004), *Modern Blackness: Nationalism, Globalization and the Politics of Culture in Jamaica*. Kingston, Jamaica: UWI Press and Duke University Press.

Thompson, K. (1982), *Emile Durkheim*. London and New York: Routledge.

Tomich, D. (2004), Atlantic History and World Economy: Concepts and Constructions. *ProtoSociology*, Vol. 20, pp. 102–121.

UWICED (2001) Vulnerability and Small Island States. *UNDP Policy Journal*, Vol. 1.

14 On the ontology of international norm diffusion

Lynn Savery*

Introduction

Whether we like it or not, there is no escaping the question of ontology. For, in order to explain how or why something occurs we must make metaphysical assumptions about the nature of social reality. This raises the question of the relation between structure and agency, a question or problem that returns with such regular insistence that it has led one scholar recently to refer to it as a dead horse that refuses to stay down.[1] Our uneasiness concerning the right approach to take regarding the structure-agency problem is the symptom of a stubborn sense that this problem is an 'undecidable paradox'.[2] The perennial problem of structure and agency is one of whether or not the two aspects of social reality are irreducible to one another. According to Walter Carlsnaes, however, the problem lies not in accepting that structures and agents are dynamically related entities but rather in the fact that we *lack a self-evident way to conceptualise these entities and their relationship*.[3] While I do not pretend to have solved the structure–agency problem, I suggest that the critical realist argument applied in this chapter to the analysis of the international diffusion of women's human rights norms offers a new and meaningful way to explain specific social change or durability in international relations. In particular, I suggest that the argument provides a useful way to analyse and explain variation in the extent to which international norms of sexual non-discrimination diffuse and affect state behaviour. By norms, I mean shared understandings of standards of behaviour held by a community of actors, in this case the international community. By diffusion, I mean the processes and mechanisms by which international norms diffuse and become incorporated in the domestic sphere. I begin by examining the limitations of existing explanations of international norms and then proceed to develop an alternative, critical realist, argument to examine and explain the way in which the interplay between various structures and agents conditions the diffusion and efficacy of international norms of sexual non-discrimination. I illustrate the usefulness of a critical realist approach to the diffusion of these norms through case studies of Germany and

*For discussion and comments I would like to thank Chris Reus-Smit, Kathy Morton, Heather Rae, and two anonymous reviewers.

Japan. Finally, I discuss some of the implications the argument has for international relations theory and for those operating in the field.

Existing explanations of international norm diffusion

Although international relations scholars have recently paid a great deal of attention to questions concerning the relationship between international norms and state behaviour, they have paid scant attention to the diffusion and efficacy of international norms of sexual non-discrimination. Existing international relations accounts of norm diffusion struggle to explain the cross-national variation in the diffusion of international norms of sexual non-discrimination, or why these norms on the whole have had a relatively limited influence on state behaviour, because they assume either that diffusion is contingent on utility maximisation or that it is purely a product of socialisation. These assumptions, in turn, are based on inadequate ontologies *vis-à-vis* structure and agency and my aim in this section is to tease out the conflationary premises of each view of norm diffusion in this regard. I begin by critically evaluating two major variants of rational-choice theory – neoliberalism and liberal intergovernmentalism. I then critically evaluate two major variants of interpretive theory – sociological institutionalism and constructivism.

Neither neoliberalism nor liberal intergovernmentalism adequately explain the diffusion of international norms of sexual non-discrimination because they erroneously assume that norm diffusion is contingent on either state or individual utility-maximisation. Neoliberalism assumes that international norms exist and function as a tool of utility-maximising states. States, neoliberals claim, create and comply with international norms in order to realise their material and economic self-interests, which are predetermined and fixed. Like neoliberalism, liberal intergovernmentalism provides a utility-maximising explanation of norms but assumes that norms and compliance are fundamentally determined by the utility-optimising behaviour of individuals in domestic society. Intergovernmentalists argue that international norms result from interstate bargains based on the domestic power and preferences of individuals or groups. They also assume that states have an interest in complying with international norms because they originate from within states or are endogenously produced. Both neoliberalism and liberal intergovernmentalism embody an individualist ontology in that they are agent-centric, with each making structures ontologically primitive entities. Neoliberalism *a priori* makes international or system structures ontologically primitive to state agents and their interactions, while liberal intergovernmentalism makes system structures ontologically primitive to individual agents within the state. In other words, system structures exist and are maintained only through the choice and actions of either states, in the case of neoliberalism, or individuals or groups inside the state, in the case of intergovernmentalism. It is not difficult to see that both propose a social reality and, thus, an explanation of norm diffusion, devoid of social or structural determinants. Consequently, both conflate structure and agency in such a fashion that structures become epiphenomena of agents. However, as we shall see, the diffusion of international norms of sexual non-discrimination is determined to some extent by social structures. Diffusion is not necessarily contingent on either state or individual utility maximisation.

In contrast to these rational-choice accounts of international norms, the interpretive accounts of sociological institutionalism and constructivism attribute diffusion to a process of socialisation. Sociological institutionalists argue that international norms are institutionalised in an ever-expanding and deepening global culture or world polity, which has a constitutive and directive effect on state identity, preferences, and behaviour. As a component of the world polity, international norms are said to diffuse in an ongoing and ubiquitous process that results in far-reaching isomorphism across states. This approach fails to explain resistance by states to incorporating international norms of sexual non-discrimination, or the persistent heterogeneity among state practices, in large part, because it reduces states to the properties of system structures. In other words, it conflates structure and agency in such a way that agents become epiphenomena of structure. Constructivism avoids this kind of reductionism and conflation by conceiving the relation between international norms and state behaviour as mutually constitutive. Constructivists argue that norms and states (structures and agents) constitute and reconstitute each other in a dynamic process of iteration. They also argue that states are socialised into incorporating patterns of behaviour and role expectations subscribed by international norms. This perspective struggles to explain domestically determined change to or continuity in state behaviour in the presence of international norms of sexual non-discrimination, as it tends to overestimate the process of socialisation and the efficacy of international norms. It also tends to conflate structure and agency in such a manner that the two aspects of social reality collapse together, becoming indivisible, and their causal interrelationships become impossible to analyse.

Since existing international relations theory cannot adequately explain the dynamic between international norms of sexual non-discrimination and state behaviour, the following section sets out to articulate a more sufficient explanation by drawing on insights from critical realism.

International norms of sexual non-discrimination and changing state practices

Between 1945 and the mid-1970s, international and European norms of sexual non-discrimination had virtually no impact on state behaviour because international and regional bodies had no expectations that states would comply with these or any other human rights norms, and because states refused to take the initiative to incorporate systemic norms of sexual non-discrimination in the absence of any external pressure. In a process apparent since about the mid-1970s, international and regional bodies have expanded and strengthened legal regimes regarding sexual non-discrimination and established concrete measures of implementation. They have also developed detailed *how to* sets of instructions in the form of action plans or programmes specifying the requisite legislative and public policy action to be taken by states.⁴ This international and regional regime strengthening, in turn, has exerted pressure on states to modify their practices accordingly. Yet, while regime strength is by itself a necessary condition for diffusion, it is not sufficient to explain either the variance in state responses to systemic norms of sexual non-discrimination or the limited overall impact these norms have had on state behaviour. Whether or not a state incorporates systemic norms of sexual non-discrimination depends also on the strength of the gender-biased corporate identity of the state, the degree of international or regional political will to use existing monitoring and enforcement resources, and the effectiveness of domestic feminist activism and private individual or group litigation. The explanation for why states respond differently to systemic norms of sexual non-discrimination lies in the complex interplay between these various structures and agents and the best way to capture this dynamic, I suggest, is to draw on some of the core ideas associated with critical realism. It must be stressed at the outset that my aim here is not to develop a general theory of norm diffusion but, rather, to develop a specific explanation of the diffusion and efficacy of international norms of sexual non-discrimination.

The critical realist explanation of the diffusion of international norms of sexual non-discrimination advanced in this chapter rests on an ontology of *emergentism*, treating structure and agency as interdependent but, at the same time, relatively autonomous entities, each possessing distinct emergent properties. It also rests squarely on a notion of time as a variable linking structure and agency. From a critical realist perspective, we can see that particular state actions are the outcome or result of a historical sequence of reciprocal structure–agency interaction involving changes in both international and domestic conditions. At any particular point in time, structure–agency interaction regarding systemic norms of sexual non-discrimination results either in the elaboration of state legislation and public policy or in the preservation of existing domestic legal and policy practices. Critical realism also allows us to explain why and how external and internal legal and political conditions generate domestic feminist activism and private individual or group litigation, which, in turn, directly or indirectly influence the efficacy of international norms of sexual non-discrimination. Critical realism enables us to explain how discourse mediates contention between dominant corporate agents – such as the state or Catholic Church – and dissident corporate agents – namely, feminist activists and litigants – over the accepted meaning of gender relations, and the consequences of this for systemic norm diffusion. It also helps us explain how contentious discursive interaction between states and international bodies affects diffusion. However, critical realism does not take us very far in analysing the operations of power in social interaction because it tends to treat it simply as the property of agents. Conceiving of power relations as relations in which *all* social actors are situated provides the remedy and allows us to examine how power impacts on the diffusion and efficacy of international norms of sexual non-discrimination.

Explaining state behavioural responses to international norms of sexual non-discrimination in critical realist terms entails a cyclical analysis of social interaction leading to state action or inaction. Change or stasis in state behaviour may be the end result of an extensive sequence of reciprocal structure–agency interaction or the outcome of a short sequence of social interaction. Analysing state behaviour in terms of dynamic cycles of social interaction involves a temporal distinction that is merely implicit in the constructivist argument of mutual constitution. By incorporating time as an actual theoretical variable we are able to explicitly ground structure–agency dialectics in historical time. Margaret Archer refers to this temporal dimension of social interaction as morphogenetic. Morphogenetic analysis treats structure and agency as distinct in all aspects – they are neither co-extensive nor co-variant – and are linked in a non-reductive analysis of the interplay between the two aspects of social reality over time.[5] This is not to say that action is not ceaseless but rather to allow the *unravelling* of the dialectical interaction between structure and agency.[6] Upholding the temporal distinction between structure and agency in order to examine their interplay depends, according to Archer, on the dual proposition that structure necessarily pre-dates the actions that reproduce or transform it, and that structural elaboration necessarily post-dates those actions.[7] However, she adds, while structure is the elaborated outcome of interaction, it is simultaneously the conditioning medium of social action: agency is systemically transformed in the process of interaction.[8] In other words, she says, a process of *double morphogenesis* takes place in which 'agency leads to structural elaboration but is itself elaborated in the process'.[9]

Upholding the temporal distinction between structure and agency also presupposes a notion of emergence, whereby socio-cultural structures and agents possess different emergent properties and powers that are relatively autonomous and irreducible to each other and yet essential to one another. As Andrew Sayer explains, emergence refers to 'situations in which the conjunction of two or more features or aspects gives rise to new phenomena, which have properties which are irreducible to those of their constituents, even though the latter are necessary for their existence'.[10] Emergence allows us to sustain the idea of the actions of agents in the past creating the socio-cultural context in which the actions of agents in the present are enabled or constrained.[11] In the process of social interaction, agents, while conditioned by socio-cultural structures, exert their own irreducible emergent powers in the shape of reflexive deliberations, which result in either structural continuity or elaboration. Structural elaboration, meanwhile, gives rise to the emergence of new structural properties and powers which, in turn, facilitate or constrain agents in various ways. For instance, the enactment of the Japanese Equal Employment Opportunity Law in 1985 can be seen as the emergent outcome of a combination of Japanese feminist activism, private individual or group litigation, and external pressure from western industrialised states criticising Japan's discriminatory employment practices. Once enacted, this legislation acquired its own emergent properties and powers, including the capacity to redefine workplace relations and conditions. These, in turn, constrained and enabled the subsequent actions of various agents such as the state, employers and employees, feminist activists, and private individual and group litigants. Of course, there are also unintended consequences or chance outcomes of social interaction, which must be accorded a degree of explanatory significance.[12]

In terms of delineating agency, Archer argues that we can distinguish between primary and corporate agents, which give rise to an individual's personal and social identity respectively and are dialectically related.[13] As primary agents (the conditioned *me*), she explains, individuals are born into a socio-cultural context and are distinguished from corporate agents (the interactive *we*) at any given time by their atomistic or uncoordinated reactions to their inherited context.[14] If, through self-reflection on their situation, primary agents seek and are able to realise collective action to either retain or re-shape existing socio-cultural structures, they become corporate agents.[15] As corporate agents, individuals pool their intra-personal deliberations about what they care about most and then subject these concerns to inter-personal scrutiny before acting.[16] The capacity of primary agents to realise collective action, however, is conditioned by structural enablements and constraints.[17] Following this line of argument, the process by which systemic norms of sexual non-discrimination diffuse or fail to diffuse into domestic state practices involves structural–agential interaction, in which the agents are corporate agents whose practices are intentionally designed to produce either societal continuity or societal change. Of course, Archer cautions, 'such intentions do not themselves determine the outcome and the result is rarely what anyone seeks'.[18] Corporate agents intent on defending or transforming gender-biased social structures include, among others, the state, the church, feminist activists, and internationally situated corporate agents such as the United Nations Committee on the Elimination of Discrimination Against Women, the European Commission, and the European Court of Justice. While it is the collective action of corporate agents that is of prime importance in the process of systemic norm diffusion and state behavioural change, the agency of small minorities and even individuals can sometimes be decisive; for instance, private individual or group sex-discrimination litigation, or the actions of a single female politician.

Having established the potential of a critical realist approach to the diffusion of international norms of sexual non-discrimination, the following section examines the particular impediments to and facilitators of diffusion. These include the gender-biased corporate identity of the state, feminist political activism and private individual litigation, contentious discursive interaction between various actors, and the dynamics of power. It does so through the empirical cases of Germany and Japan.

The gender-biased corporate identity of the state

In critical realist terms, the state as an agent is regarded, not as a singular subject or entity analogous with an individual person, but rather as a corporate agent defined as a group or collective with the capacity for articulating shared ideas or interests and organising for their pursuit. As a corporate agent, the state is thus synonymous with governmental decision-making authorities capable of engaging in concerted action 'to maintain or re-model the socio-cultural system and its institutional parts'.[19] It is reasonable then to speak in terms of the state possessing a corporate identity, which, I argue, is essential to explaining the diffusion of international norms of sexual non-discrimination. This is in stark contrast to Alexander Wendt, an international relations scholar who, having drawn a useful distinction between the corporate and social aspects of state identities, claims that it is only the social aspect that interacts with international norms. He argues that the state is a pre-social corporate entity relative to other states in that it possesses 'the intrinsic, self-organising qualities that constitute actor individuality ... and provide[s] motivation energy for engaging in action at all and, to that extent, [is] prior to interaction'. From here, he argues that the outcomes of norm diffusion depend on the social aspect of state identities, which are produced and reproduced through a mutually constitutive process of systemic interaction. Therefore, a state has an identity only to the extent that it is recognised by other states.[20] In other words, the social identities of states within the international system are constituted and reconstituted by practices and actions of mutual recognition among states. States are recognised as legitimate members of the international community by their adherence to international norms, and the legitimacy of international norms are maintained or reproduced through the ongoing practices of states. As such, a state's social identities are 'primarily external: they describe the actions of governments in a society of states'.[21] They interact with international norms and mediate between them and state preferences and practices. A state's social identities vary in salience, argues Wendt, with the salience of a particular social identity depending on how deeply the social structure that this identity instantiates penetrates a state's conceptions of self.[22]

Problematically, by attributing unitariness and intentionality to a corporate body such as the state it becomes reified; a problem that Wendt acknowledges but shrugs aside with the argument that 'even if a state has multiple personalities domestically they may manage to work together when dealing with outsiders'.[23] However, as Heather Rae points out, 'the fact that the corporate identity of the state is just that – corporate – and not an individual identity, means that we need to look at how this identity is constructed, how the "we" to which Wendt refers is constituted and maintained'.[24] By bracketing the domestic – corporate – sources of state identity and preferences, Wendt shuts out an important source of social change and state motivation. His restrictive systemic approach not only presents a narrow, mechanistic view of the process of mutual constitution between structure and agency but also renders his framework unable to explain the evident influence of interaction between domestic structures and agents on state motivations and actions regarding international norms of sexual non-discrimination. It cannot explain why and how the gender-biased corporate identity of the state frequently acts as a barrier to the diffusion of systemic norms of sexual non-discrimination. Nor can it explain why and how the gender-biased corporate identity of the state is mitigated through the diffusion of such norms.

The gender-biased corporate identity of the state, though by no means the only aspect to the modern state, is the most significant impediment to the diffusion of systemic norms of sexual non-discrimination.[25] The term 'the gender-biased corporate identity of the state' is used here to denote a particular aspect of the state's preconceived sense of self, which, in turn, political elites play a crucial, although by no means exclusive, role in producing and reproducing. They do so by pursuing, more or less consciously, policies embodying certain predominant ideas, values, and beliefs concerning the *proper* or *correct* differentiation of gender roles in both the public and private domains. Once they are institutionalised in the state legal and public policy systems, these aspects of the domestic cultural system, though often contested and historically contingent, become relatively enduring. This is so because institutionalisation, which endows norms with endurance and political influence, occurs more readily and forcefully in the domestic as opposed to the international sphere and, thus, exerts a powerful pull on state behaviour.[26] However, gender-biased corporate state identities are not fixed or immutable but vary in complexion and strength due to the particular historical junctures at which distinctive ideas of gender relations are institutionalised, and this variance results in different degrees of constraint on the diffusion of international norms of sexual non-discrimination. Domestic ideas, values, or beliefs of gender differentiation may permute through social interaction in different historical periods but they always remain linked to earlier periods and have a residual effect on the institutionalisation of successive norms. The fact that the gender-biased corporate identity of the state is internally situated does not obscure the dynamic nature of the relationship between the domestic and international spheres and the potential, therefore, for the mitigation of the gender-biased corporate state identity through the diffusion process. Since particular or specific sequences of internal social interaction constitute the state as gender-biased, the possibility of different gender-biased corporate identities portends variance in state motivations and, hence, variance in state responses to international norms of sexual non-discrimination. Through a combination of external and internal pressure exerted on the state by various actors, certain international norms of sexual non-discrimination diffuse into domestic state practices and, in the process, mitigate the gender-biased corporate identity of the state.

Germany and Japan's gender-biased corporate identities

In the wake of the Second World War, Germany and Japan's gender-biased corporate identities were politically reconstituted in such a way that, though distinct, proved equally resistant to the diffusion of international norms of sexual non-discrimination. In the case of Germany, the state explicitly set out to re-establish the principle of German paternity as the foundation of national identity and to re-domesticate German women by implementing a gender-reinforcing regime with a firm Christian-occidental dimension. The Christian Democratic government vehemently defended the *complete* Christian male-breadwinner family, arguing that equality constituted an 'assault on divinely created human nature' and would ultimately destroy the individual bodies and souls of women, as well as the nation as a whole.[27] If women were to leave the home and enter employment, the government charged, they 'would be unable to nurture their charges properly, would be unable even to reproduce' and, as such, 'the nation itself threatened to disappear'.[28] During the 1950s, the state discursively emphasised the virtue of traditional gender ascriptions as a bulwark against totalitarianism and communism, sentiments echoed by the Catholic Church. The Minister of Family Affairs, Franz Josef Wurmeling, a staunch supporter of the government's programme of *normalising* gender relations, argued that it was the responsibility of the state and society to assist women to stay at home and follow their 'true calling' as mothers and housewives.[29] The government's programme of returning Germany to normality by restoring national security and stability in the *lebensraum* (living space) of the family was promoted by politicians, clergy, academics, and the media, and was realised in the national security, industrial relations, taxation, and employment systems. Traditional gender relations were also upheld in the national legal system. Despite the post-war reality of women with or without children seeking employment out of sheer financial necessity, the government, church leaders and trades unions continued to discourage and discriminate against women in the workforce.[30] Moreover, as Germany experienced an economic surge in the late 1950s and with it a growing need for labour, the state adopted the policy of importing millions of foreign workers as *guest workers* rather than disturb the paterfamilias by integrating women into the labour force. This deeply gender-biased corporate state identity reconstituted in the post-war period survived the social and political upheavals of the late 1960s and German reunification largely intact and, thus, had a lasting inhibiting effect on the diffusion of international norms of sexual non-discrimination.

In the case of Japan, the state was determined to recreate a traditional patrilineal nation in the post-occupation period, in which the Japanese family system (*ie*) was the locus of social stability and strength.[31] Vestiges of the family system established in the Meiji period (1868–1912) survived the allied occupation and, during the 1950s and 1960s, the Japanese state introduced a series of gender-reinforcing policies explicitly aimed at eroding occupation reforms and reviving traditional social gender divisions. Discursively, the state resurrected the pre-Second World War mantra *a woman's place is in the home* and waxed lyrical about the traditional authority of paterfamilias. This vision of restoring the traditional Japanese family system was embedded in the national social security, taxation, and employment policy systems, which, in turn, built on the existing discriminatory family registration and associated resident card systems.[32] Even when Japan faced an acute labour shortage in the early 1960s, the state refused to endorse married women entering full-time employment on the grounds that their family and child-bearing responsibilities were essential to Japan.[33] In fact, the state's vision of a traditional Japanese family headed by the male-breadwinner served to legitimate the use of women as a 'flexible army of peripheral workers' subject to the disadvantages of low wages and job insecurity.[34] This extremely gender-biased corporate state identity proved decidedly resilient and, like that of the German state, had a lasting inhibiting effect on the diffusion of international norms of sexual non-discrimination. Both states were initially extremely reluctant to ratify and comply with existing international women's human rights conventions but, by the 1970s, both were under mounting internal and external pressure from a variety of actors to ratify and meet their international legal obligations. The most concerted pressure in both cases came from within the state in the form of feminist activism and private individual or group litigation, which, in turn, was generated and shaped or conditioned by the existing social context. Analysing the process by which feminist activism and private litigation are generated can explain why and how international and domestic political and legal conditions produce opportunities for and constraints on contentious action.

Feminist political activism and private individual litigation

As far as feminist political activism and private individual or group litigation is concerned, socio-cultural structures such as national legal and public policy systems, which are produced by past agential actions or practices, exert conditional influences upon the actions of contemporary activists and litigants. For, as Archer explains, socio-cultural structures do not determine the actions of agents but rather 'supply reasons for actions'.[35] With respect to the political activism of feminists advocating change to state practices, it is generated and shaped or conditioned by the existing social context. Analysing the process by which feminist activism and private individual litigation are generated can explain why and how international, regional, and domestic political and legal conditions produce opportunities for and constraints on contentious action. Thus, we can chart the influence of specific historical constellations of various opportunities and constraints that generate particular forms of feminist activism at particular points in time in each state, and examine how this activism then affects the diffusion of systemic norms of sexual non-discrimination.

The international and domestic socio-cultural context conditions the actions of domestic feminist activists in various ways. It shapes the values, beliefs and preferences that activists hold – a constitutive effect that is missing in liberal intergovernmental accounts of international politics. These collective values, beliefs and preferences then affect the strategic decisions of feminist activists, determining which actions activists will evaluate as useful or counterproductive.[36] Activists may also value a particular strategy or tactic for reasons other than its effectiveness in achieving their goal.[37] It is also important to realise that political opportunities for activism are not always recognised as such or seized on by feminist activists.[38] Furthermore, in the process of social interaction, the state or other counteragents such as the Catholic Church may react against feminist activism to protect their vested interests in maintaining gender-biased national practices, thus creating a contracting political situation for activists. At the extreme, argues Lee Ann Banaszak, it is possible for the state to so restrict the range of possible outcomes that activists cannot realise any of their objectives no matter what strategy they utilise or how many resources they expend.[39] For instance, the Japanese state has, on occasion, been particularly effective at thwarting the efforts of domestic feminist activists to effect substantive legislative and public policy changes.

Furthermore, Banaszak contends, while activists make strategies and tactical decisions based on their perceptions of political opportunities, their perceptions will not always reflect reality.[40] Activists view their society and political system through particular lenses, she says, which colour their perceptions and, in turn, their actions.[41] To an extent, this explains why the timing, form and effectiveness of feminist activism may vary from state to state. For instance, German feminist activists emerging out of the New Left in the late 1960s were divided in their perceptions of the political system between those who were sceptical of the state and those who sought political change through the state. At the time, this split left German feminist activism as a whole in a considerably weakened and marginalised position, which, as a consequence, meant that the state was less likely to initiate changes in accordance with international or European norms of sexual non-discrimination.

Critical realists have tended to think of socio-cultural interaction and its effects on the actions of agents such as feminist activists as an exclusive feature of the domestic sphere, but my comparative study shows that international, national and regional political and legal conditions interact to define the preferences of activists and create particular forms of mobilisation. Critical realists have also assumed a relatively stable state in their examination of social interaction and its effects on agency. However, this chapter demonstrates that feminist activism is also shaped by fundamental changes in the nature of the state, such as the transition to post-occupation in Japan in the 1950s, and German reunification in the 1990s. German reunification was rapid, occurred very much on West Germany's terms, and was characterised by the extension of West German norms and practices into the East, including highly discriminatory gender norms and practices. Confronted by the inevitable loss of many important social and economic rights, East German feminists tried to form an alliance with their West German counterparts against the impending reality of *Germany – united fatherland*.[42] Despite experiencing serious tensions and disagreements over a range of identity-related and logistical issues, East and West German feminists eventually managed to overcome their differences to work together to organise a series of strike actions in 1994 to draw public and political attention to the systematic dismantling of beneficial entitlements and legal guarantees of the former German Democratic Republic. Over one million women participated in the strike actions throughout unified Germany, putting considerable pressure on the federal government to adopt more progressive policies. International and regional political conditions influence both the emergence and development of domestic feminist activism by legitimating and, in some cases, shaping activists' actions and claims. For instance, in 1975, international and domestic events coincided to mobilise Japanese feminist activists to pursue changes to highly discriminatory practices of the Japanese state. The government's sensitivity to criticism of its discriminatory employment practices from Western industrialised states and an increasingly alienated female electorate provided activists with the opportunity to press the state to recognise the United Nations International Women's Year, which, in turn, lent legitimacy to Japanese feminist demands for the state to modify its employment practices in accordance with international labour standards. Here, international conditions interacted with national political conditions to generate feminist activism, which, in turn, put pressure on the state to alter its behaviour and comply with certain international norms of sexual non-discrimination.

Legal conditions – especially regional and domestic – also enable feminist activists and private individual litigants to challenge discriminatory state legislation and practices and, in the process, deliberately or inadvertently put pressure on the state to comply with international norms of sexual non-discrimination. Usually activism and litigation work in tandem because, while private individual litigation may occur in isolation, other forms of feminist activism in the political arena often accompany it.[43] Individual or group actions brought before national courts may even form part of a wider litigation strategy employed by feminist activists in their campaign to procure state legislative change. Of course, litigation is not always successful but even when cases are lost, feminist activists sometimes use the loss to exert pressure on the state for legislative reform. For example, the dismissal by Japanese courts of successive cases brought against the Japanese state by former comfort women provoked international outrage, prompting activists to convene an unofficial international war crimes tribunal in Tokyo in December 2000. During the controversial trial of the Japanese state, the tribunal heard testimonies from more than 40 comfort women and, in its final judgement found the state of Japan guilty of breaching international law by refusing to bring the perpetrators to justice or to acknowledge its own responsibility.[44] Further litigation through the United States legal system put increasing pressure on the Japanese state to compensate the victims of Japanese military prostitution during World War II – pressure that the state, unfortunately, was largely able to resist as it looked for what it called a *biological solution* to the comfort women problem.[45] For the Japanese state, a sincere apology and compensation was not an issue of justice but rather a public relations problem that it hoped would simply fade away as the survivors died of old age or the lingering effects of war-inflicted injury or disease.[46]

While the domestic legal environment on its own provides opportunities for litigation and feminist activism, regional and international legal conditions sometimes interact with national legal conditions to facilitate activism and generate change in state legal practices. This is particularly so in Europe, where violations of European Union (EU) law are brought to the European Court of Justice (ECJ) and the court's decisions are used to force member states to respect their regional legal obligations.[47] As Karen Alter explains, this makes 'European legal appeals a potent source of leverage for private litigants, groups, and the European Commission to influence national policy'.[48] Just the threat of legal suits by these actors puts pressure on member states to comply with EU law.[49] For example, the European Commission's threat to initiate infringement proceedings against the German state in 1979 for failing to implement the EU equal pay and equal treatment directives by their designated deadlines induced an amendment to national employment legislation in the form of the 1980

Adaptation Act. Prior to the mid-1970s, the European Commission rarely initiated infringement proceedings against states for non-implementation of
European law because it feared such action would 'aggravate its fragile relationship with member governments'.[50] However, as a consequence of a series of
landmark decisions by the ECJ establishing the direct effect of European equality legislation, and the court's admonishment of the commission for failing to
pursue breaches of said legislation, the European Commission began bringing
infringement proceedings against member states for defaulting on their legal
obligations. Private individual litigation at the German national level during the
1980s exerted additional pressure on the state to further modify its legal practices, as national labour courts invoked EU law in legal disputes and referred
cases to the ECJ. The case of *Bilka-Kaufhaus GmbH v. Weber Von Hartz* is particularly significant because it led to the expansion of the national legal concept
of discrimination to include indirect discrimination.[51] In the case, the plaintiff
claimed that Bilka, a large department store chain, indirectly discriminated
against women in breach of Article 119 of the European Treaty of Rome by
excluding part-time employees from its occupational pension scheme. The
Federal Labour Court referred the case to the ECJ for determination and, in May
1986, the ECJ found in favour of the plaintiff.

The international legal system lacks the enforcement mechanisms of the EU
but, nevertheless, if national courts invoke international law regarding sexual
non-discrimination in their decisions it puts indirect pressure on states to comply.
The success of plaintiffs and the invocation of international non-discriminatory
law in judicial decisions also facilitate domestic feminist activism, creating an
additional internal pressure on states. For instance, a decision in 1998 by a remote
Japanese district court described the comfort system as a fundamental violation
of international human rights. The court found the Japanese government liable to
the three plaintiffs for the legislature's failure to enact compensation legislation
for victims of militarised prostitution, putting considerable pressure on the state
to act accordingly. The plaintiffs had argued that Japan had the 'duty of a moral
state' to atone for its crimes. They invoked international law to establish a legal
obligation on the part of the Japanese government to compensate victims of
wartime aggression, including military sexual slaves. Aside from being invoked
by plaintiffs and domestic courts, the international legal regime regarding sexual
non-discrimination primarily relies on a periodic state reporting system to hold
states accountable. While not as effective as EU measures, this reporting system
still exerts pressure on states to comply with systemic norms of sexual non-discrimination. For example, in its consideration of Germany's fourth periodic
report in February 2000, the United Nations Committee on the Elimination of
Discrimination Against Women admonished the state for its continual failure to
eliminate the *persistent* wage gap between men and women, as well as other discriminatory labour practices related to recruitment and promotion, social security,
taxation and child-care. Although slow to respond, the German state did introduce
changes that brought domestic legislation and public policy closer into line with
international standards.

Contentious discursive interaction and power

To fully explain state behavioural responses to international norms of sexual non-discrimination, we need to appreciate that discourse and power mediate social interaction and, therefore, have behavioural consequences. The notion of contentious discursive interaction helps us understand how the ongoing discursive tug of war between dominant corporate agents and dissident corporate agents over the accepted meaning of gender relations indirectly affects the diffusion and efficacy of systemic norms of sexual non-discrimination. Such contentious discursive interaction commonly occurs within a discursive field generated by dominant corporate agents, who attempt to inhibit the development of meanings antagonistic to their own, and devalue, ridicule, and marginalise hostile meanings where they do develop.[52] Such discursive domination can never be total though, explains Marc Steinberg, with new discursive practices or genres emerging through resistance.[53] However, he continues, as dissident corporate agents 'seek to transform existing meanings in discursive practices, to articulate senses of injustice, make claims, and establish alternative visions, they also remain bounded by the fields and the genres within which they struggle'.[54] Moreover, he concludes, 'since discursive resistance is always a dialogue with domination, for the latter can always talk back, even the successful appropriation and reworking of discourse in one context contains the potential for resurgent dominant meanings in another'.[55] This is certainly evident in Japan in the late 1970s, where the state appropriated the discourse of domestic feminist activists and championed the cause of gender-equity in a cynical bid to cling to power and reassert itself. However, discursive dynamics are not the exclusive province of domestic politics. International and regional discourses of human rights occasionally become incorporated into domestic contentious discursive interaction. For instance, in the late 1990s, German feminists within the newly elected Social Democratic Party (SDP)–Green coalition government discursively drew on the European discourse of equal opportunity to challenge traditional notions of gender relations and articulate many of their demands for legislative change. Feminists in the government, trades unions, and the German Women Lawyer's Association also lobbied in vain to save a bill legislating equal opportunities in employment in the private sector in terms of bringing German labour law into line with international and European standards.[56]

Contentious discursive interaction contributes not only to the processes of feminist political mobilisation and action but also to the constitution and reconstitution of the gender-biased corporate identity of the state, because it is through discourse that both dominant and dissident corporate agents articulate ideational notions of appropriate gender relations. However, since contentious discursive interaction involves dialogue situated in particular historical and political contexts, the impact of this process on the diffusion of international norms of sexual non-discrimination varies from state to state. For instance, recent contentious discursive interaction between the Japanese state and Japanese feminist activists over the definition and meaning of accepted gender relations is quite different to that between the German state and German feminist activists. It is also distinct from earlier contentious discursive interaction between the post-occupation Japanese state and Japanese feminist activists, and this has different effects on the diffusion of systemic norms of sexual non-discrimination. In the post-occupation period, feminists within the Japanese Women and Minors Bureau, which had been established under the allied occupation administration in 1947, capitalised on the state's express desire to be readmitted to the UN to convince it to ratify the UN Convention on the Political Rights of Women. More recently, Japanese feminists and lawyers imported the term sexual harassment directly from the United States to put pressure on the state to take appropriate action. Prior to 1990, the concept of sexual harassment simply did not exist in Japan because there was no term in the Japanese language for sexual harassment other than the vague and rarely used phrase *seiteki iyagarase* (sex-related unpleasantness). The government tried to outlast this pressure and silence feminists by claiming that it needed time to study the issue, a tactic it had begun to use more frequently since the mid-1980s to avoid meeting its international obligations.

Inherent in the social and contentious discursive interaction surrounding norms of sexual non-discrimination is an interplay or struggle between domination and resistance that involves both pernicious and non-pernicious forms of power. In order to understand how social interaction is mediated by power requires a conception of power that is able to account for the interplay between domination and resistance, constraint and enablement. Power, of course, is a fiercely contested concept in contemporary social and political theory, with an agreement on its definition yet to be reached. Stephen Lukes argues that 'the very search for such a definition is a mistake', however, for 'what unites the various views of power is too thin and formal to provide a generally satisfying definition, applicable to all cases'.[57] In light of this and bearing in mind the ontological argument developed above, it seems important to emphasise the relational dimension of power. Power is an emergent outcome of social relations; it is not something that can be procured or possessed. Agents become more or less powerful in the process of social relations and as a result of changing socio-cultural conditions. In other words, power is to some extent an effect rather than a cause of social interaction. This is not to deny that there are asymmetries in power relations between various agents but, rather, that these asymmetries are contingently produced and reproduced through social interaction. Thus, while there is the potential at any point in history for asymmetric power relations, with certain actors exercising domination or *power over* others, there also exists the potential for the distribution of power to shift. To argue that power is, in part, an effect of social relations is also not to deny that power is embodied or cumulated in socio-cultural structures. On the contrary, structures such as international and domestic socio-legal norms, beliefs and values etc., hold the power to shape social action. At any given point in time, socio-cultural structures define and delimit the actions of not only those who seem relatively powerless but also of those who appear powerful. The question is how and why does power shift? How and why do agents resist or challenge domination? What makes resistance effective, what legitimates it, what motivates it?[58]

Both domination or *power over* and resistance or *power to* are socially generated forms of concerted action that are neither instrumental nor strategic but rather are situational, in that they are conditioned by what Archer terms *vested* or *positional* interests.[59] The motivation for both domination and resistance is derived from vested interests, which emerge within any given social situation or context and provide *strategic guidance* for agents, guidance that is not determinant but rather predisposing or conditioning.[60] It is plausible then to talk in terms of various agents having 'reasons for their commitments' or actions to dominate others and defend their social advantages or to resist and change their social disadvantages. Actors do not have calculated interests or take 'emotive leaps in the dark'.[61] The fundamental point to remember about motivation, Archer argues, is that it depends neither upon zero-sum relations nor upon maximising strategies but, rather, is relationally constituted and reconstituted.[62] Positional or vested interests are neither fixed nor predetermined but, rather, shift through social interaction. They are often multiple and sometimes conflicting or contradictory.[63] Even when they do not conflict, there is usually room for agents to interpret or act upon positional interests in a number of ways, some of which may be contrary to each other. As Roger Sibeon explains, on occasion certain positional interests are forsaken in order to satisfy other interests, needs or wants.[64] For instance, during their legal campaign against discriminatory employment practices in the 1960s, Japanese plaintiffs and lawyers forsook their initial interest in creating a new moral and political consensus for a greater interest in securing specific legislative change. Of course, forsaking one set of positional interests for another does not necessarily result in the desired change, nor does the capacity of individuals to act in *solidarity* or exercise *power-with* in the face of domination by other agents. However, the ability of individuals to act together or collectively to achieve an agreed-upon end certainly heightens the possibility of generating change. For instance, in their struggle to secure revisions to national employment legislation, Japanese feminists worked together to attain the common goal of passing an amendment to the Equal Employment Opportunity Law that included a provision prohibiting sexual harassment in the workplace that, once eventually passed in 1997, ensured employers could no longer safely ignore the problem. Taken together, this notion of power relations and analysis of social interaction present us with a distinct explanation of the diffusion of international norms of sexual non-discrimination.

Conclusion

This chapter has attempted to explain the dynamics and determinants of the diffusion and non-diffusion of international norms of sexual non-discrimination into the domestic practices of states; namely, Germany and Japan. The central argument of this chapter has been that, while the gender-biased corporate identity of the state is commonly a serious impediment to the diffusion of these norms, certain conditions arise under which particular norms do tend to diffuse and influence state behaviour. These preconditions emerge as a result of historically and locationally specific social interaction. Thus, it is crucial to understand how the gender-biased corporate identity of the state is created and maintained, and to explain the motivation of states to resist or accept incorporating international norms of sexual non-discrimination. This requires analysing the relationship between structure and agency, which are the defining components of international and domestic society and, accordingly, of the explanation of the diffusion of international norms of sexual non-discrimination. It also requires analysing a particular aspect of agency, the discursive interaction between dominant and dissident agents over the meaning of gender relations. Finally, it requires analysing the medley of power relations played out in these various interactions. Underpinning such an analysis is an ontology of emergent properties that allows us to trace how, over time, international and domestic social contexts and agents interact, with agency resulting in either state behavioural change or continuity.

This argument has several theoretical and practical implications. The most significant theoretical implication is that an analysis of the construction of the corporate aspect of state identities, and of the relationship between this aspect of state identities and various international and domestic agents pressing for state behavioural change, may produce more incisive analyses of the diffusion process than extant theories of international norms. In such an analysis, we need to acknowledge the role contentious discursive interaction plays in motivating states to act in certain ways at certain points in time. Such interaction involves a relational struggle between various agents over the meaning of social situations or issues such as the gendered social order, and family–society relations. It also involves a relational struggle between domination and resistance, or power. Such an analysis rests on a conceptualisation of structure and agency that treats the two elements of social interaction as autonomous, irreducible entities, and explicitly includes time as a variable linking structure and agency. For, although social interaction is continuous, it is necessary to accept the temporal separation of structure and agency if we are to obtain analytical purchase on those processes that are accountable for determinate state behavioural change or continuity. It is also necessary to acknowledge that socio-cultural structures and agents are relatively autonomous entities, each possessing irreducible emergent properties in order to examine their interplay over time. Ontological emergentism has significant consequences for international relations theory because it gives us good reason to doubt the widely held assumption by rationalists that the structural aspect of social reality is reducible to that of agency. It also gives us good reason to doubt the constructivist assertion that structure and agency are mutually constitutive in the sense that they are *two sides of the same coin*. If we accept an ontology of emergentism, however, the question of *how* the emergence of a new feature of social reality occurs and what relationship it bears to that from which it emerged needs further examination.

The argument presented in this chapter also has a number of important practical implications for those operating in the field. First, international and domestic agents trying to promote state behavioural change need to pay close attention to how political elites create and maintain the gender-biased corporate aspect of state identities. Second, international bodies need to find ways to generate positive attitudinal change among political elites and other dominant actors within states. Third, these bodies need to create positive incentives to encourage state compliance and support those fighting for progressive change from within states. This might take the form of outreach training programmes and advisory services, legal literacy programmes, translating international legal provisions into national languages, and facilitating information exchange between activists in various states. Fourth, these bodies need to strengthen enforcement mechanisms and, more importantly, develop the political will to apply such mechanisms and hold states accountable to their agreements. However, international bodies must remain aware that, even if they apply enforcement procedures, there is no guarantee states will fully respect their international legal obligations. In such an eventuality, international bodies must continue to pursue compliance by applying pressure by any means at their disposal. Finally, feminist activists struggling for change at the local level need to be aware that discursively challenging political elites' ideas of *proper* and *appropriate* gender roles and relations in society contributes to generating state behavioural change. If political elites within states make empty promises or misappropriate gender-equality issues, activists need to find ways to shift the terms of the debate surrounding such issues. In my view, academics and activists working together and making greater use of international law can expose and critique the discursive tactics of political elites and create new ways of thinking and talking about gender-equality issues, as well as open avenues for action.

Notes

1   See Wight (1999).
2   Ashley (1989: 279).
3   Carlsnaes (2001: 344).
4   In the case of the UN, these action plans emanated from four world conferences held between 1975 and 1995.
5   Archer (1995: 66, 87).
6   Archer (1982).
7   Archer (1995: 15).
8   Archer (1995: 247).
9   Archer (1995: 247).
10   Sayer (2000: 12).
11   Cruickshank (2002: 110).
12   See Sibeon (2004).
13   Archer (1995: 259).
14   Archer (1995: 259).
15   Archer (2000: 11).
16   Archer (2003: 133).
17   Archer (2000: 269).
18   Archer (2003: 356).
19   Archer (1995: 265).
20   Ringmar (1997: 281).
21   Katzenstein (1997: 20).
22   Wendt (1994).

23 Wendt (1999: 222).
24 Rae (2002: 22).
25 The modern sovereign state, to use Stephen Krasner's definition, is a form of political organisation consisting of government 'personnel who occupy positions of decisional authority' and a 'normative order' constructed in large part by political elites. Krasner (1984: 224).
26 Checkel (1999).
27 Weitz (2001: 227).
28 Weitz (2001: 227).
29 Schissler (2001: 364).
30 Schissler (2001: 366–367).
31 The allied occupation of Japan lasted from 1945–1952, during which time legislative changes were imposed that swept away the juridical foundations of sexual discrimination in Japan.
32 For analyses of the discriminatory aspects of the family registration and resident card systems see Sugimoto (1997) and Kamiya (1986).
33 Buckley (1993: 362).
34 Carney & O'Kelly (1990: 142).
35 Archer (1995: 209).
36 Banaszak (1996: 33).
37 Banaszak (1996: 33).
38 Banaszak (1996: 29).
39 Banaszak (1996: 29).
40 Banaszak (1996: 31).
41 Banaszak (1996: 31–32).
42 Young (1999: 143).
43 Shaw & More (1995: 267).
44 Millet (2000: 10).
45 Hahm (2001: 128).
46 Hahm (2001: 128).
47 See Alter (2001).
48 Alter (2001: 229).
49 Alter (2001: 229).
50 Ostner (1993: 100).
51 Ellis (1988: 67).
52 Collins (1996: 76).
53 Steinberg (2002: 213).
54 Steinberg (2002: 213).
55 Steinberg (2002: 213).
56 Scheele (2001).
57 Lukes (1986: 4–5).
58 These questions are taken from Allen (1999: 54).
59 Archer (1995: 203).
60 Archer (1995: 210).
61 Archer (1995: 210–211).
62 Archer (1995: 204).
63 Sibeon (2004: 143).
64 Sibeon (2004: 144).

References

Allen, A. *The Power of Feminist Theory: Domination, Resistance, Solidarity* (Boulder, Colorado: Westview Press, 1999).

Alter, K. J. *Establishing the Supremacy of European Law: The Making of an International Rule of Law in Europe* (Oxford: Oxford University Press, 2001).

Archer, M. S. 'Morphogenesis versus Structuration: On Combining Structure and Agency', *The British Journal of Sociology*, 33(4), 61, 1982.

Archer, M. S. *Realist Social Theory: The Morphogenetic Approach* (Cambridge, UK: Cambridge University Press, 1995).

Archer, M. S. *Being Human: The Problem of Agency* (Cambridge, UK: Cambridge University Press, 2000).

Archer, M. S. *Structure, Agency and the Internal Conversation* (Cambridge, UK: Cambridge University Press, 2003).

Ashley, R. K. 'Living on Border Lines: Man, Poststructuralism, and War,' in J. Der Derian and M. J. Sharpiro (eds.), *International/Intertextual Relations: Postmodern Readings of World Politics* (Lexington: Lexington Books, 1989).

Banaszak, L. A. *Why Movement's Succeed or Fail: Opportunity, Culture, and the Struggle for Woman Suffrage* (Princeton, New Jersey: Princeton University Press, 1996).

Buckley, S. 'Altered States: the Body Politics of Being-Woman,' in A. Gordon (ed.), *Postwar Japan as History* (Berkeley, California: University of California Press, 1993).

Carlsnaes, W. 'Foreign Policy,' in W. Carlsnaes, T. Risse and B. A. Simmons (eds.), *Handbook of International Relations* (London: Sage Publications, 2001).

Carney, L. S. and O'Kelly, C. G. 'Women's Work and Women's Place in the Japanese Economic Miracle,' in K. Ward (ed.), *Women Workers and Global Restructuring* (Ithaca, NY: Cornell University Press, 1990).

Checkel, J. T. 'Norms, Institutions, and National Identity in Contemporary Europe,' *International Studies Quarterly*, 43, 108, 1999.

Collins, C. 'To Concede or Contest? Language and Class Struggle,' in C. Barker and P. Kennedy (eds.), *To Make Another World: Studies in Protest and Collective Action* (Aldershot, UK: Avebury Publishing, 1996).

Cruickshank, J. *Realism and Sociology: Anti-Foundationalism, Ontology and Social Research* (London: Routledge, 2002).

Ellis, E. *Sex Discrimination Law* (Aldershot, UK: Gower Publishing Company, 1988).

Hahm, D. L. 'Urgent Matters: Redress for Surviving Comfort Women,' in M. Stetz and Bonnie B. C. Oh (eds.), *The Legacies of the Comfort Women of World War II*, pp. 128–142 (New York: M.E. Sharpe, 2001).

Kamiya, M. 'Women in Japan,' *University of British Columbia Law Review*, 20(1), 1986.

Katzenstein, P. J. 'United Germany in an Integrating Europe,' in P. J. Katzenstein (ed.), *Tamed Power: Germany in Europe* (Ithaca, NY: Cornell University Press, 1997).

Krasner, S. D. 'Approaches to the State: Alternative Conceptions and Historical Dynamics', *Comparative Politics*, 16(2), 224, 1984.

Lukes, S. 'Introduction,' in S. Lukes (ed.), *Power* pp. 4–5. (New York: New York University Press, 1986).

Millet, M. 'Hirohito Named a War Criminal', *The Age*, 13 December 2000.

Ostner, I. 'Slow Motion: Women, Work, and the Family in Germany,' in J. Lewis (ed.), *Women and Social Policies in Europe: Work, Family, and the State* (Aldershot, UK: Edward Elgar Publishing, 1993).

Rae, H. *State Identities and the Homogenisation of Peoples* (Cambridge, UK: Cambridge University Press, 2002).

Ringmar, E. 'Alexander Wendt: A Social Scientist Struggling with History', in I. B. Neumman and O. Waever (eds.), *The Future of International Relations: Masters in the Making?* (New York: Routledge, 1997).

Sayer, A. *Realism and Social Science* (London: Sage Publications, 2000).

Scheele, A. *Government-Employer Agreement Prevents Equal Opportunities Law*, WSII in der Institut in der Hans-Bockler-Stiftung, 28/07/2001.

Schissler, H. 'Normalization as a Project: Some Thoughts on Gender Relations in West Germany During the 1950s', in H. Schissler (ed.), *The Miracle Years: A Cultural History of West Germany, 1949–1968* (Princeton, New Jersey: Princeton University Press, 2001).

Shaw, J. and More, G. *New Legal Dynamics of the European Union* (Oxford: Clarendon Press, 1995).

Sibeon, R. *Rethinking Social Theory* (London: Sage Publications, 2004).

Steinberg, M. W. 'Toward a More Dialogic Analysis of Social Movement Culture,' in D. S. Meyer, N. Whittier and B. Robnett (eds.), *Social Movements: Identity, Culture, and the State* (Oxford: Oxford University Press, 2002).

Sugimoto, Y. *An Introduction to Japanese Society* (Cambridge, UK: Cambridge University Press, 1997).

Weitz, E. D. 'The Ever-Present Other: Communism in the Making of West Germany', in H. Schissler (ed.), *The Miracle Years: A Cultural History of West Germany, 1949–1968* (Princeton, New Jersey: Princeton University Press, 2001).

Wendt, A. 'Collective Identity Formation and the International State,' *American Political Science Review*, 88(2), 386, June 1994.

Wendt, A. *Social Theory of International Politics* (Cambridge, UK: Cambridge University Press, 1999).

Wight, C. 'They Shoot Dead Horses Don't They? Locating Agency in the Agent-Structure Problematique', *European Journal of International Relations*, 5(1), 109, 1999.

Young, B. *Triumph of the Fatherland: German Unification and the Marginalisation of Women* (Michigan: University of Michigan Press, 1999).

15 Realist social theorising and the emergence of state educational systems

Tone Skinningsrud

Introduction

Margaret Archer has presented a historical-sociological theory of the emergence of state educational systems which accounts for the way such systems have emerged in all Western countries, albeit at different points in history, and quite different stages of social development. The societies in which state educational systems emerged varied a great deal with regard to their political system, degree of industrialisation, urbanisation, etc.[1] Thus, Archer's theory diverges from both correspondence theory and functionalist theories in claiming that education cannot be seen as a mere reflection of the larger society of which it is a part, nor can it be assumed that it is always harmoniously integrated with its general social environment.

Archer's distinctive approach to the study of educational development and change entails a focus on the transformation of educational structures; or educational morphogenesis. The transformation of educational structures includes the transformation of external relations between education and other social institutions as well as changes in internal educational structures. The general model of morphogenesis, or the transformation of social structure through interaction, shares the same basic premises as Roy Bhaskar's transformational model of social activity (TMSA)[2] and is a meta-theory in relation to the more specific domain theory of the emergence of state educational systems. In applying the morphogenetic approach to the study of educational development in individual countries, the identification of educational structures is crucial since knowledge of structural conditioning is required in order to understand the subsequent processes of interaction that produce change. Therefore, a study of the development of the Norwegian state educational system, which aims to explain how it emerged, will have to work on identifying prior structural conditions as its first priority. In consequence, this chapter focuses on the identification of the structural integration of education in Norwegian society prior to the emergence of its state educational system.

Archer's domain theory of educational development states that during the phase prior to the emergence of state systems, education was mono-integrated with and subordinated to the church. The church was the sole provider of the material resources without which education could not exist, and the schools produced services that were uniquely suited for the church in terms of the kinds of knowledge and values they instilled in their pupils. The mono-integrated relation between education and the church was a necessary and compatible institutional relationship.[3] Archer's theory explains how state educational systems emerged through *one morphogenetic cycle,* accounting for the transition from mono-integration of education and the church to a multi-integrated state educational system providing services to a plurality of other social institutions.

The proposition of mono-integration, as a statement about the pre-existing educational structure, is the starting point of the present analysis of the emergence of the Norwegian state educational system. Since the historical development of Norwegian education deviates in significant ways from the general account provided by Archer's theory, an alternative proposition is put forward, namely that in Norway, prior to the emergence of the educational system, education was not integrated with the church only. Instead, education was integrated with the state as well as the church, in a *dual relationship.* Undoubtedly, in Norway and the Scandinavian countries in general, during The Middle Ages education was mono-integrated with the Roman Catholic Church as its sole economic provider and main beneficiary. However, the Lutheran Reformation appears to have altered this state of affairs.

If the Reformation resulted in dual integration of education with both the state and the church, the emergence of the Norwegian state educational system must have occurred through *two morphogenetic cycles rather than one.* This calls for a reformulation of Archer's theory, making it more inclusive by incorporating both one-cycle and two-cycle developmental trajectories. Also, in accounting for the development from mono-integration to system emergence through two morphogenetic cycles, the second cycle needs to be theorised in greater detail, since its initial phase of dual integration of education with the church and state represents a new type of structural conditioning, which is not covered by the established domain theory.

Historical data concerning the development of Norwegian education during the nineteenth century is examined next. The main emphasis is on substantiating my hypothesis of dual integration between education and the church and state prior to the emergence of the state educational system. I also present an outline of how the cycle that started with dual integration of education with the state and church can be theorised, by introducing concepts from the second cycle of development in Archer's theory – the cycle starting with the emergence of the state system. My attempt to elaborate the established theory shows, *inter alia*, how, in a multi-level social theory, higher level (meta-)concepts may be used in the elaboration of theories at a lower level.[4] Finally, reflecting on the kind of reasoning involved in making Archer's educational theory more inclusive, I apply her theory of cultural morphogenesis through syncretism to one of the transforms in a more encompassing process of epistemological dialectic.

Conceptualisations of state involvement in Scandinavian education

Traditionally, in Norwegian educational history, the influence of the Lutheran Reformation has been studied as the effect of ideas. There is general agreement that Lutheranism has had an enduring influence on education in all the Nordic countries, and the egalitarianism of 'the Nordic school model', in the sense of caring for the weak, has been traced to Lutheran ideas.[5] Less attention has been paid to the long-term effects of the educational structures that were established during the Reformation. When the monarch became the head of the church as well as the state, the church was deprived of virtually all its economic and political power; and the new bishops (superintendents) were made into salaried employees of the state. After the Reformation, the supervisory authority exerted by the church over education was on behalf of the monarch and authorised by church legislation passed by state authorities. The monarch assumed responsibility for educational provisions all over the land by assigning duties to local town councils, cathedral chapters and local parishes, guaranteeing that any local deficits in school provisions would be compensated by endowments from the Crown.

Recently, however, several studies of education in the Scandinavian countries have paid more attention to aspects of educational structure, and particularly the early state involvement in education.[6] The exact nature of this involvement has, however, been difficult to conceptualise. For example, in historical accounts of educational change in Norwegian elementary education during the latter half of the nineteenth century, the conjoint processes of increased state funding and secularisation of educational content and administration have been described as a paradox: 'a statification within the framework of the state'.[7]

The enduring role of the state in Norwegian education has also been described as *a tradition* of state intervention in the sense of a practice rooted in an ideology of reformism.[8] After Norway's independence from Denmark in 1814, the second generation political elite, which dominated political life for the major part of the century, adhered to a *mouvement* conception of government. Their ideology of political liberalism inclined them to restrict state power and protect individual liberty; nevertheless it did not prevent them from initiating reformative national legislation on a broad scale. Some of these reforms promoted economic liberalism by abolishing privileges of various kinds.[9] The practice of using national legislation to promote social development resembles the German tradition, but departs from it in that Norwegian political elites towards the turn of the nineteenth century formed coalitions with self-assertive new elites, and these coalitions became advocates of national and democratic values. Unlike nationalism in other parts of Europe, Norwegian nationalism was coupled with democratic ideals advocated by oppositional groups. Rune Slagstad explains the reformative role of the state in Norway from the mid-1840s to the late 1970s as the result of an enduring ideology of state interventionism, put into practice by successive political elites, regardless of their other ideological leanings.[10]

Similarly, in a recent historical-sociological study of comprehensive schooling in the Scandinavian countries, the role of the state is conceptualised as the enduring practice of state interventionism.[11] Susanne Wiborg points out that 'in Scandinavia the public elementary school and secondary school was *a result of* state intervention' and, referring to the situation during the late nineteenth century, 'both elementary and secondary schools were almost entirely public'.[12] She locates the origin of state intervention in Danish–Norwegian education to the late eighteenth century's period of reforming absolutism and sees the monarch's need for civil servants as the impetus behind reforms that ensured state funding of secondary schooling. Wiborg describes state intervention in Scandinavian education as 'a long process'.

Thus, recent studies of educational development in Scandinavia as a whole, and in Norway in particular, have noted the important role of the state and the 'long process of state intervention'. However, as already suggested, state intervention in education in Denmark–Norway can be traced even further back than to absolutism. Martin Schwarz Lausten remarks in his study of the Danish Reformation bishop Palladius that the Reformation established 'a relationship of dependency between education and the state [...] which had not existed previously'.[13] This conclusion, based on historical studies of the Reformation and early post-Reformation period in Denmark–Norway, is a strong statement about the relationship between education and the state by suggesting their structural integration in a necessary relationship.

Multi-level theorising in comparative education

The comparative study of education has traditionally been split in two research traditions. the positivist, whose aim has been to establish universal laws of educational development, and the idiographic tradition, which emphasises the uniqueness of national educational traditions and systems. Archer, in her 1979 publication, was the first to introduce a theoretical approach that transcended this divide between generalising and particularising comparative studies. Guided by a general meta-theoretical framework, she studied educational development in the four countries, England, France, Russia and Denmark, from which she developed a domain theory of 'the social origins of educational systems' as well as explanatory accounts of the development in each of these countries.

How do theories of educational development in specific countries relate to general theories of educational development? Obviously, findings about individual countries must be accommodated by the general theory. Moreover, as the conception of unilinear development, where the same trajectory is repeated in every country, is clearly contradicted by historical facts, the general theory must allow for divergent paths among individual countries. Thus, it is important to distinguish between levels of theorising. Domain theories of the emergence of state educational systems belong to a more general theoretical level than theories about the emergence of such systems in individual countries. Furthermore, the theory level of specific national case studies and that of domains are distinct from the level of general social theories. We have here three theoretical levels: (i) general theories of social change; (ii) domain theories of educational change; and (iii) specific theories of educational change in individual countries.

A domain theory of educational development must capture the general characteristics of development and its conceptions must allow divergent courses of development in individual countries. An example of the type of conceptualisations required is Archer's definition of state educational systems, which brings out common characteristics of such systems but is sufficiently general to accommodate different types of educational systems in individual countries. She defines a state educational system as:

> [A] nation wide and differentiated collection of institutions devoted to formal education, whose overall control and supervision is at least partly governmental, and whose component parts and processes are related to one another.[14]

The two main common characteristics of state educational systems brought out by this definition are (a) the integration of the system with the state as the political centre; and (b) the interconnectedness of the elements in the form of a system. This definition is sufficiently general to include educational systems that are both centralised and decentralised and based on positive (linear) as well as negative (non-linear) hierarchical principles.

Consistent with the notion of different levels of theorising, and the constraints that higher-level theory exert on the development of lower level theory, Archer's domain theory of educational development must be understood within the framework of her general morphogenetic approach to the study of social change. The morphogenetic approach conceives of structural transformation as occurring in a succession of cycles, each consisting of three phases:

structural conditioning → social interaction → structural change
(phase 1)   (phase 2)   (morphogenesis)
                                            (phase 3)

This meta-theoretical framework indicates that structural change in society, or parts of it, can be studied as sequences of morphogenetic cycles, where the last phase in one cycle constitutes the first phase in the next. The model incorporates historical time as a variable, and the different phases in a cycle extend over different but overlapping time tracts. Structure exists prior to interaction and structural change is the (often unintended) result of interaction. Thus, structural change takes time. Guided by this model, the study of structural change will entail the identification of morphogenetic cycles and their three phases: structural conditioning, social interaction and morphogenesis.

In Archer's domain theory of educational development, the emergence of state educational systems is seen as the final phase of a morphogenetic cycle that started with education having a necessary, compatible and subordinate relationship with the church. The domain theory of educational development is situated within a more general theory of social change. The elaboration of the domain theory may therefore be guided by the general theory. Thus, conceptual tools are available to repair possible inconsistencies that arise between the established domain theory and new observations pertaining to the specific study of new cases, or countries that were not included in the original study informing the established domain theory. Thus, inconsistencies may lead to the development of the theory rather than its wholesale rejection.

The conception of structural mono-integration: implications for educational interaction

A basic insight contained in the morphogenetic model of structural transformation is that social structures condition interaction, and therefore contribute in a significant way to shape the processes that produce structural change. In order to explain development and change, the identification of the conditioning structures in the first phase of a morphogenetic cycle is therefore essential. The study of the emergence of state educational systems must entail the identification of the institutional structure that conditioned the interaction that produced morphogenesis.

The assumption of the mono-integration of education and the church implies that education was integrated with the church in a necessary relationship. A necessary relationship means that education could not exist without the church, because the church provided the basic material, economic and personnel resources for educational activities, and also provided the content of instruction. Since no other providers of resources were available, education was subordinated in the relationship. The church monopoly in education ensured that provisions were tailored to the requirements of the church, and all changes had to be negotiated with the church. Since the church was the sole provider of necessary resources, external demands for change through negotiations were unlikely to succeed, and subordination to the church meant a lack of autonomy in educational activities and operations, and a lack of resources to initiate change from within schools. External demands were generated when institutional operations in other spheres of society such as trade and industry increasingly required other types of qualifications than those provided by the church schools. Demand for alternative provisions could also be initiated by ideational movements, which were related to a demand for qualifications for active citizenship, such as the folk high school movement in Scandinavia.

Mono-integration conditioned *competitive conflicts* rather than negotiations for educational change. Dominant and assertive groups struggled to obtain control over education with the intent of mutual elimination. In this interaction, agents in other institutions became potential allies with either party in the struggle. Some benefited from the education of the church schools without contributing resources to it, gaining advantage by virtue of their power over the church. An example of adventitious beneficiaries is given by Archer, mentioning the

Danish state in the 1730s, when the interest of the absolute monarchy was served by educational reforms that were administered and implemented by the church.[15]

Evidence against institutional mono-integration between education and the Church

In the following I present some aspects of Norwegian educational history that appear to contradict the general proposition of mono-integration prior to the emergence of the state educational system. The focus is on the development of secondary education and the Grundtvigian folk high school movement.[16] I discuss (1) *the structural changes in secondary education* prior to the emergence of the system; and (2) *the strategies* employed by the contestants in the political struggle over state-assisted secondary education and the folk high schools during the latter part of the nineteenth century, leading up to the emergence of the system.

Structural change in secondary education prior to the emergence of the state system

The assumption of mono-integration entails that (i) given the particular institutional structure, only minor changes in educational provisions could be obtained; and (ii) the demands for change were of great magnitude, due to the necessary and compatible relationship between education and the church. Given the mono-integration of education with the church, substantial educational change could therefore only be obtained by a destruction of the church monopoly.

However, in Denmark–Norway, the consequences of the 1809 Secondary Education Act and the subsequent reforms of Norwegian secondary education during the nineteenth century seem to contradict the assumption that, prior to the emergence of the system, only minor educational changes could be obtained. The 1809 Act effected clearer differentiation and greater autonomy for secondary education in relation to the church, reducing its economic dependency on the church and secularising the administration as well as the content of secondary education. These changes cast doubts on the assumption of the mono-integration of secondary education and the church. Long before the emergence of the state educational system, an incipient integration between secondary education and other social institutions, besides the church, was on its way.

The 1809 Secondary Education Act was initiated and implemented by the Danish Crown Prince Regent during the reform period of the absolute monarchy. Active agents in promoting the reform were prominent members of the Danish aristocratic political elite. The increased institutional differentiation between secondary education and the church and its reduced subordination to the church were manifested in many ways:

- secondary school teachers were no longer classified as ecclesiastical personnel by the ministry

- the administration of secondary education and the universities was organised in a new collegial unit in the ministry, '*Directionen for universitetet og de lærde skoler*' (which consisted of professional educators)
- new diocese school boards, the *ephorats*, were established as intermediate administrative units between the ministry and each secondary school. Here the local state representative and the bishop were members *ex officio*
- pupils and teachers from the Latin schools were relieved of their daily church duties
- the educational content was broadened by incorporating modern languages and natural science, and
- the intake of pupils was widened to include 'non-students' (i.e. pupils whose aim was not matriculation were allowed to participate in all subjects in the lower grades and in modern language and science classes in the higher grades).[17]

Changes in the funding of secondary schools also reduced the dependency of secondary education on the church. Before the 1809 Act, the participation of cathedral school pupils in church services had been a major source of income. After 1809, however, this source of income disappeared, and instead school fees were introduced. Until the end of the nineteenth century, private fees remained a major sustenance to the cathedral schools.[18] The loss of income from participation in church services was also compensated by a small state grant.[19]

After the 1809 Act, secondary education still provided services for the church, as it was required for the study of theology at university. Despite this, all the above-mentioned changes created greater autonomy for secondary education in its relation with the church: reduced economic dependency, secularised supervisory authority and secularisation of the content of instruction. Secondary education became more clearly integrated with the state bureaucracy as a whole. There was also an incipient integration with the lower bourgeoisie through the admission of 'non-students' in secondary schools.

During the 19th century, further reforms of Norwegian secondary education augmented these changes by broadening the intake of students, changing the content of instruction by further modernisation of the curriculum, and by removing the barrier preventing university entry for students who had not studied Latin. The first of these reforms, passed by the Norwegian parliament in 1848, expanded *Real*[20] education at the expense of the classical curriculum. Secondary education was to be reorganised as combined Latin and *Real* schools, and economic assistance from the state was given on the condition that the new arrangement was implemented. Thus, the state was an active promoter of a modernised curriculum through its funding arrangements.

However, major problems remained in the new combined Latin and *Real* state-assisted secondary schools. Students enrolled in the *Real* stream were not admitted to university and pupils who left school after completing the lower grades received no official recognition of their qualifications. The next secondary education Act, passed in 1869 entailed two major changes. Firstly, it allowed admission to the university for students from the *Real*-stream in secondary schools, i.e. students who had not studied Latin. Secondly, it introduced a public intermediate exam, upon the completion of the first six years of secondary education (the new middle school). The 1869 Act strengthened the sectioning of secondary education into two distinct stages: the six-year middle school without classical studies and the three-year gymnasium with a modern stream and a classical stream. The two gymnasium streams were equivalent in terms of preparing for the university, and the middle school, in practice, incorporated the previously independent *borger-skole* into state-assisted secondary education.[21]

The 1869 reform, which in effect removed the Latin wall around the university, and established a state-funded provision for the bourgeoisie and new middle classes, has been explained as the result of Grundtvigian ideas and the political efforts of the Grundtvigian movement, since they were at the forefront of the attack on Latin.[22] It has also been explained as the achievement of liberal ideas advanced by the peasant movement.[23] However, the reform was also supported by a section of the political elite, which during the 1830s had raised the issue of *Real* versus classical education and argued for a reduction of classical studies in secondary schools. Another group that was an obvious beneficiary of the reform was the bourgeoisie whose privately financed *borgerskoler* now *de facto* were incorporated in state-assisted secondary education with its own officially recognised middle school certificate. Thus, the reform was in the interests of a broad coalition, including both educationally dominant and self-assertive groups. Those who opposed the reform were members of the political elite (who were educational traditionalists and defenders of classical learning) and, on the other extreme, the vanguards of the increasingly consolidated liberal opposition in parliament; educators who, on professional grounds, felt impeded by excessive state control of secondary education, which was maintained by the act.

The arguments of the vanguards of the liberal opposition were that the reform was not in line with truly liberal principles, since the state would still be in control of secondary education. They demanded that secondary schools should become autonomous private institutions removed from state control.[24]

The expansion of secondary education after the 1869 Act, with the establishment of an increasing number of state-assisted secondary schools, confirms its successful integration with a wider range of social institutions. Towards the end of the nineteenth century, secondary education consisted of a mix of state-assisted, municipal and private secondary schools. Some were middle schools only, some were full length middle schools and gymnasiums. Modernised secondary education and in particular the new middle schools clearly met a demand. The 1869 Act continued the broader integration of secondary education with a wider range of social institutions, and also preserved its state funding and control.

Structurally conditioned strategies of self-assertive groups

The morphogenetic model implies that different types of structural conditioning generate different patterns of interaction. Specifically, the institutional structure of educational mono-integration induces interaction in the form of *competitive conflict*. The guiding principle of competitive conflict, generated by its situational logic, is mutual elimination, that is, each party trying to eliminate the other party's control. The main strategies available to self-assertive groups in such competitive struggles were *restriction* and *substitution*. The choice of strategy depended on the type of resources commanded by assertive groups. The strategy of *restriction*, i.e. closing down church controlled schools and replacing them with new provisions more in line with the requirements of assertive groups, or imposing severe restrictions on their activities, presupposed the political resources to do so. *Substitution*, which implied the establishment of alternative and competing educational provisions by assertive groups, presupposed the availability of, and willingness to apply, economic resources to establish new alternative schools. Hence, assertive groups that were dissatisfied with the church monopoly in education, tended to choose their strategy in accordance with their relative command of economic and political resources.

In England, in the competitive conflict between dominant and assertive groups, self-assertive groups used the strategy of substitution. Private denominational schools were established in competition with the established Anglican school network. State funding of schools increased during the latter half of the nineteenth century as a result of each of the contenders – the two school networks – demanding state funding for their own network, which they succeeded in obtaining through alliances with political parties. The increasingly widespread acceptance of the idea that the state should take economic responsibility for education also contributed to the resulting state involvement and the emergence of the state educational system.

In Norway, however, no dominant pattern of either restriction or substitution can be observed. Instead, several strategies were employed, and the dominant strategy was neither restriction nor substitution, but *municipalisation* in the sense of trying to remove educational control from the government bureaucracy, which was controlled by the political elite, to local politically elected bodies. During the early 1870s, the opposition went through a phase of total rejection of state funding, both for the established state secondary schools and for the alternative folk high schools. Their demand was for private and autonomous secondary schools, and in debates in the parliament their symbolically expressed strategy of restriction was *nedleggelse* (the closing down) of state secondary schools. This seems to have been more psychological warfare than real action, because the withdrawal of state funding and the closing down of state-assisted secondary schools was never put to the vote. However, it signalled a wish for the elimination of state-funded and state-controlled schools that served the educational interests of the political elite. But this does not amount to a strategy of restriction, which implies the actual constraint of educational activities through the closing down of schools, firing of teachers, etc.

During the 1870s state funding of education meant state control, favouring the educational interests of the political elite. This is most clearly expressed in the struggle over the folk high schools. The first Grundtvigian folk high school was established in Norway in 1864, and such schools proliferated during the 1870s. In 1875 there were 20 such schools in Norway; dispersed around the country, but mostly located in rural areas.[25] During a three-day public meeting in the capital in 1872, supporters and critics of the folk high school movement gathered to discuss the new educational ideas, and the issue was raised concerning public funding of the new schools, which until then had been sustained by private individuals relying on private funds. There was a strong sentiment against public funding among the members of the movement.[26] However, the schools mainly recruited among the peasant population, and as their financial situation became more difficult over the years, this attitude was reversed. Several of the folk high schools applied individually for state funding, with the proviso that they would not have to submit their educational programme for approval to state authorities.

The struggle over the folk high schools is another example of how, in Norway, the strategies of the parties conflicting on the issue of educational control differed from the strategies in England. In England, the strategy of substitution was initiated by self-assertive groups competing with established Anglican schools through the funding of their own schools competing in the same market. In Norway, the roles between the dominant and assertive groups were reversed in the battle over the Norwegian folk high schools. The already-existing private folk high schools based on Grundtvigian Christendom encountered competition from new state-initiated and state-funded schools, *amtskoler*, which were based on orthodox and Pietistic Lutheranism.[27]

The folk high schools were recruiting from a specific segment of the population, the adult male youth of peasant origin, who had not attended secondary education. This was a group that at the time had very few educational options. The folk high schools clearly met a demand for further education among those who had attended the common school. Thus, the folk high schools were not competing for recruitment in the same market as the Latin and *Real* schools, although their educational philosophy was a challenge to them, since it was based on widely publicised and hotly debated opposing educational principles. The teaching method in the folk high schools focused on oral presentations through 'the living word' and few textbooks, as opposed to the disciplined learning of a fixed curriculum. The content was secular subjects with a strong emphasis on Norwegian language, history, literature and contemporary social issues; and religion was not taught as dogma, instead the Christian spirit was to permeate all school activities. Grundtvigian Christendom was opposed to both Lutheran orthodoxy and the lay Pietistic movement, which during the latter half of the nineteenth century had formed an alliance in Norwegian church life. The Grundtvigians had strong adversaries in the established state church preventing them from getting positions in the church, and in the university, where the professors ensured that Grundtvigians were singled out among theology students through the type of exam questions that were given. Presenting a Grundtvigian interpretation in an exam in theology guaranteed a low grade, regardless of the brilliance of the essay.[28]

The folk high schools could have become a competitor to established secondary education if the idea of creating folk high schools in every municipality of the country had been followed up. However, this idea did not gain a following.[29] Instead, to ward off the threat of the folk high school movement the political elite and the established church established a new type of school, the state-approved and economically assisted county schools (*amtskoler*). Neither the folk high schools nor the county schools became part of the mainstream educational structure, and the few independent elementary schools, which were established in the localities of some of the folk high schools, were short of funds and durability.[30] Thus, the strategy of substitution, which was used in the competitive conflict between the folk high schools and the *amtskoler*, could not be considered the prevailing pattern of interaction, which was instrumental in the emergence of the educational system.[31]

The major strategy of the educational opposition, municipalisation, was signalled both in the parliamentary debate on the 1869 secondary education Act, and later, during the 1970s, in repeated moves to gather support for the withdrawal of state funding from secondary education. This strategy was clearly demonstrated in the 1877 three-day-long debate on the funding and control of the folk high schools and the county schools (*amtskoler*), when it was decided, in accordance with the demands of the opposition, that the county school boards, rather than the ministry, should decide on whether folk high schools should receive public funding. The pressure from the opposition to decentralise decision-making on the funding of folk high schools was intended to avoid the educational control of the political elite of state bureaucrats.[32]

The institutional structure prior to the emergence of the system

What can we infer about the institutional structure, which pre-dated the nineteenth century structural changes in secondary education and conditioned the strategy of municipalisation? Clearly, the assumption of mono-integration of education and the church does not hold, considering the magnitude of changes in secondary education. Firstly, there was an increased differentiation between secondary education and the church, and secondly, secondary education became integrated with a growing bourgeoisie and new middle class of lower level officials in the public and private sector. The 1809 Act initiated changes on both accounts, and further integration of secondary education with a wider range of social institutions continued throughout the 19th century. The political strategy of municipalisation, which meant the transfer of educational control from the central administration to politically elected local bodies, was distinctly different from the two strategies of self-assertive groups accounted for by Archer's theory, and therefore must have been conditioned by another type of structure than mono-integration.

In order to identify the institutional structure that conditions interaction, Archer suggests the procedure of investigation structural conditions prior to the first efforts to change the educational status quo.[33] If we look at the situation prior to the 1809 Act, secondary education was closely integrated with the church. The cathedral schools, although supported by their own funds, had obtained a major part of their income from participating in church services, and they were supervised by church officials. During the Reformation, the Latin schools had been reorganised to cater for the education of the new clergy. They were also a recruitment channel for other state officials. Besides, the clergy themselves constituted an embryonic state apparatus, as their top officials, the new bishops (superintendents), were salaried state employees who had pledged an oath of loyalty to the King before Ordination, and were directly accountable to the King. During the early post-Reformation period, a representative of secular authorities accompanied the bishops in their supervision of the Latin schools. Supervision was later left to the church alone, but remained authorised by state legislation (the 1539 Church Ordinance). Likewise, the funding arrangements for the schools were, in the final instance, the responsibility of the central authority; the King. Although funding was supplied from several sources: directly from the King, from town authorities and monasteries; and sustenance for Latin school pupils were secured by endowments from the King, employment as church deacons in neighbouring churches and through begging licensed by the King, all financial support, except for endowments from private individuals, was granted at the King's orders. Thus, the schools' recruitment to state positions, their subordination to state legislation and their funding arrangements, which in the final instance were controlled by the King, support the hypothesis that, prior to the 1809 Act, education was integrated with the state as well as the church.

This hypothesis is further strengthened by the observation that the peasant opposition and the emerging liberal Venstre-movement, increasingly, from the mid-19th century applied the strategy of municipalisation of educational control, clearly intended to avoid the control of the state bureaucracy. The strategy of municipalisation employed by the opposition in promoting the folk high schools as well as in effecting changes in secondary and elementary education was explicitly advocated as a means to avoid state control.

In the Norwegian context neither substitution nor restriction were realistic strategies for oppositional groups. Substitution was not an option because the opposition, on the whole, came from the less affluent groups in society. *Restriction* was not an option because it would require a majority vote in parliament to close down schools. This was unrealistic, and, furthermore, it required the approval of the government, which would not be forthcoming under the existing constitutional arrangements.[34] Municipalisation was the only strategy available to circumvent the dominance of the political elite who controlled the government. Besides, the strategy of municipalisation was legitimated by the ideas of liberalism; ideas that enjoyed general support in society at the time. The strategy of municipalisation required political rather than economic resources, which suited the generally poor and idealistic Grundtvigians and the peasant opposition alike, as both were among the less affluent groups in society, but had some access to central power through their representation in parliament.

In conclusion, the hypothesis that, prior to the 1809 reform, education was doubly integrated with the church and the state thus seems well founded. In England and France, the institutional structure of mono-integration and subordination of education to the church conditioned competitive conflict, as the prevailing pattern of interaction between dominant and assertive educational groups. Achieving major structural change through negotiations was not feasible under these structural conditions. In Norway, however, the integration of education with the state enabled successive changes through negotiations prior to the emergence of the system.

Theorising the new cycle: a tentative outline

If, as I have argued, Norwegian education prior to the emergence of the educational system was integrated both with the church and the state in a dual relationship, the course of development from mono-integration of education with the Catholic church during the Middle Ages to a multi-integrated state educational system must have occurred through two morphogenetic cycles, where the Lutheran Reformation represented the first morphogenesis. Furthermore, the inclusion of an additional morphogenetic cycle, starting with the dual integration of education with the church and state calls for additional theorising of the processes during this cycle. At this point I can only suggest a tentative outline of such a theory. The integration of education with the state during the initial phase of this cycle suggests that political structures and the degree of consensus among political elites will play a central role in accounting for the processes of interaction during this cycle. Thus, concepts from the second morphogenetic cycle in Archer's original domain theory will be useful in theorising the new cycle.

During the period of Norwegian educational history covered in this presentation, the political structure changed from absolutism to constitutionalism, and parliamentarianism (cabinet responsibility to the parliamentary majority) was about to emerge.[35] These changes made state power accessible to an increasingly wider range of social groups, and they fit with the typology of political centres in Archer's theory, which distinguishes between impenetrable, semi-permeable and accessible political centres. The political context of the 1809 Act, i.e. absolutism, must be characterised as impenetrable. The political context of the 1848 parliamentary decision and the 1869 Act,[36] could be seen as a semi-penetrable political centre. After 1884, the introduction of cabinet responsibility to parliament was arguably motivated by a desire to create an accessible political centre, which became even more accessible after universal suffrage for men was introduced in 1898 and for women in 1913. These political changes created a new context for subsequent educational reforms.

The hypotheses put forward by Archer[37] involving this typology seem to be confirmed by the historical evidence which has been presented above. (1) '*With an impenetrable political centre, only subsections of the governing elite will be able to negotiate educational demands by political manipulation*'. In Denmark–Norway, the 1809 Secondary Education Act was negotiated by the aristocratic political elite close to the Crown Prince. (2) *'With a semi-permeable political centre, sub-sections of the governing elite, together with government supporters, will be able to negotiate educational demands by political manipulation'*. The 1869 Norwegian secondary education Act was supported by a sub-section of the governing elite, and by the bourgeoisie, which was the political ally of the governing elite; the opposition supported some of the claims, but did not succeed in obtaining the municipalisation of educational control, which was their primary aim. And (3) *'With an accessible political centre, governmental opponents, too, will be able to negotiate educational demands by political manipulation'*. In Norway, the political centre became increasingly accessible after the introduction in 1884 of cabinet responsibility. Whether the educational reform processes, which followed this political reform, conform to the hypothesis, requires further investigation. However, the integration of education with the state seems to have allowed processes of negotiation to produce structural change before the emergence of the system.[38]

Meta-reflections on the elaboration of theory

Cultural syncretism

When scientific theories are seen as sub-systems of more encompassing cultural systems, the elaboration of scientific theories becomes a special case of cultural morphogenesis, i.e. the emergence of new cultural items.[39] The elaboration of scientific theories can be seen as a special case of cultural morphogenesis, i.e. syncretism, where novel ideas, in various ways, build upon or incorporate existing ideas. In a process of syncretism, the new cultural element, the novel idea, or, in the case of scientific theories, conceptual elaboration of the theory, emerges as the result of intellectual work that aims to repair a logical contradiction. The logical contradiction resulting in syncretism may be between pre-existing elements (propositions), which have existed for a long time, or, in the case of scientific theories, the contradiction may be between a general proposition belonging to an established theory and new observations generated within the same theoretical framework. Syncretism may either: (1) preserve the established theoretical framework by questioning and making subsequent redescriptions, or reinterpretations, of the contradictory observation, so that it becomes compatible with the theory; (2) make mutual adjustments both in the formulation of the theory and the observation to make them consistent; or (3) change the established theory to make it compatible with the contradictory observation.[40]

The general model for the various paths that lead to syncretism, through the repair of inconsistency between ideas, is outlined below, where two contradictory ideas are indicated as *A* and *B*:

1   $A \leftarrow B$; indicates that *B* is corrected so that it becomes consistent with *A*
2   $A \leftrightarrow B$; indicates that both *A* and *B* are corrected to become mutually consistent
3   $A \rightarrow B$; indicates that *A* is corrected to become consistent with B.[41]

In applying this scheme to the elaboration of scientific theories, *A* may denote a general proposition in an established theory and *B* the contradictory observation. The relationship between the two ideas, or propositions, *A* and *B*, belongs to the level of the cultural system, or subsystem, which is constituted by the logical relationship between ideas.[42] Syncretism, especially paths (2) and (3), adds new ideas to the cultural system; ideas that resolve logical contradictions and contribute to the unification of the system. Emergent properties of the cultural system, that is, either contradictions or consistency between ideas, condition socio-cultural interaction in different ways. Constraining cultural contradictions, as opposed to competitive contradictions,[43] generates repair work resulting in syncretism. A cultural contradiction between the ideas *A* and *B* is constraining, provided someone or some group wants to uphold the idea or theory *A*, which is inexorably linked to the contradictory idea, *B*. The situational logic generated by a constraining cultural contradiction is to repair the inconsistency. In elaborating scientific theories, the situational logic of a constraining contradiction is created when an observation *B*, generated within a certain theoretical framework, contradicts a general proposition *A*, within the same framework and the scientist at work is committed to preserve as much as possible of theory *A*.

Whichever method is used to correct a constraining contradiction the generic result is some form of syncretism. The main thrust emanating from its situational logic is the sinking of differences and the effecting of union between its components. In other words, the existence of constraining contradictions within the cultural system conditions ideational unification.[44]

A basic premise for the repair work of syncretism to occur is the commitment of specific agents to uphold a basic idea *A*, in face of the contradictory idea *B*. In the present case of the repair work done on Archer's domain theory of educational development, this premise lies in my commitment to the meta-theory, specifically the notion of structural transformations through morphogenetic cycles, which offers a solution to the question of how structure is preserved or transformed through social action. The commitment to work from this general idea has generated effort on my part to seek resolutions of the logical contradiction between my own empirical findings and the established educational theory.

When the model of syncretism is applied to the theoretical work that has been presented concerning the emergence of state educational systems, we can identify two contradictory propositions, representing the ideas *A* and *B* in the formula above:

A.   *Proposition from the established theory.* It is universally true that prior to the emergence of the multi-integrated state educational system, education was *mono-integrated* with one other social institution.[45]

B.   *Contradictory observation.* In Norway, prior to the emergence of the multi-integrated state educational system, there was *dual integration* between education and the state and church.

The two propositions are logically contradictory, and bound together by belonging to the same theoretical universe. The assertion (observation) of the structural integration of Norwegian education, B, has been generated through the use of the same basic conceptualisation as the one that is constitutive of A, i.e. the concept of institutional integration, and is the result of an explicitly stated research objective of identifying pre-existing institutional structures. The contradiction between A and B therefore represents a constraining contradiction. Since I cannot give up B, which has been formulated on the basis of a considerable amount of research work, and I do not see how I can possibly reformulate it to become consistent with A, I have to settle for the third path towards syncretism. I have to reformulate A to make it consistent with B. I have to formulate A_1:

A_1. *Elaboration of the established theory.* Prior to the emergence of the multi-integrated state educational system, education was either mono-integrated with the church or dually integrated with the church and state.

This more inclusive formulation of a basic proposition in the original theory has repercussions for other propositions in the theory, which are connected with it. The original theory implicitly assumes that:

a. The transition from mono-integration to multi-integration occurred through one morphogenetic cycle.

My alternative, and more inclusive, formulation is that:

a_1. The transition from mono-integration of education to a multi-integrated state system varied across countries; in some it occurred via one morphogenetic cycle, in others via two.

a_1 retains a basic element of a, namely that education was universally mono-integrated at some point, prior to the emergence of the system. The new idea is that in Norway, and perhaps other Scandinavian countries, there was an additional morphogenetic cycle in between mono-integration and system emergence. The first cycle, in Norway, and possibly other countries, started with mono-integration and ended in dual integration. The second cycle started with dual integration and ended with the emergence of the system.

In this 'repair work', I have settled for that path towards syncretism which implies the danger of a degenerative problem shift, that is, an *ad hoc* reformulation of the established theory, which may reduce its explanatory power.[46] I maintain, however, that my reformulation is progressive, rather then degenerative, because the reformulation of the theory enables it to account for a novel fact. Mono-integration can account for the strategies of substitution and restriction, but cannot account for the strategy of municipalisation. The strategy of municipalisation can, however, be explained by the integration of education with the state.

Epistemological dialectic

Archer's cultural theory enables us to see the elaboration of scientific theories as entailing repair work tending towards syncretism. The contradiction between an established theory and new observations generated within the same theoretical framework constrains the intellectual effort of the working scientist in the direction of syncretism. This effort to resolve contradictions is explained partly as conditioned by properties of the cultural system (in this case the relation of logical contradiction between cultural elements) and partly by the commitment of working scientists to save as much as possible of the established theory. However, the morphogenetic cycle of cultural emergence, which accounts for syncretism, and contains the phases

(i) constraining contradiction (cultural system) → (ii) repair work (socio-cultural interaction) → (iii) syncretism (cultural morphogenesis)

can be seen as the second transform in a more complete cycle of epistemological dialectic.

While Archer's model starts with the cultural inconsistency (constraining contradiction) as the causal factor, Bhaskar, in citing the three stages of Gödelian dialectic, includes the cause of this cause (the cultural inconsistency) in a more complete sequence, where the inconsistency is explained as caused by an absence in the established theory:

absence → inconsistency → greater completeness[47]

Archer's morphogenetic cycle of cultural emergence, which starts with a contradiction and ends with syncretism, accounts for the transition from inconsistency to greater completeness of the scientific theory. The dialectic model, in addition, explains why the contradiction arises. The morphogenetic model and the dialectic model may be joined because they both concern the development, and more specifically, the emergence of new concepts. In critical realist dialectic, adapted from Hegel, the conceptual work performed in the identification and repair of an inconsistency, leading in general to an expansion of the conceptual field, is designated the σ and τ *transform* respectively.[48]

In the present context of educational theory, the absence in the established theory was the missing identification of a determinate social structure that could explain the inconsistent observations. The inconsistency conditioned repair work tending towards syncretism and greater completeness of the theory, but it was the void in the theory which produced the contradictions. The inconsistencies encountered were (1) between the expectation, based on the established theory, that no major changes in the integration of education with other social institutions could be obtained prior to the emergence of the educational system, and the observation that Norwegian secondary education obtained considerable autonomy from the church and was integrated with other sectors of society prior to system emergence; and (2) between the expectation, based on the established theory, that only two types of strategic action were available prior to the emergence of the system, namely substitution and restriction, and the observation that municipalisation was the strategy of the Norwegian oppositional groups.

When the absence in the established theory of an additional morphogenetic cycle starting with dual integration of education with the church and state was removed (absented), the inconsistencies between the established theory and the new observations disappeared. Thus, the development of the established domain theory, through the modifications suggested here, constitutes a process of epistemological dialectic.

Notes

1 Archer (1979) contains a general theory of the historical emergence of state educational systems and specific theories of the emergence of state educational systems in four European countries. Archer (1984) is an abridged version of the 1979 publication, which presents the general theory and the specific theories of educational development in two countries, England and France. Archer (1995) contains a reformulation of the general theory of the emergence of educational systems, which clarifies its status as a domain theory, within a general social theory of structural change (morphogenesis).
2 Bhaskar (1998: 34ff) and Archer (1995: 137ff).
3 See Archer (1995: 218ff) for further clarification of the concepts necessary and compatible institutional relations.
4 Cruickshank (2003: 114).
5 Dokka (1967) sees the transformation of Norwegian elementary education during the nineteenth century as a fulfilment of the mission statement of the first elementary education Act in Norway (1741), which, strongly influenced by Pietistic ideas, established universal elementary education, in principle. Rust (1989) also traces the egalitarian tradition in Norwegian education to Luther's ideas. Markussen (1997) claims that educational egalitarianism, specifically the obligation of caring for the weak, in all the Nordic countries originated in the Lutheran practice of obliging the clergy to impart basic religious doctrines in each and every member of the congregation to ensure the salvation of their soul. Their success in fulfilling this obligation would be part of the reckoning on the day of doom.
6 Jarning (1994), Slagstad (1998, 2000), Wiborg (2004).
7 Jarning (1994: 20), ref. in Slagstad (1998: 99).
8 Slagstad (2000: 25).
9 Arup Seip (1997), Slagstad (1998).
10 Slagstad (2000).
11 Wiborg (2004: 83–93). The focus of Wiborg's article is on the early development of comprehensive schooling in the Northern part of Europe, which she sees as partly caused by early state involvement both in primary and secondary education.
12 Wiborg (2004: 85).
13 Schwarz Lausten (1987: 164).
14 Archer (1995: 328).
15 Archer (1979: 95).
16 Nicolai Fredrik Severin Grundtvig (1783–1872) was a Danish theologian, historian, poet, politician and bishop whose prolific writings and active participation in public life inspired a following in all the Scandinavian countries. His intellectual contribution was, *inter alia*, to amalgamate Christianity with nationalism, by seeing the uniqueness of folk mythology and traditions as God-given, and therefore deserving to be culti-

vated and strengthened. On this basis he rejected the dominant classical tradition in secondary education and advocated its substitution by schools, which emphasised the indigenous language and the study of national (Norse) history and mythology. The most comprehensive study of the impact of Grundtvig's ideas in the Norwegian context is Anders Skrondal (1929).

17 Sirevåg (1988).
18 Steen (1953).
19 Erichsen (1911).
20 The term *Real* education and *Real* schools was derived from the German *Real* Gymnasiums, which were schools that taught modern languages and natural sciences, i.e. things in the 'real world' as opposed to the classical languages Latin and Greek, which were 'dead' languages. 'Real subjects' is in Germanic language traditions used to denote the natural sciences, but during the 19th century modern languages were included among bodies of knowledge dealing with the 'real'.
21 Sirevåg (1988).
22 Skrondal (1929).
23 Wiborg (2004).
24 Sunnanå (1957).
25 Bjørndal (1959).
26 According to Skrondal (1929: 270) the event was attended by a large audience and by prominent academics and members of the political elite as well as young students inspired by Grundtvig's ideas. The meeting was held at the university and was reported and discussed in several Norwegian newspapers and journals.
27 Sunnanå (1957: 134) reports that the plan to establish *amtskoler* was lauched by the Ministry in 1874.
28 Skrondal (1929), Molland (1979).
29 Skrondal (1929).
30 Skrondal (1929).
31 Still, the folk high schools played an important role in fortifying the political opposition as a recruiting ground for future politicians of national and democratic leanings, the nationalistic, democratic and liberal *Venstre* movement. The Grundtvigian movement was also important in the development of elementary education, through its stronghold in teacher education institutions.
32 The strategy of municipalisation was even clearer in the struggle for the 1889 elementary education acts (*folkeskolelovene*), which is not dealt with here.
33 Archer (1984: 20).
34 Here I am referring to political arrangements before the 1884 political crisis, which resulted in the introduction of cabinet responsibility to the parliamentary majority, and which obliterated the dominance of the bureaucratic political elite, which until then had occupied government offices and refused to comply with majority decisions in the parliament.
35 Cabinet responsibility to the parliament majority was introduced in 1884.
36 I.e. a constitutional state based on limited suffrage and a constitutional practice, which ensured a balance of power between the parliament, the government and the Monarch.
37 Archer (1984: 133).
38 In the established theory processes of negotiation producing structural change only occur after the emergence of the system.
39 Archer (1996).
40 Archer (1996: 159).
41 Archer (1996).
42 Archer (1996: 104ff).
43 Archer (1995: 239). Competitive contradictions differ from constraining contradictions in the relationship between the two cultural elements, which is contingent in a competitive relationship, but necessary in a constraining relationship.
44 Archer (1996: 171).

45 Archer (1984: 11ff). This proposition is not a direct quote from the text, but is extracted from it. The universality that is claimed is restricted to educational development in countries that have not been 'subject to external intervention, via conquest, colonisation or territorial redistribution' (p. 14). I consider Norway as belonging to this category, since its union first with Denmark and then with Sweden, according to recent scholarship, cannot be considered a colonial relationship.
46 Archer (1996: 170).
47 Bhaskar (1993: 38).
48 Bhaskar (1993: 406).

References

Archer, M. S. *Social Origins of Education Systems*, London and Beverly Hills, California: Sage Publications, 1979.

Archer, M. S. *Social Origins of Educational Systems,* London: Sage Publications, University edition, 1984.

Archer, M. S. *Realist Social Theory: the Morphogenetic Approach*, Cambridge, UK: Cambridge University Press, 1995.

Archer, M. S. *Culture and Agency: The Place of Culture in Social Theory*, Cambridge, UK: Cambridge University Press, 1996, revised edition.

Bhaskar, R. *Dialectic. The Pulse of Freedom*, London and New York: Verso, 1993.

Bhaskar, R. *The Possibility of Naturalism*, London: Routledge, 1998, 3rd edition.

Bjørndal, B., *P. Voss og hans samtid*, Oslo: Universitetsforlaget, 1959.

Cruickshank, J. *Realism and Sociology,* London: Routledge, 2003.

Dokka, H.-J. *Fra almueskole til folkeskole*, Oslo, Norway: Universitetsforlaget, 1967.

Erichsen, A. L. *Trondhjems Katedralskoles historie*, Trondhjem, 1911.

Jarning, H. 'Mellom statsmakt og sosialiseringsmakt', in *Skolen 1993–1994. Årbok for norsk utdanningshistorie*, Oslo, Norway, 1994.

Lausten, M. S. *Biskop Peder Palladius og kirken (1537–1560)*, Copenhagen, Denmark: Akademisk Forlag, 1987.

Markussen, I. 'Den nordiske skolemodell', in K. Tveit, ed., *Streiftog i historisk og komparativ pedagogikk*, Universitetet i Oslo: Pedagogisk Forskningsinstitutt, Rapport no. 2, 1997.

Molland, E. *Norges kirkehistorie i det 19. århundre*, Bind I, Oslo, Norway: Gyldendal norsk forlag, 1979.

Rust, V. D. *The Democratic Tradition and the Evolution of Schooling in Norway,* New York: Greenwood Press, 1989.

Seip, J. A. *Utsyn over norsk historie*, Oslo, Norway: Gyldendal, 1997.

Sirevåg, T. *Utsyn over norsk høgre skole*, Oslo, Norway: Universitetsforlaget, 1988.

Skrondal, A. *Grundtvig og Noreg. Kyrkje og skule 1817–1875*, Bergen, Norway: A.S. Lunde & Co's Forlag, 1929.

Slagstad, R. *De nasjonale strateger*, Oslo, Norway: Pax Forlag A/S, 1998.

Slagstad, R. Kunnskapens hus i det norske system', in *NOU 2000: 14 Frihet under ansvar. Om høgre utdanning og forskning i Norge*, Vedlegg nr. 1.

Steen, J. Skolens økonomiske kår gjennom tidene, J. Steen, ed, *Bergens eldste skole: Katedralskolen 800 år*, Bergen, Norway: Bergen Katedralskole, 1953.

Sunnanå, O. *Johannes Steen. Skulemannen*, Oslo, Norway: Det norske samlaget, 1957.

Wiborg, S. 'Education and social integration: a comparative study of the comprehensive school system in Scandinavia', *London Review of Education*, vol. 2, No. 2, 2004.

16 The educational limits of critical realism? Emancipation and rational agency in the compulsory years of schooling

Brad Shipway

Introduction

This chapter has three parts. The first examines the implications for students who may lack Bhaskar's (α) cognitive, (β) empowered or (γ) dispositional components of rational agency. I argue that a dialectical critical realist perspective of education in the compulsory years of schooling emphasises two main points:

i   The criteria for rational agency can be possessed in degrees, as opposed to possessed *or not*; thus revealing the *worth* of both the agent's *emancipatory process* and the agent's *being* to be independent of the *limitations* upon them.
ii The 'opening movement' of Bhaskar's emancipatory process from *primal scream* to *cognitive emancipation* indicates that there is much important '*custodial*' work for teachers to do, as they facilitate the articulation of their students' 'assertoric utterances'.

The second part offers an example from a Kindergarten class of how key tenets of dialectical critical realism can be incorporated into even the most simple learning experiences.

In the third part, I suggest a dialectical critical realist conception of the enterprise of education is one of '*facilitating the emergent rationality of students towards emancipation*'. This conception of education is explained in terms of the key tenets of critical realism.

I would like to make the point from the outset that the purpose of this chapter is not to conduct a wide-ranging discussion of the varying views on emancipatory education in the compulsory years of schooling. Rather, it is the result of an engagement with Bhaskar's dialectical critical realism (DCR), and some reflection on what the theory of DCR might mean at the coalface of education, in this case, the primary classroom.

The issue of rational agency for education in the compulsory years of schooling

On the one hand, the emancipatory mission of DCR is most helpful in reaffirming what education should 'be about', and can provide a robust philosophical underpinning for those who wish to explore the issue of emancipatory education. On the other hand, it also raises some potentially significant problems for those working with students who, for a variety of reasons, do not possess all the criteria for rational agency. While the following discussion focuses on students in the earlier year levels of education in the compulsory years of schooling, it may also be the case that the issues raised herein may also be relevant to other groups, such as physically or mentally disabled students,[1] who for whatever reason, may not meet the criteria for rational agency.

From within a tertiary education context, Emami and Riordan (1998) have previously argued for a critical realist perspective when educating older students who are able to acknowledge their own oppression. But what are the implications for the emancipatory project of critical realism for the education of younger students? What of students who are lacking one or more of Bhaskar's criteria for rational agency (such as sufficient cognitive development) and are therefore not able to understand their own oppression? This would seem to be a significant issue for both the relevance and scope of the application of critical realism in education, and also for existing traditions in pedagogy and praxis in education. As a result, Bhaskar's definition of emancipation raises some interesting questions about the possibility of emancipating students in the compulsory years of education. These questions have the potential to challenge current conceptions of educational research and pedagogy.

The role of rational agency in emancipation

Firstly, it will be useful to briefly examine the concept of rational agency. In *Dialectic: The Pulse of Freedom* (hereafter referred to as DPF), Bhaskar mentions that the emancipation of an agent is dependent upon rational agency (DPF, p. 98). To be a 'rational agent', one must:

(α) possess the knowledge[2] to act in one's own real interests (the cognitive requirement);
(β) be able to access the skill, resources and opportunities to do so (the empowered component); and
(γ) be disposed to so act (the dispositional or motivational condition)[3] (DPF: 260).

Rational agency is dependent on autonomy, which is in turn defined by an agent's self-determination.

> The root conception of freedom with which I am working is that of autonomy in the sense of self-determination. Rational autonomy will then

incorporate cognitive, empowered and dispositional or motivational aspects. (DPF: 260).

For Bhaskar, autonomy is an important 'theoretico–practical bridge concept' which links truth to freedom (DPF: 395) and presupposes a freedom of choice, though not a complete absence of choice. In exploring this concept of autonomy, Bhaskar (DPF: 218) states that 'the most basic meaning of autonomy is self-determination'. In a somewhat circular explanation, Bhaskar outlines self-determination thus:

> Self-determination is normally a necessary condition for self-realisation, and if one's self includes potentialities, then one can reasonably be said to be alienated from them. And only a self which, in solidarity, has emancipated itself can be said to have become self-determining, i.e. autonomous (DPF: 282).

The idea here is that for an agent to make purposeful moves toward emancipation, he or she needs to be autonomous in the sense that they are self-determined.

And one can then say if one uses one's *autonomy* both *rationally* and *wisely* (i.e. in accordance with the virtue of phronesis,[4] including its connection with the criteria of mean, balance, totality, health and wholeness) then one will be able to, or tend to be able to, realise one's ideas in practice (DPF: 281).

Here, Bhaskar claims a connection between autonomy and the coherence of theory and practice *in practice*, and calls this connection 'absolute reason' (DPF: 281). However, *it is precisely this connection that many students in the compulsory years of schooling cannot make*. Any teacher who has been involved in a kindergarten craft/art/design lesson will have witnessed first-hand their students' frustration at being unable to realise their ideas in practice. Such young students may lack any or all of (α) the cognitive, (β) the empowered, or (γ) the dispositional components of rational agency.

For example, it is completely possible that:

i   a kindergarten student may possess the dispositional aspect (γ), but by virtue of their current state of motor skill or cognitive development, could lack the cognitive (α) and empowered (β) aspects respectively;
ii a disabled student may possess the cognitive (α) and dispositional (γ) aspects, but because of either the constraints of their disability,[5] or resourcing deficiencies of the school, lack the empowered aspect (β);
iii an adolescent, under the influence of peer group structures, may possess the cognitive (α) and empowered (β) aspects, but lack the dispositional aspect (γ).

Now, it can be argued that the impact of a lack of one or more of these criteria upon the emancipatory process is an issue not just for students in the compulsory years of education, but for many agents, regardless of age. However, I am interested in the implications for attempting to educate younger students in an emancipatory fashion because it presses particularly sharply on the absence of criteria (α), by virtue of the chronology of biological development. This issue raises a raft of questions for those of us who work with students who do not possess all the criteria for rational agency. These include, but are in no way limited to, questions such as:

- When do students become fully rational? – and what might the adequacy conditions for rational agency 'look like' in the classroom?
- What is the best way to cater fairly for the differing schedules, or 'timelines' of emerging rationality between individuals within the one class?
- What should teachers 'do' while they are 'waiting' for the appropriate level of cognitive development to emerge?
- If emancipation is about changing structures,[6] then how are teachers to know what structures to change for these 'pre-rational' students?

In response to such questions, the following section will argue that a dialectical critical realist perspective on education in the compulsory years of schooling reveals two main points:

1   The criteria for rational agency can be possessed in *degrees*, as opposed to possessed *or not*; thus revealing the universal moral worth of both the agent's *emancipatory process* and the agent's *being* to be independent of the *limitations* upon them;
2   The 'opening movement' of the emancipatory process from *primal scream* to *cognitive emancipation* indicates that there is much important '*custodial*' work for teachers to do.

Universal moral worth of the individual independent from their limitations

In attempting to engage with the questions posed above, perhaps a DCR perspective of the compulsory years of schooling should emphasise the possibility of holding the criteria of rational agency in *degrees*, as opposed to holding them *or not*. This idea is necessary because the only way to answer questions of when rational agency is realised, and how it is possible for another individual to tell that it has been realised, is to emphasise the *concrete singularity* of the individual.

The problem with searching for the 'adequacy conditions' of students' cognitive emancipation is that such a task can very easily degenerate into an attempt to derive an *a priori* set of conditions by which to positivistically 'determine' whether or not an agent is rational. The reduction of what is (the student's rationality) to what can be known about it (according to a pre-determined list) is the familiar *epistemic fallacy*, and the amelioration of this potential error is indicated by a close examination of Bhaskar's comment below:

… one will be free *just to the extent* that one possesses the power, knowledge and disposition to act in one's real interests …(DPF: 281, italics added).

The words 'to the extent' indicate that perhaps the criteria for rational agency (cognitive, empowered and dispositional components) should not be read as a shopping list to be 'ticked off' as they are achieved, but can be conceived as being possessed in *degrees*. It is certainly not impossible to conceive that a very young student – say 5–6 years old in kindergarten – could possess all three criteria for rational agency to a *greater or lesser extent*. That is, they may be able to (α) not only act in their own interest, but to also understand that in terms of the class, their altruistic interactions with other students are also in their own best interests in terms of creating a warm, friendly environment; (β) have the required motor skill development to complete a task, and also the knowledge that they are able to call upon the teacher as a resource to help them, and (γ) be motivated to do so. However, it is also completely possible that the next day the same student may be missing one or more of these components for a variety of reasons.

The idea of an agent possessing the criteria for rational agency in *degrees* is also supported by a postfoundationalist model of human rationality (van Huyssteen 1999). Emerging from the field of evolutionary epistemology (Plotkin 1993; Wuketits 1990), a postfoundational view sees rationality not only as a bio-logical trait, but also as a skill which can be developed.

If the criteria for rational agency can be possessed in *degrees*, then it is possi-ble to think of all agents as being involved in a process of emancipation, but at different levels, and with varying degrees of limitation. On this view, a kinder-garten student who possesses the criteria for rational agency to a lesser extent can be thought of in the same way as a fully rational, emancipated agent involved in their own process of becoming, possessing the criteria for rational agency to a greater extent.

When combined with the axiology of emancipation, the view that all agents are involved in emancipation to a greater or lesser extent supports a claim for the *equal universal moral worth* of each agent's process of emancipation. Despite the *limitations* an agent may face, or whether they are involved in the process of emancipation to a greater or lesser extent (or even at all), the process itself is of equal worth to any other agent's emancipatory process. In other words, the *worth* of each agent's emancipation is independent from the *limitations* upon it. In this way, the emancipation of an intellectually and physically disabled student – while certainly having more (biological and social) limitations and challenges than other students – is of the same *universal moral worth* as *any other* concretely sin-gular individual.

Moreover, and most importantly, if the emancipatory *process* of each agent is of the same worth, then it follows that a key claim can be made for the *universal moral worth of every agent's **being*** – regardless of their potential rationality, or potential for emancipation at all. This claim is supported by the alethic truth of every concretely singular individual. Take, for example, two individuals: (a) a most profoundly intellectually disabled child – who may never indicate any self-awareness; and (b) a Head of State – who may possess the ability and disposition to absent a variety of heteronomous social structures for many other individuals. Regardless of their emancipatory progression, or the limitations upon them, or even their potential to emancipate others, the *being* of both agents is of *equal universal moral worth*.

The 'opening movement' of emancipation indicates teachers as the custodians of students' emancipation

In DPF, there is less emphasis on the pre-cognitive part of emancipatory axiology than there is on the process of emancipation after the realisation of cognitive emancipation. Nonetheless, Bhaskar makes it quite clear that the axiology of emancipation can be discerned as early as infancy. Bhaskar speaks of the axiology of freedom being implicit in the infant's 'primal scream', resulting from the experience of a desire, which may be, for example, absenting the absence of a parent (DPF: 286). In Bhaskar's terms, the 'primal scream' is initiated by this absence (DPF: 381), and indicates the axiology of freedom toward emancipation.

Thus, the process of emancipation is already in motion *prior* to the realisation of cognitive emancipation. Bhaskar (DPF: 294) states there is a link from 'the absence implicit in elemental desire through referential detachment and acknowledgment of the reality principle to ontological stratification and alethic truth'; and represents the resulting dialectic as:

> absence (2E) – primal scream – desire – referential detachment (1M) – alethic truth – assertoric judgment – dialectical universalizability (3L) – universal human emancipation (4D) – eudaimonistic society-in-progress ... (DPF: 294–295).

If the process of emancipation is already in action *before* the stage of cognitive emancipation, then perhaps teachers and those who work with pre-rational students can be conceptualised as the '*custodians*' of their students' rationality, and facilitators of the beginnings of the dialectic of desire to freedom.[7] Room for the possibility of this custodial role for teachers of pre-rational students can be found in Bhaskar's comments below (the terms 'addressor' and 'addressee' correspond to 'teacher' and 'student' respectively):

> ... if the addressee is constrained in the satisfaction of her wanted needs, the addressor in his fiduciary judgment implies both his solidarity with her and his commitment to the content of the explanatory critical theory of her situation... Both imply a commitment to the *totalising depth praxis* and the research inquiry necessary to inform it, including practical help in the subject$_2$-addressee's self-emancipation from her current situation (DPF: 179).

This passage could lead to a radically different and complex view of what it means to be a teacher of young students. On this view, it would be incumbent upon workers in education to facilitate the preparation of their students to 'take the reigns' of their own emancipatory process at a time appropriate to each individual student. In this way, teachers help their students to more clearly articulate their 'assertoric utterances'. In effect, teachers (and others working in the educational system) become *custodians* of this beginning phase of the students' emancipation.[8]

Bhaskar delineates the beginning phase of emancipation (pre-cognitive requirement) from the long road ahead that still needs to be travelled once cognitive emancipation has begun, thus:

> There is a difference between emancipatory and emancipated action, as there is a difference between the liberation of oneself and the removal of a constraint from the outside (this is not to denigrate the value of the latter, merely to remind the reader that the former task still remains) (DPF: 297).

The teachers of younger students are working in the 'opening movement' of emancipatory axiology, concerned with the removal of constraints 'from the outside' on behalf of those who are oppressed but not in a position to realise it. As such, the primary school teacher would be working to emancipate students from specific social and educational constraints which prevent them in practical ways from realising their freedom. This work facilitates the students eventually taking part in explanatory–emancipatory discourse when cognitive emancipation is realised.

This view reveals a requirement for intricate complexity in classroom learning activities and teaching strategies if teachers are to cater to each individual student's emancipatory process. How does a teacher manage a class where some students are ready to 'take the reigns' of their own emancipatory process, while others are clearly not ready yet both students are participating in the one lesson? This issue most often arises in composite classes, or in years 5–8, where the onset of puberty brings with it significant diversity in the learning needs of students.

Another situation raised by this issue is the distinct possibility of teachers having to deal with 'backsliding' students who are on the 'cusp' of rational agency, i.e. making moves toward emancipation one day, and then 'undoing' them the next. An example would be the decision of a student to sever personally destructive peer-group connections, and then returning to the group at a later time as a result of the social pressure of that group. In this way, a critical realist perspective can support in a new way the literature which claims the emancipatory education of adolescents requires extremely skilled teachers (Beane 1993; Cumming, 1996; Hargreaves & Earl 1994).

Thus, the two main points to be made about the effect of the limits of rationality on the emancipation of students in the compulsory years of schooling are:

1 the *limits* upon emancipation are independent of the *universal moral worth* of the emancipatory process; and thus by necessity, an agent's *being*;[9]
2 because the axiology of emancipation is a tendency which is operating even *before* cognitive emancipation is realised, teachers (and other educational

workers) have important work as *custodians* of the emancipation of pre-rational students until such time as each agent is ready to become more autonomous.

Implications of rational agency for education

Viewing the education of young students through dialectical critical realist glasses, I think it is most reasonable to argue that the axiology of emancipation indicates teachers should be conditioning their students by providing them with an emancipatory environment in which to learn. The term 'conditioned' here is not used in a pejorative sense, as it is either impossible or undesirable for students to be completely socially non-conditioned.[10] The axiology of emancipation, the dialectic of desire to freedom, and the universal moral worth of each agent indicates that education workers are not abrogated from their responsibility to provide emancipatory education just because younger students may not be rational agents at a particular point in time. Such emancipatory 'conditioning' would also ameliorate the effect mentioned above of students sabotaging their own emancipation by resisting changes because of a perceived lack of social status.

However, the issue of rational agency also raises possible pedagogical problems regarding the above implication of emancipatory 'conditioning'. A DCR reading of the issue of rational agency in education indicates that teachers may need to relate to pre- and post-cognitively emancipated students in quite different ways. A specific instance of this could be the degree of autonomy allowed in students choosing what they want to learn – in other words – the way curriculum is organised. If so, this may lead to quite significant differences in classroom pedagogy between pre- and post-cognitively emancipated students. In addition, the possibility of 'pre' and 'post' students within the one class raises the pedagogical problem of teachers having to balance conditions for the optimum educational environment for one student or group that are dichotomous with the optimum conditions for another group of students.

Such a perspective on the compulsory years of education may require a reconceptualisation of the rationality of students and an attendant reconceptualisation of classroom pedagogy. Moreover, it may also challenge the way that students are thought of by educational theorists and policy-makers. It raises questions about the validity of theories and models of classroom pedagogy and management which operate on assumptions that students are already rational agents who only need to be given opportunities to exercise their rationality for an emancipatory outcome to be achieved. From a DCR perspective, such behaviour management models may be placing too much pressure on students to be self-determining before the required cognitive emancipation has been realised.

Towards an emancipatory pedagogy

The challenges and implications raised by the issue of rational agency in the compulsory years of schooling constitute perhaps the most significant and pressing direction for the further work on DCR in education. I believe the future hard work of DCR in education consists in answering the question:

How can the axiology of freedom be manifested in educational theory, praxis and pedagogy?

For those working in the compulsory years of schooling, the question can be further refined by asking:

How can the axiology of freedom from 'primal scream' to cognitive emancipation be manifested in educational theory, praxis, and pedagogy?

Applied classroom-based research in this area holds the promise of the emergence of an 'educational science'. This work could progress on two fronts, each identified by Bhaskar's definition of emancipation as (1) the move from unwanted and unneeded forms of determination to (2) wanted and needed forms of determination (Bhaskar 1986: 171). Previous research in the field of education by Corson (1995) has been concerned with point (1), namely, using critical realism to identify forms of teacher behaviour and teaching methods that are part of the preservative, structural repression of students.

However, while the explanatory critique of CR is useful in identifying 'what should not be done' in terms of existing educational structures, the axiology of freedom, and the positive valuation of action rationally directed at absenting constraints upon freedom, also indicates that is possible to chart point (2), or 'what should be done' – with the important caveat of acknowledging the non-predictive nature of CR.

The link between the notion of *emancipatory custody* and the practices of classroom pedagogy is also indicated by Bhaskar's transition from *form-to-content*. This transition is made possible by the move from *fact-to-value* and the move from *theory-to-practice*.[11] Bhaskar states that there are three ways that the transition from *form-to-content* can occur:

(i) … the reciprocity-universalisability of the content of the initial judgement…
(ii) … the action entailed by the formal requirements of solidarity and the totalising depth praxis (including inquiry); and
(iii) … the end-state process (adapted from DPF: 179–180).

Taking into account the axiology of emancipation, all three ways of moving from form to content are inherently *already existing* in any teacher–student or student–student interaction. All emancipatory classroom interaction would therefore involve: (i) judgement of truth-claims, (ii) a commitment to solidarity between agents and the engagement of praxis (inquiry resulting in change); and (iii) the implementation of a decision, which sparks off a new round of rational inquiry.

Corson (1990a, 1990b, 1991a, 1991b, 1998) has pioneered the move from form to content with critical realist perspectives in education, suggesting an approach to educational policy-making based on Bhaskar's 'logic of scientific discovery' (1978: 145). As a result of his engagement with Bhaskar, Corson offers a tentative list of emancipatory educational practices that are consistent with critical realism, thus:

- In place of a didactic teaching style for working with students from different backgrounds: a flexible and self-directed approach to diverse students rooted in the use of natural language.
- In place of a methods-based approach for handling classroom situations: a readiness to meet unusual classroom situations in imaginative and ingenious ways.
- In place of whole-class responses to conflict resolution: a person-oriented approach, sensitive to the different values and norms of diverse students.
- In place of a curriculum that binds students to abstract knowledge: a curriculum that builds critical thinkers who are in control of their lives.
- In place of a curriculum that takes the rough edges off society and its social problems: a curriculum that asks: Who makes decisions? Who benefits? Who suffers? How can change occur?
- In place of assessment methods that highlight students' weaknesses: an evaluation system that builds, extends and challenges students to higher levels of achievement.
- In place of a professional persona of objectivity and detachment: a professional engagement with diversity that celebrates difference.
- In place of an approach to accountability that blames students for their failure: a willingness to look at the school itself as the source of educational failure.
- In place of a view of the school as an isolated institution: a view that sees education in the grip of social formations that can also be changed (Corson, 1998: 215).

Corson's work in this area (1990–1998) engaged with Bhaskar's critical realism (CR). I would like to suggest that since then, the emergence of dialectical critical realism (DCR) refines and extends in new ways Corson's call for emancipatory education. In light of the above discussion on the implications of rational agency, and the lead given by Bhaskar's transition from *form-to-content*, I believe that it is possible to posit how the axiology of freedom might be manifested in the classroom.

A dialectical critical realist kindergarten?

In this section, I suggest how a 'constructivist'[12] approach to teaching primary science can be consistent with DCR, providing an example of how even very young students can participate in learning experiences which facilitate their emancipation.

Constructivist learning sequences in primary science always commence by eliciting the students' own areas of interest, and are characterised by planning learning experiences which address these areas in order to maximise interest and motivation. Great care is taken in accessing students' pre-existing, or 'alternative' conceptions of the particular scientific phenomena they chose to study. To this end, the students are engaged in an elicitation activity, where they are encouraged to make explicit and record their understanding of what is taking place as they observe a particular phenomenon. These understandings (which could be either 'scientific' or 'alternative' conceptions of the phenomena) are then recorded and collected. The students are then encouraged to examine and compare the conceptions of others with their own. From this, the students realise that there are many different ways of perceiving the same thing. Next, a scientific 'intervention' is conducted, which may take the form of an experiment or investigation.

The intervention is designed to confront and challenge the alternative science conceptions of students with the reality of the particular mechanism which causes the phenomena being studied. After the intervention, students are then given the opportunity to compare the data gathered from the intervention experience with their original alternative conception. The *concrete singularity* of the individual is acknowledged, as students are not necessarily expected to automatically change their alternative science conception of the phenomena, even if confronted with clear evidence against their original idea. Indeed, in response to the 'intervention' experience, the student has a range of available options:

(i) *accept* the scientific construction and reject their original alternative construction;
(ii) *reject* the scientific construction and hold to their original alternative construction in the face of evidence to the contrary;
(iii) construct a *hybrid* conception – an 'amalgamation' of both their original alternative construction and the accepted scientific construction.

The following example of a learning sequence is taken from actual lessons in a range of composite classes containing grades Kindergarten to Year Four (approx 5–9 years of age). The basic structure of the sequence is based on the primary science teacher text *'Teaching Primary Science Constructively'* (Skamp 1998). Throughout my description, the use of brackets {} indicates an instance or operation of key critical realist doctrines.

The class is presented with a range of topics to study which are derived from the curriculum.[13] For example, from the content strand 'Physical Phenomena', the students are presented with a choice of studying light, sound, electricity, or forces and movement. By way of a vote, or process of negotiation, the class chooses to study 'electricity' from a range of other topics *{stratified, democratic power}*.[14]

The students then generate a list of questions they have about electricity. The questions usually come from their previous experiences of the phenomena in their daily lives; e.g 'Where does electricity come from?'; 'How do they pour it into the big cans on top of the telegraph poles?'.

Guided by the teacher, the class starts classifying this long list of questions into categories which indicate how the question might be answered, e.g. 'What questions can we answer by conducting an experiment?'; 'What questions can we answer by inviting in a guest speaker?'; 'What questions can we only answer by looking up information in books?'. This process results in a collection of potential learning experiences (lessons) which have been generated by the students *{reasons as causes}*.[15]

A question such as 'What is inside a battery?' from the list is identified as being able to be answered, at least in part, by an experiment, and the students now prepare to conduct their investigation. However, before the actual experiment is conducted, each student is required to draw, describe, or represent in any way they can what they believe is inside the battery, e.g. 'I think there is fire in there, my mum said an old battery burnt her once'; '[there is] a little man riding a bike around and around in there and he makes the electricity'. Moreover, the students are given the opportunity to view and discuss the ideas of others in comparison to their own ideas *{epistemological relativism}*.[16] These data are then collected by the teacher for later reference.

Once the students' alternative conceptions are elicited, the experiment of cutting open a battery is conducted as an 'intervention', in order to challenge errors in the student's alternative concepts *{ontological realism}*. The battery is cut open, and the students draw and/or describe what they observed inside, e.g. 'it is black gooey stuff but it has a stick in the middle'; (disappointed) 'it's only grease in there, how does that make electricity?'.

A period of discussion and debate follows on what the results of the experiment mean. Here the students compare and contrast their observations, and in the process realise that there may be multiple interpretations of a single, controlled event such as cutting open a battery *{stratified, dialectical, alethic truth}*.[17] Students are asked to compare what they observed with their original conception of what was in a battery. Here, faced with the reality of the accepted scientific account of the phenomena, the students may:

(i)   reject their original construction as a result of what they observed, e.g. 'There was no wire in the battery at all';
(ii) construct a hybrid conception which blends aspects of their original conception and the accepted scientific conception, e.g. 'The black stuff could be the thing that burnt my mum';
(iii) find novel ways of tenaciously holding onto their original conception in the face of overwhelming evidence to the contrary, e.g. 'We were too slow. The man on the bike rode away when we cut it open!' *{exercise of rationality; axiology of emancipation}*.[18]

The final part of the sequence is then concerned with where the next phase of the class inquiry will lead, e.g. 'Do we need to find out more about what is in a battery?'; 'Where/how can we find out what the black gooey stuff is?'; 'Are all batteries like this inside?'; 'What is inside a transformer?'. These questions then form the basis of a new learning sequence *{stratified reality}*.[19]

From this example, it is evident that even simple learning sequences can incorporate many dialectical critical realist concepts such as:

- *stratified, democratic power* – indicated by the students choosing the subject of inquiry, while being 'scaffolded' by the teacher;
- *reasons as causes* – represented by the students' rationale for choosing a particular course of inquiry;
- *epistemological relativism* and *ontological realism* – indicated by first eliciting the students' alternative science conceptions, and then contrasting them with the accepted scientific conception;
- the process of *dialectic*, including *transformative negation* as the absenting of constraints, such as a lack of understanding;
- the *stratified nature of reality*, indicated by the results of one investigation sparking a new investigation at a different level.

The use of stratified, democratic power relations throughout the learning sequence provides opportunities for students to move towards self-determination and thus emancipation. For example, the focus on students examining their own pre- and post-intervention conceptions engages them in self-monitoring and self-evaluation, which are vital emancipatory skills for students to exercise, even though they may not yet be 'cognitively emancipated'.

All students (including those who are pre-cognitively emancipated) can be exercising and developing their rationality through engagement with processes of rational judgement (the judgement form). In other words, the rational, emancipatory thought processes learnt by a student in a kindergarten science lesson can be developed throughout the years and drawn on by the same student in a year 12 history lesson on colonisation. In this way, students become skilled in examining multiple perspectives, identifying those with greater explanatory power, and using the art of rhetoric as part of the dialectical process to defend their decision. In time, students can come to realise that scientific inquiry is 'not only initiated by partial regularities and contrasts but also through certain contradictions, inconsistencies, experiences of surprise and ultimately doubt' (Emami & Riordan 1998: 4). The goal here is to help students become agents who are conscious and deliberate in the way they arrive at their various beliefs.

'Facilitating the emergent rationality of students towards emancipation' – a dialectical critical realist perspective on the enterprise of education

So, what then is the use of dialectical critical realism for those who teach in the compulsory years of schooling? After engaging with Bhaskar's *Dialectic*, and reflecting upon the way I teach both primary students and their teachers, I have found that DCR has provided me with a powerful heuristic with which to think about and improve my own teaching.

In light of the questions and limitations posed by rational agency for younger (or disabled) students, I would like to suggest that DCR points us towards a more nuanced, but also expansive understanding of what the enterprise of education should 'be about'. This understanding is able to (i) account for the importance of the concrete singularity of the individual, regardless of their emancipatory progress and its limitations, and (ii) encompass students of all ages, and all those who work with them. I would like to suggest that a DCR conception of education can be articulated as:

facilitating[1] the emergent[2] rationality[3] of students[4] towards[5] emancipation[6].

(1) 'Facilitating' addresses the agent wherever they are in respect to *levels of rationality*, whether self-determined or not, or in the pre-compulsory, compulsory, and post-compulsory years of schooling. It also emphasises the *concrete singularity* of the agent, and by necessity, the *limit of axiology* in terms of the agent; such that to be free also contains the possibility of giving up that freedom. It reminds us that the emancipation of the individual is *not predetermined*. 'Facilitating' also emphasises the custodial role that teachers have regarding students' rationality and emancipation. Teachers cannot make students rational, or effect emancipation for them, but by virtue of their position are among the most important *custodians* of the rationality and emancipation of students.

(2) 'Emergent' indicates the influence of *evolutionary epistemology* in understanding rationality, and also the commitment to the idea of a *stratified reality*. It refers to the balance between structure and human agency in the *Transformational Model of Social Activity*, and also the concept of holism as *partial totalities*, encompassed in the concept of *dialectic* (Bhaskar 1998: 36; DPF: 271).

(3) 'Rationality' emphasises the importance of reason, and its pivotal role in the agent's emancipation. It carries with it references to both a postfoundationalist model of rationality, and the *judgement* form. It points to *ontological realism* by insisting on *judgemental rationality* as the appropriate response to epistemic relativism (DPF: 221).

(4) 'Students' focuses on educational agents as recipients. By virtue of the principle of the *free flourishing of each* being a condition of the *free flourishing of all* (DPF: 98), it intrinsically includes and is concerned with the emancipation of teachers and other workers in education – from school office staff, to administrators, right through to those in governmental bodies who determine the political face of educational policy. It is indefensible and indeed impossible for those in the field of education to take a 'neutral' stance regarding the emancipation of their students. Even a claim to be neutral in the sense of neither deliberately reinforcing, nor deliberately criticising oppressive structures is by default a perpetuation of those structures. This point has radical implications for teacher education. It provides new support

from the philosophy of science that teaching is an inherently subversive activity.

(5) 'Towards' acknowledges and emphasises the limit of axiology as a result of the characteristics of *open systems*. It includes Bhaskar's *ceteris paribus* clause, and acknowledges those 'conditions' outside the individual that must coincide for emancipation to occur. Thus it contains the critical realist focus on underlying social *structures and mechanisms* which constrain and enable human action. It realises that institutionalised education is emergent from, but irreducible to the wider society in which it is embedded, the curriculum as emergent from the institution of education, and the actions of teachers and students as emergent from (or at least co-determined by) the curriculum. As a result, it understands that education and schooling are embedded in and constrained by wider socio-cultural, political and economic interests. But, taking its cue from the *nested hierarchies* of evolutionary epistemology, it also carries with it a seed of hope for the future of education (and thus society) by virtue of the reciprocal restructuring effect education can have on society.

(6) 'Emancipation' identifies the over-riding mission of critical realism and its emphasis on the ultimate potential of the individual. It indicates the dialecticalisation of CR and thus the key category of *absence* as *transformative negation*, and the notion of *alethic truth*. It also acknowledges that this is not a destination, but a progression. It is holistic, but in the sense that teachers must work with an array of partial totalities when it comes to the emancipatory progress of their students. It also indicates the *equal universal moral worth of every agent's being*.

Perhaps the most profound implication arising from such a conception of education is a strong reaffirmation of the emancipatory power of education, and the vital role it plays in the improvement of wider society. The movement toward the eudaimonistic society is a key concern for Bhaskar's DCR, and the enterprise of education can function as either a significant hindrance, or vital impetus to this movement. I would argue that the DCR conception of education as outlined above supports Bhaskar's vision of education in the eudaimonistic society.

> Education in a creative flourishing of the arts and sciences would be at a premium in such a society. Indeed this would in essence consist in a continually *reflexive learning process* ... (DPF: 268).

A major result of a DCR view of the enterprise of education is that the popular (yet often ineffectual) claim of the human 'right' to an education is revealed to be *alethically grounded in the universal moral worth of every agent*.

> There is no reason why states of affairs such as health ... de-alienation, education, access to information, etc. should not be seen as rights and so as freedoms (DPF: 278).

Conclusion

This chapter has had three parts. The first examined some implications of the criteria for rational agency in terms of working with students in the compulsory years of schooling. The second offered an example of how key tenets of dialectical critical realism can be incorporated into even the most simple classroom lessons. In the third part, I suggested a dialectical critical realist conception of the enterprise of education could be articulated as *'facilitating the emergent rationality of students towards emancipation'*.

Critical realism offers a much-needed dynamism and balance in the field of education. The doctrines of critical realism position it as more scientifically rigorous than dominant positivist approaches to education, and more sensitive to the plurality of student needs than hermeneutical, postmodern approaches. On the one hand critical realism emphasises that engagement in the art of developing the full potential of human beings requires much more than narrow, utilitarian sets of educational practices oriented to ever-diminishing job opportunities. On the other hand, its rigour and ontological daring maintain the possibility that the art of emancipating students can be effected through a realist educational science. This ability of critical realism enables it to answer the increasingly insistent calls in education to balance visions of 'the good, beautiful, and true' with the need to address the 'institutional and public aspects of schooling' (Westbury 1999: 359).

Indeed, CR may be able to retrieve many of the noble, but often forgotten aspirations of the liberal education movement of the 1970s, sustaining them in more powerful and consistent ways with the benefit of a robust scientific realism combined with a hermeneutical sensitivity. For example, in Australia, the long-past New South Wales Department of Education document *The Aims of Primary Education in New South Wales* (1977) articulates educational values that resonate strongly with progressive work that is being done at the start of the new millennium:

> The central aim of education which, with home and community groups, the school pursues, is to guide individual development in the context of society through recognisable stages of development towards perceptive understanding, mature judgment, responsible self-direction and moral autonomy (NSW Dept. of Ed. 1977: 14).

The traditions from which the above values were espoused proved vulnerable to positivist counter-attacks throughout the 1980s and 1990s as economic rationalist forces in education became dominant. More recently, Wilmott (2002) has examined the effect of the 'new mangerialism' on education. However, the *ontological realism* and *epistemic relativism* of CR are able to sustain a defence of the above values in ways that are at once more scientifically rigorous than positivistic approaches, and more hermeneutically sensitive than previous traditions.

In this new millennium, as educational systems struggle to meet the challenges of diversity, and as the dominance of economic rationalist forces in education slowly start to wane, it is absolutely vital to ensure that judgemental relativism does not fill the void left by the old heteronomous arrangements. The judgemental rationality of critical realism is a more effective way to address the challenges of preparing students for admission into the increasing complexity of society. To this end, a significant task for critical realist researchers in education is one of untangling the intricacies of how power relations in the structures and mechanisms of society can filter into and embed themselves in educational organisations, make their way into classrooms, and then use them as a site of discourse for various socio-political and economic interests.[20]

Critical realism provides a rigorous, yet sensitive and nuanced way to think about education – the implications of which are far-reaching and all-pervasive. A dialectical critical realist perspective on the enterprise of education has the potential to revolutionise research, pedagogy and praxis – from the level of educational policy-making and funding agendas, right down to the structures which constrain the freedom of particular teachers and students in a particular classroom on a Monday morning when the bell rings. In other words, dialectical critical realism has provided me with a much clearer picture of exactly what is at stake when teaching – the emancipation of students and those who work with them, and in turn the members of future societies.

Notes

1 Williams (1999) provides a fruitful examination of a CR perspective on the chronic illness and disability debate in the field of medical sociology that may shed some light on this issue.

2 Bhaskar explains the term 'knowledge' from point (α) may be 'tacit competence, knowledge how rather than propositional knowledge that, practical not discursive' (DPF; 260)

3 Bhaskar's criteria for rational agency are strikingly similar to Evers and Lakomski's use of Simon's limits to rationality (Evers and Lakomski's work forms a significant part of the highly influential tradition of pragmatism, or 'naturalistic coherentism' in the philosophy of education):

First, an individual is limited in *skills*: dexterity, reaction times, powers of computation, thoughts and understanding. A second limitation concerns individual *values* and the *understanding* of organisational values and goals. Finally, there are limits to relevant *knowledge*, both knowledge of theory and knowledge of all the conditions that must obtain for a sound application of theory ... (Evers & Lakomski 1991: 15, italics added)

4 'Practical wisdom', see DPF, p. 401.

5 This issue is beyond the scope of this discussion, but there would seem to be *prima facie* a considerable tension here between the reality of a mentally or physically disabled agent, and the Bhaskarian emancipatory concept of an agent as already 'essentially free' (Bhaskar 2000: ix), i.e. already possessing what he/she needs to be emancipated. Williams (1999) states that the reality of critical realism maintains there are indeed 'fleshy limits' to the extent of identity reconstruction that can be achieved. However, there is little here exploring the effect and limits of chronic illness and disability for *emancipation*. Williams (1999: 815) concludes with the statement 'real bodies, real selves; real lives, real worlds', but there can also be added to this sequence 'real limits to emancipation' such that it may never get beyond the *primal scream*.

What of the situation where the emergent powers of the mind are so circumscribed by a biologically rooted disability that the agent may never have a conception of themselves? What of their emancipation? Is it to be completely custodial? There would seem to be much exploration to do in this area. Williams (1999: 805) notes that CR is an 'underdeveloped' perspective in medical sociology to date. Perhaps a CR re-reading of Foucault would also be useful here.

6 Apart from pedagogical aspects raised here, the issue of rational agency in younger students also impacts upon educational research, e.g. if the agent's reasons are the starting point for educational research, as suggested above, should researchers treat pre-rational agents' reasons any more cautiously?

7 Corson (1998) has examined the education of younger students from diverse language backgrounds and implied that the local community can also make custodial decisions for younger students. However, the limits of the students' rational agency for emancipation was not explicitly examined. In addition, Corson's focus was on the needs of students as a *group* which had diverse educational needs, and as such the implications of emancipation for rational agency at the level of the *concretely singular individual* were not examined.

8 Teachers could be motivated to facilitate the emancipation of their students by either altruism itself, or from the 'selfishness' of altruism, given that the free flourishing of each is a condition of the free flourishing of all.

It would seem that through what I will call the (12) *dialectic of material interests* agents will discover that altruism is in their purely egoistic interests (DPF: 290).

9 A much more disturbing thought is that if a particular physical disability is biologically determined (precluding disabilities which are the result of the actions of other agents, e.g. excess consumption of alcohol during pregnancy), then might there be problems in asserting a universal moral right to be free from physical disability? Bhaskar (DPF: 292) states 'The logic of my argument entails that both needs ... and resources and opportunities for the development of potentialities ... are rights, subject to reciprocal and universal recognition and democratically adjudicated global constraints'. Since biological disability is not included here, does this mean that to be free from biological disability is not a right?

10 Collier (1994: 98) elegantly explains the difference between 'in-gear freedom' and 'out-of-gear freedom'. In-gear freedom is not concerned with completely disengaging oneself from the world. If it is possible to know and act in the world, then it is necessary to be constrained by something – time, space, our own reasons, or our environment.

11 Bhaskar's fact-to-value argument comes as he is describing his 'seven levels of rationality' (1986: 181–210). The argument resides in level four ('explanatory critical rationality') of this hierarchy of rationality.

12 The term 'constructivist' in this instance is connected to a specific model of teaching primary science (Biddulph & Osbourne 1984; Skamp 1998). As a result, this specific use of the term 'constructivist' in relation to teaching primary science need not have relativist, or irrealist connotations, and can be completely consistent with a realist philosophy of science.

13 Given the idea of 'in-gear freedom' (Collier 1994: 98), I do not think it is particularly heteronomous that the teacher pre-selects a range of topics from which students can choose. However, some middle years research (Beane 1993) has indicated that formal curriculum requirements are easily covered even when these students have no constraints on choosing what they want to learn, provided the students have previously been trained in choosing areas of learning from their own concerns and interests.

14 Corson (1998).

15 Bhaskar (1998: 83).

16 Bhaskar (1989: 24).

17 DPF, p. 214 onwards.

18 DPF, p. 17; DPF, p. 238.

19 Bhaskar (1978: 14).
20 Corson has begun this work, and offers a beginning list of four things that are created by such 'filtering' of power relations into schools:
   • ideology-producing classroom processes (i.e. distortions of reality in children's minds)
   • instructional rather than educational action (i.e. confusing 'education' with 'instruction')
   • supervisory rather than relational forms of interaction (i.e. between school administrators and teachers, teachers and students, and students and administrators)
   • a reproduction of unjust sociocultural arrangements (Corson 1998: 208).

References

Beane, J. A. (1993). *A Middle School Curriculum: From Rhetoric to Reality*. Columbus, Ohio: National Middle Schools Association.

Bhaskar, R. (1978). *A Realist Theory of Science* (2nd ed.). Brighton, UK: Harvester Press.

Bhaskar, R. (1986). *Scientific Realism and Human Emancipation*. London: Verso.

Bhaskar, R. (1989). *Reclaiming Reality*. London: Verso.

Bhaskar, R. (1994). *Dialectic: The Pulse of Freedom*. London: Verso.

Bhaskar, R. (1998). *The Possibility of Naturalism* (3rd ed.). London: Routledge.

Bhaskar, R. (2000). *From East to West: Odyssey of a Soul*. London: Routledge.

Biddulph, F. and Osbourne, R. (1984). *Making Sense of Our World: An Interactive Teaching Approach*. Hamilton, NZ: University of Waikato Centre for Science and Mathematics Research.

Collier, A. (1994). *Critical Realism: An Introduction to Roy Bhaskar's Philosophy*. London: Verso.

Corson, D. J. (1990a). Old and New Conceptions of Discovery in Education. *Educational Philosophy and Theory, 22*(2), 26–49.

Corson, D. J. (1990b). Applying the Stages of a Social Epistemology to School Policy Making. *British Journal of Educational Studies, 38*(3), 259–276.

Corson, D. J. (1991a). Educational Research and Bhaskar's Conception of Discovery. *Educational Theory, 41*(2), 189–198.

Corson, D. J. (1991b). Bhaskar's Critical Realism and Educational Knowledge. *British Journal of Sociology of Education, 12*(2), 223–241.

Corson, D. J. (1995). *Discourse and Power in Educational Organizations*. Cresskill, New Jersey: Hampton Press.

Corson, D. J. (1998). *Changing Education for Diversity*. Buckingham, UK: OUP

Cumming, J. (1996). *From Alienation to Engagement: Opportunities for Reform in the Middle Years*. Canberra, Australia: Australian Curriculum Studies Association.

Emami, Z. and Riordan, T. (1998). Tony Lawson on Critical Realism: What's Teaching Got to Do With It? *Review of Social Economy, 56*(3), 311–323.

Evers, C. W. and Lakomski, G. (1991). *Knowing Educational Administration: Contemporary Methodological Controversies in Educational Administration Research*. Oxford, UK: Permagon.

Hargreaves, A. and Earl, L. (1994). Triple Transitions: Educating Early Adolescents in the Changing Canadian Context. *Curriculum Perspectives, 14*(3), 1–9.

New South Wales Department of Education (1977). *The Aims of Primary Education in New South Wales*. Sydney, Australia: Government Printer.

Plotkin, H. (1993). *Darwin Machines and the Nature of Knowledge*. Cambridge, UK: Harvard University Press.

Skamp, K. (Ed.). (1998). *Teaching Primary Science Constructively*. Sydney, Australia: Harcourt Brace.

van Huyssteen, J. W. (1999). *The Shaping of Rationality*. Grand Rapids, Michigan: Wm B Eerdmans.

Williams, S. J. (1999). Is Anybody There? Critical Realism, Chronic Illness and the Disability Debate. *Sociology of Health and Illness, 21*(6), 797–819.

Willmott, R. (2002). *Education Policy and Realist Social Theory: Primary Teachers, Child-centred Philosophy and the New Managerialism*. London: Routledge.

Westbury, I. (1999). The Burdens and the Excitement of the 'New' Curriculum Research: A Response to Hlebowitsh's 'The Burdens of the New Curricularist'. *Curriculum Inquiry, 29*(3), 355–364.

Wuketits, F. M. (1990). *Evolutionary Epistemology: Its Implications for Humankind*. Albany: SUNY Press.

17 Economics and autism: why the drive towards closure?

John Lawson

Introduction

It has been suggested that modern mainstream economics is dominated by a single approach: mathematical modelling (Lawson 1997). It has further been suggested that this approach is not particularly successful. Associations are theorised and models are constructed, associations sometimes hold for a brief period of time and then inevitably break down. The result, according to some, is a discipline 'so far removed from anything that remotely resembles the real world that it is often difficult to take the subject seriously' (Clower 1989). Some express this view even more strongly. Blaug, for example, argues that 'Modern economics is sick; Economists have converted the subject into a sort of social mathematics in which analytical rigour is everything and practical relevance is nothing' (Blaug 1997). Such was the dissatisfaction with the discipline in this respect that a group of French students organised a petition in 2000 demanding a 'return to reality' in economic methodology (Devine 2002). This movement became known as Post-Autistic Economics (PAE). The French students branded mainstream economics 'autistic' due to its (1) over-simplistic view of the world, (2) excessive reliance on mathematics and (3) refusal to integrate with other disciplines.

There are two issues of relevance to this chapter that arise from these complaints and criticisms. First, why are mainstream methods so unsuccessful and second, if the methods are so unsatisfactory, if they simply aren't working, *why* persist with them? This second point will be addressed by drawing on a theory that has been advanced to provide a psychological explanation of autism spectrum conditions on the cognitive level (Lawson 2003). The first of these issues will not be explored in depth here because of the extensive literature that already exists on this within critical realism. It is however important to provide an overview of this work in preparation for the ideas that follow.

In brief, various critical realists argue that the dissatisfaction and lack of success discussed above stems from the inappropriate application of methods which presuppose closed systems to situations that are predominantly open. The argument is therefore one that involves different ontological positions and in particular, the distinctions between what have come to be termed empirical and transcendental realist ontologies. The former is most commonly, and perhaps best, grounded in the theory of knowledge suggested by David Hume (1975).

For Hume, knowable reality is restricted to those features that are present in our direct experience. By implication, reality is reducible to events and states of affairs. Thus, according to Hume, any talk of necessary connections between events, underlying powers, internal relationality and so forth, is nothing more than a contribution of the human mind. Such conceptions have no real counterpart in the world.

If actualities such as events are all that exist, if reality is restricted to actual events and states of affairs, then the only sorts of generalities possible must consist of patterns in the succession of such events. Scientific laws, if they exist, must take the form 'if event x, then event y', or to put it another way, whenever a given event x occurs, event y will *always* follow. Despite Hume's scepticism as to whether we can ever know that such laws exist these event regularities have become known as Humean causal laws.[1] Within this broad Humean conception, reality consists of actual outcomes that may be correlated but need never be essentially connected.

In contrast to Hume's theory a second ontological perspective needs to be considered. This has, in recent years, been most thoroughly developed within critical realist accounts under the heading of Transcendental Realism. Reasoning within this perspective starts from the observation that event regularities of the sort posited by Hume occur under some conditions but not others. The ontology developed therefore encompasses the Humean model as a special case. A variety of conditions have to be in place to guarantee a closure, the most significant being the extrinsic and intrinsic condition. Achieving extrinsic closure depends upon the isolation of the target phenomena from any external confounding mechanisms that could influence outcomes, e.g. a breeze could alter the trajectory of a feather falling under the influence of gravity. Achieving intrinsic closure depends upon an absence of any mechanisms that are internal to the structure or nature of the target phenomenon that could influence outcomes on subsequent occasions, e.g. people making differing choices or having different or changing desires. If both external *and* internal conditions of closure are satisfied then the system can be said to be closed. An open system is therefore any in which event regularities do not occur.

These issues however are far from straightforward. A distinction can be made between (1) systems that are *spontaneously closed* – one possible example being astronomy); (2) systems that are open but *closable* – as in experiments carried out in the natural world; (3) systems that seem *non-closable* – one example being the social world and interactions where individual choice and internal relatedness seem to preclude closure from the outset. Thus, excluding cases of type (1), closed systems are often restricted to situations where there is a level of experimental control. It is important to note that there need not be any homogeneity among open systems. Any two open systems need not be identical. While both may be non-closable, one may tend towards closure to a greater extent. Consider as examples the earth's tidal system and human relationships, both are open systems but issues such as predictability and regularity may cause us to conclude that the former is perhaps closer to being closable than the latter.

Critical realists explain the fact that event regularities occur in some conditions but not others through the idea that in creating a closure, stable causal mechanisms can become isolated from the effects of countervailing ones. Where such an isolation is achieved the mechanism under research can be triggered and its effects measured in an unimpeded fashion. For example, a feather dropped in a vacuum will fall directly to earth under the influence of gravity. The event regularity that arises thus correlates the triggering of the mechanism with a set of reproducible effects. The importance of this analysis is that in order to explain the fact that patterns occur at times but not others it is necessary to recognise that there is more to reality than actualities such as events. Behind the events, and producing them, are 'deeper' mechanisms. This analysis is also required to make sense of the fact that theories about mechanisms can remain valid even when event regularities are not in evidence. For example, we understand that feathers are still subject to gravitational forces even though we might see them move in other directions. This observation is problematic unless we recognise that the experimental results apply not to outcomes and their patterns *per se* but to underlying mechanisms that endure both inside and outside the experiment.

To put matters another way, according to Transcendental Realism reality is *structured*. This means that it consists not only of surface phenomena but also entails underlying structures, powers, mechanisms and tendencies that govern or facilitate the actual course of events. Reality is also found to be *open* in that it does not reduce to a ubiquity of closures. Indeed we can see that experimental work presupposes that reality is open, for it is only if reality is open that laboratories and the control of variables are required in order to close it. And it is only because reality is structured that closures can sometimes be achieved. According to this view human beings are also structured. They comprise not only behaviour, but the capacities which facilitate that behaviour, including capabilities, dispositions, needs, desires, beliefs, mental states and so on. By comparison, the constraints forced by the 'if x, then y' relationship effectively preclude the notion of choice and reduce human action to the passive responding to external stimuli.

According to critical realism society too is structured. Just as the human cannot simply be reduced to behaviour, neither can society be reduced to human practices. It also includes social rules, relations, positions, institutions, etc. The social realm can be thought of as that realm of phenomena that depends at least in part on us. It therefore also includes institutions such as marriage, practices such as celebrating anniversaries, structures such as language, artefacts such as tables, pollution, and so on. The dependency of the social realm upon us indicates something of its mode of being, specifically that it is intrinsically dynamic. Consider for example, a language system. We do not create the system but are born into it, and it is given to us as a condition of our speech acts. In other words, speech acts are only possible if a language already exists. At the same time the system depends on us, it does not exist apart from our speech acts. Nor does it determine what we say or how we say it. Thus, the model of being here is one of transformation or reproduction. In critical realism this is referred to as the *transformational model of social activity* (Bhaskar 1989). Language is a (typically unacknowledged) condition of speech acts, but through the speech acts of all speech participants, the language system is (mostly unintentionally) reproduced or transformed. So its mode of being is intrinsically dynamic. This applies to all social structures such as markets, households, universities, etc. Such things as universities don't *only* exist and experience change as an external input. They are in a constant state of transformation, a process of change is essential to what a university is. And so it is for all social structure.

To summarise so far, by reducing economic science simply to methods of mathematical modelling, and thereby reducing all explanation to the application of deductive reasoning, modern mainstream economics is inappropriately applying 'closed-system methods'[2] to irreducibly open systems (i.e. social reality, where such closing off is not possible in any systematic way). This activity might usefully be termed 'misclosure'. Implicit in the use of such closed-system methods is the idea that it is possible to reduce the world to closed systems of atomistic (essentially unconnected) actualities, with processes of change reduced to differences. The inability to directly know deeper structures and internal relations precludes the existence of such things.

Now, even if this assessment can be accepted, there is nothing in this account that by itself provides an answer to our second question: why persist with such an approach if it so unsuccessful (as suggested by many theorists), and gives rise to dissatisfaction (as indicated by the post autistic movement)?

A number of answers to this question have been suggested. These have tended to involve the academic dominance of the modelling paradigm, path dependency arguments, and the perceived prestige of using more scientific methods. While these are important factors I will argue that they are bound up with and underpinned by another more fundamental reason which is located at the personal or psychological level as well as the institutional level. Specifically I suggest that there is a biologically rooted and socially accentuated bias towards closed system thinking that results in a tendency towards misclosure. This idea is evidenced by research into a group of pervasive developmental disorders known collectively as autism spectrum conditions. More specifically, from a recent theory suggesting that autism spectrum conditions involve a continuum of cognitive styles (related to open and closed systems) that extends into the general population.

Autism spectrum conditions

Autism was first documented by the Austrian psychologist Leo Kanner (1943). The term, first coined by Bleuler, was used to capture the withdrawn behaviour and separateness that seems to be at the core of the condition. Autism typically affects a person's ability to communicate and form relationships with other people and generally respond appropriately with their environment. In clinical terms it involves a tripartite of features (1) impairment in social interaction, (2) impairment in communication (3) presence of restricted, repetitive and stereotyped patterns of behaviour, interests and activities (APA 1994). Autism is normally diagnosed in childhood and cases number approximately 1 per 1000 (Fombonne 2003).

A second condition closely related to autism is Asperger syndrome (AS) (Asperger 1944). Diagnostically, the only difference between the two conditions is the absence, in AS, of any significant delay in language or cognitive development. The prevalence of AS is however significantly higher with recent estimates being as high as 5 per 1000 (Scott *et al.* 2002). Taken together, and with the possible inclusion of high-functioning autism, they are taken to constitute a continuum of relatively distinct states known as autism spectrum conditions.

The concept of a spectrum or continuum captures well the enormous behavioural variability that is a central feature of the condition. Despite this variability the three key groups of features (difficulties in social interaction, difficulties in communication and restricted patterns of behaviour and interest) remain central.

The cause of the condition is still unknown. On the biological level much current research is examining differential levels of connectivity between brain regions and hemispheres, the role of pre-natal hormones (especially testosterone) and the function of specific brain areas. All of these factors seem to be associated with the condition in some way though issues of causality and process remain unclear.

Uncertainty also exists on the cognitive level and it remains unclear as to how the condition should be conceptualised. While there is an accepted diagnostic criterion of behavioural patterns there are various different cognitive explanations or models that seek to explain these patterns in the literature. Three models in particular have dominated research over the last ten years or so. First, is the Executive Dysfunction model (Ozonoff 1995; Russell 1997) in which the condition is seen as a downstream outcome of a more general cognitive deficit that involves problem solving, flexible thinking, memory etc … Second is the Weak Central Coherence model (Frith *et al.* 1996) in which the condition is seen as an inability to switch from local to global perceptual levels. Third is the Theory of Mind/Empathising-Systemising model (Baron-Cohen *et al.* 1985, 2002) in which the condition is seen as a specific inability to effectively engage with other minds. However, it is a characteristic of each existing model that it only explains a specific subset of the overall features.[3]

More recently, and in response to this problematic situation, another model has been proposed. This model draws on the distinction between open and closed systems to move closer to accommodating all the main diagnostic elements of autism spectrum conditions and explaining the evidence from all three of the dominant models. In this, the Depth Accessibility Difficulties model, the existing theories of explanation are interpreted as special cases of the general model being proposed. This new model will be briefly outlined here although a fuller account is available elsewhere (Lawson 2003).

The depth accessibility difficulties model

The Depth Accessibility Difficulties (DAD) model draws on some of the ideas that are central in critical realism. According to the model, autism spectrum conditions can be conceptualised as involving some resistance to, or difficulty in coping with all event patterns that don't approximate the sort achieved in closed systems. Much of the previous literature has focused on the social/interactional aspects of the condition. This is in part because these aspects are of such daily importance and salience to us. In other words, it's what gets noticed first and seems to constitute the biggest part of the problem. According to the DAD model these social / interactional difficulties exist because another person's mind is such a prime example of an open system, perhaps even the ultimate one. For a genuine notion of choice to be possible another mind must be able to think or do otherwise. As a result, dealing with the thoughts, desires, emotions and beliefs that exist in other people's minds can be a challenge for all of us. The DAD model however is also able to explain difficulties associated with autism spectrum conditions that exist beyond the social/interactional realm. In fact, difficulties would be expected in *any* situation where uncertainty and change are prevalent.

For people with autism spectrum conditions, being presented with such states of affairs results in a tendency to simply treat open-system situations as though they are closed; misclosure. The fact that such ways of understanding their environment, and ways of interacting with it, are fundamentally inappropriate then leads to the host of behavioural problems that are associated with the condition. This applies to the clearly interpersonal deficits but it also explains the less social (in a psychological sense) problems, e.g. coping with the fact that buses are sometimes five minutes late or early.

Conceptualising autism spectrum conditions in this way has several advantages. Most importantly for current purposes, such a conceptualisation allows for the explanation of the seemingly disparate research findings that currently exist in the field. As a result the DAD model has the ability to explain more fully the characteristics identified in the other models. First, regarding the Empathising-Systemising model, the ideas in the DAD model can explain *why* people with the condition find interacting with other minds and life in an irreducibly social world, so difficult. Second, regarding the Executive Dysfunction model, the DAD model can explain why people with the condition perform badly in tasks that require flexible thinking and reaction to a new situation. The DAD model also explains why people with the condition don't perform poorly at *all* such tasks; some tasks have high executive demands but simultaneously approximate closed systems. Third, ideas from the DAD model can also explain some of the problematic aspects of the Weak Central Coherence model. As with executive function, there does not seem to be a universal deficit in central coherence. Again the distinction between open and closed systems seems to lead to a better explanation.[4]

There are certain aspects of the DAD model that need to be made explicit. The distinction between open and closed systems exists on an ontological level; it concerns how the world is characterised. The DAD model is suggesting a biologically rooted condition that manifests on the psychological level in a specific cognitive and behavioural pattern. This pattern includes difficulties with social interaction, non verbal communication, dealing with change in the environment, and flexible thinking. The pattern simultaneously often includes proficiency in other areas such as mathematics, engineering and deductive logic. This pattern also results in a psychological need for, or comfort with, sameness and regularity in the environment. Such a desire for routine and dislike of change among people with autism spectrum conditions is well documented. The condition gives rise to a reduced ability in dealing with open systems. As a result, the approaches used by people with the condition in negotiating the world tend to be atomistic and focused on the surface level. In other words, there is a tendency towards misclosure. An interesting illustration of this point comes from research regarding Applied Behaviour Analysis (ABA) (Lovaas 1987, 1993; Lovaas & Smith 1988). ABA is considered to be the most successful intervention currently available for autism spectrum conditions. It involves intensive one-on-one therapy sessions during which complex situations are broken down into smaller rule-based components: the expression if x, then y jumps to mind here. Despite some degrees of success one of the most persistent limitations with ABA concerns the issue of generalising learning. For example, a child with the condition may complete task 1 at time 1 with facilitator 1 in room 1. However they may well fail task 1 at time 2 if they're working with another facilitator, or even with the same facilitator but in a different room. If generalised learning fails to negotiate a room change it perhaps comes as no surprise to learn that skills learned during ABA sessions are often unsuccessfully transferred to the social world.

Simultaneously we need to remember that on occasions such atomistic, surface level approaches can be both appropriate and highly successful. For example, when repairing a fault in an electrical system it would be a mistake to consider the systems' *desire* to work or not. This issue of appropriateness to the situation is perhaps crucial in understanding why so often the talents and successes of people with Asperger syndrome are expressed in fields such as mathematics, engineering, computing and physics. Likewise it becomes clear why the deficits of the condition always manifests most in the individual's social relationships and negotiation of the social world.

It is important at this point to return to the issue of prevalence in autism spectrum conditions. Prevalence rates were discussed earlier as being in the region of 1–5 per 1000. These figures were based on the number of diagnoses within a certain geographical area. More recently, epidemiological work has been undertaken to examine the presence of the condition in a large section of the general population. The initial suggestion from this work based around the Cambridge area suggests a prevalence rate among school children of 13 per 1000 or 1 in 80.[5]

The implications following from this work are significant. If nearly two per cent of the population fulfil the diagnostic criteria, and the condition is known to be on a continuum, it suggests that a great many people in the general population, to differing degrees, have some kind of difficulty in dealing with open systems. To some extent this may be true of all of us. We may all need to apply a certain level of closure to enable us to function effectively in the social world. These closures might be what we refer to as routines? On a psychological level dealing with novelty and change is highly draining on the cognitive system and cannot be maintained for long periods without consequence. Of course the tendency to impose closure where possible may manifest in a host of different ways. For example, on an individual level many people construct and seem to have a real psychological need for daily routines. Adherence to these may not be to the extreme degree as seen in autism spectrum conditions (where any deviation from routine simply can't be coped with) but they are still an important factor in day-to-day life. On a wider level there may exist other more general attempts to impose closure on the social world by constructing frameworks of rules and codes. Overall, these ideas taken together seem to suggest a human psychological disposition or bias towards sometimes using approaches that might be more appropriate in dealing with closed systems.

The main point that I am making here is that if this conceptualisation of autism spectrum conditions is accepted, then there may indeed be a personal or psychological level explanation for the persistent use of inappropriate and unsuccessful methodology in mainstream economics, as witnessed by those such as critical realists and the PAE. There are a number of corollaries to this idea that are beyond the scope of this chapter but worth mentioning nonetheless. These include the influence of such a bias on the social sciences more generally. For example, the drive towards using methods more appropriate to dealing with closed systems has manifested in other areas of social science such as psychology (e.g. behaviourism and early cognitive modelling) and geography (e.g. regional science). Another corollary involves how such a bias has shaped societal values and practices more generally. Both of these issues are being explored in work currently underway.

Let me be clear about the argument being made here. If the DAD account of autism spectrum conditions is correct it seems possible to argue that the problems occurring in contemporary mainstream economics stem from a general human tendency to impose closures. Specifically, according to the DAD model, the (mistaken) dominance of mathematical modelling is rooted in a drive to use methods oriented towards closed systems irrespective of their appropriateness to the object being studied. It is of course problematic to specify where a tendency to impose closure becomes a tendency towards misclosure. Given that the DAD model is evidenced by the existence of autism spectrum conditions it seems that the use of the term 'post-autistic' by the French students seems to have a certain amount of validity and appropriateness, perhaps more than was originally intended. It is unclear however, whether the term was chosen with autism spectrum conditions, as a specific psychiatric condition, in mind, or whether the French students, like Bleuler were drawing on the Greek origins of the term to signify different aspects of detachment and focus on the self.

The DAD model is a relatively new one and at the moment many of the issues discussed are highly speculative with little more than instances of congruent evidence for support. There are also some significant aspects of the theory that require further development. For example, as mentioned earlier, the distinction between open and closed systems is an ontological one describing types of phenomena in the world. The DAD model involves the idea that such a distinction corresponds in some way to distinct processes or styles on the cognitive level.

This is clearly a large assumption to make and whilst it might make some degree of intuitive sense its justification requires further work.

There is however new evidence emerging from other areas of autism research that seems to support the DAD model. For example, on the physiological and neurological level, studies involving structural brain imaging and functional magnetic resonance imaging have found that people with the condition seem to have less white brain matter than people without the condition. White matter is crucial in terms of connectivity between brain hemispheres and different brain regions and these findings have led to physiological conceptions of the condition being forwarded that centre on connectivity deficits (Just *et al.* 2004). My point here is that a reduction in connectivity would probably make dealing with open systems increasingly problematic. Incidentally, sex differences in connectivity levels have also been found (males having less) and while this issue is clearly of huge importance given the greater incidence of autism spectrum conditions in males it is also beyond the scope of this chapter.

Another issue that is beyond the remit of this chapter involves implications regarding the future direction of mainstream economics. They are however important issues that need to be addressed. The work certainly raises the question of whether this misclosure will persist. In a recent issue of *New Scientist*, work was reported where functional magnetic resonance imaging had been used to explore the relationship between neuronal response in specific brain networks and behaviour so that choices could become predictable (Spinney 2004). Related work was reported describing a 21st century version of game theory, where people's choice making was predicted by the firing rates of individual neurons (Glimcher & Dorris, in press). Although these are just a few examples they seem to suggest that the drive towards misclosure is far from dead in current mainstream economics.

Conclusion

This chapter has examined the issue of *why* inappropriate research methods continue to dominate mainstream economics despite their lack of success and the dissatisfaction caused (as so clearly demonstrated by the PAE movement among others). A possible explanation has been suggested in the form of the DAD model which was primarily devised to conceptualise autism spectrum conditions but also carries implications for the general population. According to this model autism spectrum conditions can fruitfully be conceptualised as an inability or great difficulty in dealing with open systems. As a result some aspects of the world become highly problematic, others less so. The DAD model seems to be the first conceptualisation that is able to account for all of the behavioural features of autism spectrum conditions. The model simultaneously suggests the existence of a general human tendency towards imposing closure on open systems. As discussed, this tendency is highly variable from person to person and may manifest in very different ways. Likewise, such a tendency will give rise to outcomes that vary in appropriateness depending on the event at hand. In sum, the persistent application of inappropriate methods in mainstream economics stems from a variable human bias towards enforcing closure on open systems that sometimes results in misclosure.

Notes

1 In critical realism the systems in which such event regularities occur are referred to as 'closed' systems.
2 Here I mean those methods appropriate where it is possible to close off aspects of reality.
3 For a more detailed description and critique of these theories see Lawson (2003).
4 See Lawson *et al.* (2004).
5 It should be noted here that the increased numbers of the condition in the Cambridge area are already well documented and referred to as the 'silicone fen effect'. It has been estimated that this may be responsible for a doubling of the prevalence levels. Even so, this work still implies a national rate of approximately 1 in 160.

References

APA (1994). *DSM-IV Diagnostic and Statistical Manual of Mental Disorders, 4th Edition.* Washington DC: American Psychiatric Association.

Asperger, H. (1944). 'Die 'Autistischen Psychopathen' im Kindesalter.' *Archiv fur Psychiatrie und Nervenkrankheiten* 117: 76–136.

Baron-Cohen, S., Leslie, A. M. and Frith, U. (1985). 'Does the autistic child have a 'theory of mind'?' *Cognition* 21: 37–46.

Baron-Cohen, S., Wheelwright, S., Lawson, J., Griffin, R. and Hill, J. (2002). The exact mind: Empathising and systemising in autism spectrum conditions. *Handbook of Cognitive Development.* U. Goswami. Oxford, UK: Blackwell.

Bhaskar, R. (1989). *The Possibility of Naturalism.* London: Harvester-Wheatsheaf.

Blaug, M. (1997). 'Ugly Currents in Modern Economics.' *Policy Options (Montreal, Canada, Institute for Research on Public Policy)* http://www.irpp.org, September 1997), p. 3.

Clower, R. W. (1989). The state of economics: hopeless but not serious? *The Spread of Economic Ideas.* D. Colander and A. W. Coates. Cambridge, UK: CUP.

Devine, J. (2002). 'Psychological Autism, Institutional Autism and Economics.' *Post-autistic economics review* (16).

Fleetwood, S., Ed. (1999). *Critical realism in economics: development and debate. Economics as social theory.* London: Routledge.

Fombonne, E. (2003). 'The prevalence of autism.' *Journal of the American Medical Association* 1(289): 87–89.

Frith, U., Morton, J. and Leslie, A. (1991). 'The cognitive basis of a biological disorder: autism.' *Trends in Neuroscience* 14: 433–438.

Glimcher, P. W., Dorris, M. C. and Bayer, H. M. (2005) Physiological utility theory and the neuroeconomics of choice, *Games and Economic Behavior*, 52, 213–256.

Happe, F. (1996). 'Studying weak central coherence at low levels: children with autism do not succumb to visual illusions. A research note.' *Journal of Child Psychology and Psychiatry* 37: 873–877.

Hume, D. (1975). *Enquiries concerning human understanding and concerning the principles of morals.* Oxford, UK: Clarendon Press.

Just, M. A., Cherkassky, V. L., Keller, T. A. and Minshew, N. J. (2004). 'Cortical activation and synchronization during sentence comprehension in high-functioning autism: evidence of underconnectivity.' *Brain* 127: 1811–1821.

Kanner, L. (1943). 'Autistic disturbance of affective contact.' *Nervous Child* 2: 217–250.

Lawson, J. (2003). 'Depth Accessibility Difficulties: An alternative conceptualisation of autism spectrum conditions'. *Journal for the Theory of Social Behaviour* 33(2): 189–202.

Lawson, J., Baron-Cohen, S. and Wheelwright, S. (2004). 'Empathising and Systemising in Adults With and Without Asperger Syndrome.' *Journal of Autism and Developmental Disorders.*

Lawson, T. (1997). *Economics and Reality.* London: Routledge.

Lovaas, O. (1987). 'Behavioural Treatment and Normal Educational and Intellectual Functioning in Young Autistic Children.' *Journal of Consulting and Clinical Psychology* 55: 3–9.

Lovaas, O. (1993). 'The Development of a Treatment-research Project for Developmentally Disabled and Autistic Children.' *Journal of Applied Behaviour Analysis* 26: 617–630.

Lovaas, O. and Smith, T. (1988). Intensive behavioural treatment for young autistic children. *Advances in Clinical Child Psychology.* B. Lahey and A. Kazdin, Plenum Publishing. II.

Ozonoff, S. (1995). Executive functions in autism. *Learning and Cognition in Autism.* E. Schopler and G. Mesibov. New York: Plenum Press.

Russell, J., Ed. (1997). *Autism as an Executive Disorder.* Oxford: Oxford University Press.

Scott, F. J., Baron-Cohen, S., Bolton, P. and Brayne, C. (2002). 'Prevalence of autism spectrum conditions in children aged 5–11 years in Cambridgeshire, UK.' *Autism* 6(3): 231–237.

Spinney, L. (2004). Why we do what we do. *New Scientist* 183: 32–35.

18 Applying critical realism: re-conceptualising the emergent English early music performer labour market

Nicholas Wilson

Introduction

As a professional classical musician beginning my freelance singing career in the mid-1980s, I took a very minor role in the early music movement which was enjoying its 'golden age' at about that time. Early music recordings regularly topped the classical music CD charts and a new breed of early music performer now worked exclusively in historically informed performance. Although musicians had long held an interest in 'older' repertoire[1] and the question of 'authenticity',[2] it was only in the late 1960s and particularly early 1970s that historically informed performance began to take off on a professional level in England. The launch of such ensembles as the *Academy of Ancient Music* and *The English Concert* alongside the first publication of the specialist *Early Music* magazine (all in 1973) represents an important milestone in this development. As a musician familiar with the established practices, norms, traditions, etc. of gaining employment in both the wider classical music field and the specific area of early music performance, it became apparent that, though the two 'markets' shared many similarities, there were also differences in terms of how employment, movement between jobs, development and differentiation of job skills, or wages, were structured. Putting this another way, there seemed to be two separate labour markets in operation.

In making this distinction between the 'new' early music performer labour market (which reasonably could not be held to exist before some date in the early 1970s) and that for classical musicians in general (which has existed for hundreds of years albeit in varied forms) I was particularly struck by a question that is both simple in form and yet rather difficult to answer. If a labour market did not exist *yesterday*, but it does *today*, what happened in between to make this possible?

As I will seek to demonstrate in this paper, the answer to this question matters for a number of significant reasons – and has a seminal bearing on how we conceptualise 'the labour market'. At this point, however, it is worth highlighting two issues. Firstly, no-one appears to have tried to answer this question before. Secondly, and perhaps more importantly, given the particular theme of this book, it would seem that, with the exception of critical realism, there are few, if any, appropriate approaches that might be considered adequate for undertaking such a task. To explain labour market emergence requires a social ontology that can account for both transformation and emergence of social structures – and the role that agents play in this respect. As Archer (1995) has observed, 'there is a glaring absence of bold social theories which uncompromisingly make "emergence" their central tenet' (1998: 356). Critical realist meta-theory and realist social ontology, in particular, can be put forward as offering the researcher a suitable approach from which to face up to the 'vexatious' (Archer 1995: 1) task of explaining the relationship between structure and agency in this specific context.

This chapter therefore presents an account of how critical realism has been applied in a particular empirical context – the study of the English early music performer labour market. In so doing, I also hope to highlight some of the methodological challenges that face the researcher when undertaking research from a critical realist perspective. In the next section I outline the importance of making explicit the ontological and epistemological assumptions which underpin this type of study. The case for adopting a social ontology that is both transformational (taking into account how things change) and stratified (allowing for the existence of emergent causal powers that operate at different levels of reality) is put forward. This lays the foundation for the introduction of critical realist meta-theory, and realist social ontology in particular, as an appropriate approach from which to conceptualise a labour market and its emergence. In the fourth and fifth sections I present a re-conceptualisation of the labour market and labour market emergence, based on the retroductive argument (Sayer 1992: 107) and Archer's adaptation of the transformational model of social activity – the morphogenetic approach (1995) respectively. This prepares the ground for an outline causal explanatory account of the emergence of the early music performer labour market. The chapter concludes with a discussion of the key insights which result from using critical realism as a 'philosophical underlabourer' in this enquiry.

Key ontological assumptions

The inability to analytically distinguish between structure and agency, and therefore account for the relationship between them, may well be responsible for much of the ongoing disagreement on conceptual issues relating to the origins of new markets and the introduction of new economic activity (see Shane 2003: 2–3). In fact, of course, this problem is not specific to the study of labour markets, but has been central to pretty much everything considered under the umbrella of sociological theory. Two schools of thought, represented above all by Weber and Durkheim, present social objects as being *either* the results of intentional or meaningful human behaviour, *or* as possessing a life of their own, external to the individual (Bhaskar 1989: 31). In focusing on the social *object* of a new labour market, therefore, we are compelled to take some position – ranging from individualist to relational – on the nature of its existence. It is worth noting, of course, that all researchers bring with them a particular ontological perspective. We cannot escape ontology – even if we don't make it explicit. In other words, any meaningful conceptualisation of a labour market and its emergence is necessarily contingent on the author's assumptions as to the nature of social reality. This, as I shall reveal, is what makes the application of critical realist meta-theory so powerful. But this is not all – for while our understanding of a social object is necessarily dependent upon our underlying assumptions about its existence (i.e. our ontological perspective) it is also contingent upon our subjective interests and knowledge of the subject in studying it (i.e. our epistemological perspective). As both a professional musician actively involved in the early music performance labour market and a University lecturer with specific research interests in innovation and entrepreneurship, I have a particular (and at one level inescapable) *vantage* point from which to explore this phenomenon. Related to this vantage point is the particular level of abstraction (Lawson 1997) that I will use in my analysis. As will become apparent, I believe that all labour markets share common features and the process of labour market emergence can be generalised across different empirical contexts. However, the particular 'mechanisms' that account for individual labour market emergence can only be discussed in relation to the specific context of the case at hand. This discussion forms the final analytical section of the chapter.

Critical realist meta-theory and realist social ontology

Before focusing on the early music performer labour market, we need to introduce some key elements of critical realist meta-theory and realist social ontology. Fundamental to realist philosophy (Harré 1972, 1986; Bhaskar 1978; Sayer 1992) is the belief that the world exists independently of us and our investigations of it. In other words, while it is the case that all knowledge is conceptually mediated, and therefore all our observations of the world are 'theory laden', this does not determine what reality is like – rather, it exists independently of our knowledge of it (Danermark *et al.* 2002). This is an important starting point and forms the basis for our understanding of realist social ontology. In particular, it has significant bearing on how we go about researching social objects such as labour markets. For if we assume that our theory laden observations are in fact what reality is like, we commit the 'epistemic fallacy' and reduce what *is* to what we can *know* about it (Bhaskar 1978: 36). I suggest that the assumption that a labour market is *only* made up of actual buyers and sellers of labour power is primarily derived from this type of thinking, for example (and elaborate on this further below). To avoid committing this fallacy, we must seek to explain how the world is by considering those generative mechanisms in the 'real' ontological domain (Bhaskar 1978: 56) which can produce events which we experience, directly or indirectly, in the 'empirical' domain, or which happen, whether we experience them or not, in the 'actual' domain.

The purpose of realist social science then becomes the discovery and explanation of the 'mechanisms' that account for the particular events under scrutiny. Fundamental to this task is the process of conceptualisation. Critical realist writers have emphasised the importance of conceptualising the object of study (Sayer 1992; Danermark *et al.* 2002). Indeed, Danermark *et al.* state that 'conceptualization stands out as the most central social scientific activity' (p. 41). So how do we undertake such a process? The guiding principle of the approach taken in this paper is the retroductive argument. This involves, in the words of Sayer (2001a), 'to try and work out what is necessarily the case about' the labour market in order for it to exist. Such an argument almost always involves *abstraction*. As Sayer notes (1992: 87) this 'isolates in thought a *one-sided* or partial aspect of an object'.

It is in the nature of abstractions, however, that they 'freeze the moment' (Danermark *et al.*: 52). As a consequence, they cannot tell us anything directly about processes and change. In researching labour market emergence, therefore, we also require an analysis of causal conditions. For critical realists, causality is conceptualised in terms of *natural necessity*. This is to say that a thing behaves in certain ways under certain circumstances, 'in virtue of its intrinsic nature' (Harré & Madden 1975: 86). We can explain what is meant by this natural necessity within critical realist social ontology by referring to three concepts – social structures, powers and generative mechanisms. Social structures (the connections among agents causally affecting their actions and in turn causally affected by them – see Porpora 1998) possess the *powers* that they have (i.e. to enable or constrain) in virtue of their intrinsic natures. Furthermore, *generative mechanisms* exist and are what they are because of this structure. There is then an internal and necessary relation between the nature of an object and its causal powers. We can explain events in terms of the compound effect of influences drawn from different mechanisms (see Danermark *et al.* 2002: 55–56). It is important to add, however, that the existence of powers and mechanisms does not mean that they *will* be exercised or triggered, for this is a matter of contingency. For example, a match has the causal power to flare up if triggered, but this depends on someone striking it, and that it is dry, etc. This has very important implications for our understanding of the causality behind the formation of new labour markets. For it implies that 'causal laws ... must be analysed as tendencies' (Bhaskar 1978: 50). This in turn further cautions any attempt to explain phenomena in the world in terms of empirical observations alone. Rather, the researcher must ask 'transfactual' questions which look beyond the event by postulating and identifying generative mechanisms which made the event possible (Danermark *et al.* 2002: 58). This is the retroductive argument.

How then might we retroduce the mechanisms responsible for the emergence of a new labour market? It is the capacity of realist social ontology to provide a *transformational* model of social activity that provides us with the means of doing this. For in treating the duality of structure and praxis as analytically separable we can isolate structure and agency as operating over different time periods. Structure necessarily predates the actions which transform it; and structural elaboration necessarily post-dates those actions (Archer 1995: 90). At the heart of critical realism, therefore, there is a commitment to an explanatory framework that acknowledges and incorporates pre-existent structures as generative mechanisms (Archer *et al.* 1998: 377–378). This has important implications for our understanding of labour market emergence.

Before moving on to re-conceptualise the labour market using the retroductive argument, one further feature of reality, that has very significant implications for how we understand such social objects, needs to be outlined. This is its *stratified* nature.

To explain this feature of reality we return once more to the relationship between structure and agency. This is because when we undertake analysis of social phenomena we are obliged to do so with particular respect to how they are expressed through individuals. Empirical studies in labour markets, for example, necessarily revolve around research of those people we take to be involved (usually focusing primarily on the employers' (Rubery 1988) or the employees' (Fevre 1992) perspective). Unfortunately, our understanding of 'the whole' (the social object) cannot be gleaned from simply summing 'the parts' (properties relating to individuals). This is because causal mechanisms operate at more than one level below the 'surface' of events (Danermark *et al.* 2002: 59). For example, we might explain language in terms of being an emergent outcome of the practical engagement of the cognitive and reflexive powers of human beings with the properties and powers of the world (Carter & New 2004). Crucially, each new stratum is formed by powers and mechanisms from the underlying strata. As such, new objects come in to being, each with their own specific structures, powers and generative mechanisms. We refer to these new occurrences as *emergence*, since the new objects possess emergent properties. The phenomenon of emergence can then be simply thought of as the relationship which makes it possible for a whole to be more than the sum of its parts (Elder-Vass 2004: 103).

Archer (2003) notes that 'the primary distinguishing feature of any emergent property is the natural necessity of its internal relations, for what the entity is and its very existence depends upon them' (1995: 173). Most importantly, the emergent property 'has the generative capacity to modify the powers of its constituents in fundamental ways and to exercise causal influences sui generis' (p. 174). Archer talks of structural and cultural emergent properties as having the generative power to facilitate projects of different kinds (p. 7). We can think of structural emergent properties (SEPs) in terms of distributions, roles, organisations and institutions. Cultural emergent properties (CEPs) include propositions, theories or doctrines (Archer 2003: 5). In the particular empirical context of the early music movement – where ideas about how people should perform music appear to drive the agenda – we might expect to find that the generative powers of CEPs have a key role to play in 'facilitating' particular projects. A particularly fruitful way of thinking about such generative powers – and one that forms the focus for my outline causal explanatory account of labour market emergence – is in terms of enablements and constraints which act on agential projects.

An agential project 'involves an end that is desired, however tentatively or nebulously, and also some notion, however imprecise, of the course of action through which to accomplish it' (ibid: 6). The concept of the 'project' is extremely useful for our re-conceptualisation of the labour market and its emergence. This is because it gives us a way of grounding explanation in terms of how certain individuals turn ideas into practice. The ability of individuals to be reflex-

ive about the situations in which they find themselves, and make intentional decisions in the light of the conditional influence of pre-existing structural and cultural emergent properties, is a central element of this process. Archer describes
personal reflexivity as the 'missing link in mediation' (ibid: 9). It has its own
causal efficacy and therefore represents one of the most important personal emergent properties (PEPs).

Having briefly outlined the most salient elements of the critical realist general
meta-theory and realist social ontology, we now turn to its application in respect
of our conceptualisation of the labour market and its emergence. My approach
follows Cruickshank (2003: 143–5) in developing an immanent critique of existing literature, or what he terms the construction of domain-specific meta-theory.

Re-conceptualising the labour market

A general way of conceptualising labour markets is as 'arenas' (Freedman 1976)
where employment, movement between jobs, development and differentiation of
job skills, or wages, are similarly structured (Althauser & Kalleberg 1981).
Orthodox or mainstream economists' accounts of the labour market seek to predict labour market outcomes and, therefore, employ, as a central analytical
device, functional relations between wage rates and the quantities of labour
demanded and supplied (Fleetwood 2003: 3). Unfortunately for mainstream
accounts, functional relations presuppose a Humean account of causality that is
based on the constant conjunction of events, rather than natural necessity.
Furthermore, such accounts are forced to engineer closed systems when, as critical realists have argued strongly, social systems are more likely to be open systems.

Fleetwood (2003) has argued that despite many positive observations and
comments, institutionalists and mainstream commentators from other schools and
subjects have not provided a viable alternative to the neoclassical approach. This
is because whereas social structures are treated as 'problematic residuals' in the
mainstream account, the opposite is the case in heterodox accounts: labour markets become problematic residuals. In other words 'heterodox analysis ...
defaults to a mode wherein labour markets remain sites where some kind of relation between wages, supply and demand for labour exists, even if the precise
nature of this relation is underelaborated' (p. 7).

Fleetwood (2003) has re-defined labour markets as 'synonymous with the
social structures that constitute them' (p. 1). Yet, this step forward is not enough
to clarify the nature of the labour market, and remains incomplete. For there is a
danger that treating the labour market as synonymous with the social structures
that constitute it, may then lead to both the actions and beliefs of agents as being
considered external to, but dependent upon, the labour market. As such, we will
not be able to explain how individual actors that participate in the labour market
become participants. We would limit our analysis to those people who are 'in' (or
'out') of the labour market, not those who had the potential to be, or did not have
the potential to be.

To adequately explain the labour market, therefore, we must provide an account that conveys how a particular set of social structures are actively drawn upon by human agents, so that these structures can be said to 'facilitate' the exchange of the commodity labour power. In so doing, we will also be able to account for the (emergent) process by which the structures that, in part, constitute the labour market are themselves either reproduced or transformed, through the mediation of human agency. It is my view that such an account is best served by explicitly referring to *both* the structures and agents involved.

It follows on from this view that the labour market constitutes both structural and cultural emergent properties *and* the agential projects upon which these emergent properties' causal powers act. The labour market can then be defined as comprising:

> the social structures that enable and constrain those agential projects which have the exchange of labour power as their intended outcome.[3]

The definition of the labour market put forward, including as it does human agency, now allows for an explanation of the phenomenon in terms of both those humans that participate in it and those that have the potential to participate in it. For example, it could be the case that the labour market acts to constrain a particular individual's project from reaching its intended outcome, thus resulting in no exchange of labour power. To the extent that a labour market can be thought of as 'real' as a result of its capacity to make a difference or have an effect on those involved, we can see that its power to constrain or even prevent individuals from acting in some way could be a particularly important feature of its existence (and one that is often overlooked by labour market theory).

Allied to this inclusive definition of the labour market, attention might also be drawn to the implicit assumption that labour markets can exist outside of the market economy. For example, even where a labour market is constituted solely by freelance self-employed providers there remains a sense in which their labour power is 'exchanged', and the possibility (or likelihood) of agential projects involving the exchange of labour power with others being constrained by certain social structures. Similarly, even where 'free' labour markets do not exist[4] – for example in some state-controlled economies – there are still the ingredients in place for a labour market to be present.

The conceptualisation of the labour market, as laid out above, now begs two further related transcendental questions:

1   *Which* particular social structures might be involved?
2   *What type of* agential projects are enabled or constrained?

To answer the first question we can pose another – what does the existence of the labour market (in this form) presuppose (Sayer 1992: 91)? Essentially we must undertake counterfactual thinking (or what Sayer calls structural analysis) to uncover those relations that *must* be present in order for the labour market to exist.

Focusing on what is 'necessary' is to consider the internally related nature of human action. The distinction between external or contingent relations and internal or necessary relations (see Bhaskar 1989: 42) is important here. For we can theorise that the existence of a labour market is itself dependent (minimally) on two necessary and internal relations. The first of these is the relation between a buyer and seller of labour power (which I will call the Labour power exchange structure – LxS). The second is the relation between the buyer and seller of the product for which labour power is required (the Product exchange structure – PxS).[5] We can usefully begin by conceptualising the labour market in terms of these two structural emergent properties and their causal powers, which condition (i.e. enable and/or constrain) the particular projects of agents who intend to exchange labour power. Any notion of the labour market without both these internal and necessary relations being present appears implausible.

Yet, this again is only part of the story. The juxtaposition of necessity and contingency is complex (Sayer 1992: 108). Whether or not the causal powers of these emergent properties are activated, resulting in concrete labour market behaviours and processes being observed, is itself contingent on the conditions (other structures and practices) which are actually present. Indeed, much of labour market theory has focused on this aspect of its existence. For example, issues of gender, race, labour market segmentation, etc. are all concerned with these contingent aspects of labour markets.[6] In the case of the state-controlled economy, given above, the regulatory structures that constrain free labour power exchange can also be seen as contingent structures (albeit very important ones) rather than necessary ones for the very existence of a labour market.

Conceptualising labour market emergence

To answer the second question posed above – what type of agential projects are enabled or constrained? – we need to consider how new labour markets emerge for the first time.[7] In other words, we need to look at the link between the 'introduction of new economic activity' (often referred to as 'entrepreneurship')[8] and the emergence of new labour markets. As we have already observed, it is implausible to conceive of a labour market's existence without the possibility of exchange between the buyer and seller of a related product (PxS). In the case of a new labour market, therefore, this will also involve the production of a new product. It is apparent that the 'agential project' of our labour market definition (i.e. with the exchange of labour power as its intended outcome) is not an 'end that is desired' in its own right, but rather reflects the means by which the production of a new product or service will be affected. We can think of the agential project as being 'entrepreneurial' – not least in the sense that it requires the recombination of resources (including labour power), and it gives rise to new productive use.[9]

As described, the focus of attention here rests squarely on the demand-side of the labour market (even though labour power is itself the quasi-commodity[10] being *supplied*). This fits with those contemporary segmentation theories that give primacy to the demand-side of the labour market, 'as the area where job structures are shaped and the level and form of demand is determined' (Peck 2000: 224). However, labour market theory's traditional separation of demand-side and supply-side influences ignores a more nuanced reality. For the individuals involved in agential projects that give rise to the introduction of new economic activity (i.e. the labour market demand-side) are themselves most likely to have been acting on the supply-side up until that point, and may well continue to do so in the 'new' labour market context. The cases of two leading early music ensemble music directors serve to demonstrate this. Christopher Hogwood (Academy of Ancient Music) and Trevor Pinnock (The English Concert) were leading performers (keyboard players) in their own right in the wider classical music field before setting up their own orchestras. Their experiences and contacts as classical musicians 'employed' by others inevitably (intentionally and unintentionally) had significant bearing on their subsequent 'demand-side' roles in the new early music performer labour market. The concepts of 'labour power' and 'product' overlap here. To some extent, this is reflected in how the labour market is structured. For example, in the case of the early music orchestras described above, one of the unintended consequences of setting up their respective ensembles was that both Hogwood and Pinnock became synonymous with their orchestra's 'product'. It became very difficult to sell the Academy of Ancient Music, for example, without Christopher Hogwood being present to direct the ensemble.

The insights described above about demand-side and supply-side influences relating to previous, albeit related, labour markets (i.e. the market for classical music performers) are significant when we focus explicitly on how a new labour market emerges for the first time (such as that of the early music performer). Recalling Archer's morphogenetic approach (1995), structure necessarily pre-dates the actions which transform it, and structural elaboration necessarily post-dates those actions. A new labour market, therefore, will necessarily post-date the actions of agents (i.e. the undertaking of 'demand-side' projects involving the exchange of labour power) which are themselves conditioned by existing structures. These existing structures include labour power structures $(L \times S)$, which involve both the demand and supply of labour power, and product exchange structures $(P \times S)$ belonging to existing labour markets – since we know them to operate on projects of this kind.

The key insight from this argument is that 'new' labour markets (and related product markets) are reproduced via an emergent process from existing labour markets (and related product markets). Unlike in evolution – where the survival of the fittest sees existing species mutate and evolve into new species, usually causing the demise of the existing species, here the pre-existing labour market continues to exist alongside the new labour market. The classical musician labour market co-exists (and competes) with the early music performer labour market. Crucially, the 'new' labour market is differentiated from the existing labour market in terms of its structural and cultural emergent properties – which contain causal powers of their own which are irreducible to those operating in the pre-existing structure(s). It is in this respect in particular that we can legitimately speak of separate labour markets that have the capacity to effect or make a difference to those involved. The key premise underlying my presentation of the following causal explanatory account of labour market emergence is that through understanding these emergent properties in more detail and how they came to exist, we will be better able to conceptualise the labour market itself. The outline account now presented is not intended to be exhaustive by any means, but is offered as an illustrative example of the approach being taken.[11]

Outline causal explanatory account of the emergence of the English early music performer labour market

Figure 18.1 provides a conceptual model of the emergence of the new labour market, which forms the basis of the account that follows. The model owes some allegiance to Archer's morphogenetic approach (see 1995: 160), most notably in the analytical separation of the process of change (morphogenesis) into three stages or part cycles. However, this model seeks to introduce further insights relating to agential projects and the role of reflexivity in mediating between agency and structure. The process of emergence can be separated into six key analytical stages (conditioning; conception of agential project; reflexivity; practice; competition and emergence; elaboration).

Stage 1: conditioning

At our arbitrary starting point in time (T^0) there existed a particular set of individual labour markets, all of which are structured differently (see Fine, 1998, p. 16). Common to each, however, are the existence of L × S and P × S structures

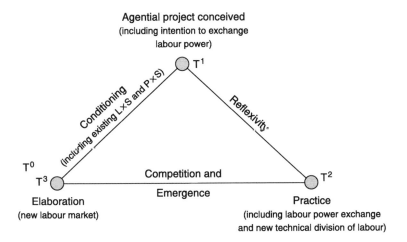

Figure 18.1 Conceptualising labour market emergence.

which either enable or constrain specific agential projects with the exchange of labour power as their intended outcome. These structures represent, in part at least, the conditions under which an 'entrepreneurial' agential project is conceived (T^1).

In the case of early music performers, structures relating to the production and performance of classical music represent conditioning factors. Taking the labour power exchange structure ($L \times S$) first, the majority of classical musicians are freelance players or singers who move from job to job on a project basis. As is the case in many other areas of the cultural sector, the exchange of labour power is characterised by flexible working arrangements (Blair 2001; Feist 2001). Often performers engage agents or diary services, who provide an employment service, dealing with 'fixers' of orchestras, or promoters of concerts, broadcasts and recording sessions. These 'middlemen' contribute to a network, or grapevine, which offers an important means of economising on search and information costs (see Towse 2001). Such a network is particularly important given the fact that there are generally many more musicians trained to a very high level of competence than there are secure jobs available. 'Over-supply' is a prevailing characteristic of the classical music field (see Caves 2000). A related problem that has concerned cultural economists for some years is the observation that artists' earnings do not appear to be raised by training. In other words, neither the human capital model nor the screening hypothesis (where formal training is seen as a screening device for sorting students within the labour market) appears to provide a satisfactory economic explanation for the market response to training in the arts (Towse 1995). What is highlighted here, and in more recent studies on artists' earnings (see Abbing 2002) is the particular importance of intrinsic motivation (the love of performing music) rather than extrinsic motivation (the desire to gain financial reward). Performing music is not an exclusively professional occupation, of course. Many amateur classical musicians regularly perform – and often there is a modest 'fee' involved.[12] This amateur music-making is an important aspect of the early history of early music performance. Prior to the late 1960s there were many musicians experimenting with early music repertoire and instruments in private circles. The repertoire being played was chiefly from the renaissance period or earlier (i.e. written before 1600) – whereas the professional early music ensembles launched in the early 1970s performed Baroque and later Classical music (i.e. written after 1600).

Given the competitive nature of the job market for classical musicians it is not surprising to find that there was some hostility to the idea of musicians devoting themselves to early music – which was seen as 'amateurish' or even 'dangerous' by many of those working and teaching in the classical music field. It was ostensibly for this reason that Trevor Pinnock had his scholarship taken away at the Royal College of Music for devoting too much attention to playing the harpsichord rather than the organ – which was his first instrument of study. Elsewhere, Christopher Hogwood explains the thinking behind such a decision: 'the paid conservatoire teachers who saw it [early music] … I don't think they were against it being period music. I think they were very much trying to train people to a regular career. Their job was to put you in a job ... and it should be a job as secure as *their* job – a lifetime contract playing in a professional orchestra'.

The situation was rather different for singers, since 'early music' embraced repertoire that had been sung in English cathedrals and Oxbridge chapels for hundreds of years. There was an unbroken tradition of choral music which made historical performance less of a challenging idea to accept. Nevertheless, there were also few opportunities for professional careers in singing outside of the cathedral circuit.

Ultimately, of course, the exchange of classical music performers' labour power would not have been possible without adequate resources to pay them. Traditionally, the cultural sector (including classical music as a major recipient) has received subsidy to underpin its activities. This is not the place to go in to any detail concerning the public good/market failure arguments for why the state has intervened (see O'Hagan 1998 for a detailed discussion). However, the Arts Council's involvement in supporting classical music represents another conditioning factor in the development of the early music performer labour market.

In terms of the buyers and sellers of classical music product (P×S), one should not underestimate the importance of record companies in providing the resources necessary to make a career in classical music a viable option for many. This is despite the fact that royalties for recorded performances seldom percolate to individual 'rank and file' orchestral players. The development of the CD as the leading format for distributing music in the 1980s had a very significant impact on the early music movement. In what can be seen as a prime example of 'historical specificity' (Hodgson 2001) the CD represented the opportunity for record companies to re-record much of their catalogue – including music written before 1750. In other words, this was a very happy accident of timing for those involved in early music performance.

Stage 2: conception of agential project

The 'agential project' conceived in this case can be thought of as the establishment of a new period instrument orchestra or ensemble. We automatically think of the 'pioneers' of the early music movement (such as David Munrow, Christopher Hogwood, Trevor Pinnock and Roger Norrington) as being the prime movers and shakers in this respect. However, closer scrutiny reveals a cast of silent 'corporate agents' (Archer 1995) whose influence is as great, if not greater in some cases. These are individuals who, because of their particular positions or roles in the classical music field, were able to play an active role in changing the status quo. An example is the record producer Peter Wadland at Decca. He met with Christopher Hogwood at a recording session for the successful classical music chamber orchestra, the Academy of St Martin in the Fields. As Hogwood recalls, Wadland asked whether he could conceive of a period instrument group of about the same size playing to anything like the same standard. The agential project itself was not initiated by early music performers but by a representative of a recording company. To the extent that Wadland represents the buyer of services some way down an industry value chain, this distinction is important.

Stage 3: reflexivity

The next crucial stage in this process of labour market emergence (between T^1 and T^2) is when the individual(s) conceiving of the agential project reflects on whether to undertake the project or not, in the light of their (imperfect) knowledge of the conditions that will influence its success. This might include knowledge about existing labour markets and product markets. Of course, this process of reflection can take many forms and last anywhere from a moment's thought to many years of deliberation. Much of the entrepreneurship field's interest in the role of information and decision-making (see Casson 1982; Palich & Bagby 1995) relates to this 'mediating' stage of reflection. It is here that people's emergent properties (PEPs) have the potential for considerable causal efficacy, since ultimately these determine whether any actions are taken.

Performing early music was not, of itself, a new phenomenon. As we have observed, there was a significant level of amateur music-making going on, and there were also professional ensembles performing and recording in continental Europe. The work of European performers in the 1950s and 1960s in Amsterdam, Vienna and elsewhere, represented an important precedent. As Hogwood notes 'the evidence of Harnoncourt and Leonhardt showed that bigger groups could be put together. The reason we knew that was that we heard their recordings'.

Early music performance also required the availability of appropriate editions and musical instruments. One leading musicologist and publisher observed, for example, that 'discovering the early music repertoire came about a decade before the instruments'.

Early music performers were faced with some suspicion from the classical music establishment. These suspicions were not altogether unfounded. At a basic level, there was the unpalatable truth that playing music on period instruments often sounded 'interesting' at best. It was not possible for classically trained musicians to simply pick up an original instrument and master it technically overnight. As those involved in the early years of its development recall, there were major problems in learning the instruments and playing in tune. Nevertheless, as one early music orchestra manager comments 'it is like the four minute mile … no one could do it for years. All of a sudden one person does it, and everyone can! It was the same with playing these instruments'.

The process of reflection, therefore, needed to take account of what performers were able to perform given the constraints of existing resources, skills, training and raw materials (published editions and instruments). Archer (2003) highlights the potential of agents to act strategically under such conditions. With significant levels of uncertainty for performers, record companies and audiences alike, it is not surprising to note that the establishment of early music as a new 'product' took some time to stabilise. So too, as agential projects gave way to

'practice' the employment of early music performers began to take on a more routinised form, building on a set of common behaviours and norms.

Stage 4: practice

This 'practice' involved the *recombination of resources* (including performers'
labour power), the *use of new technology*, i.e. the new arrangement of people (such
as early music performers), ideas (such as historically informed practice), and
objects (such as original instruments) for the accomplishment of a particular
goal,[13] and the *organisation of tasks* (the division of labour), in order to accomplish the desired 'end'. Despite the over-supply of classical musicians, those
involved in the first professional period instrument ensembles were faced by a
shortage of skilled (and suitably motivated) players. After all, there had been no
didactic paths for training musicians in early music performance. The existing
classical music channels were not able to provide the necessary knowledge about
which performers to employ. Music directors' *personal* networks were essential
for bringing together players. Interestingly, this involved engaging some musicians with rather different motivations to those behind the agential project. Early
music performance for some was something of an experiment – a bit of fun –
rather than anything to do with authenticity. Some well-established classical musicians were enticed to play on their 'Sunday instruments' simply because they were
available, talented, and able to pick it up quickly. Brass players 'fixed' themselves
– to the annoyance of some orchestral managers. In order to engage such players,
however, the ensembles quickly established fees that were above the classical
music performer going rate (as agreed by the Musicians Union) on the basis of
being a specialist activity. This was a precedent that has remained to this day.

It is here (T2) that there first appears the possibility of having a transformative
effect on the existing classical music performer labour market. This is because the
elaboration of representative labour market structures (L×S and P×S) post-dates
the actions which transform it. The actions associated with the entrepreneurial
agential project give rise to emergent properties, resulting from the recombination of resources, use of new technology, and the technical division of labour.

Stage 5: competition and emergence

The model presented in Figure 18.1 takes as its focus a single agential project.
Nevertheless, subsequent competition and emergence involves multiple 'entrepreneurial' projects being enacted. These can take place simultaneously or out of
phase with each other. The detail of their interaction will, of course, be potentially
very complex. However, the basic temporal features that underlie Archer's morphogenetic model hold throughout.

With competition come the issues of loyalty and allegiance. In the early days
of the early music movement in England there were simply not enough players to
go round. For this reason it was not uncommon to find the same performers playing regularly with three or four different ensembles. As the market grew, how-

ever, this led to the need for some governance to avoid timetable clashes. The management of the leading groups regularly got together to discuss their diaries and to avoid performing on the same night. Such meetings would naturally be good opportunities for sharing experiences and practices concerned with employing musicians. The increased workload also saw an increasing separation between the founders' personal input into the management and hiring of players and their artistic contribution to their ensembles. Specialist managers and fixers were hired to look after this aspect of the new orchestras. From the players' perspective too there was a need to 'belong' to a particular ensemble (even though contracts for engagement remained on a project basis only).

Underpinning much of this account has been the importance of personal networks and informal contacts. These constitute key emergent properties such as the relations between the buyers and sellers of labour power (i.e. founders and their ensembles, and between these new music directors and record companies, promoters, venues, agents and fixers), and between the buyers and sellers of the early music product (including the BBC, record companies, festivals in the UK and abroad, and the public in general). A host of further contingent structures are also important here, however. These reflect the activities and ideas of musicologists, publishers, instrument makers, instrument retailers, teachers, Arts Council representatives and other interested parties. Further to the earlier discussion concerning demand-side and supply-side influences on labour markets, therefore, it is important to highlight the fact that labour market structuring is also dependent on the influences that arise out of the emergence of new organisations and the introduction of new economic activity (i.e. entrepreneurship). This is not least because the future activities of those individuals involved in the early music performer labour market were at least to some extent path dependent or 'locked-in' (see David 1986).

Stage 6: elaboration

Finally (T³) we can see the interaction of these emergent properties and contingent structures as representing the mechanisms and specific context behind the elaboration of the existing labour market structures. It should be remembered, of course, that it remains a matter of contingency whether or not emergent properties are, in fact, exercised, and thus whether they do indeed give rise to new (and subsequently emerging) labour markets.

We can usefully point to some key cases of elaboration within the early music performer labour market which cannot adequately be explained without understanding how the early music performance market and labour market developed in the first place. For example, one of the reasons that early music performers themselves have stated for launching their own democratically elected player-led orchestra (the Orchestra of the Age of Enlightenment) in the mid 1980s was to move away from the dominance they felt was exerted by the founder music directors of the leading English early music ensembles. The emergence of this new orchestra had a significant bearing on the activities of all the other professional early music groups. Shortly after its launch the orchestra gained the contract to perform Mozart operas at Glyndebourne Festival Opera under the leadership of Simon Rattle. This signalled a major landmark in the gradual 'mainstreaming' of early music – one that has seen the meeting of ideas as classical music orchestras increasingly play in a historically informed style, often under the leadership of early music specialists (Archer has described this type of situation as 'ideational unification'). By the mid 1980s, all the UK music colleges provided specialist training in early music performance. There now existed an over-supply of early music performers. Along with the shrinking classical music market in general, however, the opportunities for students of early music to gain a foothold in the profession have more recently become few and far between.

Discussion

Before concluding with a summary of the key benefits accruing from this application of critical realist meta-theory, we need to make some important qualifications about the insights outlined here. In pointing to the importance of discovering and explaining the 'mechanisms' that account for particular events, we are making claims not about some data of appearance, but rather about something that goes beyond them. These transfactual claims are therefore always open to refutation by *further* information. This, of course, highlights the problem of how we assert that any particular causal explanation is more convincing (or, indeed, more 'practically adequate' (Sayer 1992)) than any other. As Runde (1998) has observed 'principles used to assess causal explanations ... will often not have sufficient bite, to discriminate unambiguously between competing causal explanations ... there will always be situations in which it is not possible to identify one explanation as unambiguously superior to its rivals' (p. 168). It is on these grounds that Hodgson (2004) calls for 'some much needed modesty' in terms of what can be claimed for the critical realist philosophy (p. 63). While I agree with this sentiment, I do not agree with the assertion that critical realism 'gives us little guidance to assess the importance of one causal link compared with another' (ibid). I hope to have demonstrated that the retroductive argument does, in fact, provide a powerful tool for emphasising underlying social structures. This is, not least, because it is based on an immanent critique of existing literature. In my view, therefore, it does not have to be the case that it 'fails at the crucial point of comparative causal assessment of rival and potentially complementary theories' as is suggested by Hodgson (2004: 68). Nevertheless, it is recognised that the account presented here is both fallible and corrigible.

In conclusion, therefore, let me (modestly) summarise the key benefits of the approach being laid out in this paper. From an ontological perspective, I have sought to show the benefit of 'theorising ontology' – of bringing into the open our assumptions about the existence of social objects. In particular, I have sought to account for the role of structure and agency and their interaction in the specific case of the labour market. This builds on Archer's concept of analytical dualism and provides a purchase on the structuring of social systems over time (see Carter

& New 2004: 17). The re-conceptualisation of the labour market in terms of both structures and agency is particularly important in this respect, since it provides for a more inclusive definition that does not exclude those that *appear* to be non-participants. Providing an outline causal explanation of the emergence of a labour market also makes a first contribution to our (up until now rather limited) understanding of how a new labour market comes into being. This, in turn, offers us some further insight as to the nature of the mechanisms behind the functioning of labour markets – though it is accepted that further analysis will be required to pinpoint these mechanisms more clearly.

At an epistemological level, the presentation of a realist conception of labour markets encourages a re-evaluation of existing labour market theory. The ground has also been prepared for a richer understanding of the interdependency between theories of firm formation, labour markets, entrepreneurship, and markets in general. For example, the strong implication of what has been presented in this chapter is that entrepreneurship theory can offer some important insights into the process of labour market emergence. However, up until now, very few commentators in the entrepreneurship field have made this connection. Equally, labour market theory, and particularly some of the richer institutionalist approaches that focus on what I consider to be contingent labour market structures, will no doubt have much to offer the entrepreneurship field.

Finally, at a methodological level, the potential benefit of applying the retroductive argument and counterposing counterfactual thinking, with its concern for which social objects necessarily depend on one another, to associational thinking, with its 'suspicion of abstraction' (Sayer 2001b: 967), has been highlighted. The importance of Archer's morphogenetic model as a methodological foundation for the analysis of the interplay between structure and agency has also been demonstrated. This is not to deny that the approach taken is without its challenges. In developing a causal explanatory account of labour market emergence the researcher is confronted by a potentially overwhelming level of data. One of the major insights of undertaking such a study is the unearthing of so many contingent factors and examples of historical specificity that demand careful analysis to determine their true impact. There is necessarily a need to sift data and be selective in terms of what to focus on. This, of course, is the very essence of what abstraction is all about. Used wisely, the process offers 'a procedure that can facilitate the illumination of the open social world in which we live' (Lawson 1997: 237).

To pose the question of 'what properties must be necessary in order for a social phenomenon to be a possible object of knowledge for us?' is to force the enquirer to step back from tacitly accepting theory-laden and path-dependent conceptualisations of social objects. This, in turn, makes looking in a new light at phenomena such as labour markets and their emergence, a real possibility.

Notes

1 'Early music' is a relative term. For some, it refers to music written before J. S. Bach's death in 1750. However, historically informed performance now also embraces music composed as recently as the late 19th century.

2 That is, performing music in keeping with the composer's original intentions – including the use of original instruments and historically informed musical performance practice.

3 This use of the term *social structures* is broad enough to include *both* structural emergent properties, which are internal and necessary relations entailing material resources, and cultural emergent properties, which involve logical relations between items constituting the Cultural System (Archer 1995: 179).

4 Arguably there is no such thing as a 'free' labour market – given the influence of Trade Unions, monopolies, and other market imperfections.

5 It is noted that the existence of this product exchange structure is itself necessarily dependent on the existence of the idea of the product itself (i.e. a Cultural Emergent Property).

6 Sayer has described the gendering of organisations and markets as an example of 'associational thinking' which focuses associations between social phenomena without asking counterfactual questions about the status of these relationships (2000: 707).

7 'It is noted that *emergence* in this chapter is used primarily to infer the appearance of a labour market for the first time. It is important to distinguish this emergence from on-going emergence of social structures (which is also consistent with Archer's use of the term).

8 See Herbert Simon in Sarasvathy (1999) pp. 2, 11.

9 I define entrepreneurship as a particular process of social change in which the undertaking of an agential project, requiring the recombination of resources, new technology, and the technical division of labour, gives rise to new productive use and the extension of the social division of labour.

10 Labour power is not reproduced 'capitalistically' – i.e. the domestic labour that goes to reproduce labour power is unpaid.

11 The account is based on intensive interviews held with early music ensemble founders, managers and performers, and other experts, as part of the author's doctoral research. A more complete causal explanatory account is being compiled as part of this doctoral thesis.

12 The distinction between amateur and professional is problematic, not least for this reason.

13 See Hargadon (2003).

References

Abbing, H. (2002) *Why are Artists Poor? The Exceptional Economy of the Arts,* Amsterdam University Press, Amsterdam.

Althauser, R. P. and Kalleberg, A. L. (1981) 'Firms, Occupations, and the Structure of Labor Markets: A Conceptual Analysis', In: Berg, I. (ed.) *Sociological Perspectives on Labor Markets,* Academic Press, New York, pp. 119–149.

Archer, M. S. (1995) *Realist Social Theory: the Morphogenetic Approach,* Cambridge University Press, Cambridge, UK.

Archer, M. S. (1998) "Realism and Morphogenesis", In: Archer, M. S., Bhaskar, R., Collier, A., Lawson, T. and Norrie, A. (eds.) *Critical Realism: Essential Readings,* Routledge, London, pp. 356–382.

Archer, M. S. (2003) *Structure, Agency and the Internal Conversation,* Cambridge University Press, Cambridge, UK.

Bhaskar, R. (1978) *A Realist Theory of Science,* 2nd edn., Harvester Press, Brighton, UK.

Bhaskar, R. (1989) *The Possibility of Naturalism,* 2nd edn., Harvester Wheatsheaf, Hemel Hempstead, UK (first published 1979).

Blair, H. (2001) 'You're Only as Good as Your Last Job: the Labour Process and Labour Market in the British Film Industry, *Work Employment & Society*, 15(1): 149–169.

Carter, B. and New, C. (Eds.) (2004) *Making Realism Work: Realist Social Theory and Empirical Research*, Routledge, London.

Casson, M. C. (1982) *The Entrepreneur: An Economic Theory*, Martin Robertson, Oxford.

Caves, R. (2000) *Creative Industries: Contracts Between Art and Commerce*, Harvard University Press, Boston, MA.

Cruickshank, J. (2003) *Realism and Sociology: Anti-foundationalism, Ontology and Social Research*, Routledge, London.

Danermark, B., Ekström, M., Jakobsen, L. and Karlsson, J. (2002) *Explaining Society: Critical Realism in the Social Sciences*, Routledge, London.

David, P. A. (1986) 'Understanding the Economics of QWERTY: The Necessity of History', In: Parker, W.N. (ed.) *Economic History and the Modern Economist*, Blackwell, Oxford, UK.

Elder-Vass, D. (2004) 'Re-examining Bhaskar's Three Ontological Domains: The Lessons from Emergence', In: *The 2004 Annual Conference of the International Association for Critical Realism Conference Proceedings*, pp. 100–120, Cambridge, UK.

Feist, A. (2001) 'The Relationship Between the Subsidised and the Wider Cultural Sector', In: Selwood, S. (ed.) *The UK Cultural Sector*, pp. 189–201, Policy Studies Institute, London.

Fevre, R. (1992) *The Sociology of Labour Markets*, Simon & Schuster, Hemel Hemstead, UK.

Fine, B. (1998) *Labour Market Theory A Constructive Reassessment*, Routledge, London.

Fleetwood, S. (2003) 'Preparing the Ground for A Viable Account of Labour Markets', unpublished paper submitted to *Class and Capital*, March.

Freedman, M. (1976) *Labor Markets: Segments and Shelters*, Allanheld Osman, New York.

Hargadon, A. (2003) *How Breakthroughs Happen*, Harvard Business School Press, Boston, MA.

Harré, R. (1972) *The Philosophies of Science*, Oxford University Press, Oxford.

Harré, R. (1986) *Varieties of Realism*, Blackwell, Oxford.

Harré, R. and Madden, E. H. (1975) *Causal Powers. A Theory of Natural Necessity*, Blackwell, Oxford.

Hodgson, G. M. (2001) *How Economics Forgot History*, Routledge, London.

Hodgson, G. M. (2004) 'Some Claims Made for Critical Realism in Economics: Two Case Dtudies', *Journal of Economic Methodology*, 11(1) 53–73.

Lawson, T. (1997) *Economics and Reality*, Routledge, London.

O'Hagan, J. W. (1998) *The State and the Arts: An Analysis of Key Economic Policy Issues in Europe and the United States*, Edward Elgar, Cheltenham, UK.

Palich, L. E. and Bagby, D. R. (1995) 'Using Cognitive Theory to Explain Entrepreneurial Risk Taking: Challenging Conventional Wisdom', *Journal of Business Venturing*, 10, 425–438.

Peck, J. (2000) 'Structuring the Labour Market: a Segmentation Approach', In: S. Ackroyd and S. Fleetwood (eds.) pp. 220–244, *Realist Perspectives on Management and Organisations*, Routledge, London.

Porpora, D. (1998) 'Four Concepts of Social Structure', In M. S. Archer, R. Bhaskar, A. Collier, T. Lawson, and A. Norrie (Eds.), *Critical Realism: Essential Readings*, pp. 339–355, Routledge, London.

Rubery, J. (1988) 'Employers and the Labour Market', In: D. Gallie, (ed.) *Employment in Britain*, pp. 251–280, Blackwell, Oxford, UK.

Runde, J. H. (1998) 'Assessing Causal Economic Explanations', *Oxford Economic Papers*, 50(1): 151–172.

Sarasvathy, S. (1999) 'Seminar on Research Perspectives in Entrepreneurship', *Journal of Business Venturing*, 15; 1–57.

Sayer, A. (1992) *Method in Social Science: A Realistic Approach*, Routledge, London.

Sayer, A. (2000) 'System, Lifeworld and Gender: Associational Versus Counterfactual Thinking', *Sociology*, 34(4): 707–725.

Sayer, A. (2001a) 'For a Critical Cultural Political Economy', *Antipode*, 33(4): 687–708.

Sayer, A. (2001b) 'Reply to Holmwood', *Sociology*, 35(4): 967–984.

Shane, S. (2003) *A General Theory of Entrepreneurship: The Individual-Opportunity Nexus*, Edward Elgar, Cheltenham, UK.

Towse, R. (1995) *The Economics of Artists' Labour Markets*, Arts Council of England, London.

Towse, R. (2001) *Creativity, Incentive and Reward*, Edward Elgar, Cheltenham, UK.

Index

Diagrams are given in italics